Late Have I Loved Thee

VINTAGE SPIRITUAL CLASSICS

General Editors
John F. Thornton
Susan B. Varenne

ALSO AVAILABLE

Late Have I Loved Thee

SELECTED WRITINGS OF

Saint Augustine

ON LOVE

EDITED BY

John F. Thornton and *Susan B. Varenne*

PREFACE BY

James J. O'Donnell

VINTAGE SPIRITUAL CLASSICS

VINTAGE BOOKS
A DIVISION OF RANDOM HOUSE, INC.
NEW YORK

A VINTAGE SPIRITUAL CLASSICS ORIGINAL, DECEMBER 2006
FIRST EDITION

About the Vintage Spiritual Classics, Preface to the Vintage Spiritual
Classics Edition, Chronology of the Life of Saint Augustine,
and Suggestions for Further Reading
Copyright © 2006 by Random House, Inc.

For permission to reprint, acknowledgment is gratefully made to the following:

Reprinted with permission from Augustine, Saint. *Tractates on the Gospel of
John 55–111,* edited and translated by John W. Rettig (The Catholic University
of America Press, 1994: "Tractate 65").

From *Augustine: Later Works* (Library of Christian Classics Series) edited by John Burnaby.
Used by permission of Westminster John Knox Press: "Ten Homilies on the
First Epistle of St. John": First, Second, Fifth, Sixth, Ninth, and Tenth Homilies.

From the Augustinian Heritage Institute/New City Press, *The Works of Saint Augustine: A
Translation for the 21st Century* series (John E. Rotelle, O.S.A., Editor) volumes as follows:

1. *The Confessions.* Translated by Maria Boulding, O.S.B. (1997): Book I: 1, 1; 5, 5:6. Book II:
1, 1; 2, 2; 5, 10; 6, 13&14; 7, 15. Book III: 1, 1. Book IV: 8, 13; 9, 14; 12, 18. Book V: 1, 1; 2, 2.
Book VI: 15, 25; 16, 26. Book X: 5, 7; 6, 8; 9; 27, 38; 28, 39; 43, 69. Book XI: 2, 2; 3.
Book XIII: 7, 8; 8, 9; 9, 10.

2. *Part III—Sermons:* Sermon 33; Sermon 34; Sermon 344; Sermon 349; Sermon 350;
Sermon 350A; Sermon 368; Sermon 382; Sermon 385, Sermon 386.

The Cataloging-in-Publication Data is on file at the Library of Congress.

www.vintagebooks.com

Book design by Fritz Metsch

Printed in the United States of America.
10 9 8 7 6 5 4 3 2 1

CONTENTS

FROM *THE CITY OF GOD*

Book XXII

FROM *ON CHRISTIAN DOCTRINE*

Book I

FROM *THE ENCHIRIDION ON FAITH, HOPE, AND LOVE*

FROM *AUGUSTINE'S LETTERS*

FROM *EXPOSITIONS OF THE PSALMS*

From *The Trinity*

FROM *TRACTATES ON THE GOSPEL OF JOHN*

FROM *HOMILIES ON THE FIRST EPISTLE OF SAINT JOHN*

SELECTED SERMONS

Lord Jesus, let me know myself and know You,
And desire nothing save only You.
Let me hate myself and love You.
Let me do everything for the sake of You.
Let me humble myself and exalt You.
Let me think of nothing except You.
Let me die to myself and live in You.
Let me accept whatever happens as from You.
Let me banish self and follow You,
And ever desire to follow You.
Let me fly from myself and take refuge in You,
That I may deserve to be defended by You.
Let me fear for myself, let me fear You,
And let me be among those who are chosen by You.
Let me distrust myself and put my trust in You.
Let me be willing to obey for the sake of You.
Let me cling to nothing save only to You,
And let me be poor because of You.
Look upon me, that I may love You.
Call me that I may see You,
And forever enjoy You. Amen.

— PRAYER OF SAINT AUGUSTINE

ABOUT THE
VINTAGE SPIRITUAL CLASSICS

by John F. Thornton and Susan B. Varenne, General Editors

A turn or shift of sorts is becoming evident in the reflections of men and women today on their life experiences. Not quite as adamantly secular and, perhaps, a little less insistent on material satisfactions, the reading public has recently developed a certain attraction to testimonies that human life is leavened by a Presence that blesses and sanctifies. Recovery, whether from addictions or personal traumas, illness, or even painful misalignments in human affairs, is evolving from the standard therapeutic goal of enhanced self-esteem. Many now seek a deeper healing that embraces the whole person, including the soul. Contemporary books provide accounts of the invisible assistance of angels. The laying on of hands in prayer has made an appearance at the hospital bedside. Guides for the spiritually perplexed have risen to the tops of best-seller lists. The darkest shadows of skepticism and unbelief, which have eclipsed the presence of the Divine in our rationalistic age, are beginning to lighten and part.

If the power and presence of God are real and effective, what do they mean for human experience? What does He offer to men and women, and what does He ask in return? How do we recognize Him? Know Him? Respond to Him? God has a reputation for being both benevolent and wrathful. Which will He be for me and when? Can these aspects of the Divine somehow be reconciled? Where is God when I suffer? Can I lose Him? Is God truthful, and are His promises to be trusted?

Are we really as precious to God as we are to ourselves and our loved ones? Do His providence and amazing grace guide our faltering steps toward Him, even in spite of ourselves? Will God abandon us if the sin is serious enough, or if we have episodes of resistance and forgetfulness? These are fundamental questions any person might address to God during a lifetime. They are pressing and difficult, often becoming wounds in the soul of the person who yearns for the power and courage of hope, especially in stressful times.

The Vintage Spiritual Classics present the testimony of writers across the centuries who have considered all these difficulties and who have pondered the mysterious ways, unfathomable mercies, and deep consolations afforded by God to those who call upon Him from out of the depths of their lives. These writers, then, are our companions, even our champions, in a common effort to discern the meaning of God in personal experience. For God is personal to us. To whom does He speak if not to us, provided we have the desire to hear Him deep within our hearts?

Each volume opens with a specially commissioned essay by a well-known contemporary writer that offers the reader an appreciation of its intrinsic value. A chronology of the general historical context of each author and his work is provided, as are suggestions for further reading.

We offer a final word about the act of reading these spiritual classics. From the very earliest accounts of monastic practice—dating back to the fourth century—it is evident that a form of reading called *lectio divina* ("divine" or "spiritual reading") was essential to any deliberate spiritual life. This kind of reading is quite different from that of scanning a text for useful facts and bits of information, or advancing along an exciting plot line to a climax in the action. It is, rather, a meditative approach by which the reader seeks to savor and taste the beauty and truth of every phrase and passage. This process of contemplative reading has the effect of enkindling in the reader compunction for past behavior that has been less than beautiful and true. At the same time, it increases the desire to seek a realm where all that is lovely and unspoiled may be found. There are four steps in *lectio divina*: first, to read, next to meditate, then to rest in the sense of God's nearness, and, ultimately, to resolve to govern one's actions in the light of new understanding. This kind of reading is itself an act of prayer. And, indeed, it is in prayer that God manifests His Presence to us.

PREFACE TO THE VINTAGE SPIRITUAL CLASSICS EDITION

by James J. O'Donnell

"My weight is my love": *pondus meum amor meus.*[1] Those words stand a few pages before the end of the one book, more than any other of his many books, that has made Augustine, the Christian bishop of Hippo Regius (modern Annaba, Algeria), famous through sixteen centuries. They arrest our attention because, as heirs of Newton, we think differently about weight, *gravitas*, than the ancients did, but even in his time, they made a bold claim—that the constellation of emotions and behaviors that carries the name of "love" is not something external, extrinsic, contingent, or unnecessary to a human being. Nor is "love" identical with the yen for sexual contact with another or the contact itself. For Augustine, love is an essential feature of what we are—of who we are, inside, in the inner space of which he wrote with a poet's insight and accuracy. The selections from his writings collected in this volume are meant to give the reader an understanding of how that could be so for Augustine and an opportunity for rehearsing what it would be like to think that way ourselves.

His words come to us across a vast distance, and their impact and relevance are more impressive for the distance they have traveled. Born into modest prosperity in Roman Africa in 354 C.E., Augustine famously abandoned a worldly career at the heart of Roman power in Italy to make himself over as a man of his religion and from 395 to 430 was the bishop of the second largest city (after Carthage) of Roman Africa and the undoubted central figure in the religious and political history of Rome's wealthiest province.

1. *Confessions*, 13.9.10.

He remade the structures of Christian power there and wrote books that shaped and continued to shape Christian doctrine well beyond the places where he was ordained to act. When he died, his city was surrounded by an army that had come from northern Germany, beyond the Roman borders, passed through Gaul and Spain, crossed the straits of Gibraltar, and made its way along the African coast, seeking power and a place for themselves inside the Roman world. They would capture his city shortly after his death and all of Roman Africa not long after, thereby decisively unmaking and remaking the western Roman Empire. Augustine's story has often been told,[2] but one part of it will need recounting briefly here.

Augustine's impact on Christian thought began with the spoken word, in the thousands of sermons he gave during his lifetime, many of which were taken down by stenographers and copied for a wider audience. His letters to private and ecclesiastical persons created a network of awareness that went well beyond the Africa where he lived, and it smoothed the way for his many books to find an eager audience. Five million words survive from his pen to this day, far more than any other literary figure of late antiquity managed to produce and transmit to us. Though he had adversaries in his lifetime, his reputation prevailed and made him an authoritative figure in Latin Christianity ever after. His books were copied and recopied in medieval scriptoria, printed and reprinted by the earliest generations of impresarios of movable type, and read by men and women inside and outside his church in every generation. Few have ever been found who might be said to agree with everything he wrote—and he changed his mind often enough to make such agreement probably impossible—but many are those who have found him a reference point, guide, and provocateur, whether they end in substantial agreement or, as is more often the case today, far from the positions Augustine himself would take.

When Augustine comes to write of love, he inherits an ancient tradition that is both part of us and often strikingly dissonant with our traditions. At the same time, he is innocent of a long medieval and modern tradition of courtly and romantic love that moderns take for granted as inextricably part of any conception of love. Be-

2. Most recently by the present writer, in *Augustine: A New Biography* (New York, 2005).

tween the ancient and the modern, Augustine's contribution to the long dialogue of the ages is itself an essential constituent of our half-understood inheritance. He had been taught to distrust love as the ancients knew it (Greek *eros*, Latin *amor*), and from early in his career he was more aware than most other Christian writers of antiquity that the distrust needed to be made explicit and an alternate theory supplied.[3]

He had, of course, places to go in the Christian Scriptures that could give him a starting point and directions to follow. The special form of love that Paul speaks of in 1 Corinthians 13 and elsewhere (Greek *agape*, Latin *caritas*) spoke across the pages of the New Testament to the commandment that Jesus extracted from the Torah to make his own, the dual law of love of God and love of neighbor.[4] In this volume we shall see that the letter to the Parthians attributed to the Apostle John came to be the place where Augustine found himself able to work out in moving and powerful language his own variations on the themes that Jesus and Paul gave him to meditate.

But the defect of the scriptural heritage for Augustine was that it offered ethics without mechanics. It told Christians what to do, but it did not make it clear how the dynamics of love played out in a human person or a human society. Augustine's distinctive contribution is what some have called his "anthropology"—that is, his understanding of the human person and its spiritual components and energies. The inquiry that led to this understanding was at the center of Augustine's life and experience. It allowed him to propose a model of human experience that is fully temporal and transformative. Where ancient ethics regarded the individual as a kind of statue in the making, refined by ethical teaching to an unchanging perfection of self, Augustine's view of the human being always takes into account change over time, change for the better and change for the worse. The weight of love explained—again, in pre-Newtonian terms—the inertia, the headlong rush, and the collisions that love engenders.

The centrality of love arose from Augustine's understanding of man's resemblance to God. Augustine belonged to that line of

---

3. For the history of distrust and alternatives, see Peter Brown, *The Body and Society* (New York, 1988).

4. Mt 22:37–39, depending on Dt 6:5 and Lv 19:18.

ancient thought that found man a small, fragile, short-lived thing in contrast to a well-envisioned Divine Being. For such a thinker, the notion that the mighty God had made man in his own image and likeness (Gn 1:26) was cause for gasping surprise, in the face of a gap between the divine and the human that otherwise seemed incomprehensibly vast. Anthropomorphism—the doctrine of a God with hair and fingernails and emotions like ours—was never a risk for such a thinker, and so Augustine found a different path to understanding image and likeness, one that ennobled humankind rather than belittled God.

The generations between the conversion of the emperor Constantine to Christianity (c. 312) and Augustine's rise to ecclesiastical prominence had been preoccupied with fixing the Christian doctrine of the Trinity, that is, the evolving language used to explain the divine economy that made Father, Son, and Spirit somehow both three and one at the same time. On Trinitarian matters, Augustine presents himself as an heir of a settled tradition, even in the long and ambitiously argued book he devoted to the topic. The lingering brushfires of controversy on the topic in his lifetime were being dealt with elsewhere. The spark of uncertainty and dispute would jump, late in Augustine's life, to the new and poisonously obsessive topic of Christology, for if Jesus's divinity was now officially settled, his relationship to humankind became the focus of angry debates whose real subtext was the underlying incongruity between Christian belief and Scripture and the philosophical expectations of serious thinkers trained in the ancient traditions. Those wars, however, were fought mainly among Greek-speaking theologians and in the eastern empire, far from Augustine's direct ken.[5]

Between Trinitarian debates and Christological ones, Augustine's most abstract speculations stay remarkably close to the ground. What, he asked, did it mean for a mortal human being to stand in the image and likeness of God? His answer was trinitarian in form.

Just as the divine being, one and eternal, could be approached by three paths, so too the human. In God, Augustine argued, the

---

5. This history can be explored by following the people who quarreled or by following the ideas they deployed. For the latter approach, see J. J. Pelikan, *The Emergence of the Catholic Tradition: 100–600* (Chicago, 1971).

Father represented the power of being itself, the creator and sustainer of all that is contingent, fragile, and destined to destruction in the material world, and again of all that is eternal in the domain of the spirit. God the Father expresses that which is original and creative in the divine, as God the Son expresses that which is wise and knowing, and as God the Spirit embodies the love that Dante found at the center of the universe. So, then, a human being, reflecting the image and likeness of God, exists, knows . . . and loves. In so doing, the human being shares with angelic creation the two characteristic powers of knowing and loving. The love, moreover, is the means by which human beings act on and in the world.

For every action, to Augustine, is an act of love. We act, he holds, out of love of the objective for which we act. That love may be base or sublime, but every action depends on it, and it is at the heart of human and religious existence: "No, really, if you see love, then you are seeing the Trinity."[6]

But love goes wrong sometimes, and there are at bottom two loves in the world: "Two loves created two cities,"[7] the rightful love of the heavenly city and the wrongful love of the earthly. When we begin to ask how men and women choose their loves, we come to the heart of the issues that perplexed Augustine and divided his readers most deeply late in his life, issues of freedom, grace, and predestination. This is not the place for another study of the "Pelagian controversy," but instead I will try to outline the main positions Augustine himself *tried* to take—not always succeeding in making them his main points in the face of withering criticism.

Love originates for Augustine in delight, in pleasure. He is at bottom a hedonist in principle, but he holds that everything depends on the right kind of disembodied pleasure, on the right ordering of one's inmost affections. In the opening pages of *On Christian Doctrine*, he makes his most systematic exposition of right and wrong love sound abstract, centering on notions of "use" and "enjoyment." There is "love," he argues, for things that are only a means to an end, things that we use. I love my house for what it means for family, not for itself—but if I begin to love the house for its own

6. *The Trinity*, 8.8.12, quoted recently with approval by Pope Benedict XVI in his encyclical, *God Is Love* (*Deus est caritas*), 2.19.

7. *City of God*, 14.28.

sake and neglect my family, something has gone wrong. On that model, I *use* my house and *enjoy* my family. On a larger scale, and this is challenging, I really only *use* my family, and the only final enjoyment that is appropriate is love of God. This is a tough doctrine, not at all incompatible with the New Testament's urgings to leave family behind in some circumstances, but it can be bleak or warm depending on the treatment.

The implications of that doctrine for the human family are what get worked out in *The City of God*, where we are encouraged, in language that returns from the first book of *On Christian Doctrine* written twenty years earlier, to think of everything about life in this world as an experience of homelessness and alienation, to be "pilgrims" in this world, sighing ever for the authentic life of the next. The heavenly city promises fulfillment in a world we cannot see, while the earthly city is condemned to live only in the one here visible. Pilgrims "use" the places they pass through as means to an end, and in this manner the virtuous are to use this world. That too can be a hard doctrine for its impact on human behavior, and we moderns are well prepared to resent the notion that we are to "use" other people, but Augustine means it seriously.

His seriousness is evident in one of his most memorable and often-quoted, but challenging, sentences: "Love—and do whatever you like."[8] The implication is that if you love and truly love, and have the right ordering of loves, then the action that follows (since action is only the expression of love) will be the right action. This internalizes ethics to intention and state of mind and relativizes commandment and law. It's relatively easy to connect that teaching of the two great commandments of Matthew's gospel but potentially difficult to embody and preach it in a world in which insistence on specific rights and wrongs of particular kinds of behavior is still the order of the day, especially in traditional Christian church communities.

That fundamental teaching of love abides with Augustine throughout his episcopal career, but he came early in that career to an important turn in the road. Not long after his ordination, about the time he was abandoning *On Christian Doctrine* unfinished (he revisited and completed it thirty years later), a letter from his old

8. *Homilies on 1 John*, 7.8.

mentor, Simplicianus of Milan, put him to reading Paul again. Paul had been a puzzle to Augustine from his Milan days forward. He had gone to Paul very likely then in Milan to find out what someone who had actually been to heaven—for so he interpreted Paul's account of his own visions—had to say about God. The story told in *The Confessions* of conversion in the garden in Milan[9] is connected to a passage of Paul (Rom 13:13) commanding radical change and the abandonment of sensuality for "putting on the Lord Jesus," but if we look closely at Augustine's writing and thinking in the decade after, Paul makes relatively little impression. Even two attempts at writing commentaries, on Romans and on Galatians, come to nothing very quickly. Afterward, Augustine would understand that he was reading Paul too optimistically. Pessimism is what he found in 396.

The mature Augustine, after his reply to Simplicianus, is a man who believes in the starkest reading of Paul. We know what is right, and we do not do what is right. Two laws (and Augustine would say, two loves) wrestle within us for control, and the better often loses. Our experience of ourself is an experience of intention at war with action, indeed of intention at war with intention. The saving grace of faith and baptism has not yet healed the soul. The deferral of expectation of that healing until the next life is something we can see Augustine accepting, reluctantly, in 396, and then learning to understand. It meant for him that he would distrust his sense of his own autonomy, and he would elevate that distrust to doctrine.

How had he gone wrong? He could never answer that. Love had been disordered by sin in the garden of Eden at the beginning of history and would only be put right at the end of history by the second coming of Christ and the resurrection of bodies. In the meantime—"in this time between times," he would say—sin continues to struggle for and often achieves mastery. The human will goes wrong by choosing the lesser good over the higher, not because there is anything better to be chosen but because the sinner "defects" from the good for what is less good. Such sin is ubiquitous (i.e., every person commits sin) but voluntary (i.e., there is no determinism, no outside force that makes us sin)—but in *some* sense unavoidable, in some sense predestined.

9. *Confessions*, 8.12.29.

Defining that sense is what cost Augustine more pain and work than anything else in the last two decades of his life, and opinions will differ how far he succeeded. This is not, as I said, the place to explore those troubling years. What is remarkable is that the underlying view of how a human being, created in the image and likeness of God, actually *works* remains the same. In the midst of contentious arguments against his ecclesiastical opponents, he will find time, as in his *Homilies on 1 John* or in his late sermons on the Psalms, to speak in memorably poetic and persuasive terms of the fundamental power of love in the universe and in humankind. Indeed, the placement of the theme of two loves at the center of *City of God* has the effect of making all of human society a macrocosm imitating, on the one hand, the microcosmic experience of the individual person, but on the other hand, that imitation is really an imitation of the experience of the inmost relations between the three Persons of the Trinity.

So I will close these notes by suggesting three surprising aspects of Augustine's teachings and beliefs on love, human and divine. First, the most intimate experience of the individual human person—the inner torment and delight of one who loves, loses, seeks, finds—is of fundamental cosmic importance and is at the heart of all history. The most "modern" feature of Augustine's view of human society is that it is firmly rooted in the value and experience of the person. A great empire is only of any value at all if it is a commonality of people who are themselves seeking and achieving what is good for themselves. This is a profoundly democratic view, hardly understood in Augustine's own imperial times, but the thing more than any other that makes his social and political views seem to resonate with modern expectations of the world.

Second, however, that intimate experience is curiously isolated and lonely. Augustine is much weaker in speaking of the way love connects human beings with one another in the household and in the community. Leaving aside polemics over his view of women and sexuality, it is undeniable that his writing is notably lacking in text that captures what it is about the love of sexual partners and the love of family members that can make human experience vibrant and valuable. He does write short treatises on marriage, and he can be quoted saying good things, but the magic we find in other places in his writings is not there, and that is a great loss to all of us. That Augustine himself lived essentially alone in a community of other clerics suggests—from what his earliest biographer, who spent time with him there, says—a man for whom the challenges of establishing intimacy and warm personal relations with friends, family, and others grew more difficult over time rather than easier. Whatever his bond with the woman who was for all legal purposes his wife in the days before his conversion, modern readers have been attracted to it because it does seem to show an Augustine who might have been, an Augustine who might have found a way to be the theologian of human love as well of divine. Augustine *on* love is easy to know and to write about; Augustine *in* love is far more elusive for us, as perhaps he was for himself.

Third and finally, what must also be seen is the sensuality of Augustine's love—not always on display, but unmistakable when it appears, as in this passage that culminates in the mystical ascent that his *Confessions* embodies and encourages:

> I was late in loving you, beauty so ancient and so new, I was late in loving you. You were inside me and I was outside myself, and I was looking for you out there and went rushing headlong among all the beautiful things you had made, me in my self-made ugliness. You were there for me and I was not with you. All sorts of things distracted me from you, things that wouldn't have had any meaning without you giving it to them. So you called out to me and shouted and broke through my deafness! You flashed, you gleamed, you chased away my blindness! Your odor flooded me and I took a deep breath and sucked you in! I took a taste, and I hungered and thirsted the more! And then you touched me, and I was all on fire for your peace.[10]

That Augustine is a man for whom the world of the senses is a powerful and seductive place. He spent his mature life struggling to make sure that he was seduced in the right way. The struggle makes him a poet of divine love with deep influence in many

10. *Confessions*, 10.27.38.

later centuries: Aelred of Rievaulx, Bernard of Clairvaux, Dante, Petrarch—the theologians and poets of the medieval world caught a sense of his imagination and his poetry and made it their own, to the lasting benefit of the societies for which they wrote. The anthology here in your hands is meant to allow that imagination to come alive again, even if we late postmoderns will feel the need to resist it, at least for a while.

Bishop of Hippo, 354–430 A.D.

Early Life

337 The death of Emperor Constantine was followed by the division of the Roman Empire into East and West. Constans, an orthodox Catholic, ruled the West from 337–50. Constantius II, an Arian who disputed the divinity of Christ, acquired the East. He became sole emperor in 350.

354 Born November 13 in Thagaste in the province of Numidia in North Africa (today Souk Ahras in Algeria), Aurelius Augustinus was the son of a pagan father, Patricius, and a Berber Christian mother, Monica. The family was respectable but somewhat impoverished.

354–65 The infancy and early schooling of Augustine. Determined to secure a future for his intelligent son, Patricius made great financial sacrifices to see that Augustine received a classical Latin education in the local school. Augustine delighted in Latin literature, but he detested the brutally enforced rote learning of arithmetic and Greek.

361 Following the death of Constantius II in 361, Julian the Apostate ruled as Roman emperor until 363, fostering the dominance of paganism even though freedom of worship for all religions had been proclaimed by Constantine in 313.

364 Valentinian I succeeded Julian as emperor in the West until 378. He reestablished toleration for Christian practice. He was the last emperor to subscribe to Arianism.

366 Augustine's education continued at Madaura, a center of learning in Roman North Africa twenty miles south of Thagaste, where he was sent to study rhetoric at age twelve. A formal command of rhetorical art, that is, expressive, ornamented, and persuasive speech, was in classical times fundamental to any professional career, such as law or public life.

370 Augustine had to return home for a year while Patricius saved money for his further education. A year of idleness led the adolescent student into acts of dissipation and sexual adventure, vividly recounted in Book II of *The Confessions*.

371 Augustine left home again to study at Carthage, which he described as "a caldron of shameful loves." He frequented the theater and kept company with a group of coarse friends whom he called "the wreckers." Here he entered into a long-term relationship with a woman whom he came to love dearly but whose name we do not know.

372 Augustine's unnamed lover bore him a son, Adeodatus, "God-given." Augustine's father died, baptized a Christian on his deathbed. At the time he merited cold contempt from his son for marital infidelity and for failing to give Augustine the guidance and sense of self-discipline he needed during his turbulent adolescence. It is clear, however, that Augustine's extraordinary gift for affection and generosity in friendship was a legacy from his sociable, openhanded father. At the conclusion of Book IX of *The Confessions*, Augustine beseeches his readers that both his parents be remembered in prayer with "devout affection."

At this time Augustine became a Manichaean "hearer." Manichaeism was a pseudo-Christian sect that emerged in the third century A.D. Its founder, Mani, drew its principles from Babylonian, Jewish, and Christian sources. It was a gnostic religious system based on a fundamental concept of the duality of light and darkness. Goodness was thought to be manifested in what belongs to the realm of light: knowledge, spirit, and soul. Evil, or darkness, was associated with ignorance, matter, and the body. Redemption was to be achieved through a special, intuitive knowledge and through moral practices that included abstinence from meat, wine, and sex for those who were fully initiated. Augustine was attracted to its dualistic concept of human nature because it allowed him to evade accepting full responsibility for his moral failures by taking refuge in the rational aspect of his being—through a spurious detachment from the activities of his bodily self. He accepted the Manichaean rejection of the Hebrew Bible along with its highly critical approach to the New Testament.

373 On reading Cicero's *Hortensius*, a strong desire for true wisdom was awakened in Augustine. This dialogue on the necessity of philosophical thinking inspired him to dedicate himself to the study of philosophy. He abandoned a career as a lawyer in the imperial civil service, a career planned for him by his father and by Romanianus, a wealthy patron who had supported his studies. The *Hortensius* counseled against the pursuit of sensual pleasure as inimical to the discipline of thought. However, Augustine stayed with his lover and continued to be influenced by Manichaeism for the next nine years. He began to question deeply the meaning of evil and the power of sin.

Teaching Career

374 Augustine returned home to Thagaste to teach grammar, the underlying foundation for the study of rhetoric. Monica, appalled at his alliance with the heretical Manichees, at first refused to allow him to enter her house. She prayed unceasingly for his conversion to the Catholic Church.

376 Augustine returned to Carthage following the death of a dear friend in Thagaste, which had made the associations of that city unbearable to him. In Carthage he opened a school of rhetoric. The rowdiness and pranks of the students made teaching extremely difficult and wore on his nerves. He persisted, however, in this career for eight years.

379 Theodosius I became emperor of the Roman Empire and ruled until 395. During this period, orthodox Christianity was established as the official state religion, and Arianism was suppressed. All subjects of the Roman Empire were enjoined to accept the Nicene

Creed, formulated at the Council of Nicea in 325, which is still in use today to express Catholic Trinitarian theology.

383 Augustine left for Rome to teach rhetoric after several good friends, including Alypius, a former student of his, wrote urging him to join them there and promising him serious students and better pay. He deceived Monica about his departure so that she could not follow him, in an effort to escape both her scrutiny and criticism of his manner of life. After suffering a siege of illness upon arrival, Augustine then had to endure cheating students who skipped out on him when it was time to pay their fees. But good fortune came his way when Symmachus, prefect of the city, chose Augustine for a post in Milan as professor of rhetoric.

Conversion

384 Augustine moved to Milan and took up the study of the Neo-platonists, especially Plotinus (205–70 A.D.), who had taught that one is awakened to a sense of divine destiny through purification from carnal appetites. He became increasingly disillusioned with Manichaean materialism and with skepticism about certitude, which had become fashionable at the time in the form of the New Academy. (This was a Greek school of thought that had its origin in pre-Socratic philosophy; it insisted that no certainty about truth can ever be attained, that there are only degrees of probability, and that all judgments are thereby relative. Augustine would write *Contra academicos* in the fall of 387 to refute these ideas.) The basic Christian principles his mother had taught him remained intact.

Augustine eventually decided to become a catechumen in the Catholic church of Milan after being impressed by the sermons of its bishop, Ambrose (c. 340–97), who showed him how to appreciate the Bible in spiritual terms and whose discourses were mystical, with Neoplatonic concepts of the soul. Augustine recognized clearly now that his carnal activity weakened his efforts at introspective contemplation.

385 Monica arrived in Milan a year after Augustine and set about arranging a marriage for him with a Catholic woman of an appropriate rank and means to further his career. As a condition for the marriage, the woman's family insisted that Augustine be separated from his concubine for at least two years before the ceremony could take place. He had been faithful to his lover for some fourteen years, and this separation was emotionally wrenching for both of them. However, instead of accepting the period of celibacy, Augustine soon after replaced her with another woman to satisfy his needs. By now, Augustine's carnal appetites were in deep conflict with his spiritual desire to seek metaphysical truth.

386 In late summer, Augustine and his companion Alypius entertained a visitor, Ponticianus, who spoke to them about St. Anthony and the other desert monks of Egypt who had left all they had in the world to devote themselves to lives of asceticism and prayer. Augustine began to feel his heart burn in his breast with the power that the call to a life of renunciation was exerting on him. He repaired to the garden of the house where he wrestled with the demands of his flesh and wept with great, tormented sobs over his inability to accept the challenge of continence.

Hearing an unseen child say, "Take up and read. Take up and read," Augustine opened St. Paul's Epistle to the Romans, which he had been studying, to chapter 13, where he read: "Let us live honorably as in daylight; not in carousing and drunkenness, not in sexual excess and lust, not in quarreling and jealousy. Rather, put on the Lord Jesus Christ and make no provision for the desires of the flesh."

At this moment, confidence and peace flooded into his heart and dispelled the anguish that had overwhelmed him in the garden. Paul's question, "Who will free me from this body of death?" became Augustine's question. Paul's answer, "Thanks be to God through Jesus Christ our Lord!" became precisely the truth he had long sought. Augustine reported all this to his mother, who rejoiced in God for his answer to her lifelong prayer for her son.

387 In the fall of 386 Augustine, with Adeodatus, Monica, Alypius, and several other friends, retired to Cassiciacum near Lake Como, where they stayed through the winter. Augustine had been ill with a chest condition similar to asthma and needed quiet rest. Here he wrote dialogues on metaphysical questions and enjoyed the natural beauty of the country setting. When winter turned harsh, Augustine returned to Milan and, with Alypius and Adeodatus, presented himself for baptism at Easter from Bishop Ambrose (c. 339–97). They were baptized together on April 24, Easter Sunday.

Ambrose was described by Augustine thus: "He was one of those who speak the truth, and speak it well, judiciously, pointedly, and with beauty and power of expression" (*On Christian Doctrine*, Book IV, 21). Like Augustine, he would be declared a Doctor of the Church.

Augustine was drawn deeply into the implications of his conversion and baptism. His emotions overflowed in tears of joy under the loving influence of Ambrose and Monica. He decided to return home to Africa with his group of friends, his mother and son, and live a life of austere seclusion. He had, by this time, given up any thought of marriage or professional career.

387 That summer Augustine, Monica, and their fellow companions had to remain in the port of Ostia while the harbors of Rome were blockaded because of an ongoing civil war. Here Augustine and his mother, standing together as they looked out into a garden, shared a mystical vision as they talked about the utter silence in which God may be heard once the clamor of the flesh, the appeals of the world, and even the sounds of the heavens and soul are stilled.

A few days later, Monica fell ill with a fever and died, age fifty-six, leaving Augustine deeply aggrieved over her death. Her last request to her son, as recounted in *The Confessions* (Book IX, 8) was that he could "Bury my body anywhere, and trouble not yourselves for it; only one thing I ask, that you remember me at the altar of my God, wherever you may be."

Book IX of *The Confessions* ends here with the description of his mother's death and Augustine's prayer for both Monica and his father, Patricius. It brings to a close Augustine's account of his purgation from sin, the illumination of his conversion and baptism, and the complete surrender of himself in unity with God. In Book X, Augustine gives an account of his state of mind at the time when he was composing *The Confessions*. Books XI–XIII set forth his own theological position on creation, time, and eternity, and the destiny of man to know himself and to know God.

388 Augustine remained for about a year in Rome, where he investigated several monastic communities. He then returned to

Thagaste in Africa with Alypius and Adeodatus, settled his property, established his own monastic community, and began to live a contemplative life as a lay "servant of God."

390 Augustine's tranquil life of prayer and study in community was soon shattered by the deaths of his gifted son, Adeodatus, at age seventeen, and of another dear friend, Nebridius.

Bishop of Hippo

391 Grief made Augustine restless, and he visited Hippo to see about setting up another monastery there. While at Mass one day, when Bishop Valerius was describing the urgent needs of the Catholic minority, besieged and persecuted by heretical sects, the congregation turned to Augustine and importuned him to accept ordination. He was made a priest on the spot. Augustine remained in Hippo for the rest of his life.

393 In December, the General Council of Hippo met, providing an occasion for the assembly of Catholic bishops to see and hear Augustine. He spoke to them clearly and eloquently "On the Faith and the Creed." It was highly unusual for an ordinary priest to preach to bishops in this manner, since the privilege of preaching was then reserved for bishops or those to whom they granted permission.

During this period and through 405, Augustine wrote against the Manichaean heresy, which he now completely repudiated.

394 For the next eight years, Augustine will campaign vigorously against the Donatists, members of a North African schism that bitterly disputed the validity of the election of Caecilian as bishop of Carthage in 311. Bishop Donatus had opposed Caecilian, who was further legitimized by the Synod of Milan in 316. Augustine, a Caeilianist, fought the Donatists over their extreme rigorism by which they held that any sacrament administered by a priest who was a *traditore* was thereby invalid. *Traditores* were those Christians who, under the threat of death during the persecution of Emperor Diocletian, had handed over their sacred books for burning. The implication was that if one's baptism was retroactively invalidated because of the sins of the priest performing it, then one has in fact never become a member of the communion of saints and must be rebaptized.

Augustine repudiated the Donatist theory with the doctrine *ex opere operato* ("from the work itself"), which means that the validity of the sacraments lies in their own inherent quality and is not determined by the merits of the person who performs the rite. The Donatists, considering themselves the "pure" Church, insisted on rigorously observing ritual actions to the point of fanaticism. They also turned away from the world to face inwardly toward their own static community of an elite chosen few who vigorously and violently persecuted nonmembers. In contrast to the separatism practiced by the Donatists, Augustine held that the Church must be coextensive with society as a kind of leaven in the world and insisted on the universal dimension of Catholicism.

395 Augustine was ordained coadjutor (assistant) bishop of Hippo. In less than two years he would be made bishop. During his episcopate, he drove the Donatists and other heretical Christian rivals out of Hippo. He led the community like a father heads a family, adjudicating disputes, intervening for prisoners to save them from torture and execution, advocating for the poor, buying freedom for badly treated slaves, and charging religious women with the care of abandoned and orphaned children. He preached abundantly and wrote *On Christian Doctrine*. By 410 Augustine had written thirty-three books.

395 Arcadius became emperor in the Roman East until 408.
Honorius, a devout Catholic, became emperor in the West until 423. He granted legal recognition to the Orthodox Catholic Church in Africa. This gave Augustine political power in his struggle with the Donatists.

396 Bishop Valerius died and Augustine succeeded him as bishop of Hippo. He remained in this office until his own death in 430.

397 Augustine began to write *The Confessions*, which were completed in 401. This work expresses three main concerns. One is Augustine's frank and detailed acknowledgment of his personal

sinfulness and the power he came to recognize as God's provident grace—protective, creative, salvific—in every moment of his life. He also wrote in order to confess his own Christian faith and to clearly repudiate any supposed lingering connections on his part with Manichaeism. Finally, *The Confessions* are a heartfelt paean of praise and thanksgiving in honor of God's glory.

This extraordinary memoir is a formidable act of memory by which Augustine reveals, vividly and specifically, the personal deeds, events, men and women, and ideas that formed the texture of his life. *The Confessions* are written in the form of a long prayer addressed directly to God and are an exercise in scrupulous honesty and candor. The theme is stated in the opening paragraph: "You have made us for Yourself, and our heart is restless until it rests in You."

399 For twenty years Augustine labored over *On the Trinity*, his most profound theological treatise. In it he exposed the errors of the Manichaeans, Donatists, Pelagians, and Arians. It included exegetical works and commentaries on Scripture.

408 The eastern German Visigoths crossed over the borders of the Roman Empire seeking refuge from the Huns and looting Roman cities as they came. Rome was besieged twice during this time and its citizens starved into acts of cannibalism. In the year 410, on August 24, the Gothic military leader Alaric and his men sacked Rome, burning parts of the city.

c. 410 Pelagius (c. 350–c. 425), a British monk, had taught an austere and reformed ideal of the Christian church for about ten years in Rome. He had gathered a small but devoted group of followers when Alaric's army forced him to flee to Africa. The battle against the Donatist heresy, which Augustine had fought vigorously for years, would be succeeded by his controversies with Pelagianism. Contrary to Augustine, Pelagius taught that human beings achieve salvation through personal acts of will by which they take total responsibility for their actions. He denied the doctrine of original sin, which held that the human will was weakened by sin and in need of divine assistance. With no concession in his system for "amazing grace," Pelagius placed on each individual the burden and blame for every sin as a fully deliberate act. A person can be saved if he or she makes up his or her mind to live a correct, moral life by exercising self-control. One must choose the good and reject what is evil. One is born free to make one's choices as one will, and is to be held completely responsible for them. In Pelagius's view, Jesus is more model than savior.

Augustine, on the contrary, accepted a fallen, flawed human nature, helpless in sin without the intervention of God's provident and salvific grace. His compassionate tolerance for the weakness of human nature contrasted sharply with the Pelagian stoic puritanism, which allowed no excuse for personal sin. For Augustine, true freedom is achieved only through a long process by which the individual's knowledge and will are healed by grace. Pelagius ultimately moved on to the Holy Land without ever meeting Augustine face-to-face. The Bishop of Hippo fought with Pelagius on the basis of his written works.

412 An imperial decree was issued from Rome banning the Donatist church.

413 For the next thirteen years, until 426, Augustine worked on his masterpiece, *The City of God*, a summation of his Christian philosophy of history, occasioned by Alaric's sack of Rome. In the wake of that disaster, the charge had come from all corners of the empire that it was the result of the forsaking of old pagan deities in favor of the Christian religion. Augustine refuted this charge by citing the fall of Troy, "the parent of Rome," which had remained faithful to all its gods.

Augustine, instead, viewed the immense suffering caused by the invasion as a necessary discipline, or remediation, of human society. Envy, pride, and the lust to dominate lead to the misery of the human race and are tendencies present in every human heart. But in disasters, souls are sifted by what they endure. Those who are evil blaspheme against God, while those who are humble and pious reverence him. However, both good and evil persons are similarly taught that the goods of this world, all gifts from God but liable to misuse, are temporary and will pass away. True and lasting riches are to be found only in God's kingdom. The rewards of heaven will eclipse with their splendor all the brilliance of creation as we know it now.

415 The synod at Diospolis in Palestine pronounced the writings of Pelagius to be orthodox.

416 Jerome (c. 347–420), biblical scholar and famous for his translation of the Bible into Latin from Greek and Hebrew (known as the Vulgate), had long had a contentious relationship with Augustine. They reconciled their differences and united together to fight their common enemy, Pelagianism. Jerome's monastery in Bethlehem had been attacked and burned by Pelagian thugs.

417 The teachings of Pelagius were condemned in Italy. He and all of his supporters were forbidden to remain in Rome.

418 The Council of Carthage, with over two hundred bishops under Augustine's leadership, pronounced Pelagianism heretical.

Final Years

423 Valentinian III became emperor in the West. He ruled until 455.

426 On September 26, Augustine nominated Eraclius to be his successor.

427 Augustine began work on his *Reconsiderations*, in which he revised and corrected the theological works he had produced both before and during the years of his bishopric.

429 Vandals, who were Arian Christians led by Genseric, invaded Africa from Spain.

430 The North African coastal provinces of Mauretania and Numidia were ravaged by Vandals, who raped, tortured, and pillaged, burning Catholic churches along the way. Catholic bishops and refugees fled to Hippo, which was a fortified city.

On August 28, Augustine died after suffering a fever for several days. He spent these final days of his life alone in his room, weeping and praying over the seven penitential psalms that were written on the wall over his bed.

*   *   *

Augustine had prayed with his frightened flock for the gift of perseverance in the faith by which the weak individual can come to share in the eternal stability of Christ. Bound as a father to his family, the Bishop of Hippo stood firm until the end, while all his world and life's work were destroyed in the violence around him. Though Hippo was partly burned, the library of Augustine was preserved from destruction. It contained much of what he felt and believed and has been handed down to us as our priceless inheritance. It comprised some 100 books, some 240 letters, and more than 500 sermons, making him the most prolific author of classical times. He composed no will for he had no property to dispose of except the library, which he left to the Church.

Augustine was declared a Doctor of the Church in 1298. He is one of the four Latin Doctors, together with SS. Ambrose, Jerome, and Gregory the Great. His feast day is celebrated on August 28.

A NOTE ON THE TEXTS

When reading the works of Saint Augustine, it is advisable to have a Bible on hand. So suffused was Augustine's thought with the words of Scripture, that—as the proliferation of citations to it in this book attest—he not only quotes liberally on every page from the Hebrew Bible and the New Testament, he also weaves into his own sentences numerous (uncited) biblical phrases and ideas.

The Augustine texts for this volume have been chosen from both older and more modern translations. For the sources of the modern selections, see the Acknowledgments on the copyright page. Many of the other selections are taken from the eight volumes of *Nicene and Post-Nicene Fathers*, edited by Philip Schaff (1885; see Suggestions for Further Reading). A complete scholarly edition of all the works of Augustine is under way under the aegis of the Augustinian Heritage Institute, but it will be many years before it is complete. Bear in mind that Augustine was the most prolific of the classical Latin and Greek authors, leaving us, as the Introduction points out, some five million words to deal with.

For *Late Have I Loved Thee*, the Editors have done their best to harmonize these disparate sources by imposing Americanized spelling and punctuation. Presentation of the various texts as to design, headings, notes, etc., are consistent with the rest of the Vintage Spiritual Classics series. The decision to retain occasional archaisms (*loveth*, *doth*) is deliberate, as is the sometimes varying use of capitalization for references to God or Christ in different selections. All has been ordered for what we hope will be the reader's best interests. The numbering of various "chapters" and subsections of the selections conforms to their original sources, but these are by no means consistent for all of Augustine's works, which have been edited and arranged by different hands over the centuries since Gutenberg.

Late Have I Loved Thee

He brought me into the cellar of wine and he set in order charity in me.

—Commentary of St. Augustine on the
Canticle of Canticles, 2:4

*He didn't abolish love of parents, wife, children, but put them in their
right order. He didn't say, "Whoever loves" but "whoever loves above me."
(Mt 10:37) That's what the church is saying in the Song of Songs: "He
put charity in order for me." Love your father, but not above your Lord;
love the one who begot you, but not above the one who created you.*

—Sermon 344.2

*But if the Creator is truly loved, that is, if He Himself is loved and not
another thing in His stead, He cannot be evilly loved; for love itself is to
be ordinately loved, because we do well to love that which, when we
love it, makes us live well and virtuously. So it seems to me that it is a
brief but true definition of virtue to say, it is the order of love; and on
this account, in the Canticles, the bride of Christ, the city of God, sings,
"Order love within me."*

—From *The City of God*, Book XV, Chapter 22,
"Of the Fall of the Sons of God"

*Now he is a man of just and holy life who forms an unprejudiced
estimate of things, and keeps his affections also under strict control, so
that he neither loves what he ought not to love, nor fails to love what he
ought to love, nor loves that more which ought to be loved less, nor
loves that equally which ought to be loved either less or more, nor loves
that less or more which ought to be loved equally. No sinner is to be
loved as a sinner; and every man is to be loved as a man for God's sake;
but God is to be loved for His own sake. And if God is to be loved more
than any man, each man ought to love God more than himself.
Likewise we ought to love another man better than our own body,
because all things are to be loved in reference to God, and another man
can have fellowship with us in the enjoyment of God, whereas our body*

cannot; for the body only lives through the soul, and it is by the soul that we enjoy God.

—FROM *On Christian Doctrine*, CHAPTER 27,
"THE ORDER OF LOVE"

If your heart is occupied by love of the world, the love of God will not be in it. Hold to the love of God, that you may stand fast for ever as God stands: for the being of every man is according to his love.

—FROM *Tractates on the Gospel of John*,
SECOND HOMILY, I JOHN 2:12–17

From The Confessions

Book I

1, 1. Great are you, O Lord, and exceedingly worthy of praise;[11] your power is immense and your wisdom beyond reckoning.[12] And so we humans, who are a due part of your creation, long to praise you—we who carry our mortality about with us,[13] carry the evidence of our sin and with it the proof that you thwart the proud.[14] Yet these humans, due part of your creation as they are, still do long to praise you. You arouse us so that praising you may bring us joy, because you have made us and drawn us to yourself, and our heart is unquiet until it rests in you.

Grant me to know and understand, Lord, which comes first: to call upon you or to praise you? To know you or to call upon you? Must we know you before we can call upon you? Anyone who invokes what is still unknown may be making a mistake. Or should you be invoked first, so that we may then come to know you? But how can people call upon someone in whom they do not yet believe? And how can they believe without a preacher?[15] But Scripture tells us that those who seek the Lord will praise him,[16] for as they seek they find him,[17] and on finding him they will praise him. Let me seek you, then, Lord, even while I am calling upon you, and call upon you even as I believe in you; for to us you have indeed been preached. My faith calls upon you, Lord, this faith which is your gift to me, which you have breathed into me through the humanity of your Son and the ministry of your preacher.

5, 5. Who will grant me to find peace in you? Who will grant me this grace, that you would come into my heart and inebriate it, enabling me to forget the evils that beset me[18] and embrace you, my only good? What are you to me? Have mercy on me, so that I may tell. What indeed am I to you, that you should command me to love you, and grow angry with me if I do not, and threaten me with

11. See Ps 47:2 (48:1); 95 (96):4; 144 (145):3.   12. See Ps 146 (147):5.

13. See 2 Cor 4:10.   14. See 1 Pt 5:5.   15. See Rom 10:14.

16. See Ps 21:27 (22:26).   17. See Mt 7:7–8; Lk 11:10.   18. See Jer 44:9.

enormous woes? Is not the failure to love you woe enough in itself? Alas for me! Through your own merciful dealings with me, O Lord my God, tell me what you are to me. Say to my soul, "I am your salvation."[19] Say it so that I can hear it. My heart is listening, Lord; open the ears of my heart and say to my soul, "I am your salvation." Let me run toward this voice and seize hold of you. Do not hide your face from me:[20] let me die so that I may see it, for not to see it would be death to me indeed.[21]

6. The house of my soul is too small for you to enter: make it more spacious by your coming. It lies in ruins: rebuild it. Some things are to be found there which will offend your gaze; I confess this to be so and know it well. But who will clean my house? To whom but yourself can I cry, "Cleanse me of my hidden sins, O Lord, and for those incurred through others pardon your servant"[22]? I believe, and so I will speak.[23] You know everything, Lord.[24] Have I not laid my own transgressions bare before you to my own condemnation, my God, and have you not forgiven the wickedness of my heart?[25] I do not argue my case against you,[26] for you are truth itself; nor do I wish to deceive myself, lest my iniquity be caught in its own lies.[27] No, I do not argue the case with you, because "if you, Lord, keep the score of our iniquities, then who, Lord, can bear it?"[28]

Book II

1, 1. Now I want to call to mind the foul deeds I committed, those sins of the flesh that corrupted my soul, not in order to love them, but to love you, my God. Out of love for loving you I do this, recalling my most wicked ways and thinking over the past with bitterness so that you may grow ever sweeter to me; for you are a sweetness that deceives not, a sweetness blissful and serene. I will try now to give a coherent account of my disintegrated self, for when I turned

19. Ps 34 (35):3.   20. See Dt 32:20.   21. See Ex 33:23.   22. Ps 18 (19):13.

23. Ps 115 (116):10; 2 Cor 4:13.   24. See Jn 21:17.   25. See Ps 31 (32):5.

26. See Jb 9:2–3.   27. See Ps 26 (27):12.   28. Ps 129 (130):3.

away from you, the one God, and pursued a multitude of things, I went to pieces. There was a time in adolescence when I was afire to take my fill of hell. I boldly thrust out rank, luxuriant growth in various furtive love affairs; my beauty wasted away and I rotted in your sight, intent on pleasing myself and winning favor in the eyes of men.

2, 2. What was it that delighted me? Only loving and being loved. But there was no proper restraint, as in the union of mind with mind, where a bright boundary regulates friendship. From the mud of my fleshly desires[29] and my erupting puberty belched out murky clouds that obscured and darkened my heart until I could not distinguish the calm light of love from the fog of lust. The two swirled about together and dragged me, young and weak as I was, over the cliffs of my desires, and engulfed me in a whirlpool of sins. Your anger had grown hot at my doings, yet I did not know. I was deafened by that clanking chain of my mortal state which was the punishment for my soul's pride, and I was wandering away from you, yet you let me go my way. I was flung hither and thither, I poured myself out, frothed and floundered in the tumultuous sea of my fornications; and you were silent.[30] O my joy, how long I took to find you! At that time you kept silence as I continued to wander far from you and sowed more and more sterile seeds to my own grief, abased by my pride and wearied by my restlessness.

5, 10. The beautiful form of material things attracts our eyes, so we are drawn to gold, silver, and the like. We are powerfully influenced by the feel of things agreeable to the touch; and each of our other senses finds some quality that appeals to it individually in the variety of material objects. There is the same appeal in worldly rank, and the possibility it offers of commanding and dominating other people: this too holds its attraction, and often provides an opportunity for settling old scores. We may seek all these things, O Lord, but in seeking them we must not deviate from your law. The life we live here is open to temptation by reason of a certain measure and harmony between its own splendor and all these beautiful things of low degree. Again, the friendship which draws human beings together in a tender bond is sweet to us because out of many minds it forges a unity. Sin gains entrance through these

29. See 1 Jn 2:16.   30. See Is 42:14.

and similar good things when we turn to them with immoderate desire, since they are the lowest kind of goods and we thereby turn away from the better and higher: from you yourself, O Lord our God, and your truth and your law. These lowest goods hold delights for us indeed, but no such delights as does my God, who made all things; for in him the just man finds delight, and for upright souls[31] he himself is joy.

6, 13. For in vice there lurks a counterfeit beauty: pride, for instance—even pride apes sublimity, whereas you are the only God, most high above all things. As for ambition, what does it crave but honors and glory, while you are worthy of honor beyond all others, and eternally glorious? The ferocity of powerful men aims to inspire fear; but who is to be feared except the one God? Can anything be snatched from his power or withdrawn from it—when or where or whither or by whom? Flirtatiousness aims to arouse love by its charming wiles, but nothing can hold more charm than your charity, nor could anything be loved to greater profit than your truth, which outshines all else in its luminous beauty. Curiosity poses as pursuit of knowledge, whereas you know everything to a supreme degree. Even ignorance or stupidity masquerades as simplicity and innocence, but nothing that exists is simpler than yourself; and what could be more innocent than you, who leave the wicked to be hounded by their own sins? Sloth pretends to aspire to rest, but what sure rest is there save the Lord? Lush living likes to be taken for contented abundance, but you are the full and inexhaustible store of a sweetness that never grows stale. Extravagance is a bogus generosity, but you are the infinitely wealthy giver of all good things. Avarice strives to amass possessions, but you own everything. Envy is contentious over rank accorded to another, but what ranks higher than you? Anger seeks revenge, but whoever exacts revenge with greater justice than yourself? Timidity dreads any unforeseen or sudden threat to the things it loves, and takes precautions for their safety; but is anything sudden or unforeseen to you? Who can separate what you love from you?[32] Where is ultimate security to be found, except with you? Sadness pines at the loss of the good things with which greed took its pleasure, because it wants to be like you, from whom nothing can be taken away.

31. See Ps 63:11 (64:10).   32. See Rom 8:35.

6, 14. A soul that turns away from you therefore lapses into fornication[33] when it seeks apart from you what it can never find in pure and limpid form except by returning to you. All those who wander far away and set themselves up against you are imitating you, but in a perverse way; yet by this very mimicry they proclaim that you are the creator of the whole of nature, and that in consequence there is no place whatever where we can hide from your presence.

With regard to my theft, then: what did I love in it, and in what sense did I imitate my Lord, even if only with vicious perversity? Did the pleasure I sought lie in breaking the law at least in that sneaky way, since I was unable to do so with any show of strength? Was I, in truth, a prisoner, trying to simulate a crippled sort of freedom, attempting a shady parody of omnipotence by getting away with something forbidden? How like that servant of yours who fled from his Lord and hid in the shadows! What rottenness, what a misshapen life! Rather a hideous pit of death! To do what was wrong simply because it was wrong—could I have found pleasure in that?

7, 15. How can I repay the Lord[34] for my ability to recall these things without fear? Let me love you, Lord, and give thanks to you and confess to your name, because you have forgiven my grave sins and wicked deeds. By your sheer grace and mercy you melted my sins away like ice.[35] To your grace also do I ascribe whatever sins I did not commit, for what would I not have been capable of, I who could be enamored even of a wanton crime? I acknowledge that you have forgiven me everything, both the sins I willfully committed by following my own will, and those I avoided through your guidance.

Is there anyone who can take stock of his own weakness and still dare to credit his chastity and innocence to his own efforts? And could such a person think to love you less, on the pretext that he has had smaller need of your mercy, that mercy with which you forgive the sins of those who turn back to you? If there is anyone whom you have called, who by responding to your summons has avoided those sins which he finds me remembering and confessing in my own life as he reads this, let him not mock me; for I have been healed by the same doctor who has granted him the grace not to fall

33. See Ps 72 (73):27.   34. See Ps 115 (116):12.   35. See Sir 3:17.

ill, or at least to fall ill less seriously. Let such a person therefore love you just as much, or even more, on seeing that the same physician who rescued me from sinful diseases of such gravity has kept him immune.

Book III

1, 1. So I arrived at Carthage, where the din of scandalous love affairs raged cauldron-like around me. I was not yet in love, but I was enamored with the idea of love, and so deep within me was my need that I hated myself for the sluggishness of my desires. In love with loving, I was casting about for something to love; the security of a way of life free from pitfalls seemed abhorrent to me, because I was inwardly starved of that food which is yourself, O my God. Yet this inner famine created no pangs of hunger in me. I had no desire for the food that does not perish, not because I had my fill of it, but because the more empty I was, the more I turned from it in revulsion. My soul's health was consequently poor. It was covered with sores and flung itself out of doors, longing to soothe its misery by rubbing against sensible things; yet these were soulless, and so could not be truly loved. Loving and being loved were sweet to me, the more so if I could also enjoy a lover's body; so I polluted the stream of friendship with my filthy desires and clouded its purity with hellish lusts; yet all the while, befouled and disgraced though I was, my boundless vanity made me long to appear elegant and sophisticated. I blundered headlong into the love which I hoped would hold me captive, but in your goodness, O my God, my mercy,[36] you sprinkled bitter gall over my sweet pursuits. I was loved, and I secretly entered into an enjoyable liaison, but I was also trammeling myself with fetters of distress, laying myself open to the iron rods and burning scourges of jealousy and suspicion, of fear, anger, and quarrels.[37]

36. See Ps 58:18 (59:17).   37. See Gal 5:20.

Book IV

8, 13. Time does not stand still, nor are the rolling seasons useless to us, for they work wonders in our minds. They came and went from day to day, and by their coming and going implanted in me other hopes and other memories. Little by little they set me up again and turned me toward things that had earlier delighted me, and before these my sorrow began to give ground. Yet its place was taken, not indeed by fresh sorrows, but by the seeds of fresh sorrows; for how had that sorrow been able so easily to pierce my inmost being, if not because I had poured out my soul into the sand by loving a man doomed to death as though he were never to die? What restored and re-created me above all was the consolation of other friends, in whose company I loved what I was loving as a substitute for you. This was a gross fable and a long-sustained lie, and as our minds itched to listen, they were corrupted by its adulterous excitation, but the fable did not die for me when any of my friends died.

There were other joys to be found in their company which still more powerfully captivated my mind—the charms of talking and laughing together and kindly giving way to each other's wishes, reading elegantly written books together, sharing jokes and delighting to honor one another, disagreeing occasionally but without rancor, as a person might disagree with himself, and lending piquancy by that rare disagreement to our much more frequent accord. We would teach and learn from each other, sadly missing any who were absent and blithely welcoming them when they returned. Such signs of friendship sprang from the hearts of friends who loved and knew their love returned, signs to be read in smiles, words, glances, and a thousand gracious gestures. So were sparks kindled and our minds were fused inseparably, out of many becoming one.

9, 14. This is what we esteem in our friends, and so highly do we esteem it that our conscience feels guilt if we fail to love someone who responds to us with love, or do not return the love of one who offers love to us, and this without seeking any bodily gratification from the other save signs of his goodwill. From this springs our grief if someone dies, from this come the darkness of sorrow and the heart drenched with tears because sweetness has turned to bitterness, so that as the dying lose their life, life becomes no better than death for those who live on. Blessed is he who loves you, and loves his friend in you, and his enemy for your sake.[38] He alone loses no one dear to him, to whom all are dear in the One who is never lost. And who is this but our God, the God who made heaven and earth and fills them, because it was by filling them that he made them? No one loses you unless he tries to get rid of you, and if he does try to do that, where can he go, whither does he flee,[39] but from you in your tranquillity to you in your anger? Does he not encounter your law everywhere, in his own punishment? Your law is truth, as you yourself are truth.[40]

12, 18. If sensuous beauty delights you, praise God for the beauty of corporeal things, and channel the love you feel for them onto their Maker, lest the things that please you lead you to displease him. If kinship with other souls appeals to you, let them be loved in God, because they too are changeable and gain stability only when fixed in him; otherwise they would go their way and be lost. Let them be loved in him, and carry off to God as many of them as possible with you, and say to them:

Let us love him, for he made these things and he is not far off,[41] for he did not make them and then go away: they are from him but also in him. You know where he is, because you know where truth tastes sweet. He is most intimately present to the human heart, but the heart has strayed from him. Return to your heart, then, you wrongdoers, and hold fast to him who made you. Stand with him and you will stand firm, rest in him and you will find peace. Where are you going, along your rough paths? Tell me, where are you going? The good which you love derives from him, and insofar as it is referred to him it is truly good and sweet, but anything that comes from him will justly turn bitter if it is unjustly loved by people who forsake him. Why persist in walking difficult and toilsome

38. See Mt 5:44; Lk 6:27.   39. See Ps 138 (139:7).

40. See Ps 118 (119):142; Jn 14:6.   41. See Ps 99 (100):3; Acts 17:27.

paths?[42] There is no repose where you are seeking it. Search as you like, it is not where you are looking. You are seeking a happy life in the realm of death, and it will not be found there. How could life be happy, where there is no life at all?

Book V

1, 1. Accept the sacrifice of my confessions, offered to you by the power of this tongue of mine which you have fashioned and aroused to confess to your name;[43] bring healing to all my bones[44] and let them exclaim, "Lord, who is like you?"[45] A person who confesses to you is not informing you about what goes on within him, for a closed heart does not shut you out, nor is your hand pushed away by human obduracy; you melt it when you choose, whether by showing mercy or by enforcing your claim, and from your fiery heat no one can hide.[46]

But allow my soul to give you glory that it may love you the more, and let it confess to you your own merciful dealings,[47] that it may give you glory. Your whole creation never wearies of praising you, never falls silent; never a breath from the mouth[48] of one who turns to you but gives you glory, never is praise lacking from the universe of living creatures and corporeal beings as they laud you through the mouths of those who contemplate them. Supported by these things you have made, let the human soul rise above its weariness and pass through these creatures to you, who have made them so wonderfully. There it will find refreshment, there is its true strength.

2, 2. Wicked, restless folk may go their way and flee from you as they will. You see them, for your eyes pierce their darkness, and how lovely is the whole of which they are part, lovely though they are foul! And how have they harmed you? Have they in any point

---

42. See Ws 5:7.   43. See Prv 18:21.   44. See Ps 6:3 (2).

45. Ps 34 (35):10.   46. See Ps 18:7 (19:6).   47. See Ps 106 (107):8.

48. See Ps 150:7 (6).

brought your rule into disrepute, that rule which is just and perfect
from highest heaven to the lowest of creatures? Where have they
fled, in fleeing from your face? Is there any place where you cannot
find them?[49] They have fled all the same, to avoid seeing you who
see them, and so in their blindness they have stumbled over you—
for you abandon nothing you have made; yes, stumbled over you,
these unjust folk, and justly hurt themselves; for they distanced
themselves from your gentleness only to trip over your probity and
fall upon the rough edges of your anger.[50] Clearly they do not know
that you are everywhere, for you are not confined to any place, and
you alone are present to those who run far away from you.

> Let them turn back, and seek you,
> for you do not forsake your creation
> as they have forsaken their creator.
> Let them only turn back,
> see! there you are in their hearts,
> in the hearts of all those who confess to you,
> who fling themselves into your arms
> and weep against your breast after their difficult journey,
> while you so easily will wipe away their tears.[51]
> At this they weep the more,
> yet even their laments are matter for joy,
> because you, Lord, are not some human being of flesh
>   and blood,
> but the Lord who made them,
> and now make them anew and comfort them.

And what of myself: where was I as I sought you? You were
straight ahead of me, but I had roamed away from myself and
could not find even myself, let alone you!

---

49. See Ps 138 (139):7–8.   50. Echoes of Rom 11:7–11.
51. See Is 25:8; Rv 7:17; 21:4.

Book VI

15, 25. Meanwhile my sins were multiplying, for the woman with whom I had been cohabiting was ripped from my side, being regarded as an obstacle to my marriage. So deeply was she engrafted into my heart that it was left torn and wounded and trailing blood. She had returned to Africa, vowing to you that she would never give herself to another man, and the son I had fathered by her was left with me. But I was too unhappy to follow a woman's example: I faced two years of waiting before I could marry the girl to whom I was betrothed, and I chafed at the delay, for I was no lover of marriage but the slave of lust. So I got myself another woman, in no sense a wife, that my soul's malady might be sustained in its pristine vigor or even aggravated, as it was conducted under the escort of inveterate custom into the realm of matrimony.

The wound inflicted on me by the earlier separation did not heal either. After the fever and the immediate acute pain had dulled, it putrefied, and the pain became a cold despair.

16, 26. Praise be to you, glory be to you,[52] O fount of all mercy! As I grew more and more miserable, you were drawing nearer. Already your right hand was ready to seize me and pull me out of the filth, yet I did not know it. The only thing that restrained me from being sucked still deeper into the whirlpool of carnal lusts was the fear of death and of your future judgment, which throughout all the swings of opinion had never been dislodged from my heart. With my friends Alypius and Nebridius I argued about the fate of the good and the wicked: I maintained that, as I saw it, Epicurus would have won the debate had I not believed that after death life remains for the soul, and so do the consequences of our moral actions; this Epicurus refused to believe. I posed this question: if we were immortal and lived in a state of perpetual bodily pleasure without any fear of losing it, why should we not be happy? Would there be anything else to seek? I did not know that it was symptomatic of my vast misery that I had sunk so low, and was so blind, as to be incapable of even conceiving the light of a goodness, a beauty,

52. See 1 Chr 29:11–12.

which deserved to be embraced for its own sake, which the bodily eye sees not, though it is seen by the spirit within. Nor did I in my wretchedness consider what stream it was whence flowed to me the power to discuss even these distasteful things with my friends and still find sweetness in our talk, or whence came my inability to be happy, even in the sense in which I then understood happiness, without my friends, however lavishly supplied I might be with carnal luxuries. I loved these friends for their own sake, and felt myself loved by them for mine.

Oh, how tortuous were those paths! Woe betide the soul which supposes it will find something better if it forsakes you! Toss and turn as we may, now on our back, now side, now belly—our bed is hard at every point, for you alone are our rest. But lo! Here you are;[53] you rescue us from our wretched meanderings and establish us on your way;[54] you console us and bid us, "Run:[55] I will carry you, I will lead you and I will bring you home."[56]

Book X

5, 7. For it is you, Lord, who judge me. No one knows what he himself is made of, except his own spirit within him,[57] yet there is still some part of him which remains hidden even from his own spirit; but you, Lord, know everything about a human being because you have made him. And though in your sight I may despise myself and reckon myself dust and ashes,[58] I know something about you which I do not know about myself. It is true that we now see only a tantalizing reflection in a mirror,[59] and so it is that while I am on pilgrimage far from you,[60] I am more present to myself than to you; yet I do know that you cannot be defiled in any way whatever, whereas I do not know which temptations I may have the strength to resist, and to which ones I shall succumb. Our hope is that, because you are trustworthy, you do not allow us to be tempted

---

53. See Ps 138 (139):8.   54. See Ps 31 (32):8; 85 (86):11.   55. See 1 Cor 9:24.

56. See Is 46:4.   57. See 1 Cor 2:11.   58. See Jb 42:6; Sir 10:9, Gn 18:27.

59. See 1 Cor 13:12.   60. See 2 Cor 5:6.

more fiercely than we can bear, but along with the temptation you ordain the outcome of it, so that we can endure.[61] Let me, then, confess what I know about myself, and confess too what I do not know, because what I know of myself I know only because you shed light on me, and what I do not know I shall remain ignorant about until my darkness becomes like bright noon before your face.[62]

6, 8. I love you, Lord, with no doubtful mind but with absolute certainty. You pierced my heart with your Word, and I fell in love with you. But the sky and the earth too, and everything in them— all these things around me are telling me that I should love you; and since they never cease to proclaim this to everyone, those who do not hear are left without excuse.[63] But you, far above, will show mercy to anyone with whom you have already determined to deal mercifully, and will grant pity to whomsoever you choose.[64] Were this not so, the sky and the earth would be proclaiming your praises to the deaf.

But what am I loving when I love you? Not beauty of body nor transient grace, not this fair light which is now so friendly to my eyes, not melodious song in all its lovely harmonies, not the sweet fragrance of flowers or ointments or spices, not manna or honey, not limbs that draw me to carnal embrace: none of these do I love when I love my God. And yet I do love a kind of light, a kind of voice, a certain fragrance, a food, and an embrace, when I love my God: a light, voice, fragrance, food, and embrace for my inmost self, where something limited to no place shines into my mind, where something not snatched away by passing time sings for me, where something no breath blows away yields to me its scent, where there is savor undiminished by famished eating, and where I am clasped in a union from which no satiety can tear me away. This is what I love, when I love my God.

9. And what is this?
I put my question to the earth, and it replied, "I am not he";
I questioned everything it held, and they confessed the same.
I questioned the sea and the great deep,[65]

---

61. See 1 Cor 10:13.   62. See Is 58:10; Ps 89 (90):8.   63. See Rom 1:20.

64. See Rom 9:15; Ex 33:19.   65. See Jb 28:14.

and the teeming live creatures that crawl,[66]
and they replied,
"We are not God; seek higher."
I questioned the gusty winds,
and every breeze with all its flying creatures told me,
"Anaximenes was wrong: I am not God."
To the sky I put my question, to sun, moon, stars,
but they denied me: "We are not the God you seek."
And to all things which stood around the portals of my flesh
    I said,
"Tell me of my God.
You are not he, but tell me something of him."
Then they lifted up their mighty voices and cried,
"He made us."[67]
My questioning was my attentive spirit,
and their reply, their beauty.

Then toward myself I turned and asked myself, "Who are you?"
And I answered my own question: "A man." See, here are the body
and soul that make up myself, the one outward and the other
within. Through which of these should I seek my God? With my
body's senses I had already sought him from earth to heaven, to the
farthest place whither I could send the darting rays of my eyes; but
what lay within me was better, and to this all those bodily messen-
gers reported back, for it controlled and judged the replies of sky
and earth, and of all the creatures dwelling in them, all those who
had proclaimed, "We are not God" and "He made us." My inner
self[68] recognized them all through the service of the outer. I, who was
that inmost self, I, who was mind, knew them through the senses
of my body; and so I questioned the vast frame of the world concerning my God, and it answered, "I am not he, but he made me."

27, 38. Late have I loved you, Beauty so ancient and so new,
late have I loved you!
Lo, you were within,

---

66. See Gn 1:20.   67. See Ps 99 (100):3.
68. See Rom 7:22; 2 Cor 4:16; Eph 3:16.

but I outside, seeking there for you,
and upon the shapely things you have made I rushed
   headlong,
I, misshapen.
You were with me, but I was not with you.
They held me back far from you,
those things which would have no being
were they not in you.
You called, shouted, broke through my deafness;
you flared, blazed, banished my blindness;
you lavished your fragrance, I gasped, and now I pant for
   you;
I tasted you, and I hunger and thirst;
you touched me, and I burned for your peace.

28, 39. When at last I cling to you[69] with my whole being there will be no more anguish or labor for me,[70] and my life will be alive indeed, because filled with you. But now it is very different. Anyone whom you fill you also uplift, but I am not full of you, and so I am a burden to myself. Joys over which I ought to weep do battle with sorrows that should be matter for joy, and I know not which will be victorious. But I also see griefs that are evil at war in me with joys that are good, and I know not which will win the day. This is agony, Lord, have pity on me! It is agony! See, I do not hide my wounds; you are the physician and I am sick; you are merciful, I in need of mercy. Is not human life on earth a time of testing?[71]

43, 69. How you loved us, O good Father, who spared not even your only Son, but gave him up for us evildoers![72] How you loved us, for whose sake he who deemed it no robbery to be your equal was made subservient, even to the point of dying on the cross![73] Alone of all he was free among the dead,[74] for he had power to lay down his life and power to retrieve it.[75] For our sake he stood to you as both victor and victim, and victor because victim;[76] for us he stood to you as priest and sacrifice, and priest because sacrifice,[77]

69. See Ps 62:9 (63:8).   70. See Ps 89 (90):10.   71. See Jb 7:1, Old Latin.

72. See Rom 8:32.   73. See Phil 2:6, 8.   74. See Ps 87:6 (88:5).

75. See Jn 10:18.   76. See Heb 9:28.   77. See Heb 7:27.

making us sons and daughters to you instead of servants[78] by being born of you to serve us. With good reason is there solid hope for me in him, because you will heal all my infirmities[79] through him who sits at your right hand and intercedes for us.[80] Were it not so, I would despair. Many and grave are those infirmities, many and grave; but wider-reaching is your healing power. We might have despaired, thinking your Word remote from any conjunction with humankind, had he not become flesh and made his dwelling among us.[81]

70. Filled with terror by my sins and my load of misery I had been turning over in my mind a plan to flee into solitude, but you forbade me, and strengthened me by your words, "To this end Christ died for all," you reminded me, "that they who are alive may live not for themselves, but for him who died for them."[82] See, then, Lord: I cast my care upon you[83] that I may live, and I will contemplate the wonders you have revealed.[84] You know how stupid and weak I am:[85] teach me and heal me.[86] Your only Son, in whom are hidden all treasures of wisdom and knowledge,[87] has redeemed me with his blood. Let not the proud disparage me,[88] for I am mindful of my ransom. I eat it, I drink it,[89] I dispense it to others, and as a poor man I long to be filled[90] with it among those who are fed and feasted. And then do those who seek him praise the Lord.[91]

Book XI

2, 2. My pen serves me as a tongue,[92] but when will it find eloquence enough to recount all those exhortations and threats, all that encouragement and guidance, by which you led me to this position where I must preach the word and administer the sacrament to

78. See Gal 4:7.   79. See Ps 102 (103):3.   80. See Rom 8:34.

81. See Jn 1:14.   82. 2 Cor 5:15.   83. See Ps 54:23 (55:22).

84. See Ps 118 (119):17–18.   85. See Ps 68:6 (69:5).

86. See Ps 24 (25):5; 6:3 (2).   87. See Col 2:3.   88. See Ps 118 (119):22.

89. See Jn 6:55, 57; 1 Cor 10:31; 11:29.   90. See Lk 16:21.

91. See Ps 21:27 (22:26).   92. See Ps 44:2 (45:1).

your people? Furthermore, even had I skill to relate it all in order, the dripping moments of time are too precious to me. I have long burned with desire to meditate on your law,[93] that there I may confess to you both what I know and what I still find baffling, your dawning light in me and the residual darkness that will linger until my weakness is swallowed up by your strength. I am chary of frittering away on anything else the hours I find free from such needful activities as bodily refreshment, mental concentration, the duties I owe to the people and others which I do not owe but render nonetheless.

3. O Lord my God, hear my prayer,[94]
may your mercy hearken to my longing,[95]
a longing on fire not for myself alone
but to serve the brethren I dearly love;
you see my heart and know this is true.
Let me offer in sacrifice to you the service of my heart and
    tongue,
but grant me first what I can offer you;
for I am needy and poor,[96]
but you are rich unto all who call upon you,[97]
and you care for us though no care troubles you.
Circumcise all that is within me from presumption
and my lips without from falsehood.[98]
Let your Scriptures be my chaste delight,
let me not be deceived in them
nor through them deceive others.
Hearken, O Lord, have mercy, my Lord and God,[99]
O Light of the blind, Strength of the weak—
who yet are Light to those who see and Strength to the
    strong—
hearken to my soul,
hear me as I cry from the depths,[100]
for unless your ears be present in our deepest places

93. See Ps 1:2.   94. See Ps 60:2 (61:1).   95. See Ps 9B:38 (10:17).

96. See Ps 85 (86):1.   97. See Rom 10:12.   98. See Ex 6:12.

99. See Jer 18:19; Ps 26 (27):7.   100. See Ps 129 (130):1.

where shall we go[101] and whither cry?
Yours is the day, yours the night,[102]
a sign from you sends minutes speeding by;
spare in their fleeting course a space for us
to ponder the hidden wonders of your law:
shut it not against us as we knock.[103]
Not in vain have you willed so many pages to be written,
pages deep in shadow, obscure in their secrets;
not in vain do harts and hinds seek shelter in those woods,
to hide and venture forth,
roam and browse, lie down and ruminate.
Perfect me too, Lord, and reveal those woods to me.[104]
Lo, your voice is joy to me,
your voice that rings out above a flood of joys.
Give me what I love;
for I love indeed, and this love you have given me.
Forsake not your gifts, disdain not your parched grass.
Let me confess to you all I have found in your books,
Let me hear the voice of praise,[105]
and drink from you,
and contemplate the wonders of your law[106]
from the beginning when you made heaven and earth
to that everlasting reign when we shall be with you in
    your holy city.

Book XIII

7, 8. Anyone with enough mental agility should here follow your apostle, who tells us that "the love of God has been poured out into our hearts through the Holy Spirit who has been given us."[107] But then, minded to instruct us on spiritual matters,[108] the apostle points

---

101. See Ps 138 (139):7–8.   102. See Ps 73 (74):16.

103. See Mt 7:7–8; Lk 11:9–10.   104. See Ps 28 (29):9.

105. See Ps 25 (26):7.   106. See Ps 118 (119):18.   107. Rom 5:5.

108. See 1 Cor 12:1.

out a way of loftiest excellence, the way of charity;[109] and he kneels before you[110] on our behalf, entreating you to grant us some understanding of the charity of Christ, which is exalted above all knowledge.[111] This is why the Spirit, who is supereminent Love, was said to be poised above the waters at the beginning.

To whom should I speak, and how express myself, about the passion that drags us headlong into the deep, and the charity that uplifts us through your Spirit, who hovered over the waters? To whom should I say this, and in what terms? These are not literally places, into which we plunge and from which we emerge: what could seem more placelike than they, yet what is in reality more different? They are movements of the heart, they are two loves. One is the uncleanness of our own spirit, which like a flood tide sweeps us down, in love with restless cares; the other is the holiness of your Spirit, which bears us upward in a love for peace beyond all care, that our hearts may be lifted up to you,[112] to where your Spirit is poised above the waters, so that once our soul has crossed over those waters on which there is no reliance we may reach all-surpassing rest.[113]

8, 9. An angel was swept away, the human soul was swept away; and they had shown that all spiritual creatures would have been engulfed in darkness, had you not said at that first moment, "Let there be light,"[114] and brought light into being; and had not every obedient intelligence in your heavenly city clung fast to you and found its rest in your Spirit, who unchangingly broods over everything subject to change. Otherwise the very heaven above our heaven would have been a dark abyss in itself, whereas now it is light in the Lord.[115] When spirits slide away from you they are stripped of their vesture of light and exposed in their native darkness, and then their unhappy restlessness amply proves to us how noble is each rational creature you have made, for nothing less than yourself can suffice to give it any measure of blessed rest, nor indeed can it be its own satisfaction. For it is you, Lord, who will

109. See 1 Cor 12:31.   110. See Eph 3:14.   111. See Eph 3:19.

112. See Col 3:1–2.   113. See Ps 123 (124):5.   114. Gn 1:3.

115. See Eph 5:8.

light up our darkness.[116] From you derives our garment of light, and in you our darkness will be bright as noon.[117]

Give me yourself, O my God, give yourself back to me. Lo, I love you, but if my love is too mean, let me love more passionately. I cannot gauge my love, nor know how far it fails, how much more love I need for my life to set its course straight into your arms, never swerving until hidden in the covert of your face.[118] This alone I know, that without you all to me is misery, woe outside myself and woe within, and all wealth but penury, if it is not my God.

9, 10. It cannot be denied, surely, that the Father too was borne aloft over the waters, and the Son? If the expression means poised in a place, after the manner of a body, then the Holy Spirit was not poised there either; but if it means that the eminence of unchangeable Godhead is far above all that is changeable, then certainly the one God, Father, Son, and Holy Spirit, was poised above the waters. Why, then, was this stated of your Spirit only? Why of him alone, as though he were in a place, when it is no place; and why only of him who alone is said to be your Gift?[119]

Because, I think, in your Gift we find rest, and there we enjoy you. Our true place is where we find rest. We are borne toward it by love, and it is your good Spirit[120] who lifts up our sunken nature from the gates of death.[121] In goodness of will is our peace.[122] A body gravitates to its proper place by its own weight. This weight does not necessarily drag it downward, but pulls it to the place proper to it: thus fire tends upward, a stone downward. Drawn by their weight, things seek their rightful places. If oil is poured into water, it will rise to the surface, but if water is poured onto oil it will sink below the oil: drawn by their weight, things seek their rightful places. They are not at rest as long as they are disordered, but once brought to order they find their rest. Now, my weight is my love, and wherever I am carried, it is this weight that carries me. Your Gift sets us afire and we are borne upward; we catch his flame and

116. See Ps 17:29 (18:28).   117. See Is 58:10.

118. See Col 3:3; Ps 30:21 (31:20).   119. See Acts 2:38.

120. See Ps 142 (143):10.   121. See Ps 9:14–15 (13).   122. See Lk 2:14.

up we go. In our hearts we climb those upward paths,[123] singing the songs of ascent. By your fire, your beneficent fire, are we inflamed, because we are making our way up to "the peace of Jerusalem." For "I rejoiced when I was told, 'We are going to the Lord's house.'"[124] There shall a good will find us a place, that we may have no other desire but to abide there forever.[125]

123. See Ps 83:6 (84:5).   124. Ps 121 (122):6, 1.   125. See Ps 60:8 (61:7).

From The City of God

Book XIV

Chapter 6 Of the Character of the Human Will Which Makes the Affections of the Soul Right or Wrong.

But the character of the human will is of moment; because, if it is wrong, these motions of the soul will be wrong, but if it is right, they will be not merely blameless, but even praiseworthy. For the will is in them all; yea, none of them is anything else than will. For what are desire and joy but a volition of consent to the things we wish? And what are fear and sadness but a volition of aversion from the things which we do not wish? But when consent takes the form of seeking to possess the things we wish, this is called desire; and when consent takes the form of enjoying the things we wish, this is called joy. In like manner, when we turn with aversion from that which we do not wish to happen, this volition is termed fear; and when we turn away from that which has happened against our will, this act of will is called sorrow. And generally in respect of all that we seek or shun, as a man's will is attracted or repelled, so it is changed and turned into these different affections. Wherefore the man who lives according to God, and not according to man, ought to be a lover of good, and therefore a hater of evil. And since no one is evil by nature, but whoever is evil is evil by vice, he who lives according to God ought to cherish toward evil men a perfect hatred, so that he shall neither hate the man because of his vice, nor love the vice because of the man, but hate the vice and love the man. For the vice being cursed, all that ought to be loved, and nothing that ought to be hated, will remain.

Chapter 7 That the Words Love and Regard (*amor* and *dilectio*) Are in Scripture Used Indifferently of Good and Evil Affection.

He who resolves to love God, and to love his neighbor as himself, not according to man but according to God, is on account of this love said to be of a good will; and this is in Scripture more commonly called charity, but it is also, even in the same books, called love. For the apostle says that the man to be elected as a ruler of the people must be a lover of good.[126] And when the Lord himself had asked Peter, "Hast thou a regard for me (*diligis*) more than these?" Peter replied, "Lord, Thou knowest that I love (*amo*) Thee." And again a second time the Lord asked not whether Peter loved (*amaret*) him, but whether he had a regard (*diligeret*) for him, and, he again answered, "Lord, Thou knowest that I love (*amo*) Thee." But on the third interrogation the Lord himself no longer says, "Hast thou a regard (*diligis*) for me," but "Lovest thou (*amas*) me?" And then the evangelist adds, "Peter was grieved because He said unto him the third time, 'Lovest thou (*amas*) me?'" though the Lord had not said three times but only once, "Lovest thou (*amas*) me?" and twice "*Diligis* me?" from which we gather that, even when the Lord said "*diligis*," he used an equivalent for "*amas.*" Peter, too, throughout used one word for the one thing, and the third time also replied, "Lord, Thou knowest all things, Thou knowest that I love (*amo*) Thee."[127]

I have judged it right to mention this, because some are of the opinion that charity or regard (*dilectio*) is one thing, love (*amor*) another. They say that *dilectio* is used of a good affection, *amor* of an evil love. But it is very certain that even secular literature knows no such distinction. However, it is for the philosophers to determine whether and how they differ, though their own writings sufficiently testify that they make great account of love (*amor*) placed on good objects, and even on God himself. But we wished to show that the Scriptures of our religion, whose authority we prefer to all writings whatsoever, make no distinction between *amor*, *dilectio*, and *caritas*; and we have already shown that *amor* is used in a good connection. And if anyone fancy that *amor* is no doubt used both of good and bad loves, but that *dilectio* is reserved for the good only, let him remember what the psalm says, "He that loveth (*diligit*) iniquity hateth his own soul";[128] and the words of the Apostle John, "If any man love (*diligere*) the world, the love (*dilectio*) of the Father is not in him.[129] Here you have in one passage *dilectio* used both in a good and a bad sense. And if anyone demands an instance of *amor* being used in a bad sense (for we have already shown its use in a

---

126. Ti 1:8, according to Greek and Vulgate.   127. Jn 21:15–17.

128. Ps 11:5.   129. 1 Jn 2:15.

good sense) let him read the words, "For men shall be lovers (*amantes*) of their own selves, lovers (*amatores*) of money."[130]

The right will is, therefore, well-directed love, and the wrong will is ill-directed love. Love, then, yearning to have what is loved, is desire; and having and enjoying it, is joy; fleeing what is opposed to it, it is fear; and feeling what is opposed to it, when it has befallen it, it is sadness. Now these motions are evil if the love is evil; good if the love is good. What we assert let us prove from Scripture. The apostle "desires to depart, and to be with Christ."[131] And, "My soul desired to long for Thy judgments";[132] or if it is more appropriate to say, "My soul longed to desire Thy judgments." And, "The desire of wisdom bringeth to a kingdom."[133] Yet there has always obtained the usage of understanding desire and concupiscence in a bad sense if the object be not defined. But joy is used in a good sense: "Be glad in the Lord, and rejoice, ye righteous."[134] And, "Thou hast put gladness in my heart."[135] And, "Thou wilt fill me with joy with Thy countenance."[136] Fear is used in a good sense by the apostle when he says, "Work out your salvation with fear and trembling."[137] And, "Be not high-minded, but fear."[138] And, "I fear, lest by any means, as the serpent beguiled Eve through his subtilty, so your minds should be corrupted from the simplicity that is in Christ."[139] But with respect to sadness, which Cicero prefers to call sickness (*ægritudo*), and Virgil pain (*dolor*) (as he says, *"Dolent gaudentque"*),[140] but which I prefer to call sorrow, because sickness and pain are more commonly used to express bodily suffering—with respect to this emotion, I say, the question whether it can be used in a good sense is more difficult.

Chapter 9   Of the Perturbations of the Soul Which Appear as Right Affections in the Life of the Righteous.

But so far as regards this question of mental perturbations, we have answered these philosophers in the ninth book[141] of this work, showing that it is rather a verbal than a real dispute, and that they

130. 2 Tm 3:2.   131. Phil 1:23.   132. Ps 119:20.   133. Ws 6:20.

134. Ps 32:11.   135. Ps 4:7.   136. Ps 16:11.   137. Phil 2:12.

138. Rom 11:20.   139. 2 Cor 11:3.   140. *Aeneid* 6.733.

141. Chaps. 4, 5.

seek contention rather than truth. Among ourselves, according to the sacred Scriptures and sound doctrine, the citizens of the holy city of God, who live according to God in the pilgrimage of this life, both fear and desire, and grieve and rejoice. And because their love is rightly placed, all these affections of theirs are right. They fear eternal punishment, they desire eternal life; they grieve because they themselves groan within themselves, waiting for the adoption, the redemption of their body;[142] they rejoice in hope, because there "shall be brought to pass the saying that is written, Death is swallowed up in victory."[143] In like manner they fear to sin, they desire to persevere; they grieve in sin, they rejoice in good works. They fear to sin, because they hear that "because iniquity shall abound, the love of many shall wax cold."[144] They desire to persevere, because they hear that it is written, "He that endureth to the end shall be saved."[145] They grieve for sin, hearing that "If we say that we have no sin, we deceive ourselves, and the truth is not in us."[146] They rejoice in good works, because they hear that "the Lord loveth a cheerful giver."[147] In like manner, according as they are strong or weak, they fear or desire to be tempted, grieve or rejoice in temptation. They fear to be tempted, because they hear the injunction, "If a man be overtaken in a fault, ye which are spiritual restore such an one in the spirit of meekness; considering thyself, lest thou also be tempted."[148] They desire to be tempted, because they hear one of the heroes of the city of God saying, "Examine me, O Lord, and tempt me: try my reins and my heart."[149] They grieve in temptations, because they see Peter weeping;[150] they rejoice in temptations, because they hear James saying, "My brethren, count it all joy when ye fall into divers temptations."[151]

And not only on their own account do they experience these emotions, but also on account of those whose deliverance they desire and whose perdition they fear, and whose loss or salvation affects them with grief or with joy. For if we who have come into the Church from among the Gentiles may suitably instance that noble and mighty hero who glories in his infirmities, the teacher (*doctor*)

---

142. Rom 8:23.   143. 1 Cor 15:54.   144. Mt 24:12.   145. Mt 10:22.

146. 1 Jn 1:8.   147. 2 Cor 9:7.   148. Gal 6:1.   149. Ps 26:2.

150. Mt 26:75.   151. Jas 1:2.

of the nations in faith and truth, who also labored more than all his fellow apostles, and instructed the tribes of God's people by his Epistles, which edified not only those of his own time, but all those who were to be gathered in—that hero, I say, and athlete of Christ, instructed by him, anointed of his Spirit, crucified with him, glorious in him, lawfully maintaining a great conflict on the theater of this world, and being made a spectacle to angels and men,[152] and pressing onward for the prize of his high calling[153]—very joyfully do we with the eyes of faith behold him rejoicing with them that rejoice, and weeping with them that weep;[154] though hampered by fightings without and fears within;[155] desiring to depart and to be with Christ;[156] longing to see the Romans, that he might have some fruit among them as among other Gentiles;[157] being jealous over the Corinthians, and fearing in that jealousy lest their minds should be corrupted from the chastity that is in Christ;[158] having great heaviness and continual sorrow of heart for the Israelites,[159] because they, being ignorant of God's righteousness, and going about to establish their own righteousness, have not submitted themselves unto the righteousness of God;[160] and expressing not only his sorrow, but bitter lamentation over some who had formally sinned and had not repented of their uncleanness and fornications.[161]

If these emotions and affections, arising as they do from the love of what is good and from a holy charity, are to be called vices, then let us allow these emotions which are truly vices to pass under the name of virtues. But since these affections, when they are exercised in a becoming way, follow the guidance of right reason, who will dare to say that they are diseases or vicious passions? Wherefore even the Lord himself, when he condescended to lead a human life in the form of a slave, had no sin whatever, and yet exercised these emotions where he judged they should be exercised. For as there was in him a true human body and a true human soul, so was there also a true human emotion. When, therefore, we read in the Gospel that the hard-heartedness of the Jews moved him to sorrowful indignation,[162] that he said, "I am glad for your sakes, to the intent ye may

---

152. 1 Cor 4:9.   153. Phil 3:14.   154. Rom 12:15.   155. 2 Cor 7:5.

156. Phil 1:23.   157. Rom 1:11–13.   158. 2 Cor 11:1–3.

159. Rom 9:2.   160. Rom 10:3.   161. 2 Cor 12:21.   162. Mk 3:5.

believe,"[163] that when about to raise Lazarus he even shed tears,[164] that he earnestly desired to eat the Passover with his disciples,[165] that as his passion drew near his soul was sorrowful,[166] these emotions are certainly not falsely ascribed to him. But as he became man when it pleased him, so, in the grace of his definite purpose, when it pleased him he experienced those emotions in his human soul.

But we must further make the admission, that even when these affections are well regulated, and according to God's will, they are peculiar to this life, not to that future life we look for, and that often we yield to them against our will. And thus sometimes we weep in spite of ourselves, being carried beyond ourselves, not indeed by culpable desire; but by praiseworthy charity. In us, therefore, these affections arise from human infirmity; but it was not so with the Lord Jesus, for even his infirmity was the consequence of his power. But so long as we wear the infirmity of this life, we are rather worse men than better if we have none of these emotions at all. For the apostle vituperated and abominated some who, as he said, were "without natural affection."[167] The sacred psalmist also found fault with those of whom he said, "I looked for some to lament with me, and there was none."[168] For to be quite free from pain while we are in this place of misery is only purchased, as one of this world's literati perceived and remarked,[169] at the price of blunted sensibilities both of mind and body. And therefore that which the Greeks call ἀπάθεια, and what the Latins would call, if their language would allow them, *"impassibilitas,"* if it be taken to mean an impassibility of spirit and not of body, or, in other words, a freedom from those emotions which are contrary to reason and disturb the mind, then it is obviously a good and most desirable quality, but it is not one which is attainable in this life. For the words of the apostle are the confession, not of the common herd, but of the eminently pious, just, and holy men: "If we say we have no sin, we deceive ourselves, and the truth is not in us."[170] When there shall be no sin in a man, then there shall be this ἀπάθεια. At present it is

163. Jn 11:15.   164. Jn 11:35.   165. Lk 22:15.   166. Mt 26:38.
167. Rom 1:31.   168. Ps 69:20.
169. Crantor, an Academic philosopher quoted by Cicero, *Tusc. Quaest.* 3.6.
170. 1 Jn 1:8.

enough if we live without crime, and he who thinks he lives without sin puts aside not sin, but pardon. And if that is to be called apathy, where the mind is the subject of no emotion, then who would not consider this insensibility to be worse than all vices? It may, indeed, reasonably be maintained that the perfect blessedness we hope for shall be free from all sting of fear or sadness, but who that is not quite lost to truth would say that neither love nor joy shall be experienced there? But if by apathy a condition be meant in which no fear terrifies nor any pain annoys, we must in this life renounce such a state if we would live according to God's will, but may hope to enjoy it in that blessedness which is promised as our eternal condition.

For that fear of which the Apostle John says, "There is no fear in love; but perfect love casteth out fear, because fear hath torment. He that feareth is not made perfect in love"[171]—that fear is not of the same kind as the Apostle Paul felt lest the Corinthians should be seduced by the subtlety of the serpent, for love is susceptible of this fear, yea, love alone is capable of it. But the fear which is not in love is of that kind of which Paul himself says, "For ye have not received the spirit of bondage again to fear."[172] But as for that "clean fear which endureth for ever,"[173] if it is to exist in the world to come (and how else can it be said to endure forever?), it is not a fear deterring us from evil which may happen, but preserving us in the good which cannot be lost. For where the love of acquired good is unchangeable, there certainly the fear that avoids evil is, if I may say so, free from anxiety. For under the name of "clean fear" David signifies that will by which we shall necessarily shrink from sin, and guard against it, not with the anxiety of weakness, which fears that we may strongly sin, but with the tranquillity of perfect love. Or if no kind of fear at all shall exist in that most imperturbable security of perpetual and blissful delights, then the expression, "The fear of the Lord is clean, enduring for ever," must be taken in the same sense as that other, "The patience of the poor shall not perish for ever."[174] For patience, which is necessary only where ills are to be borne, shall not be eternal, but that which patience leads us to will be eternal. So perhaps this "clean fear" is said to endure forever, because that to which fear leads shall endure.

And since this is so—since we must live a good life in order to attain to a blessed life, a good life has all these affections right, a bad life has them wrong. But in the blessed life eternal there will be love and joy, not only right, but also assured; but fear and grief there will be none. Whence it already appears in some sort what manner of persons the citizens of the city of God must be in this their pilgrimage, who live after the spirit, not after the flesh—that is to say, according to God, not according to man—and what manner of persons they shall be also in that immortality whither they are journeying. And the city or society of the wicked, who live not according to God, but according to man, and who accept the doctrines of men or devils in the worship of a false, and contempt of the true, divinity, is shaken with those wicked emotions as by diseases and disturbances. And if there be some of its citizens who seem to restrain and, as it were, temper those passions, they are so elated with ungodly pride, that their disease is as much greater as their pain is less. And if some, with a vanity monstrous in proportion to its rarity, have become enamored of themselves because they can be stimulated and excited by no emotion, moved or bent by no affection, such persons rather lose all humanity than obtain true tranquillity. For a thing is not necessarily right because it is inflexible, nor healthy because it is insensible.

Chapter 13   That in Adam's Sin an Evil Will Preceded the Evil Act.

Our first parents fell into open disobedience because already they were secretly corrupted, for the evil act had never been done had not an evil will preceded it. And what is the origin of our evil will but pride? For "pride is the beginning of sin."[175] And what is pride but the craving for undue exaltation? And this is undue exaltation, when the soul abandons him to whom it ought to cleave as its end, and becomes a kind of end to itself. This happens when it becomes its own satisfaction. And it does so when it falls away from that unchangeable good which ought to satisfy it more than itself. This falling away is spontaneous, for if the will had remained steadfast in the love of that higher and changeless good by which it was illumined to intelligence and kindled into love, it would not have

175. Ecclus 10:13.

turned away to find satisfaction in itself, and so become frigid and benighted; the woman would not have believed the serpent spoke the truth, nor would the man have preferred the request of his wife to the command of God, nor have supposed that it was a venial transgression to cleave to the partner of his life even in a partner-ship of sin. The wicked deed, then—that is to say, the transgression of eating the forbidden fruit—was committed by persons who were already wicked. That "evil fruit"[176] could be brought forth only by "a corrupt tree." But that the tree was evil was not the result of nature, for certainly it could become so only by the vice of the will, and vice is contrary to nature. Now, nature could not have been de-praved by vice had it not been made out of nothing. Consequently, that it is a nature, this is because it is made by God, but that it falls away from him, this is because it is made out of nothing. But man did not so fall away as to become absolutely nothing, but being turned toward himself, his being became more contracted than it was when he clave to him who supremely is. Accordingly, to exist in himself, that is, to be his own satisfaction after abandoning God, is not quite to become a nonentity, but to approximate to that. And therefore the holy Scriptures designate the proud by another name, "self-pleasers." For it is good to have the heart lifted up, yet not to one's self, for this is proud, but to the Lord, for this is obedient, and can be the act only of the humble. There is, therefore, something in humility which, strangely enough, exalts the heart, and something in pride which debases it. This seems, indeed, to be contradictory, that loftiness should debase and lowliness exalt. But pious humility enables us to submit to what is above us, and nothing is more ex-alted above us than God, and therefore humility, by making us subject to God, exalts us. But pride, being a defect of nature, by the very act of refusing subjection and revolting from him who is supreme, falls to a low condition, and then comes to pass what is written: "Thou castedst them down when they lifted up them-selves."[177] For he does not say, "when they had been lifted up," as if first they were exalted, and then afterward cast down, but "when they lifted up themselves" even then they were cast down—that is to say, the very lifting up was already a fall. And therefore it is that humility is specially recommended to the city of God as it sojourns

176. Mt 7:18.   177. Ps 73:18.

in this world, and is specially exhibited in the city of God, and in the person of Christ its King; while the contrary vice of pride, according to the testimony of the sacred writings, specially rules his adversary the devil. And certainly this is the great difference which distinguishes the two cities of which we speak, the one being the society of the godly men, the other of the ungodly, each associated with the angels that adhere to their party, and the one guided and fashioned by love of self, the other by love of God.

The devil, then, would not have ensnared man in the open and manifest sin of doing what God had forbidden, had man not already begun to live for himself. It was this that made him listen with pleasure to the words, "Ye shall be as gods,"[178] which they would much more readily have accomplished by obediently adhering to their supreme and true end than by proudly living to themselves. For created gods are gods not by virtue of what is in themselves, but by a participation of the true God. By craving to be more, man becomes less, and by aspiring to be self-sufficing, he fell away from him who truly suffices him. Accordingly, this wicked desire which prompts man to please himself as if he were himself light, and which thus turns him away from that light by which, had he followed it, he would himself have become light—this wicked desire, I say, already secretly existed in him, and the open sin was but its consequence. For that is true which is written "Pride goeth before destruction, and before honor is humility";[179] that is to say, secret ruin precedes open ruin, while the former is not counted ruin. For who counts exaltation ruin, though no sooner is the highest forsaken than a fall is begun? But who does not recognize it as ruin, when there occurs an evident and indubitable transgression of the commandment? And consequently, God's prohibition had reference to such an act as, when committed, could not be defended on any pretense of doing what was righteous.[180] And I make bold to say that it is useful for the proud to fall into an open and indisputable transgression, and so displease themselves, as already, by pleasing themselves, they had fallen. For Peter was in a healthier condition when he wept and was dissatisfied with himself, than when he boldly presumed and satisfied himself. And this is averred

178. Gn 3:5.   179. Prv 18:12.

180. That is to say, it was an obvious and indisputable transgression.

by the sacred psalmist when he says, "Fill their faces with shame, that they may seek Thy name, O Lord";[181] that is, that they who have pleased themselves in seeking their own glory may be pleased and satisfied with Thee in seeking Thy glory.

Chapter 22 Of the Conjugal Union as It Was Originally Instituted and Blessed by God.

But we, for our part, have no manner of doubt that to increase and multiply and replenish the earth in virtue of the blessing of God, is a gift of marriage as God instituted it from the beginning before man sinned, when he created them male and female—in other words, two sexes manifestly distinct. And it was this work of God on which his blessing was pronounced. For no sooner had Scripture said, "Male and female created He them,"[182] than it immediately continues, "And God blessed them, and God said unto them, Increase, and multiply, and replenish the earth, and subdue it," etc. And though all these things may not unsuitably be interpreted in a spiritual sense, yet "male and female" cannot be understood of two things in one man, as if there were in him one thing which rules, another which is ruled, but it is quite clear that they were created male and female, with bodies of different sexes, for the very purpose of begetting offspring, and so increasing, multiplying, and replenishing the earth, and it is great folly to oppose so plain a fact. It was not of the spirit which commands and the body which obeys, nor of the rational soul which rules and the irrational desire which is ruled, nor of the contemplative virtue which is supreme and the active which is subject, nor of the understanding of the mind and the sense of the body, but plainly of the matrimonial union by which the sexes are mutually bound together, that our Lord, when asked whether it were lawful for any cause to put away one's wife (for on account of the hardness of the hearts of the Israelites Moses permitted a bill of divorcement to be given), answered and said, "Have ye not read that He which made them at the beginning made them male and female, and said, For this cause shall a man leave father and mother, and shall cleave to his wife, and they twain shall be one flesh? Wherefore they are no more twain, but

181. Ps 83:16.   182. Gn 1:27, 28.

one flesh. What, therefore, God hath joined together, let not man put asunder."[183] It is certain, then, that from the first men were created, as we see and know them to be now, of two sexes, male and female, and that they are called one, either on account of the matrimonial union, or on account of the origin of the woman, who was created from the side of the man. And it is by this original example, which God himself instituted, that the apostle admonishes all husbands to love their own wives in particular.[184]

Chapter 28   Of the Nature of the Two Cities, the Earthly and the Heavenly.

Accordingly, two cities have been formed by two loves: the earthly by the love of self, even to the contempt of God; the heavenly by the love of God, even to the contempt of self. The former, in a word, glories in itself, the latter in the Lord. For the one seeks glory from men, but the greatest glory of the other is God, the witness of conscience. The one lifts up its head in its own glory; the other says to its God, "Thou art my glory, and the lifter up of mine head."[185] In the one, the princes and the nations it subdues are ruled by the love of ruling; in the other, the princes and the subjects serve one another in love, the latter obeying, while the former take thought for all. The one delights in its own strength, represented in the persons of its rulers; the other says to its God, "I will love Thee, O Lord, my strength."[186] And therefore the wise men of the one city, living according to man, have sought for profit to their own bodies or souls, or both, and those who have known God "glorified Him not as God, neither were thankful, but became vain in their imaginations, and their foolish heart was darkened; professing themselves to be wise"—that is, glorying in their own wisdom and being possessed by pride—"they became fools, and changed the glory of the incorruptible God into an image made like to corruptible man, and to birds, and four-footed beasts, and creeping things." For they were either leaders or followers of the people in adoring images, "and worshipped and served the creature more than the Creator, who is blessed for ever."[187] But in the other city there is no human wisdom,

183. Mt 19:4, 5.   184. Eph 5:25.   185. Ps 3:3.   186. Ps 18:1.
187. Rom 1:21–25.

but only godliness, which offers due worship to the true God, and looks for its reward in the society of the saints, of holy angels as well as holy men, "that God may be all in all."[188]

Book XV

Chapter 22   Of the Fall of the Sons of God Who Were Captivated by the Daughters of Men, Whereby All, with the Exception of Eight Persons, Deservedly Perished in the Deluge.

When the human race, in the exercise of this freedom of will, increased and advanced, there arose a mixture and confusion of the two cities by their participation in a common iniquity. And this calamity, as well as the first, was occasioned by woman, though not in the same way, for these women were not themselves betrayed, neither did they persuade the men to sin, but having belonged to the earthly city and society of the earthly, they had been of corrupt manners from the first, and were loved for their bodily beauty by the sons of God, or the citizens of the other city which sojourns in this world. Beauty is indeed a good gift of God, but that the good may not think it a great good, God dispenses it even to the wicked. And thus, when the good that is great and proper to the good was abandoned by the sons of God, they fell to a paltry good which is not peculiar to the good, but common to the good and the evil; and when they were captivated by the daughters of men, they adopted the manners of the earthly to win them as their brides, and forsook the godly ways they had followed in their own holy society. And thus beauty, which is indeed God's handiwork, but only a temporal, carnal, and lower kind of good, is not fitly loved in preference to God, the eternal, spiritual, and unchangeable good. When the miser prefers his gold to justice, it is through no fault of the gold, but of the man; and so with every created thing. For though it be good, it may be loved with an evil as well as with a good love: it is loved rightly when it is loved ordinately; evilly, when inordinately. It is this which someone has briefly said in these verses in praise of

188. 1 Cor 15:28.

the Creator: "These are Thine, they are good, because Thou art good who didst create them. There is in them nothing of ours, unless the sin we commit when we forget the order of things, and instead of Thee love that which Thou hast made."

But if the Creator is truly loved, that is, if he himself is loved and not another thing in his stead, he cannot be evilly loved, for love itself is to be ordinately loved, because we do well to love that which, when we love it, makes us live well and virtuously. So that it seems to me that it is a brief but true definition of virtue to say, it is the order of love; and on this account, in the Canticles, the bride of Christ, the city of God, sings, "Order love within me."[189] It was the order of this love, then, this charity or attachment, which the sons of God disturbed when they forsook God, and were enamored of the daughters of men.[190] And by these two names (sons of God and daughters of men) the two cities are sufficiently distinguished. For though the former were by nature children of men, they had come into possession of another name by grace. For in the same Scripture in which the sons of God are said to have loved the daughters of men, they are also called angels of God; whence many suppose that they were not men but angels.

Book XIX

Chapter 4   What the Christians Believe Regarding the Supreme Good and Evil, in Opposition to the Philosophers, Who Have Maintained That the Supreme Good Is in Themselves.

If, then, we be asked what the city of God has to say upon these points, and, in the first place, what its opinion regarding the supreme good and evil is, it will reply that life eternal is the supreme good, death eternal the supreme evil, and that to obtain the one and escape the other we must live rightly. And thus it is written, "The just lives by faith,"[191] for we do not as yet see our good, and must therefore live by faith; neither have we in ourselves power to

189. Sg 2:4.   190. See *On Christian Doctrine*, Book I, Chap. 28.
191. Hb 2:4.

live rightly, but can do so only if he who has given us faith to believe in his help do help us when we believe and pray. As for those who have supposed that the sovereign good and evil are to be found in this life, and have placed it either in the soul or the body, or in both, or, to speak more explicitly, either in pleasure or in virtue, or in both; in repose or in virtue, or in both; in pleasure and repose, or in virtue, or in all combined; in the primary objects of nature, or in virtue, or in both—all these have, with a marvelous shallowness, sought to find their blessedness in this life and in themselves. Contempt has been poured upon such ideas by the Truth, saying by the prophet, "The Lord knoweth the thoughts of men" (or, as the Apostle Paul cites the passage, "The Lord knoweth the thoughts of the *wise*") "that they are vain."[192]

For what flood of eloquence can suffice to detail the miseries of this life? Cicero, in the *Consolation* on the death of his daughter, has spent all his ability in lamentation, but how inadequate was even his ability here? For when, where, how, in this life, can these primary objects of nature be possessed so that they may not be assailed by unforeseen accidents? Is the body of the wise man exempt from any pain which may dispel pleasure, from any disquietude which may banish repose? The amputation or decay of the members of the body puts an end to its integrity, deformity blights its beauty, weakness its health, lassitude its vigor, sleepiness or sluggishness its activity—and which of these is it that may not assail the flesh of the wise man? Comely and fitting attitudes and movements of the body are numbered among the prime natural blessings, but what if some sickness makes the members tremble? What if a man suffers from curvature of the spine to such an extent that his hands reach the ground, and he goes upon all fours like a quadruped? Does not this destroy all beauty and grace in the body, whether at rest or in motion? What shall I say of the fundamental blessings of the soul, sense and intellect, of which the one is given for the perception, and the other for the comprehension of truth? But what kind of sense is it that remains when a man becomes deaf and blind? Where are reason and intellect when disease makes a man delirious? We can scarcely, or not at all, refrain from tears, when we think of or see the actions and words of such frantic persons, and consider how

192. Ps 94:11; 1 Cor 3:20.

different from and even opposed to their own sober judgment and ordinary conduct their present demeanor is. And what shall I say of those who suffer from demoniacal possession? Where is their own intelligence hidden and buried while the malignant spirit is using their body and soul according to his own will? And who is quite sure that no such thing can happen to the wise man in this life? Then, as to the perception of truth, what can we hope for even in this way while in the body, as we read in the true book of Wisdom, "The corruptible body weigheth down the soul, and the earthly tabernacle presseth down the mind that museth upon many things"?[193] And eagerness, or desire of action, if this is the right meaning to put upon the Greek ὁρμή, is also reckoned among the primary advantages of nature, and yet is it not this which produces those pitiable movements of the insane, and those actions which we shudder to see, when sense is deceived and reason deranged?

In fine, virtue itself, which is not among the primary objects of nature, but succeeds to them as the result of learning, though it holds the highest place among human good things, what is its occupation save to wage perpetual war with vices—not those that are outside of us, but within; not other men's, but our own—a war which is waged especially by that virtue which the Greeks call σωφροσύνη, and we temperance,[194] and which bridles carnal lusts, and prevents them from winning the consent of the spirit to wicked deeds? For we must not fancy that there is no vice in us, when, as the apostle says, "The flesh lusteth against the spirit,"[195] for to this vice there is a contrary virtue, when, as the same writer says, "The spirit lusteth against the flesh." "For these two," he says, "are contrary one to the other, so that you cannot do the things which you would." But what is it we wish to do when we seek to attain the supreme good, unless that the flesh should cease to lust against the spirit, and that there be no vice in us against which the spirit may lust? And as we cannot attain to this in the present life, however ardently we desire it, let us by God's help accomplish at least this, to preserve the soul from succumbing and yielding to the flesh that lusts against it, and to refuse our consent to the perpetration of sin. Far be it from us, then, to fancy that while we are still engaged in this intestine war, we have already found the happiness

193. Ws 9:15.   194. Cicero, *Tusc. Quaest.* 3.8.   195. Gal 5:17.

which we seek to reach by victory. And who is there so wise that he has no conflict at all to maintain against his vices?

What shall I say of that virtue which is called prudence? Is not all its vigilance spent in the discernment of good from evil things, so that no mistake may be admitted about what we should desire and what avoid? And thus it is itself a proof that we are in the midst of evils, or that evils are in us, for it teaches us that it is an evil to consent to sin and a good to refuse this consent. And yet this evil, to which prudence teaches and temperance enables us not to consent, is removed from this life neither by prudence nor by temperance. And justice, whose office it is to render to every man his due, whereby there is in man himself a certain just order of nature, so that the soul is subjected to God, and the flesh to the soul, and consequently both soul and flesh to God—does not this virtue demonstrate that it is as yet rather laboring toward its end than resting in its finished work? For the soul is so much the less subjected to God as it is less occupied with the thought of God, and the flesh is so much the less subjected to the spirit as it lusts more vehemently against the spirit. So long, therefore, as we are beset by this weakness, this plague, this disease, how shall we dare to say that we are safe? And if not safe, then how can we be already enjoying our final beatitude? Then that virtue which goes by the name of fortitude is the plainest proof of the ills of life, for it is these ills which it is compelled to bear patiently. And this holds good, no matter though the ripest wisdom coexists with it. And I am at a loss to understand how the Stoic philosophers can presume to say that these are no ills, though at the same time they allow the wise man to commit suicide and pass out of this life if they become so grievous that he cannot or ought not to endure them. But such is the stupid pride of these men who fancy that the supreme good can be found in this life, and that they can become happy by their own resources, that their wise man, or at least the man whom they fancifully depict as such, is always happy, even though he become blind, deaf, dumb, mutilated, racked with pains, or suffer any conceivable calamity such as may compel him to make away with himself; and they are not ashamed to call the life that is beset with these evils happy. O happy life, which seeks the aid of death to end it? If it is happy, let the wise man remain in it; but if these ills drive him out of it, in what sense is it happy? Or how can they say that these are not evils which conquer the virtue of fortitude, and force it not only to yield, but so to rave that it in one breath calls life happy and recommends it to be given up? For who is so blind as not to see that if it were happy it would not be fled from? And if they say we should flee from it on account of the infirmities that beset it, why then do they not lower their pride and acknowledge that it is miserable? Was it, I would ask, fortitude or weakness which prompted Cato to kill himself? For he would not have done so had he not been too weak to endure Caesar's victory. Where, then, is his fortitude? It has yielded, it has succumbed, it has been so thoroughly overcome as to abandon, forsake, flee this happy life. Or was it no longer happy? Then it was miserable. How, then, were these not evils which made life miserable, and a thing to be escaped from?

And therefore those who admit that these are evils, as the Peripatetics do, and the Old Academy, the sect which Varro advocates, express a more intelligible doctrine; but theirs also is a surprising mistake, for they contend that this is a happy life which is beset by these evils, even though they be so great that he who endures them should commit suicide to escape them. "Pains and anguish of body," says Varro, "are evils, and so much the worse in proportion to their severity; and to escape them you must quit this life." What life, I pray? This life, he says, which is oppressed by such evils. Then it is happy in the midst of these very evils on account of which you say we must quit it? Or do you call it happy because you are at liberty to escape these evils by death? What, then, if by some secret judgment of God you were held fast and not permitted to die, nor suffered to live without these evils? In that case, at least, you would say that such a life was miserable. It is soon relinquished, no doubt, but this does not make it not miserable, for were it eternal, you yourself would pronounce it miserable. Its brevity, therefore, does not clear it of misery; neither ought it to be called happiness because it is a brief misery. Certainly there is a mighty force in these evils which compel a man—according to them even a wise man—to cease to be a man that he may escape them, though they say, and say truly, that it is as it were the first and strongest demand of nature that a man cherish himself, and naturally therefore avoid death, and should so stand his own friend as to wish and vehemently aim at continuing to exist as a living creature, and subsisting in this union of soul and body. There is a mighty force in these evils to overcome this natural instinct by which death is by every means and with all a man's efforts avoided, and to overcome it so completely that what was avoided is desired, sought after, and if it cannot in any other way be obtained, is inflicted by the man on himself. There is a mighty force in these evils which make fortitude a homicide—if, indeed, that is to be called fortitude which is so thoroughly overcome by these evils, that it not only cannot preserve by patience the man whom it undertook to govern and defend, but is itself obliged to kill him. The wise man, I admit, ought to bear death with patience, but when it is inflicted by another. If, then, as these men maintain, he is obliged to inflict it on himself, certainly it must be owned that the ills which compel him to this are not only evils, but intolerable evils. The life, then, which is either subject to accidents, or environed with evils so considerable and grievous, could never have been called happy, if the men who give it this name had condescended to yield to the truth and to be conquered by valid arguments, when they inquired after the happy life, as they yield to unhappiness, and are overcome by overwhelming evils, when they put themselves to death, and if they had not fancied that the supreme good was to be found in this mortal life; for the very virtues of this life, which are certainly its best and most useful possessions, are all the more telling proofs of its miseries in proportion as they are helpful against the violence of its dangers, toils, and woes. For if these are true virtues—and such cannot exist save in those who have true piety—they do not profess to be able to deliver the men who possess them from all miseries; for true virtues tell no such lies, but they profess that by the hope of the future world this life, which is miserably involved in the many and great evils of this world, is happy as it is also safe. For if not yet safe, how could it be happy? And therefore the Apostle Paul, speaking not of men without prudence, temperance, fortitude, and justice, but of those whose lives were regulated by true piety, and whose virtues were therefore true, says, "For we are saved by hope: now hope which is seen is not hope; for what a man seeth, why doth he yet hope for? But if we hope for that we see not, then do we with patience wait for it."[196] As, therefore, we are saved, so we are made happy by hope. And as we do not as yet possess a present, but look

196. Rom 8:24.

for a future salvation, so is it with our happiness, and this "with patience," for we are encompassed with evils, which we ought patiently
to endure, until we come to the ineffable enjoyment of unmixed
good; for there shall be no longer anything to endure. Salvation, such
as it shall be in the world to come, shall itself be our final happiness.
And this happiness these philosophers refuse to believe in, because
they do not see it, and attempt to fabricate for themselves a happiness
in this life, based upon a virtue which is as deceitful as it is proud.

Chapter 20   That the Saints Are in This Life Blessed in Hope.

Since, then, the supreme good of the city of God is perfect and eternal peace, not such as mortals pass into and out of by birth and death,
but the peace of freedom from all evil, in which the immortals ever
abide, who can deny that that future life is most blessed, or that, in
comparison with it, this life which now we live is most wretched,
be it filled with all blessings of body and soul and external things?
And yet, if any man uses this life with a reference to that other which
he ardently loves and confidently hopes for, he may well be called
even now blessed, though not in reality so much as in hope. But the
actual possession of the happiness of this life, without the hope of
what is beyond, is but a false happiness and profound misery. For
the true blessings of the soul are not now enjoyed, for that is no true
wisdom which does not direct all its prudent observations, manly
actions, virtuous self-restraint, and just arrangements, to that end in
which God shall be all and all in a secure eternity and perfect peace.

Book XXI

Chapter 15   That Everything Which the Grace of God Does in the Way of Rescuing Us from the Inveterate Evils in Which We Are Now Sunk, Pertains to the Future World, in Which All Things Are Made New.

Nevertheless, in the "heavy yoke that is laid upon the sons of
Adam, from the day that they go out of their mother's womb to the
day that they return to the mother of all things," there is found an

admirable though painful monitor teaching us to be sober-minded, and convincing us that this life has become penal in consequence of that outrageous wickedness which was perpetrated in paradise, and that all to which the New Testament invites belongs to that future inheritance which awaits us in the world to come, and is offered for our acceptance, as the earnest that we may, in its own due time, obtain that of which it is the pledge. Now, therefore, let us walk in hope, and let us by the spirit mortify the deeds of the flesh, and so make progress from day to day. For "the Lord knoweth them that are His";[197] and "as many as are led by the Spirit of God, they are sons of God,"[198] but by grace, not by nature. For there is but one Son of God by nature, who in his compassion became Son of man for our sakes, that we, by nature sons of men, might by grace become through him sons of God. For he, abiding unchangeable, took upon him our nature, that thereby he might take us to himself; and, holding fast his own divinity, he became partaker of our infirmity, that we, being changed into some better thing, might, by participating in his righteousness and immortality, lose our own properties of sin and mortality, and preserve whatever good quality he had implanted in our nature perfected now by sharing in the goodness of his nature. For as by the sin of one man we have fallen into a misery so deplorable, so by the righteousness of one Man, who also is God, shall we come to a blessedness inconceivably exalted. Nor ought anyone to trust that he has passed from the one man to the other until he shall have reached that place where there is no temptation, and have entered into the peace which he seeks in the many and various conflicts of this war, in which "the flesh lusteth against the spirit, and the spirit against the flesh."[199] Now, such a war as this would have had no existence if human nature had, in the exercise of free will, continued steadfast in the uprightness in which it was created. But now in its misery it makes war upon itself, because in its blessedness it would not continue at peace with God; and this, though it be a miserable calamity, is better than the earlier stages of this life, which do not recognize that a war is to be maintained. For better is it to contend with vices than without conflict to be subdued by them. Better, I say, is war with the hope of peace everlasting than captivity without any thought of deliverance.

197. 2 Tm 2:19.   198. Rom 8:14.   199. Gal 5:17.

We long, indeed, for the cessation of this war, and, kindled by the flame of divine love, we burn for entrance on that well-ordered peace in which whatever is inferior is forever subordinated to what is above it. But if (which God forbid) there had been no hope of so blessed a consummation, we should still have preferred to endure the hardness of this conflict, rather than, by our nonresistance, to yield ourselves to the dominion of vice.

Chapter 27   Against the Belief of Those Who Think That the Sins Which Have Been Accompanied with Almsgiving Will Do Them No Harm.

It remains to reply to those who maintain that those only shall burn in eternal fire who neglect alms-deeds proportioned to their sins, resting this opinion on the words of the Apostle James, "He shall have judgment without mercy that hath showed no mercy."[200] Therefore, they say, he that hath showed mercy, though he has not reformed his dissolute conduct, but has lived wickedly and iniquitously even while abounding in alms, shall have a merciful judgment, so that he shall either be not condemned at all, or shall be delivered from final judgment after a time. And for the same reason they suppose that Christ will discriminate between those on the right hand and those on the left, and will send the one party into his kingdom, the other into eternal punishment, on the sole ground of their attention to or neglect of works of charity. Moreover, they endeavor to use the prayer which the Lord himself taught as a proof and bulwark of their opinion, that daily sins which are never abandoned can be expiated through alms-deeds, no matter how offensive or of what sort they be. For, say they, as there is no day on which Christians ought not to use this prayer, so there is no sin of any kind which, though committed every day, is not remitted when we say, "Forgive us our debts," if we take care to fulfill what follows, "as we forgive our debtors."[201] For, they go on to say, the Lord does not say, "If ye forgive men their trespasses, your heavenly Father will forgive you your little daily sins," but "will forgive you your sins." Therefore, be they of any kind or magnitude what-

---

200. Jas 2:13.   201. Mt 6:12.

ever, be they perpetrated daily and never abandoned or subdued in this life, they can be pardoned, they presume, through alms-deeds.

But they are right to inculcate the giving of alms proportioned to past sins, for if they said that any kind of alms could obtain the divine pardon of great sins committed daily and with habitual enormity, if they said that such sins could thus be daily remitted, they would see that their doctrine was absurd and ridiculous. For they would thus be driven to acknowledge that it were possible for a very wealthy man to buy absolution from murders, adulteries, and all manner of wickedness, by paying a daily alms of ten paltry coins. And if it be most absurd and insane to make such an acknowledgment, and if we still ask what are those fitting alms of which even the forerunner of Christ said, "Bring forth therefore fruits meet for repentance,"[202] undoubtedly it will be found that they are not such as are done by men who undermine their life by daily enormities even to the very end. For they suppose that by giving to the poor a small fraction of the wealth they acquire by extortion and spoliation they can propitiate Christ, so that they may with impunity commit the most damnable sins, in the persuasion that they have bought from him a license to transgress, or rather do buy a daily indulgence. And if they for one crime have distributed all their goods to Christ's needy members, that could profit them nothing unless they desisted from all similar actions, and attained charity which worketh no evil; He therefore who does alms-deeds proportioned to his sins must first begin with himself. For it is not reasonable that a man who exercises charity toward his neighbor should not do so toward himself, since he hears the Lord saying, "Thou shalt love thy neighbor as thyself,"[203] and again, "Have compassion on thy soul, and please God."[204] He then who has not compassion on his own soul that he may please God, how can he be said to do alms-deeds proportioned to his sins? To the same purpose is that written, "He who is bad to himself, to whom can he be good?"[205] We ought therefore to do alms that we may be heard when we pray that our past sins may be forgiven, not that while we continue in them we may think to provide ourselves with a license for wickedness by alms-deeds.

202. Mt 3:8.   203. Mt 22:39.   204. Ecclus 30:24.   205. Ecclus 21:1.

The reason, therefore, of our predicting that he will impute to those on his right hand the alms-deeds they have done, and charge those on his left with omitting the same, is that he may thus show the efficacy of charity for the deletion of past sins, not for impunity in their perpetual commission. And such persons, indeed, as decline to abandon their evil habits of life for a better course cannot be said to do charitable deeds. For this is the purport of the saying, "Inasmuch as ye did it not to one of the least of these, ye did it not to me."[206] He shows them that they do not perform charitable actions even when they think they are doing so. For if they gave bread to a hungering Christian because he is a Christian, assuredly they would not deny to themselves the bread of righteousness, that is, Christ himself, for God considers not the person to whom the gift is made, but the spirit in which it is made. He therefore who loves Christ in a Christian extends alms to him in the same spirit in which he draws near to Christ, not in that spirit which would abandon Christ if it could do so with impunity. For in proportion as a man loves what Christ disapproves does he himself abandon Christ. For what does it profit a man that he is baptized, if he is not justified? Did not he who said, "Except a man be born of water and of the Spirit, he shall not enter into the kingdom of God."[207] say also, "Except your righteousness shall exceed the righteousness of the scribes and Pharisees, ye shall not enter into the kingdom of heaven"?[208] Why do many through fear of the first saying run to baptism, while few through fear of the second seek to be justified? As therefore it is not to his brother a man says, "Thou fool," if when he says it he is indignant not at the brotherhood, but at the sin of the offender—or otherwise he were guilty of hellfire—so he who extends charity to a Christian does not extend it to a Christian if he does not love Christ in him. Now he does not love Christ who refuses to be justified in him. Or, again, if a man has been guilty of this sin of calling his brother Fool, unjustly reviling him without any desire to remove his sin, his alms-deeds go a small way toward expiating this fault, unless he adds to this the remedy of reconciliation which the same passage enjoins. For it is there said, "Therefore, if thou bring thy gift to the altar, and there rememberest that thy brother hath aught against thee; leave there thy gift before the altar, and go thy way;

206. Mt 25:45.   207. Jn 3:5.   208. Mt 5:20.

first be reconciled to thy brother, and then come and offer thy gift."[209] Just so it is a small matter to do alms-deeds, no matter how great they be, for any sin, so long as the offender continues in the practice of sin.

Then as to the daily prayer which the Lord himself taught, and which is therefore called the Lord's Prayer, it obliterates indeed the sins of the day, when day by day we say, "Forgive us our debts," and when we not only say but act out that which follows, "as we forgive our debtors";[210] but we utter this petition because sins have been committed, and not that they may be. For by it our Savior designed to teach us that, however righteously we live in this life of infirmity and darkness, we still commit sins for the remission of which we ought to pray, while we must pardon those who sin against us that we ourselves also may be pardoned. The Lord then did not utter the words, "If ye forgive men their trespasses, your Father will also forgive you your trespasses,"[211] in order that we might contract from this petition such confidence as should enable us to sin securely from day to day, either putting ourselves above the fear of human laws, or craftily deceiving men concerning our conduct, but in order that we might thus learn not to suppose that we are without sins, even though we should be free from crimes; as also God admonished the priests of the old law to this same effect regarding their sacrifices, which he commanded them to offer first for their own sins, and then for the sins of the people. For even the very words of so great a Master and Lord are to be intently considered. For he does not say, "If ye forgive men *their* sins, your Father will also forgive you your sins," no matter of what sort they be, but he says, "*your* sins"; for it was a daily prayer he was teaching, and it was certainly to disciples already justified he was speaking. What, then, does he mean by "your sins," but those sins from which not even you who are justified and sanctified can be free? While, then, those who seek occasion from this petition to indulge in habitual sin maintain that the Lord meant to include great sins, because he did not say he will forgive you your small sins, but "your sins," we, on the other hand, taking into account the character of the persons he was addressing, cannot see our way to interpret the expression "your sins" of anything but small sins, because such persons are no

209. Mt 5:23, 24.   210. Mt 6:12.   211. Mt 6:14.

longer guilty of great sins. Nevertheless not even great sins themselves—sins from which we must flee with a total reformation of
life—are forgiven to those who pray, unless they observe the ap-
pended precept, "as ye also forgive your debtors." For if the very
small sins which attach even to the life of the righteous be not remitted without that condition, how much further from obtaining
indulgence shall those be who are involved in many great crimes,
if, while they cease from perpetrating such enormities, they still in-
exorably refuse to remit any debt incurred to themselves, since the
Lord says, "But if ye forgive not men their trespasses, neither will
your Father forgive your trespasses"?[212] For this is the purport of
the saying of the Apostle James also, "He shall have judgment
without mercy that hath showed no mercy."[213] For we should remember that servant whose debt of ten thousand talents his lord
canceled, but afterward ordered him to pay up, because the servant
himself had no pity for his fellow servant, who owed him a hundred pence.[214] The words which the Apostle James subjoins, "And
mercy rejoiceth against judgment,"[215] find their application among
those who are the children of the promise and vessels of mercy. For
even those righteous men, who have lived with such holiness that
they receive into the eternal habitations others also who have won
their friendship with the mammon of unrighteousness,[216] became
such only through the merciful deliverance of him who justifies the
ungodly, imputing to him a reward according to grace, not according to debt. For among this number is the apostle, who says, "I obtained mercy to be faithful."[217]

But it must be admitted that those who are thus received into the
eternal habitations are not of such a character that their own life
would suffice to rescue them without the aid of the saints, and consequently in their case especially does mercy rejoice against judgment. And yet we are not on this account to suppose that every
abandoned profligate, who has made no amendment of his life, is
to be received into the eternal habitations if only he has assisted the
saints with the mammon of unrighteousness—that is to say, with
money or wealth which has been unjustly acquired, or, if rightfully

---

212. Mt 6:15.   213. Jas 2:13.   214. Mt 18:23.   215. Jas 2:13.
216. Lk 16:9.   217. 1 Cor 7:25.

acquired, is yet not the true riches, but only what iniquity counts riches, because it knows not the true riches in which those persons abound, who even receive others also into eternal habitations. There is then a certain kind of life, which is neither, on the one hand, so bad that those who adopt it are not helped toward the kingdom of heaven by any bountiful almsgiving by which they may relieve the wants of the saints, and make friends who could receive them into eternal habitations, nor, on the other hand, so good that it of itself suffices to win for them that great blessedness, if they do not obtain mercy through the merits of those whom they have made their friends. And I frequently wonder that even Virgil should give expression to this sentence of the Lord, in which he says, "Make to yourselves friends of the mammon of unrighteousness, that they may receive you into everlasting habitations";[218] and this very similar saying, "He that receiveth a prophet, in the name of a prophet, shall receive a prophet's reward; and he that receiveth a righteous man, in the name of a righteous man, shall receive a righteous man's reward."[219] For when that poet described the Elysian fields, in which they suppose that the souls of the blessed dwell, he placed there not only those who had been able by their own merit to reach that abode, but added—

> And they who grateful memory won
> By services to others done;[220]

that is, they who had served others, and thereby merited to be remembered by them. Just as if they used the expression so common in Christian lips, where some humble person commends himself to one of the saints, and says, "Remember me," and secures that he do so by deserving well at his hand. But what that kind of life we have been speaking of is, and what those sins are which prevent a man from winning the kingdom of God by himself, but yet permit him to avail himself of the merits of the saints, it is very difficult to ascertain, very perilous to define. For my own part, in spite of all investigation, I have been up to the present hour unable to discover this. And possibly it is hidden from us, lest we should become careless in avoiding such sins, and so cease to make progress. For if it

218. Lk 16:9.   219. Mt 10:41.   220. *Aeneid* 6.664.

were known what these sins are which, though they continue, and be not abandoned for a higher life, do yet not prevent us from seeking and hoping for the intercession of the saints, human sloth would presumptuously wrap itself in these sins, and would take no steps to be disentangled from such wrappings by the deft energy of any virtue, but would only desire to be rescued by the merits of other people, whose friendship had been won by a bountiful use of the mammon of unrighteousness. But now that we are left in ignorance of the precise nature of that iniquity which is venial, even though it be persevered in, certainly we are both more vigilant in our prayers and efforts for progress, and more careful to secure with the mammon of unrighteousness friends for ourselves among the saints.

But this deliverance, which is effected by one's own prayers, or the intercession of holy men, secures that a man be not cast into eternal fire, but not that, when once he has been cast into it, he should after a time be rescued from it. For even those who fancy that what is said of the good ground bringing forth abundant fruit, some thirty, some sixty, some a hundredfold, is to be referred to the saints, so that in proportion to their merits some of them shall deliver thirty men, some sixty, some a hundred—even those who maintain this are yet commonly inclined to suppose that this deliverance will take place at, and not after, the day of judgment. Under this impression, someone who observed the unseemly folly with which men promise themselves impunity on the ground that all will be included in this method of deliverance is reported to have very happily remarked that we should rather endeavor to live so well that we shall be all found among the number of those who are to intercede for the liberation of others, lest these should be so few in number that, after they have delivered one thirty, another sixty, another a hundred, there should still remain many who could not be delivered from punishment by their intercessions, and among them everyone who has vainly and rashly promised himself the fruit of another's labor. But enough has been said in reply to those who acknowledge the authority of the same sacred Scriptures as ourselves, but who, by a mistaken interpretation of them, conceive of the future rather as they themselves wish, than as the Scriptures teach. And having given this reply, I now, according to promise, close this book.

Book XXII

Chapter 22   Of the Miseries and Ills to Which the Human Race Is Justly Exposed Through the First Sin, and from Which None Can Be Delivered Save by Christ's Grace.

That the whole human race has been condemned in its first origin, this life itself, if life it is to be called, bears witness by the host of cruel ills with which it is filled. Is not this proved by the profound and dreadful ignorance which produces all the errors that enfold the children of Adam, and from which no man can be delivered without toil, pain, and fear? Is it not proved by his love of so many vain and hurtful things, which produces gnawing cares, disquiet, griefs, fears, wild joys, quarrels, lawsuits, wars, treasons, angers, hatreds, deceit, flattery, fraud, theft, robbery, perfidy, pride, ambition, envy, murders, parricides, cruelty, ferocity, wickedness, luxury, insolence, impudence, shamelessness, fornications, adulteries, incests, and the numberless uncleannesses and unnatural acts of both sexes, which it is shameful so much as to mention; sacrileges, heresies, blasphemies, perjuries, oppression of the innocent, calumnies, plots, falsehoods, false witnessings, unrighteous judgments, violent deeds, plunderings, and whatever similar wickedness has found its way into the lives of men, though it cannot find its way into the conception of pure minds? These are indeed the crimes of wicked men, yet they spring from that root of error and misplaced love which is born with every son of Adam. For who is there that has not observed with what profound ignorance, manifesting itself even in infancy, and with what superfluity of foolish desires, beginning to appear in boyhood, man comes into this life, so that, were he left to live as he pleased, and to do whatever he pleased, he would plunge into all, or certainly into many of those crimes and iniquities which I mentioned, and could not mention?

But because God does not wholly desert those whom he condemns, nor shuts up in his anger his tender mercies, the human race is restrained by law and instruction, which keep guard against the ignorance that besets us, and oppose the assaults of vice, but are themselves full of labor and sorrow. For what mean those multifarious threats which are used to restrain the folly of children? What mean pedagogues, masters, the birch, the strap, the cane, the schooling which Scripture says must be given a child, "beating him on the sides lest he wax stubborn,"[221] and it be hardly possible or not possible at all to subdue him? Why all these punishments, save to overcome ignorance and bridle evil desires—these evils with which we come into the world? For why is it that we remember with difficulty, and without difficulty forget, learn with difficulty, and without difficulty remain ignorant, are diligent with difficulty, and without difficulty are indolent? Does not this show what vitiated nature inclines and tends to by its own weight, and what succor it needs if it is to be delivered? Inactivity, sloth, laziness, negligence, are vices which shun labor, since labor, though useful, is itself a punishment.

But, besides the punishments of childhood, without which there would be no learning of what the parents wish—and the parents rarely wish anything useful to be taught—who can describe, who can conceive the number and severity of the punishments which afflict the human race—pains which are not only the accompaniment of the wickedness of godless men, but are a part of the human condition and the common misery—what fear and what grief are caused by bereavement and mourning, by losses and condemnations, by fraud and falsehood, by false suspicions, and all the crimes and wicked deeds of other men? For at their hands we suffer robbery, captivity, chains, imprisonment, exile, torture, mutilation, loss of sight, the violation of chastity to satisfy the lust of the oppressor, and many other dreadful evils. What numberless casualties threaten our bodies from without—extremes of heat and cold, storms, floods, inundations, lightning, thunder, hail, earthquakes, houses falling; or from the stumbling, or shying, or vice of horses; from countless poisons in fruits, water, air, animals; from the painful or even deadly bites of wild animals; from the madness which a mad dog communicates, so that even the animal which of all others is most gentle and friendly to its own master becomes an object of intenser fear than a lion or dragon, and the man whom it has by chance infected with this pestilential contagion becomes so rabid that his

221. Ecclus 30:12.

parents, wife, children, dread him more than any wild beast! What disasters are suffered by those who travel by land or sea! What man can go out of his own house without being exposed on all hands to unforeseen accidents? Returning home sound in limb, he slips on his own doorstep, breaks his leg, and never recovers. What can seem safer than a man sitting in his chair? Eli the priest fell from his and broke his neck. How many accidents do farmers, or rather all men, fear that the crops may suffer from the weather, or the soil, or the ravages of destructive animals? Commonly they feel safe when the crops are gathered and housed. Yet, to my certain knowledge, sudden floods have driven the laborers away and swept the barns clean of the finest harvest. Is innocence a sufficient protection against the various assaults of demons? That no man might think so, even baptized infants, who are certainly unsurpassed in innocence, are sometimes so tormented, that God, who permits it, teaches us hereby to bewail the calamities of this life, and to desire the felicity of the life to come. As to bodily diseases, they are so numerous that they cannot all be contained even in medical books. And in very many, or almost all of them, the cures and remedies are themselves tortures, so that men are delivered from a pain that destroys by a cure that pains. Has not the madness of thirst driven men to drink human urine, and even their own? Has not hunger driven men to eat human flesh, and that the flesh not of bodies found dead, but of bodies slain for the purpose? Have not the fierce pangs of famine driven mothers to eat their own children, incredibly savage as it seems? In fine, sleep itself, which is justly called repose, how little of repose there sometimes is in it when disturbed with dreams and visions; and with what terror is the wretched mind overwhelmed by the appearances of things which are so presented, and which, as it were so stand out before the senses, that we cannot distinguish them from realities! How wretchedly do false appearances distract men in certain diseases! With what astonishing variety of appearances are even healthy men sometimes deceived by evil spirits, who produce these delusions for the sake of perplexing the senses of their victims, if they cannot succeed in seducing them to their side!

From this hell upon earth there is no escape, save through the grace of the Savior Christ, our God and Lord. The very name Jesus shows this, for it means Savior; and he saves us especially from passing out of this life into a more wretched and eternal state, which is rather a death than a life. For in this life, though holy men and holy pursuits afford us great consolations, yet the blessings which men crave are not invariably bestowed upon them, lest religion should be cultivated for the sake of these temporal advantages, while it ought rather to be cultivated for the sake of that other life from which all evil is excluded. Therefore, also, does grace aid good men in the midst of present calamities, so that they are enabled to endure them with a constancy portioned to their faith. The world's sages affirm that philosophy contributes something to this—that philosophy which, according to Cicero, the gods have bestowed in its purity only on a few men. They have never given, he says, nor can ever give, a greater gift to men. So that even those against whom we are disputing have been compelled to acknowledge, in some fashion, that the grace of God is necessary for the acquisition, not, indeed, of any philosophy, but of the true philosophy. And if the true philosophy—this sole support against the miseries of this life—has been given by heaven only to a few, it sufficiently appears from this that the human race has been condemned to pay this penalty of wretchedness. And as, according to their acknowledgment, no greater gift has been bestowed by God, so it must be believed that it could be given only by that God whom they themselves recognize as greater than all the gods they worship.

Chapter 23   Of the Miseries of This Life Which Attach Peculiarly to the Toil of Good Men, Irrespective of Those Which Are Common to the Good and Bad.

But, irrespective of the miseries which in this life are common to the good and bad, the righteous undergo labors peculiar to themselves, insofar as they make war upon their vices, and are involved in the temptations and perils of such a contest. For though sometimes more violent and at other times slacker, yet without intermission does the flesh lust against the spirit and the spirit against the flesh, so that we cannot do the things we would,[222] and extirpate all lust, but can only refuse consent to it, as God gives us ability, and so keep it under, vigilantly keeping watch lest a semblance of truth deceive us, lest a subtle discourse blind us, lest error involve us in

222. Gal 5:17.

darkness, lest we should take good for evil or evil for good, lest fear should hinder us from doing what we ought, or desire precipitate us into doing what we ought not, lest the sun go down upon our wrath, lest hatred provoke us to render evil for evil, lest unseemly or immoderate grief consume us, lest an ungrateful disposition make us slow to recognize benefits received, lest calumnies fret our conscience, lest rash suspicion on our part deceive us regarding a friend, or false suspicion of us on the part of others give us too much uneasiness, lest sin reign in our mortal body to obey its desires, lest our members be used as the instruments of unrighteousness, lest the eye follow lust, lest thirst for revenge carry us away, lest sight or thought dwell too long on some evil thing which gives us pleasure, lest wicked or indecent language be willingly listened to, lest we do what is pleasant but unlawful, and lest in this warfare, filled so abundantly with toil and peril, we either hope to secure victory by our own strength, or attribute it when secured to our own strength, and not to his grace of whom the apostle says, "Thanks be unto God, who giveth us the victory through our Lord Jesus Christ";[223] and in another place he says, "In all these things we are more than conquerors through Him that loved us."[224] But yet we are to know this, that however valorously we resist our vices, and however successful we are in overcoming them, yet as long as we are in this body we have always reason to say to God, "Forgive us our debts."[225] But in that kingdom where we shall dwell forever, clothed in immortal bodies, we shall no longer have either conflicts or debts—as indeed we should not have had at any time or in any condition, had our nature continued upright as it was created. Consequently even this our conflict, in which we are exposed to peril, and from which we hope to be delivered by a final victory, belongs to the ills of this life, which is proved by the witness of so many grave evils to be a life under condemnation.

Chapter 24   Of the Blessings with Which the Creator Has Filled This Life, Obnoxious Though It Be to the Curse.

But we must now contemplate the rich and countless blessings with which the goodness of God, who cares for all he has created,

223. 1 Cor 15:57.   224. Rom 8:37.   225. Mt 6:12.

has filled this very misery of the human race, which reflects his ret-
ributive justice. That first blessing which he pronounced before the
fall, when he said, "Increase, and multiply, and replenish the
earth,"[226] he did not inhibit after man had sinned, but the fecundity
originally bestowed remained in the condemned stock; and the
vice of sin, which has involved us in the necessity of dying, has yet
not deprived us of that wonderful power of seed, or rather of that
still more marvelous power by which seed is produced, and which
seems to be as it were inwrought and inwoven in the human body.
But in this river, as I may call it, or torrent of the human race, both
elements are carried along together—both the evil which is derived from him who begets, and the good which is bestowed by
him who creates us. In the original evil there are two things, sin
and punishment; in the original good, there are two other things,
propagation and conformation. But of the evils, of which the one,
sin, arose from our audacity, and the other, punishment, from
God's judgment, we have already said as much as suits our present
purpose. I mean now to speak of the blessings which God has conferred or still confers upon our nature, vitiated and condemned as
it is. For in condemning it he did not withdraw all that he had
given it, else it had been annihilated; neither did he, in penally sub-
jecting it to the devil, remove it beyond his own power, for not even
the devil himself is outside of God's government, since the devil's
nature subsists only by the supreme Creator who gives being to all
that in any form exists.

Of these two blessings, then, which we have said flow from
God's goodness, as from a fountain, toward our nature, vitiated by
sin and condemned to punishment, the one, propagation, was conferred by God's benediction when he made those first works, from
which he rested on the seventh day. But the other, conformation, is
conferred in that work of his wherein "He worketh hitherto."[227]
For were he to withdraw his efficacious power from things, they
should neither be able to go on and complete the periods assigned
to their measured movements, nor should they even continue in
possession of that nature they were created in. God, then, so created man that he gave him what we may call fertility, whereby he
might propagate other men, giving them a congenital capacity to

226. Gn 1:28.   227. Jn 5:17.

propagate their kind, but not imposing on them any necessity to do so. This capacity God withdraws at pleasure from individuals, making them barren, but from the whole race he has not withdrawn the blessing of propagation once conferred. But though not withdrawn on account of sin, this power of propagation is not what it would have been had there been no sin. For since "man placed in honor fell, he has become like the beasts,"[228] and generates as they do, though the little spark of reason, which was the image of God in him, has not been quite quenched. But if conformation were not added to propagation, there would be no reproduction of one's kind. For even though there were no such thing as copulation, and God wished to fill the earth with human inhabitants, he might create all these as he created one without the help of human generation. And, indeed, even as it is, those who copulate can generate nothing save by the creative energy of God. As, therefore, in respect of that spiritual growth whereby a man is formed to piety and righteousness, the apostle says, "Neither is he that planteth anything, neither he that watereth, but God that giveth the increase,"[229] so also it must be said that it is not he that generates that is anything, but God that giveth the essential form; that it is not the mother who carries and nurses the fruit of her womb that is anything, but God that giveth the increase. For he alone, by that energy wherewith "He worketh hitherto," causes the seed to develop, and to evolve from certain secret and invisible folds into the visible forms of beauty which we see. He alone, coupling and connecting in some wonderful fashion the spiritual and corporeal natures, the one to command, the other to obey, makes a living being. And this work of his is so great and wonderful, that not only man, who is a rational animal, and consequently more excellent than all other animals of the earth, but even the most diminutive insect, cannot be considered attentively without astonishment and without praising the Creator.

It is he, then, who has given to the human soul a mind, in which reason and understanding lie as it were asleep during infancy, and as if they were not destined, however, to be awakened and exercised as years increase, so as to become capable of knowledge and of receiving instruction, fit to understand what is true and to love

228. Ps 49:20.   229. 1 Cor 3:7.

what is good. It is by this capacity the soul drinks in wisdom, and becomes endowed with those virtues by which, in prudence, fortitude, temperance, and righteousness, it makes war upon error and the other inborn vices, and conquers them by fixing its desires upon no other object than the supreme and unchangeable Good. And even though this be not uniformly the result, yet who can competently utter or even conceive the grandeur of this work of the Almighty, and the unspeakable boon he has conferred upon our rational nature, by giving us even the capacity of such attainment? For over and above those arts which are called virtues, and which teach us how we may spend our life well, and attain to endless happiness—arts which are given to the children of the promise and the kingdom by the sole grace of God which is in Christ—has not the genius of man invented and applied countless astonishing arts, partly the result of necessity, partly the result of exuberant invention, so that this vigor of mind, which is so active in the discovery not merely of superfluous but even of dangerous and destructive things, betokens an inexhaustible wealth in the nature which can invent, learn, or employ such arts? What wonderful—one might say stupefying—advances has human industry made in the arts of weaving and building, of agriculture and navigation! With what endless variety are designs in pottery, painting, and sculpture produced, and with what skill executed! What wonderful spectacles are exhibited in the theaters, which those who have not seen them cannot credit! How skillful the contrivances for catching, killing, or taming wild beasts! And for the injury of men, also, how many kinds of poisons, weapons, engines of destruction, have been invented, while for the preservation or restoration of health the appliances and remedies are infinite! To provoke appetite and please the palate, what a variety of seasonings have been concocted! To express and gain entrance for thoughts, what a multitude and variety of signs there are, among which speaking and writing hold the first place! What ornaments has eloquence at command to delight the mind! What wealth of song is there to captivate the ear! How many musical instruments and strains of harmony have been devised! What skill has been attained in measures and numbers! With what sagacity have the movements and connections of the stars been discovered! Who could tell the thought that has been spent upon nature, even though, despairing of recounting it in detail, he endeavored only to give a general view of it? In fine, even the defense of errors and misapprehensions, which has illustrated the genius of heretics and philosophers, cannot be sufficiently declared. For at present it is the nature of the human mind which adorns this mortal life which we are extolling, and not the faith and the way of truth which lead to immortality. And since this great nature has certainly been created by the true and supreme God, who administers all things he has made with absolute power and justice, it could never have fallen into these miseries, nor have gone out of them to miseries eternal—saving only those who are redeemed—had not an exceeding great sin been found in the first man from whom the rest have sprung.

Moreover, even in the body, though it dies like that of the beasts, and is in many ways weaker than theirs, what goodness of God, what providence of the great Creator, is apparent! The organs of sense and the rest of the members, are not they so placed, the appearance, and form, and stature of the body as a whole, is it not so fashioned, as to indicate that it was made for the service of a reasonable soul? Man has not been created stooping toward the earth, like the irrational animals, but his bodily form, erect and looking heavenward, admonishes him to mind the things that are above. Then the marvelous nimbleness which has been given to the tongue and the hands, fitting them to speak, and write, and execute so many duties, and practice so many arts, does it not prove the excellence of the soul for which such an assistant was provided? And even apart from its adaptation to the work required of it, there is such a symmetry in its various parts, and so beautiful a proportion maintained, that one is at a loss to decide whether, in creating the body, greater regard was paid to utility or to beauty. Assuredly no part of the body has been created for the sake of utility which does not also contribute something to its beauty. And this would be all the more apparent, if we knew more precisely how all its parts are connected and adapted to one another, and were not limited in our observations to what appears on the surface, for as to what is covered up and hidden from our view, the intricate web of veins and nerves, the vital parts of all that lies under the skin, no one can discover it. For although, with a cruel zeal for science, some medical men, who are called anatomists, have dissected the bodies of the dead, and sometimes even of sick persons who died under their knives, and have inhumanly pried into the secrets of the human body to learn the nature of the disease and its exact seat, and how it might be cured, yet those relations of which I speak, and which form the concord, or, as the Greeks call it, "harmony," of the whole body outside and in, as of some instrument, no one has been able to discover, because no one has been audacious enough to seek for them. But if these could be known, then even the inward parts, which seem to have no beauty, would so delight us with their exquisite fitness, as to afford a profounder satisfaction to the mind—and the eyes are but its ministers—than the obvious beauty which gratifies the eye. There are some things, too, which have such a place in the body, that they obviously serve no useful purpose, but are solely for beauty, as e.g., the teats on a man's breast, or the beard on his face; for that this is for ornament, and not for protection, is proved by the bare faces of women, who ought rather, as the weaker sex, to enjoy such a defense. If, therefore, of all those members which are exposed to our view, there is certainly not one in which beauty is sacrificed to utility, while there are some which serve no purpose but only beauty, I think it can readily be concluded that in the creation of the human body comeliness was more regarded than necessity. In truth, necessity is a transitory thing, and the time is coming when we shall enjoy one another's beauty without any lust—a condition which will specially redound to the praise of the Creator, who, as it is said in the psalm, has "put on praise and comeliness."[230]

How can I tell of the rest of creation, with all its beauty and utility, which the divine goodness has given to man to please his eye and serve his purposes, condemned though he is, and hurled into these labors and miseries? Shall I speak of the manifold and various loveliness of sky, and earth, and sea; of the plentiful supply and wonderful qualities of the light; of sun, moon, and stars; of the shade of trees; of the colors and perfume of flowers; of the multitude of birds, all differing in plumage and in song; of the variety of animals, of which the smallest in size are often the most wonderful—the works of ants and bees astonishing us more than the huge bodies of whales? Shall I speak of the sea, which itself is so grand a spectacle, when it arrays itself as it were in vestures of various colors, now running through every shade of green, and again becom-

230. Ps 104:1.

ing purple or blue? Is it not delightful to look at it in storm, and experience the soothing complacency which it inspires, by suggesting
that we ourselves are not tossed and shipwrecked? What shall I say
of the numberless kinds of food to alleviate hunger, and the variety
of seasonings to stimulate appetite which are scattered everywhere
by nature, and for which we are not indebted to the art of cookery?
How many natural appliances are there for preserving and restoring health! How grateful is the alternation of day and night! How
pleasant the breezes that cool the air! How abundant the supply of
clothing furnished us by trees and animals! Who can enumerate all
the blessings we enjoy? If I were to attempt to detail and unfold
only these few which I have indicated in the mass, such an enumeration would fill a volume. And all these are but the solace of the
wretched and condemned, not the rewards of the blessed. What
then shall these rewards be, if such be the blessings of a condemned
state? What will he give to those whom he has predestined to life,
who has given such things even to those whom he has predestined
to death? What blessings will he in the blessed life shower upon
those for whom, even in this state of misery, he has been willing
that his only-begotten Son should endure such sufferings even to
death? Thus the apostle reasons concerning those who are predestined to that kingdom: "He that spared not His own Son, but delivered Him up for us all, how shall He not with Him also give us all
things?"[231] When this promise is fulfilled, what shall we be? What
blessings shall we receive in that kingdom, since already we have
received as the pledge of them Christ's dying? In what condition
shall the spirit of man be, when it has no longer any vice at all;
when it neither yields to any, nor is in bondage to any, nor has to
make war against any, but is perfected, and enjoys undisturbed
peace with itself? Shall it not then know all things with certainty,
and without any labor or error, when unhindered and joyfully it
drinks the wisdom of God at the fountainhead? What shall the
body be, when it is in every respect subject to the spirit, from which
it shall draw a life so sufficient as to stand in need of no other nutri-
ment? For it shall no longer be animal, but spiritual, having indeed
the substance of flesh, but without any fleshly corruption.

231. Rom 8:32.

Chapter 30   Of the Eternal Felicity of the City of God, and of the Perpetual Sabbath.

How great shall be that felicity, which shall be tainted with no evil, which shall lack no good, and which shall afford leisure for the praises of God, who shall be all in all! For I know not what other employment there can be where no lassitude shall slacken activity, nor any want stimulate to labor. I am admonished also by the sacred song, in which I read or hear the words, "Blessed are they that dwell in Thy house, O Lord; they will be still praising Thee."[232] All the members and organs of the incorruptible body, which now we see to be suited to various necessary uses, shall contribute to the praises of God, for in that life necessity shall have no place, but full, certain, secure, everlasting felicity. For all those parts of the bodily harmony, which are distributed through the whole body, within and without, and of which I have just been saying that they at present elude our observation, shall then be discerned; and, along with the other great and marvelous discoveries which shall then kindle rational minds in praise of the great Artificer, there shall be the enjoyment of a beauty which appeals to the reason. What power of movement such bodies shall possess, I have not the audacity rashly to define, as I have not the ability to conceive. Nevertheless I will say that in any case, both in motion and at rest, they shall be, as in their appearance, seemly, for into that state nothing which is unseemly shall be admitted. One thing is certain, the body shall forthwith be wherever the spirit wills, and the spirit shall will nothing which is unbecoming either to the spirit or to the body. True honor shall be there, for it shall be denied to none who is worthy, nor yielded to any unworthy; neither shall any unworthy person so much as sue for it, for none but the worthy shall be there. True peace shall be there, where no one shall suffer opposition either from himself or any other. God himself, who is the Author of virtue, shall there be its reward, for, as there is nothing greater or better, he has promised himself. What else was meant by his word through the prophet, "I will be your God, and ye shall be my people,"[233] than, "I shall be their satisfaction, I shall be all that men honorably desire—life, and health, and nourishment, and plenty,

232. Ps 84:4.   233. Lv 26:12.

and glory, and honor, and peace, and all good things"? This, too, is the right interpretation of the saying of the apostle, "That God may be all in all."[234] He shall be the end of our desires who shall be seen without end, loved without cloy, praised without weariness. This outgoing of affection, this employment, shall certainly be, like eternal life itself, common to all.

But who can conceive, not to say describe, what degrees of honor and glory shall be awarded to the various degrees of merit? Yet it cannot be doubted that there shall be degrees. And in that blessed city there shall be this great blessing, that no inferior shall envy any superior, as now the archangels are not envied by the angels, because no one will wish to be what he has not received, though bound in strictest concord with him who has received, as in the body the finger does not seek to be the eye, though both members are harmoniously included in the complete structure of the body. And thus, along with his gift, greater or less, each shall receive this further gift of contentment to desire no more than he has.

Neither are we to suppose that because sin shall have no power to delight them, free will must be withdrawn. It will, on the contrary, be all the more truly free, because set free from delight in sinning to take unfailing delight in not sinning. For the first freedom of will which man received when he was created upright consisted in an ability not to sin, but also in an ability to sin, whereas this last freedom of will shall be superior, inasmuch as it shall not be able to sin. This, indeed, shall not be a natural ability, but the gift of God. For it is one thing to be God, another thing to be a partaker of God. God by nature cannot sin, but the partaker of God receives this inability from God. And in this divine gift there was to be observed this gradation, that man should first receive a free will by which he was able not to sin, and at last a free will by which he was not able to sin—the former being adapted to the acquiring of merit, the latter to the enjoying of the reward.[235] But the nature thus constituted, having sinned when it had the ability to do so, it is by a more abundant grace that it is delivered so as to reach that freedom in which it cannot sin. For as the first immortality which Adam lost by sinning consisted in his being able not to die, while the last shall consist in

234. 1 Cor 15:28.

235. Or, the former to a state of probation, the latter to a state of reward.

his not being able to die; so the first free will consisted in his being able not to sin, the last in his not being able to sin. And thus piety and justice shall be as indefeasible as happiness. For certainly by sinning we lost both piety and happiness, but when we lost happiness, we did not lose the love of it. Are we to say that God himself is not free because he cannot sin? In that city, then, there shall be free will, one in all the citizens, and indivisible in each, delivered from all ill, filled with all good, enjoying indefeasibly the delights of eternal joys, oblivious of sins, oblivious of sufferings, and yet not so oblivious of its deliverance as to be ungrateful to its Deliverer.

The soul, then, shall have an intellectual remembrance of its past ills, but, so far as regards sensible experience, they shall be quite forgotten. For a skillful physician knows, indeed, professionally almost all diseases, but experientially he is ignorant of a great number which he himself has never suffered from. As, therefore, there are two ways of knowing evil things—one by mental insight, the other by sensible experience, for it is one thing to understand all vices by the wisdom of a cultivated mind, another to understand them by the foolishness of an abandoned life—so also there are two ways of forgetting evils. For a well-instructed and learned man forgets them one way, and he who has experientially suffered from them forgets them another—the former by neglecting what he has learned, the latter by escaping what he has suffered. And in this latter way the saints shall forget their past ills, for they shall have so thoroughly escaped them all that they shall be quite blotted out of their experience. But their intellectual knowledge, which shall be great, shall keep them acquainted not only with their own past woes, but with the eternal sufferings of the lost. For if they were not to know that they had been miserable, how could they, as the psalmist says, forever sing the mercies of God? Certainly that city shall have no greater joy than the celebration of the grace of Christ, who redeemed us by his blood. There shall be accomplished the words of the psalm, "Be still, and know that I am God."[236] There shall be the great Sabbath which has no evening, which God celebrated among his first works, as it is written, "And God rested on the seventh day from all His works which He had made. And God

236. Ps 46:10.

blessed the seventh day, and sanctified it; because that in it He had rested from all His work which God began to make."[237] For we shall ourselves be the seventh day, when we shall be filled and replenished with God's blessing and sanctification. There shall we be still, and know that he is God; that he is that which we ourselves aspired to be when we fell away from him, and listened to the voice of the seducer, "Ye shall be as gods,"[238] and so abandoned God, who would have made us as gods, not by deserting him, but by participating in him. For without him what have we accomplished, save to perish in his anger? But when we are restored by him, and perfected with greater grace, we shall have eternal leisure to see that he is God, for we shall be full of him when he shall be all in all. For even our good works, when they are understood to be rather his than ours, are imputed to us that we may enjoy this Sabbath rest. For if we attribute them to ourselves, they shall be servile; for it is said of the Sabbath, "Ye shall do no servile work in it."[239] Wherefore also it is said by Ezekiel the prophet, "And I gave them my Sabbaths to be a sign between me and them, that they might know that I am the Lord who sanctify them."[240] This knowledge shall be perfected when we shall be perfectly at rest, and shall perfectly know that he is God.

This Sabbath shall appear still more clearly if we count the ages as days, in accordance with the periods of time defined in Scripture, for that period will be found to be the seventh. The first age, as the first day, extends from Adam to the deluge; the second from the deluge to Abraham, equalling the first, not in length of time, but in the number of generations, there being ten in each. From Abraham to the advent of Christ there are, as the evangelist Matthew calculates, three periods, in each of which are fourteen generations—one period from Abraham to David, a second from David to the captivity, a third from the captivity to the birth of Christ in the flesh. There are thus five ages in all. The sixth is now passing, and cannot be measured by any number of generations, as it has been said, "It is not for you to know the times, which the Father hath put in His own power."[241] After this period God shall rest

237. Gn 2:2, 3.   238. Gn 3:5.   239. Dt 5:14.   240. Ez 20:12.

241. Acts 1:7.

as on the seventh day, when he shall give us (who shall be the seventh day) rest in himself.[242] But there is not now space to treat of these ages; suffice it to say that the seventh shall be our Sabbath, which shall be brought to a close, not by an evening, but by the Lord's day, as an eighth and eternal day, consecrated by the resurrection of Christ, and prefiguring the eternal repose not only of the spirit, but also of the body. There we shall rest and see, see and love, love and praise. This is what shall be in the end without end. For what other end do we propose to ourselves than to attain to the kingdom of which there is no end?

I think I have now, by God's help, discharged my obligation in writing this large work. Let those who think I have said too little, or those who think I have said too much, forgive me; and let those who think I have said just enough join me in giving thanks to God. Amen.

242. On Augustine's view of the millennium and the first resurrection, see Bk. XX, 6–10.—P.S.

From On Christian Doctrine

Book I

Chapter 3   Some Things Are for Use, Some for Enjoyment.

3. There are some things, then, which are to be enjoyed, others which are to be used, others still which enjoy and use. Those things which are objects of enjoyment make us happy. Those things which are objects of use assist, and (so to speak) support us in our efforts after happiness, so that we can attain the things that make us happy and rest in them. We ourselves, again, who enjoy and use these things, being placed among both kinds of objects, if we set ourselves to enjoy those which we ought to use, are hindered in our course, and sometimes even led away from it; so that, getting entangled in the love of lower gratifications, we lag behind in, or even altogether turn back from, the pursuit of the real and proper objects of enjoyment.

Chapter 4   Difference of Use and Enjoyment.

4. For to enjoy a thing is to rest with satisfaction in it for its own sake. To use, on the other hand, is to employ whatever means are at one's disposal to obtain what one desires, if it is a proper object of desire, for an unlawful use ought rather to be called an abuse. Suppose, then, we were wanderers in a strange country, and could not live happily away from our fatherland, and that we felt wretched in our wandering, and wishing to put an end to our misery, determined to return home. We find, however, that we must make use of some mode of conveyance, either by land or water, in order to reach that fatherland where our enjoyment is to commence. But the beauty of the country through which we pass, and the very pleasure of the motion, charm our hearts, and turning these things which we ought to use into objects of enjoyment, we become unwilling to hasten the end of our journey, and becoming engrossed in a factitious delight, our thoughts are diverted from that home whose delights would make us truly happy. Such is a picture of our condition in this life of mortality. We have wandered far from

God; and if we wish to return to our Father's home, this world must be used, not enjoyed, that so the invisible things of God may be clearly seen, being understood by the things that are made[243]— that is, that by means of what is material and temporary we may lay hold upon that which is spiritual and eternal.

Chapter 22　　God Alone to Be Enjoyed.

20. Among all these things, then, those only are the true objects of enjoyment which we have spoken of as eternal and unchangeable. The rest are for use, that we may be able to arrive at the full enjoyment of the former. We, however, who enjoy and use other things are things ourselves. For a great thing truly is man, made after the image and similitude of God, not as respects the mortal body in which he is clothed, but as respects the rational soul by which he is exalted in honor above the beasts. And so it becomes an important question, whether men ought to enjoy, or to use, themselves, or to do both. For we are commanded to love one another: but it is a question whether man is to be loved by man for his own sake, or for the sake of something else. If it is for his own sake, we enjoy him; if it is for the sake of something else, we use him. It seems to me, then, that he is to be loved for the sake of something else. For if a thing is to be loved for its own sake, then in the enjoyment of it consists a happy life, the hope of which at least, if not yet the reality, is our comfort in the present time. But a curse is pronounced on him who places his hope in man.[244]

21. Neither ought anyone to have joy in himself, if you look at the matter clearly, because no one ought to love even himself for his own sake, but for the sake of him who is the true object of enjoyment. For a man is never in so good a state as when his whole life is a journey toward the unchangeable life, and his affections are entirely fixed upon that. If, however, he loves himself for his own sake, he does not look at himself in relation to God, but turns his mind in upon himself, and so is not occupied with anything that is unchangeable. And thus he does not enjoy himself at his best, because he is better when his mind is fully fixed upon, and his affections wrapped up in, the unchangeable good, than when he turns

243. Rom 1:20.　　　244. Jer 17:5.

from that to enjoy even himself. Wherefore if you ought not to love even yourself for your own sake, but for his in whom your love finds its most worthy object, no other man has a right to be angry if you love him too for God's sake. For this is the law of love that has been laid down by Divine authority: "Thou shall love thy neighbor as thyself"; but, "Thou shall love God with all thy heart, and with all thy soul, and with all thy mind";[245] so that you are to concentrate all your thoughts, your whole life, and your whole intelligence upon him from whom you derive all that you bring. For when he says, "With all thy heart, and with all thy soul, and with all thy mind," he means that no part of our life is to be unoccupied, and to afford room, as it were, for the wish to enjoy some other object, but that whatever else may suggest itself to us as an object worthy of love is to be borne into the same channel in which the whole current of our affections flows. Whoever, then, loves his neighbor aright, ought to urge upon him that he too should love God with his whole heart, and soul, and mind. For in this way, loving his neighbor as himself, a man turns the whole current of his love both for himself and his neighbor into the channel of the love of God, which suffers no stream to be drawn off from itself by whose diversion its own volume would be diminished.

Chapter 23   Man Needs No Injunction to Love Himself and His Own Body.

22. Those things which are objects of use are not all, however, to be loved, but those only which are either united with us in a common relation to God, such as a man or an angel, or are so related to us as to need the goodness of God through our instrumentality, such as the body. For assuredly the martyrs did not love the wickedness of their persecutors, although they used it to attain the favor of God. As, then, there are four kinds of things that are to be loved—first, that which is above us; second, ourselves; third, that which is on a level with us; fourth, that which is beneath us—no precepts need be given about the second and fourth of these. For, however far a man may fall away from the truth, he still continues to love himself, and to love his own body. The soul which flies away from the

245. Mt 22:37–39. Compare Lv 19:18; Dt 6:5.

unchangeable Light, the Ruler of all things, does so that it may rule over itself and over its own body; and so it cannot but love both itself and its own body.

23. Moreover, it thinks it has attained something very great if it is able to lord it over its companions, that is, other men. For it is inherent in the sinful soul to desire above all things, and to claim as due to itself, that which is properly due to God only. Now such love of itself is more correctly called hate. For it is not just that it should desire what is beneath it to be obedient to it while itself will not obey its own superior; and most justly has it been said, "He who loveth iniquity hateth his own soul."[246] And accordingly the soul becomes weak, and endures much suffering about the mortal body. For, of course, it must love the body, and be grieved at its corruption, and the immortality and incorruptibility of the body spring out of the health of the soul. Now the health of the soul is to cling steadfastly to the better part, that is, to the unchangeable God. But when it aspires to lord it even over those who are by nature its equals—that is, its fellow men—this is a reach of arrogance utterly intolerable.

Chapter 24   No Man Hates His Own Flesh, Not Even Those Who Abuse It.

24. No man, then, hates himself. On this point, indeed, no question was ever raised by any sect. But neither does any man hate his own body. For the apostle says truly, "No man ever yet hated his own flesh."[247] And when some people say that they would rather be without a body altogether, they entirely deceive themselves. For it is not their body, but its corruptions and its heaviness, that they hate. And so it is not no body, but an uncorrupted and very light body, that they want. But they think a body of that kind would be no body at all, because they think such a thing as that must be a spirit. And as to the fact that they seem in some sort to scourge their bodies by abstinence and toil, those who do this in the right spirit do it not that they may get rid of their body, but that they may have it in subjection and ready for every needful work. For they strive by a kind of

246. Ps 10:5 (Septuagint).   247. Eph 5:29.

toilsome exercise of the body itself to root out those lusts that are hurtful to the body, that is, those habits and affections of the soul that lead to the enjoyment of unworthy objects. They are not destroying themselves; they are taking care of their health.

25. Those, on the other hand, who do this in a perverse spirit, make war upon their own body as if it were a natural enemy. And in this matter they are led astray by a mistaken interpretation of what they read: "The flesh lusteth against the spirit, and the spirit against the flesh, and these are contrary the one to the other."[248] For this is said of the carnal habit yet unsubdued, against which the spirit lusteth, not to destroy the body, but to eradicate the lust of the body—i.e., its evil habit—and thus to make it subject to the spirit, which is what the order of nature demands. For as, after the resurrection, the body, having become wholly subject to the spirit, will live in perfect peace to all eternity; even in this life we must make it an object to have the carnal habit changed for the better, so that its inordinate affections may not war against the soul. And until this shall take place, "the flesh lusteth against the spirit, and the spirit against the flesh"; the spirit struggling, not in hatred, but for the mastery, because it desires that what it loves should be subject to the higher principle; and the flesh struggling, not in hatred, but because of the bondage of habit which it has derived from its parent stock, and which has grown in upon it by a law of nature till it has become inveterate. The spirit, then, in subduing the flesh, is working as it were to destroy the ill-founded peace of an evil habit, and to bring about the real peace which springs out of a good habit. Nevertheless, not even those who, led astray by false notions, hate their bodies would be prepared to sacrifice one eye, even supposing they could do so without suffering any pain, and that they had as much sight left in one as they formerly had in two, unless some object was to be attained which would overbalance the loss. This and other indications of the same kind are sufficient to show those who candidly seek the truth how well-founded is the statement of the apostle when he says, "No man ever yet hated his own flesh." He adds too, "but nourisheth and cherisheth it, even as the Lord the Church."[249]

248. Gal 5:17.   249. Eph 5:29.

Chapter 25   A Man May Love Something More Than His Body, But Does Not Therefore Hate His Body.

26. Man, therefore, ought to be taught the due measure of loving, that is, in what measure he may love himself so as to be of service to himself. For that he does love himself, and does desire to do good to himself, nobody but a fool would doubt. He is to be taught, too, in what measure to love his body, so as to care for it wisely and within due limits. For it is equally manifest that he loves his body also, and desires to keep it safe and sound. And yet a man may have something that he loves better than the safety and soundness of his body. For many have been found voluntarily to suffer both pains and amputations of some of their limbs that they might obtain other objects which they valued more highly. But no one is to be told not to desire the safety and health of his body because there is something he desires more. For the miser, though he loves money, buys bread for himself—that is, he gives away money that he is very fond of and desires to heap up—but it is because he values more highly the bodily health which the bread sustains. It is superfluous to argue longer on a point so very plain, but this is just what the error of wicked men often compels us to do.

Chapter 26   The Command to Love God and Our Neighbor Includes a Command to Love Ourselves.

27. Seeing, then, that there is no need of a command that every man should love himself and his own body—seeing, that is, that we love ourselves, and what is beneath us but connected with us, through a law of nature which has never been violated, and which is common to us with the beasts (for even the beasts love themselves and their own bodies)—it only remained necessary to lay injunctions upon us in regard to God above us, and our neighbor beside us. "Thou shalt love," he says, "the Lord thy God with all thy heart, and with all thy soul, and with all thy mind; and thou shalt love thy neighbor as thyself. On these two commandments hang all the Law and the Prophets."[250] Thus the end of the commandment is love, and that twofold, the love of God and the love of our neighbor. Now, if you

250. Mt 22:37–40.

take yourself in your entirety—that is, soul and body together—
and your neighbor in his entirety, soul and body together (for man
is made up of soul and body), you will find that none of the classes
of things that are to be loved is overlooked in these two commandments. For though, when the love of God comes first, and the measure of our love for him is prescribed in such terms that it is evident
all other things are to find their center in him, nothing seems to be
said about our love for ourselves; yet when it is said, "Thou shall
love thy neighbor as thyself," it at once becomes evident that our
love for ourselves has not been overlooked.

Chapter 27   The Order of Love.

28. Now he is a man of just and holy life who forms an unprejudiced estimate of things, and keeps his affections also under strict
control, so that he neither loves what he ought not to love, nor fails
to love what he ought to love, nor loves that more which ought to
be loved less, nor loves that equally which ought to be loved either
less or more, nor loves that less or more which ought to be loved
equally. No sinner is to be loved as a sinner, and every man is to be
loved as a man for God's sake, but God is to be loved for his own
sake. And if God is to be loved more than any man, each man
ought to love God more than himself. Likewise we ought to love
another man better than our own body, because all things are to be
loved in reference to God, and another man can have fellowship
with us in the enjoyment of God, whereas our body cannot, for
the body only lives through the soul, and it is by the soul that we
enjoy God.

Chapter 28   How We Are to Decide Whom to Aid.

29. Further, all men are to be loved equally. But since you cannot do
good to all, you are to pay special regard to those who, by the accidents of time, or place, or circumstance, are brought into closer
connection with you. For, suppose that you had a great deal of
some commodity, and felt bound to give it away to somebody who
had none, and that it could not be given to more than one person; if
two persons presented themselves, neither of whom had either
from need or relationship a greater claim upon you than the other,

you could do nothing fairer than choose by lot to which you would give what could not be given to both. Just so among men: since you cannot consult for the good of them all, you must take the matter as decided for you by a sort of lot, according as each man happens for the time being to be more closely connected with you.

Chapter 29   We Are to Desire and Endeavor That All Men May Love God.

30. Now of all who can with us enjoy God, we love partly those to whom we render services, partly those who render services to us, partly those who both help us in our need and in turn are helped by us, partly those upon whom we confer no advantage and from whom we look for none. We ought to desire, however, that they should all join with us in loving God, and all the assistance that we either give them or accept from them should tend to that one end. For in the theaters, dens of iniquity though they be, if a man is fond of a particular actor and enjoys his art as a great or even as the very greatest good, he is fond of all who join with him in admiration of his favorite, not for their own sakes, but for the sake of him whom they admire in common; and the more fervent he is in his admiration, the more he works in every way he can to secure new admirers for him, and the more anxious he becomes to show him to others; and if he find anyone comparatively indifferent, he does all he can to excite his interest by urging his favorite's merits: if, however, he meet with anyone who opposes him, he is exceedingly displeased by such a man's contempt of his favorite, and strives in every way he can to remove it. Now, if this be so, what does it become us to do who live in the fellowship of the love of God, the enjoyment of whom is true happiness of life, to whom all who love him owe both their own existence and the love they bear him, concerning whom we have no fear that anyone who comes to know him will be disappointed in him, and who desires our love, not for any gain to himself, but that those who love him may obtain an eternal reward, even himself whom they love? And hence it is that we love even our enemies. For we do not fear them, seeing they cannot take away from us what we love, but we pity them rather, because the more they hate us the more are they separated from

him whom we love. For if they would turn to him, they must of necessity love him as the supreme good, and love us too as partakers with them in so great a blessing.

Chapter 36 That Interpretation of Scripture Which Builds Us up in Love Is Not Perniciously Deceptive Nor Mendacious, Even Though It Be Faulty. The Interpreter, However, Should Be Corrected.

40. Whoever, then, thinks that he understands the Holy Scriptures, or any part of them, but puts such an interpretation upon them as does not tend to build up this twofold love of God and our neighbor, does not yet understand them as he ought. If, on the other hand, a man draws a meaning from them that may be used for the building up of love, even though he does not happen upon the precise meaning which the author whom he reads intended to express in that place, his error is not pernicious, and he is wholly clear from the charge of deception. For there is involved in deception the intention to say what is false, and we find plenty of people who intend to deceive, but nobody who wishes to be deceived. Since, then, the man who knows practices deceit, and the ignorant man is practiced upon, it is quite clear that in any particular case the man who is deceived is a better man than he who deceives, seeing that it is better to suffer than to commit injustice. Now every man who lies commits an injustice, and if any man thinks that a lie is ever useful, he must think that injustice is sometimes useful. For no liar keeps faith in the matter about which he lies. He wishes, of course, that the man to whom he lies should place confidence in him, and yet he betrays his confidence by lying to him. Now every man who breaks faith is unjust. Either, then, injustice is sometimes useful (which is impossible), or a lie is never useful.

41. Whoever takes another meaning out of Scripture than the writer intended goes astray, but not through any falsehood in Scripture. Nevertheless, as I was going to say, if his mistaken interpretation tends to build up love, which is the end of the commandment, he goes astray in much the same way as a man who by mistake quits the high road, but yet reaches through the fields the same place to which the road leads. He is to be corrected, however,

and to be shown how much better it is not to quit the straight road, lest, if he get into a habit of going astray, he may sometimes take crossroads, or even go in the wrong direction altogether.

Chapter 37   Dangers of Mistaken Interpretation.

For if he takes up rashly a meaning which the author whom he is reading did not intend, he often falls in with other statements which he cannot harmonize with this meaning. And if he admits that these statements are true and certain, then it follows that the meaning he had put upon the former passage cannot be the true one: and so it comes to pass, one can hardly tell how, that, out of love for his own opinion, he begins to feel more angry with Scripture than he is with himself. And if he should once permit that evil to creep in, it will utterly destroy him. "For we walk by faith, not by sight."[251] Now faith will totter if the authority of Scripture begin to shake. And then, if faith totter, love itself will grow cold. For if a man has fallen from faith, he must necessarily also fall from love, for he cannot love what he does not believe to exist. But if he both believes and loves, then through good works, and through diligent attention to the precepts of morality, he comes to hope also that he shall attain the object of his love. And so these are the three things to which all knowledge and all prophecy are subservient: faith, hope, love.

Chapter 38   Love Never Faileth.

42. But sight shall displace faith, and hope shall be swallowed up in that perfect bliss to which we shall come; love, on the other hand, shall wax greater when these others fail. For if we love by faith that which as yet we see not, how much more shall we love it when we begin to see! And if we love by hope that which as yet we have not reached, how much more shall we love it when we reach it! For there is this great difference between things temporal and things eternal, that a temporal object is valued more before we possess it, and begins to prove worthless the moment we attain it, because it does not satisfy the soul, which has its only true and sure resting-

251. 2 Cor 5:7.

place in eternity; an eternal object, on the other hand, is loved with greater ardor when it is in possession than while it is still an object of desire, for no one in his longing for it can set a higher value on it than really belongs to it, so as to think it comparatively worthless when he finds it of less value than he thought; on the contrary, however high the value any man may set upon it when he is on his way to possess it, he will find it, when it comes into his possession, of higher value still.

Chapter 39   He Who Is Mature in Faith, Hope, and Love, Needs Scripture No Longer.

43. And thus a man who is resting upon faith, hope, and love, and who keeps a firm hold upon these, does not need the Scriptures except for the purpose of instructing others. Accordingly, many live without copies of the Scriptures, even in solitude, on the strength of these three graces. So that in their case, I think, the saying is already fulfilled: "Whether there be prophecies, they shall fail; whether there be tongues, they shall cease; whether there be knowledge, it shall vanish away."[252] Yet by means of these instruments (as they may be called), so great an edifice of faith and love has been built up in them, that, holding to what is perfect, they do not seek for what is only in part perfect—of course, I mean, so far as is possible in this life, for, in comparison with the future life, the life of no just and holy man is perfect here. Therefore the apostle says, "Now abideth faith, hope, charity, these three; but the greatest of these is charity":[253] because, when a man shall have reached the eternal world, while the other two graces will fail, love will remain greater and more assured.

Chapter 40   What Manner of Reader Scripture Demands.

44. And, therefore, if a man fully understands that "the end of the commandment is charity, out of a pure heart, and of a good conscience, and of faith unfeigned,"[254] and is bent upon making all his understanding of Scripture to bear upon these three graces, he may come to the interpretation of these books with an easy mind. For

252. 1 Cor 13:8.   253. 1 Cor 13:13.   254. 1 Tm 1:5.

while the apostle says "love," he adds "out of a pure heart," to provide against anything being loved but that which is worthy of love.
And he joins with this "a good conscience," in reference to hope,
for if a man has the burden of a bad conscience, he despairs of ever
reaching that which he believes in and loves. And in the third place
he says, "and of faith unfeigned." For if our faith is free from all
hypocrisy, then we both abstain from loving what is unworthy of
our love, and by living uprightly we are able to indulge the hope
that our hope shall not be in vain.

For these reasons I have been anxious to speak about the objects
of faith, as far as I thought it necessary for my present purpose, for
much has already been said on this subject in other volumes, either
by others or by myself. And so let this be the end of the present
book. In the next I shall discuss, as far as God shall give me light,
the subject of signs.

From The Enchiridion on Faith, Hope, and Love

Chapter 31 — Love

117. And now regarding *love*, which the apostle says is greater than the other two—that is, faith and hope—for the more richly it dwells in a man, the better the man in whom it dwells. For when we ask whether someone is a good man, we are not asking what he believes, or hopes, but what he loves. Now, beyond all doubt, he who loves aright believes and hopes rightly. Likewise, he who does not love believes in vain, even if what he believes is true; he hopes in vain, even if what he hopes for is generally agreed to pertain to true happiness, unless he believes and hopes for this: that he may through prayer obtain the gift of love. For, although it is true that he cannot hope without love, it may be that there is something without which, if he does not love it, he cannot realize the object of his hopes. An example of this would be if a man hopes for life eternal—and who is there who does not love that?—and yet does not love *righteousness*, without which no one comes to it.

Now this is the true faith of Christ which the apostle commends: faith that works through love. And what it yet lacks in love it asks that it may receive, it seeks that it may find, and knocks that it may be opened unto it.[255] For faith achieves what the law commands [*fides namque impetrat quod lex imperat*]. And, without the gift of God—that is, without the Holy Spirit, through whom love is shed abroad in our hearts—the law may bid but it cannot aid [*jubere lex poterit, non juvare*]. Moreover, it can make of man a transgressor, who cannot then excuse himself by pleading ignorance. For appetite reigns where the love of God does not.[256]

118. When, in the deepest shadows of ignorance, he lives according to the flesh with no restraint of reason—this is the primal state of man.[257] Afterward, when "through the law the knowledge of sin"[258] has come to man, and the Holy Spirit has not yet come to his aid—so that even if he wishes to live according to the law, he is

---

255. Mt 7:7.   256. Another wordplay on *cupiditas* and *caritas*.

257. An interesting resemblance here to Freud's description of the id, the primal core of our unconscious life.   258. Rom 3:20.

vanquished—man sins knowingly and is brought under the spell and made the slave of sin, "for by whatever a man is vanquished, of this master he is the slave."[259] The effect of the knowledge of the law is that sin works in man the whole round of concupiscence, which adds to the guilt of the first transgression. And thus it is that what was written is fulfilled: "The law entered in, that the offense might abound."[260] This is the *second* state of man.[261]

But if God regards a man with solicitude so that he then believes in God's help in fulfilling his commands, and if a man begins to be led by the Spirit of God, then the mightier power of love struggles against the power of the flesh.[262] And although there is still in man a power that fights against him—his infirmity being not yet fully healed—yet he [the righteous man] lives by faith and lives righteously insofar as he does not yield to evil desires, conquering them by his love of righteousness. This is the *third* stage of the man of good hope.

A final peace is in store for him who continues to go forward in this course toward perfection through steadfast piety. This will be perfected beyond this life in the repose of the spirit, and, at the last, in the resurrection of the body.

Of these four different stages of man, the first is before the law, the second is under the law, the third is under grace, and the fourth is in full and perfect peace. Thus, also, the history of God's people has been ordered by successive temporal epochs, as it pleased God, who "ordered all things in measure and number and weight."[263] The first period was before the law; the second under the law, which was given through Moses; the next, under grace which was revealed through the first Advent of the Mediator.[264] This grace was not previously absent from those to whom it was to be imparted, although, in conformity to the temporal dispensations, it was veiled and hidden. For none of the righteous men of antiquity could find salvation apart from the faith of Christ. And, unless Christ had also been known to them, he could not have been prophesied to us—sometimes openly and sometimes obscurely—through their ministry.

259. 2 Pt 2:19.   260. Rom 5:20.

261. Compare the psychological notion of the effect of external moral pressures and their power to arouse guilt feelings, as in Freud's notion of "superego."

262. Gal 5:17.   263. Ws 11:21 (Vulgate).   264. Cf. Jn 1:17.

119. Now, in whichever of these four "ages"—if one can call them that—the grace of regeneration finds a man, then and there all his past sins are forgiven him and the guilt he contracted in being born is removed by his being reborn. And so true is it that "the Spirit breatheth where he willeth"[265] that some men have never known the second "age" of slavery under the law, but begin to have divine aid directly under the new commandment.

120. Yet, before a man can receive the commandment, he must, of course, live according to the flesh. But, once he has been imbued with the sacrament of rebirth, no harm will come to him even if he then immediately depart this life—"Wherefore on this account Christ died and rose again, that he might be the Lord of both the living and the dead."[266] Nor will the kingdom of death have dominion over him for whom he, who was "free among the dead,"[267] died.

Chapter 32 — The End of All the Law

121. All the divine precepts are, therefore, referred back to *love*, of which the apostle says, "Now the end of the commandment is love, out of a pure heart, and a good conscience and a faith unfeigned."[268] Thus every commandment harks back to love. For whatever one does either in fear of punishment or from some carnal impulse, so that it does not measure up to the standard of love which the Holy Spirit sheds abroad in our hearts—whatever it is, it is not yet done as it should be, although it may seem to be. Love, in this context, of course includes both the love of God and the love of our neighbor and, indeed, "on these two commandments hang all the Law and the Prophets"[269]—and, we may add, the Gospel and the apostles, for from nowhere else comes the voice, "The end of the commandment is love,"[270] and, "God is love."[271]

Therefore, whatsoever things God commands (and one of these is, "Thou shalt not commit adultery")[272] and whatsoever things are

---

265. Jn 3:8.   266. Rom 14:9.   267. Cf. Ps 88:5.   268. 1 Tm 1:5.

269. Mt 22:40.   270. 1 Tm 1:5.   271. 1 Jn 4:16.

272. Ex 20:14; Mt 5:27; etc.

not positively ordered but are strongly advised as good spiritual counsel (and one of these is, "It is a good thing for a man not to touch a woman")[273]—all of these imperatives are rightly obeyed only when they are measured by the standard of our love of God and our love of our neighbor in God [*propter Deum*]. This applies both in the present age and in the world to come. Now we love God in faith; then, at sight. For, though mortal men ourselves, we do not know the hearts of mortal men. But then "the Lord will illuminate the hidden things in the darkness and will make manifest the cogitations of the heart; and then shall each one have his praise from God"[274]—for what will be praised and loved in a neighbor by his neighbor is just that which, lest it remain hidden, God himself will bring to light. Moreover, passion decreases as love increases until love comes at last to that fullness which cannot be surpassed, "for greater love than this no one has, that a man lay down his life for his friends."[275] Who, then, can explain how great the power of love will be, when there will be no passion [*cupiditas*] for it to restrain or overcome? For, then, the supreme state of true health [*summa sanitas*] will have been reached, when the struggle with death shall be no more.

Chapter 33 — Conclusion

122. But somewhere this book must have an end. You can see for yourself whether you should call it an enchiridion[276] or use it as one. But since I have judged that your zeal in Christ ought not to be spurned and since I believe and hope for good things for you through the help of our Redeemer, and since I love you greatly as one of the members of his body, I have written this book for you— may its usefulness match its prolixity!—on Faith, Hope, and Love.

273. 1 Cor 7:1.   274. 1 Cor 4:5.   275. Jn 15:23.
276. I.e., a handbook.

From Augustine's Letters

Letter 20
[390 A.D.]

To Antoninus Augustine Sends Greeting.

1. As letters are due to you by two of us, a part of our debt is repaid with very abundant usury when you see one of the two in person; and since by his voice you, as it were, hear my own, I might have refrained from writing, had I not been called to do it by the urgent request of the very person whose journey to you seemed to me to make this unnecessary. Accordingly I now hold converse with you even more satisfactorily than if I were personally with you, because you both read my letter, and you listen to the words of one in whose heart you know that I dwell. I have with great joy studied and pondered the letter sent by Your Holiness, because it exhibits both your Christian spirit unsullied by the guile of an evil age, and your heart full of kindly feeling toward myself.

2. I congratulate you, and I give thanks to our God and Lord, because of the hope and faith and love which are in you, and I thank you, in him, for thinking so well of me as to believe me to be a faithful servant of God, and for the love which with guileless heart you cherish toward that which you commend in me; although, indeed, there is occasion rather for congratulation than for thanks in acknowledging your goodwill in this thing. For it is profitable for yourself that you should love for its own sake that goodness which he of course loves who loves another because he believes him to be good, whether that other be or be not what he is supposed to be. One error only is to be carefully avoided in this matter, that we do not think otherwise than truth demands, not of the individual, but of that which is true goodness in man. But, my brother well beloved, seeing that you are not in any degree mistaken either in believing or in knowing that the great good for men is to serve God cheerfully and purely, when you love any man because you believe him to share this good, you reap the reward, even though the man be not what you suppose him to be. Wherefore it is fitting that you

should on this account be congratulated; but the person whom you love is to be congratulated, not because of his being for that reason loved, but because of his being truly (if it is the case) such a one as the person who for this reason loves him esteems him to be. As to our real character, therefore, and as to the progress we may have made in the divine life, this is seen by him whose judgment, both as to that which is good in man, and as to each man's personal character, cannot err. For your obtaining the reward of blessedness so far as this matter is concerned, it is sufficient that you embrace me with your whole heart because you believe me to be such a servant of God as I ought to be. To you, however, I also render many thanks for this, that you encourage me wonderfully to aspire after such excellence, by your praising me as if I had already attained it. Many more thanks still shall be yours, if you not only claim an interest in my prayers, but also cease not to pray for me. For intercession on behalf of a brother is more acceptable to God when it is offered as a sacrifice of love.

3. I greet very kindly your little son, and I pray that he may grow up in the way of obedience to the salutary requirements of God's law. I desire and pray, moreover, that the one true faith and worship, which alone is catholic, may prosper and increase in your house; and if you think any labor on my part necessary for the promotion of this end, do not scruple to claim my service, relying upon him who is our common Lord, and upon the law of love which we must obey. This especially would I recommend to your pious discretion, that by reading the word of God, and by serious conversation with your partner, you should either plant the seed or foster the growth in her heart of an intelligent fear of God. For it is scarcely possible that anyone who is concerned for the soul's welfare, and is therefore without prejudice resolved to know the will of the Lord, should fail, when enjoying the guidance of a good instructor, to discern the difference which exists between every form of schism and the one Catholic Church.

Letter 27
[395 A.D.]

To My Lord, Holy and Venerable, and Worthy of Highest Praise in Christ, My Brother Paulinus, Augustine Sends Greeting in the Lord.

1. O excellent man and excellent brother, there was a time when you were unknown to my mind; and I charge my mind to bear patiently your being still unknown to my eyes, but it almost—nay, altogether—refuses to obey. Does it indeed bear this patiently? If so, why then does a longing for your presence rack my inmost soul? For if I were suffering bodily infirmities, and these did not interrupt the serenity of my mind, I might be justly said to bear them patiently, but when I cannot bear with equanimity the privation of not seeing you, it would be intolerable were I to call my state of mind patience. Nevertheless, it would perhaps be still more intolerable if I were to be found patient while absent from you, seeing that you are such a one as you are. It is well, therefore, that I am unsatisfied under a privation which is such that, if I were satisfied under it, everyone would justly be dissatisfied with me. What has befallen me is strange, yet true: I grieve because I do not see you, and my grief itself comforts me, for I neither admire nor covet a fortitude easily consoled under the absence of good men such as you are. For do we not long for the heavenly Jerusalem? And the more impatiently we long for it, do we not the more patiently submit to all things for its sake? Who can so withhold himself from joy in seeing you, as to feel no pain when you are no longer seen? I at least can do neither, and seeing that if I could, it could only be by trampling on right and natural feeling, I rejoice that I cannot, and in this rejoicing I find some consolation. It is therefore not the removal, but the contemplation, of this sorrow that consoles me. Blame me not, I beseech you, with that devout seriousness of spirit which so eminently distinguishes you; say not that I do wrong to grieve because of my not yet knowing you, when you have disclosed to my sight your mind, which is the inner man. For if, when sojourning in any place, or in the city to which you belong, I had come to know you as my brother and friend, and as one so eminent as a Christian, so noble as a man, how could you think that it would be no disappointment to me if I were not permitted to know your

dwelling? How, then, can I but mourn because I have not yet seen your face and form, the dwelling-place of that mind which I have come to know as if it were my own?

2. For I have read your letter, which flows with milk and honey, which exhibits the simplicity of heart wherewith, under the guidance of piety, you seek the Lord, and which brings glory and honor to him. The brethren have read it also, and find unwearied and ineffable satisfaction in those abundant and excellent gifts with which God has endowed you. As many as have read it carry it away with them, because, while they read, it carries them away. Words cannot express how sweet is the savor of Christ which your letter breathes. How strong is the wish to be more fully acquainted with you which that letter awakens by presenting you to our sight! For it at once permits us to discern and prompts us to desire you. For the more effectually that it makes us in a certain sense realize your presence, the more does it render us impatient under your absence. All love you as seen therein, and wish to be loved by you. Praise and thanksgiving are offered to God, by whose grace you are what you are. In your letter, Christ is awakened that he may be pleased to calm the winds and the waves for you, directing your steps toward his perfect steadfastness. In it the reader beholds a wife[277] who does not bring her husband to effeminacy, but by union to him is brought herself to share the strength of his nature; and unto her in you, as completely one with you, and bound to you by spiritual ties which owe their strength to their purity, we desire to return our salutations with the respect due to Your Holiness. In it, the cedars of Lebanon, leveled to the ground, and fashioned by the skillful craft of love into the form of the Ark, cleave the waves of this world, fearless of decay. In it, glory is scorned that it may be secured, and the world given up that it may be gained. In it, the little ones, yea, the mightier sons of Babylon, the sins of turbulence and pride, are dashed against the rock.

3. These and other such most delightful and hallowed spectacles are presented to the readers of your letter—that letter which exhibits a true faith, a good hope, a pure love. How it breathes to us your thirst, your longing and fainting for the courts of the Lord! With what holy love it is inspired! How it overflows with the

277. Therasia.

abundant treasure of a true heart! What thanksgivings it renders to God! What blessings it procures from him! Is it elegance or fervor, light or life-giving power, which shines most in your letter? For how can it at once soothe us and animate us? How can it combine fertilizing rains with the brightness of a cloudless sky? How is this? I ask; or how shall I repay you, except by giving myself to be wholly yours in him whose you wholly are? If this be little, it is at least all I have to give. But you have made me think it not little, by your deigning to honor me in that letter with such praises, that when I requite you by giving myself to you, I would be chargeable if I counted the gift a small one, with refusing to believe your testimony. I am ashamed, indeed, to believe so much good spoken of myself, but I am yet more unwilling to refuse to believe you. I have one way of escape from the dilemma: I shall not credit your estimate of my character, because I do not recognize myself in the portrait you have drawn, but I shall believe myself to be beloved by you, because I perceive and feel this beyond all doubt. Thus I shall be found neither rash in judging of myself, nor ungrateful for your esteem. Moreover, when I offer myself to you, it is not a small offering, for I offer one whom you very warmly love, and one who, though he is not what you suppose him to be, is nevertheless one for whom you are praying that he may become such. And your prayers I now beg the more earnestly, lest, thinking me to be already what I am not, you should be less solicitous for the supply of that which I lack.

4. The bearer of this letter[278] to Your Excellency and most eminent Charity is one of my dearest friends, and most intimately known to me from early years. His name is mentioned in the treatise *De Religione*, which Your Holiness, as you indicate in your letter, has read with very great pleasure, doubtless because it was made more acceptable to you by the recommendation of so good a man as he who sent it to you.[279] I would not wish you, however, to give credence to the statements which, perchance, one who is so intimately my friend may have made in praise of me. For I have often observed, that, without intending to say what was untrue, he was, by the bias of friendship, mistaken in his opinion concerning me, and that he thought me to be already possessed of many things, for

278. Romanianus.   279. Alypius.

the gift of which my heart earnestly waited on the Lord. And if he did such things in my presence, who may not conjecture that out of the fullness of his heart he may utter many things more excellent than true concerning me when absent? He will submit to your esteemed attention and review all my treatises, for I am not aware of having written anything, either addressed to those who are beyond the pale of the Church, or to the brethren, which is not in his possession. But when you are reading these, my holy Paulinus, let not those things which Truth has spoken by my weak instrumentality so carry you away as to prevent your carefully observing what I myself have spoken, lest, while you drink in with eagerness the things good and true which have been given to me as a servant, you should forget to pray for the pardon of my errors and mistakes. For in all that shall, if observed, justly displease you, I myself am seen, but in all which in my books is justly approved by you, through the gift of the Holy Spirit bestowed on you, he is to be loved, he is to be praised, with whom is the fountain of life, and in whose light we shall see light,[280] not darkly as we do here, but face-to-face.[281] When, in reading over my writings, I discover in them anything which is due to the working of the old leaven in me, I blame myself for it with true sorrow, but if anything which I have spoken is, by God's gift, from the unleavened bread of sincerity and truth, I rejoice therein with trembling. For what have we that we have not received? Yet it may be said, his portion is better whom God has endowed with larger and more numerous gifts, than his on whom smaller and fewer have been conferred. True; but, on the other hand, it is better to have a small gift, and to render to him due thanks for it, than, having a large gift, to wish to claim the merit of it as our own. Pray for me, my brother, that I may make such acknowledgments sincerely, and that my heart may not be at variance with my tongue. Pray, I beseech you, that, not coveting praise to myself, but rendering praise to the Lord, I may worship him, and I shall be safe from mine enemies.

5. There is yet another thing which may move you to love more warmly the brother who bears my letter, for he is a kinsman of the venerable and truly blessed bishop Alypius, whom you love with your whole heart, and justly: for whoever thinks highly of that

280. Ps 36:10.   281. 1 Cor 13:12.

man, thinks highly of the great mercy and wonderful gifts which God has bestowed on him. Accordingly, when he had read your request, desiring him to write for you a sketch of his history, and, while willing to do it because of your kindness, was yet unwilling to do it because of his humility, I, seeing him unable to decide between the respective claims of love and humility, transferred the burden from his shoulders to my own, for he enjoined me by letter to do so. I shall therefore, with God's help, soon place in your heart Alypius just as he is, for this I chiefly feared, that he would be afraid to declare all that God has conferred on him, lest (since what he writes would be read by others besides you) he should seem to any who are less competent to discriminate to be commending not God's goodness bestowed on men, but his own merits, and that thus you, who know what construction to put on such statements, would, through his regard for the infirmity of others, be deprived of that which to you as a brother ought to be imparted. This I would have done already, and you would already be reading my description of him, had not my brother suddenly resolved to set out earlier than we expected. For him I bespeak a welcome from your heart and from your lips as kindly as if your acquaintance with him was not beginning now, but of as long-standing as my own. For if he does not shrink from laying himself open to your heart, he will be in great measure, if not completely, healed by your lips, for I desire him to be often made to hear the words of those who cherish for their friends a higher love than that which is of this world.

6. Even if Romanianus had not been going to visit Your Charity, I had resolved to recommend to you by letter his son [Licentius], dear to me as my own (whose name you will find also in some of my books), in order that he may be encouraged, exhorted, and instructed, not so much by the sound of your voice, as by the example of your spiritual strength. I desire earnestly that while his life is yet in the green blade, the tares may be turned into wheat, and he may believe those who know by experience the dangers to which he is eager to expose himself. From the poem of my young friend, and my letter to him, your most benevolent and considerate wisdom may perceive my grief, fear, and care on his account. I am not without hope that, by the Lord's favor, I may through your means be set free from such disquietude regarding him.

As you are now about to read much that I have written, your

love will be much more gratefully esteemed by me, if, moved by compassion, and judging impartially, you correct and reprove whatever displeases you. For you are not one whose oil anointing my head would make me afraid.[282]

The brethren, not those only who dwell with us, and those who, dwelling elsewhere, serve God in the same way as we do, but almost all who are in Christ our warm friends, send you salutations, along with the expression of their veneration and affectionate longing for you as a brother, as a saint, and as a man.[283] I dare not ask, but if you have any leisure from ecclesiastical duties, you may see for what favor all Africa, with myself, is thirsting.

Letter 58
[401 A.D.]

To My Noble and Worthy Lord Pammachius, My Son, Dearly Beloved in the Bowels of Christ, Augustine Sends Greeting in the Lord.

1. The good works which spring from the grace of Christ in you have given you a claim to be esteemed by us his members, and have made you as truly known and as much beloved by us as you could be. For even were I daily seeing your face, this could add nothing to the completeness of the acquaintance with you which I now have, when in the shining light of one of your actions I have seen your inner being, fair with the loveliness of peace, and beaming with the brightness of truth. Seeing this has made me know you, and knowing you has made me love you, and therefore, in addressing you, I write to one who, notwithstanding our distance from each other, has become known to me, and is my beloved friend. The bond which binds us together is indeed of earlier date, and we were living united under One Head: for had you not been rooted in his love, the Catholic unity would not have been so dear to you, and you would not have dealt as you have done with your African

---

282. The reference is to Ps 141:5, the words of which are translated from the Septuagint version.

283. This may approximate to a translation of the three titles in the original, "Germanitas, Beatitudo, Humanitas tua."

tenants[284] settled in the midst of the consular province of Numidia, the very country in which the folly of the Donatists began, addressing them in such terms, and encouraging them with such enthusiasm, as to persuade them with unhesitating devotion to choose that course which they believed that a man of your character and position would not adopt on other grounds than truth ascertained and acknowledged, and to submit themselves, though so remote from you, to the same Head, so that along with yourself they are reckoned forever as members of him by whose command they are for the time dependent upon you.

2. Embracing you, therefore, as known to me by this transaction, I am moved by joyful feelings to congratulate you in Christ Jesus our Lord, and to send you this letter as a proof of my heart's love toward you, for I cannot do more. I beseech you, however, not to measure the amount of my love by this letter, but by means of this letter, when you have read it, pass on by the unseen inner passage which thought opens up into my heart, and see what is there felt toward you. For to the eye of love that sanctuary of love shall be unveiled which we shut against the disquieting trifles of this world when there we worship God, and there you will see the ecstasy of my joy in your good work, an ecstasy which I cannot describe with tongue or pen, glowing and burning in the offering of praise to him by whose inspiration you were made willing, and by whose help you were made able to serve him in this way. "Thanks be unto God for His unspeakable gift!"[285]

3. Oh how we desire in Africa to see such work as this by which you have gladdened us done by many, who are, like yourself, senators in the state, and sons of the holy Church! It is, however, hazardous to give them this exhortation: they may refuse to follow it, and the enemies of the Church will take advantage of this to deceive the weak, as if they had gained a victory over us in the minds of those who disregarded our counsel. But it is safe for me to express gratitude to you, for you have already done that by which, in the emancipation of those who were weak, the enemies of the Church are confounded. I have therefore thought it sufficient to ask you to read this letter with friendly boldness to any to whom you can do so on the ground of their Christian profession. For thus

284. *Coloni.*   285. 1 Cor 9:15.

learning what you have achieved, they will believe that that, about which as an impossibility they are now indifferent, can be done in Africa. As to the snares which these heretics contrive in the perversity of their hearts, I have resolved not to speak of them in this letter, because I have been only amused at their imagining that they could gain any advantage over your mind, which Christ holds as his possession. You will hear them, however, from my brethren, whom I earnestly commend to Your Excellency: they fear lest you should disdain some things which to you might seem unnecessary in connection with the great and unlooked-for salvation of those men over whom, in consequence of your work, their Catholic Mother rejoices.

Letter 130
[412 A.D.]

To Proba,[286] *a Devoted Handmaid of God, Bishop Augustine, a Servant of Christ and of Christ's Servants, Sends Greeting in the Name of the Lord of Lords.*

1. Recollecting your request and my promise, that as soon as time and opportunity should be given by him to whom we pray, I would write you something on the subject of prayer to God, I feel it

---

286. Anicia Faltonia Proba, the widow of Sextus Petronius Probus, belonged to a Roman family of great wealth and noble lineage. Three of her sons held the consulship, two of them together in 395 A.D., and the third in 406 A.D. When Rome was taken by Alaric in 410, Proba and her family were in the city, and narrowly escaped from violence during the six days in which the Goths pillaged the city. About this time one of the sons of Proba died, and very soon after this sad event she resolved to quit Rome, as the return of Alaric was daily expected. Having realized her ample fortune, she sailed to Africa, accompanied by her daughter-in-law Juliana (the widow of Anicus Hermogenianus Olybrius), and the daughter of Juliana Demetrias, the well-known *religieuse*, whose taking of the veil in 413 produced so profound an impression throughout the ecclesiastical world. A considerable retinue of widows and younger women, seeking protection under her escort, accompanied the distinguished refugee to Carthage. After paying a large sum to secure the protection of Heraclianus, Count of Africa, she was permitted to establish herself with her community of pious women in Carthage. Her piety led her to seek the friendship and counsel of Augustine. How readily it was given is seen here.

my duty now to discharge this debt, and in the love of Christ to minister to the satisfaction of your pious desire. I cannot express in words how greatly I rejoiced because of the request, in which I perceived how great is your solicitude about this supremely important matter. For what could be more suitably the business of your widowhood than to continue in supplications night and day, according to the apostle's admonition, "She that is a widow indeed, and desolate, trusteth in God, and continueth in supplications night and day"?[287] It might, indeed, appear wonderful that solicitude about prayer should occupy your heart and claim the first place in it, when you are, so far as this world is concerned, noble and wealthy, and the mother of such an illustrious family, and, although a widow, not desolate, were it not that you wisely understand that in this world and in this life the soul has no sure portion.

2. Wherefore he who inspired you with this thought is assuredly doing what he promised to his disciples when they were grieved, not for themselves, but for the whole human family, and were despairing of the salvation of anyone, after they heard from him that it was easier for a camel to go through the eye of a needle than for a rich man to enter into the kingdom of heaven. He gave them this marvelous and merciful reply: "The things which are impossible with men are possible with God."[288] He, therefore, with whom it is possible to make even the rich enter into the kingdom of heaven, inspired you with that devout anxiety which makes you think it necessary to ask my counsel on the question how you ought to pray. For while he was yet on earth, he brought Zaccheus,[289] though rich, into the kingdom of heaven, and, after being glorified in his resurrection and ascension, he made many who were rich to despise this present world, and made them more truly rich by extinguishing their desire for riches through his imparting to them his Holy Spirit. For how could you desire so much to pray to God if you did not trust in him? And how could you trust in him if you were fixing your trust in uncertain riches, and neglecting the wholesome exhortation of the apostle: "Charge them that are rich in this world that they be not high-minded, nor trust in uncertain riches, but in the living God, who giveth us richly all things to enjoy; that they do good, that they be rich in good works, ready to distribute, willing

287. 1 Tm 5:5.   288. Mt 19:21–26.   289. Lk 19:9.

to communicate, laying up in store for themselves a good foundation, that they may lay hold on eternal life"?[290]

CHAPTER 2

3. It becomes you, therefore, out of love to this true life, to account
yourself "desolate" in this world, however great the prosperity of
your lot may be. For as that is the true life, in comparison with
which the present life, which is much loved, is not worthy to be
called life, however happy and prolonged it be, so is it also the true
consolation promised by the Lord in the words of Isaiah, "I will
give him the true consolation, peace upon peace,"[291] without which
consolation men find themselves, in the midst of every mere
earthly solace, rather desolate than comforted. For as for riches and
high rank, and all other things in which men who are strangers to
true felicity imagine that happiness exists, what comfort do they
bring, seeing that it is better to be independent of such things than
to enjoy abundance of them, because, when possessed, they occasion, through our fear of losing them, more vexation than was
caused by the strength of desire with which their possession was
coveted? Men are not made good by possessing these so-called
good things, but, if men have become good otherwise, they make
these things to be really good by using them well. Therefore true
comfort is to be found not in them, but rather in those things in
which true life is found. For a man can be made blessed only by the
same power by which he is made good.

4. It is true, indeed, that good men are seen to be the sources of
no small comfort to others in this world. For if we be harassed by
poverty, or saddened by bereavement, or disquieted by bodily pain,
or pining in exile, or vexed by any kind of calamity, let good men
visit us, men who cannot only rejoice with them that rejoice, but also
weep with them that weep,[292] and who know how to give profitable
counsel, and win us to express our feelings in conversation: the effect
is, that rough things become smooth, heavy burdens are lightened,
and difficulties vanquished most wonderfully. But this is done in and
through them by him who has made them good by his Spirit. On the
other hand, although riches may abound, and no bereavement befall

290. 1 Tm 6:17–19.   291. Is 56:18, 19 (Septuagint).

292. Rom 12:15.

us, and health of body be enjoyed, and we live in our own country in peace and safety, if, at the same time, we have as our neighbors wicked men, among whom there is not one who can be trusted, not one from whom we do not apprehend and experience treachery, deceit, outbursts of anger, dissensions, and snares, in such a case are not all these other things made bitter and vexatious, so that nothing sweet or pleasant is left in them? Whatever, therefore, be our circumstances in this world, there is nothing truly enjoyable without a friend. But how rarely is one found in this life about whose spirit and behavior as a true friend there may be perfect confidence! For no one is known to another so intimately as he is known to himself, and yet no one is so well known even to himself that he can be sure as to his own conduct on the morrow; wherefore, although many are known by their fruits, and some gladden their neighbors by their good lives, while others grieve their neighbors by their evil lives, yet the minds of men are so unknown and so unstable, that there is the highest wisdom in the exhortation of the apostle: "Judge nothing before the time until the Lord come, who both will bring to light the hidden things of darkness, and will make manifest the counsels of the hearts; and then shall every man have praise of God."[293]

5. In the darkness, then, of this world, in which we are pilgrims absent from the Lord as long as "we walk by faith and not by sight,"[294] the Christian soul ought to feel itself desolate, and continue in prayer, and learn to fix the eye of faith on the word of the divine sacred Scriptures, as "on a light shining in a dark place, until the day dawn, and the day-star arise in our hearts."[295] For the ineffable source from which this lamp borrows its light is the Light which shineth in darkness, but the darkness comprehendeth it not—the Light, in order to seeing which our hearts must be purified by faith, for "blessed are the pure in heart, for they shall see God";[296] and "we know that when He shall appear, we shall be like Him, for we shall see Him as He is."[297] Then after death shall come the true life, and after desolation the true consolation, that life shall deliver our "souls from death" that consolation shall deliver our "eyes from tears," and, as follows in the psalm, our feet shall be delivered from falling, for there shall be no temptation there.[298]

293. 1 Cor 4:15.   294. 2 Cor 5:6, 7.   295. 2 Pt 1:19.   296. Mt 5:8.
297. 1 Jn 3:2.   298. Ps 116:8.

Moreover, if there be no temptation, there will be no prayer; for there we shall not be waiting for promised blessings, but contemplating the blessings actually bestowed, wherefore he adds, "I will walk before the Lord in the land of the living,"[299] where we shall then be—not in the wilderness of the dead, where we now are: "For ye are dead," says the apostle, "and your life is hid with Christ in God; when Christ, who is our life, shall appear, then shall ye also appear with Him in glory."[300] For that is the true life on which the rich are exhorted to lay hold by being rich in good works, and in it is the true consolation, for want of which, meanwhile, a widow is "desolate" indeed, even though she has sons and grandchildren, and conducts her household piously, entreating all dear to her to put their hope in God: and in the midst of all this, she says in her prayer, "My soul thirsteth for Thee; my flesh longeth in a dry and thirsty land, where no water is,"[301] and this dying life is nothing else than such a land, however numerous our mortal comforts, however pleasant our companions in the pilgrimage, and however great the abundance of our possessions. You know how uncertain all these things are, and even if they were not uncertain, what would they be in comparison with the felicity which is promised in the life to come!

6. In saying these things to you, who, being a widow, rich and noble, and the mother of an illustrious family, have asked from me a discourse on prayer, my aim has been to make you feel that, even while your family are spared to you, and live as you would desire, you are desolate so long as you have not attained to that life in which is the true and abiding consolation, in which shall be fulfilled what is spoken in prophecy: "We are satisfied in the morning with Thy mercy, we rejoice and are glad all our days; we are made glad according to the days wherein Thou hast afflicted us, and the years wherein we have seen evil."[302]

CHAPTER 3

7. Wherefore, until that consolation come, remember, in order to your "continuing in prayers and supplications night and day," that, however great the temporal prosperity may be which flows around you, you are desolate. For the apostle does not ascribe this gift to

299. Ps 116:9. In the Septuagint, εὐαρεστήσω; in Augustine, "placebo."

300. Col 3:3, 4.   301. Ps 63:1.   302. Ps 90:14, 15 (Septuagint).

every widow, but to her who, being a widow indeed, and desolate, "trusteth in God, and continueth in supplication night and day." Observe, however, most vigilantly the warning which follows: "But she that liveth in pleasure is dead while she liveth";[303] for a person lives in those things which he loves, which he greatly desires, and in which he believes himself to be blessed. Wherefore, what Scripture has said of riches, "If riches increase, set not your heart upon them,"[304] I say to you concerning pleasures: "If pleasures increase, set not your heart upon them." Do not, therefore, think highly of yourself because these things are not wanting, but are yours abundantly, flowing, as it were, from a most copious fountain of earthly felicity. By all means look upon your possession of these things with indifference and contempt, and seek nothing from them beyond health of body. For this is a blessing not to be despised, because of its being necessary to the work of life until "this mortal shall have put on immortality"[305] in other words, the true, perfect, and everlasting health, which is neither reduced by earthly infirmities nor repaired by corruptible gratification, but, enduring with celestial rigor, is animated with a life eternally incorruptible. For the apostle himself says, "Make not provision for the flesh, to fulfill the lusts thereof,"[306] because we must take care of the flesh, but only insofar as is necessary for health; "For no man ever yet hated his own flesh,"[307] as he himself likewise says. Hence, also, he admonished Timothy, who was, as it appears, too severe upon his body, that he should "use a little wine for his stomach's sake, and for his often infirmities."[308]

8. Many holy men and women, using every precaution against those pleasures in which she that liveth, cleaving to them, and dwelling in them as her heart's delight, is dead while she liveth, have cast from them that which is as it were the mother of pleasures, by distributing their wealth among the poor, and so have stored it in the safer keeping of the treasury of heaven. If you are *hindered* from doing this by some consideration of duty to your family, you know yourself what account you can give to God of your use of riches. For no one knoweth what passeth within a man, "but the spirit of the man which is in him."[309] We ought not to

---

303. 1 Tm 5:5, 6.   304. Ps 62:10.   305. 1 Cor 15:54.   306. Rom 13:14.

307. Eph 5:39.   308. 1 Tm 5:23.   309. 1 Cor 2:11.

judge anything "before the time until the Lord come who both will bring to light the hidden things of darkness, and will make manifest the counsels of the hearts, and then shall every man have praise of God."[310] It pertains, therefore, to your care as a widow, to see to it that if pleasures increase you do not set your heart upon them, lest that which ought to rise that it may live, die through contact with their corrupting influence. Reckon yourself to be one of those of whom it is written, "Their hearts shall live for ever."[311]

CHAPTER 4

9. You have now heard what manner of person you should be if you would pray; hear, in the next place, what you ought to pray for. This is the subject on which you have thought it most necessary to ask my opinion, because you were disturbed by the words of the apostle: "We know not what we should pray for as we ought";[312] and you became alarmed lest it should do you more harm to pray otherwise than you ought, than to desist from praying altogether. A short solution of your difficulty may be given thus: "Pray for a happy life." This all men wish to have, for even those whose lives are worst and most abandoned would by no means live thus, unless they thought that in this way they either were made or might be made truly happy. Now what else ought we to pray for than that which both bad and good desire, but which only the good obtain?

CHAPTER 5

10. You ask, perchance, What is this happy life? On this question the talents and leisure of many philosophers have been wasted, who, nevertheless, failed in their researches after it just in proportion as they failed to honor him from whom it proceeds and were unthankful to him. In the first place, then, consider whether we should accept the opinion of those philosophers who pronounce that man happy who lives according to his own will. Far be it, surely, from us to believe this, for what if a man's will inclines him to live in wickedness? Is he not proved to be a miserable man in proportion to the facility with which his depraved will is carried out? Even philosophers who were strangers to the worship of God have rejected this sentiment with deserved abhorrence. One of them,

310. 1 Cor 4:5.   311. Ps 22:26.   312. Rom 8:26.

a man of the greatest eloquence, says, "Behold, however, others, not philosophers indeed, but men of ready power in disputation, who affirm that all men are happy who live according to their own will. But this is certainly untrue, for to wish that which is unbecoming is itself a most miserable thing; nor is it so miserable a thing to fail in obtaining what you wish as to wish to obtain what you ought not to desire."[313] What is your opinion? Are not these words, by whomso-ever they are spoken, derived from the Truth itself? We may there-fore here say what the apostle said of a certain Cretan poet[314] whose sentiment had pleased him: "This witness is true."[315]

11. He, therefore, is truly happy who has all that he wishes to have, and wishes to have nothing which he ought not to wish. This being understood, let us now observe what things men may with-out impropriety wish to have. One desires marriage; another, having become a widower, chooses thereafter to live a life of continence; a third chooses to practice continence though he is married. And al-though of these three conditions one may be found better than an-other, we cannot say that any one of the three persons is wishing what he ought not: the same is true of the desire for children as the fruit of marriage, and for life and health to be enjoyed by the chil-dren who have been received—of which desires the latter is one with which widows remaining unmarried are for the most part occu-pied; for although, refusing a second marriage, they do not now wish to have children, they wish that the children that they have may live in health. From all such care those who preserve their vir-ginity intact are free. Nevertheless, all have some dear to them whose temporal welfare they do without impropriety desire. But when men have obtained this health for themselves, and for those whom they love, are we at liberty to say that they are now happy? They have, it is true, something which it is quite becoming to de-sire, but if they have not other things which are greater, better, and more full both of utility and beauty, they are still far short of pos-sessing a happy life.

CHAPTER 6

12. Shall we then say that in addition to this health of body men may desire for themselves and for those dear to them honor and

313. Cicero, *Hortensius*.   314. Epimenides.   315. Ti 1:13.

power? By all means, if they desire these in order that by obtaining them they may promote the interest of those who may be their dependants. If they seek these things not for the sake of the things themselves, but for some good thing which may through this means be accomplished, the wish is a proper one, but if it be merely for the empty gratification of pride and arrogance, and for a superfluous and pernicious triumph of vanity, the wish is improper. Wherefore, men do nothing wrong in desiring for themselves and for their kindred the competent portion of necessary things, of which the apostle speaks when he says, "Godliness with a competency [contentment in English version] is great gain; for we brought nothing into this world, and it is certain we can carry nothing out: and having food and raiment, let us be therewith content. But they that will be rich fall into temptation, and a snare, and into many foolish and hurtful lusts, which drown men in destruction and perdition; for the love of money is the root of all evil, which while some coveted after, they have erred from the faith, and pierced themselves through with many sorrows."[316] This competent portion he desires without impropriety who desires it and nothing beyond it, for if his desires go beyond it, he is not desiring it, and therefore his desire is improper. This was desired and was prayed for by him who said, "Give me neither poverty nor riches: feed me with food convenient for me: lest I be full, and deny Thee, and say, Who is the Lord? or lest I be poor, and steal, and take the name of my God in vain."[317] You see assuredly that this competency is desired not for its own sake, but to secure the health of the body, and such provision of house and clothing as is befitting the man's circumstances, that he may appear as he ought to do among those among whom he has to live, so as to retain their respect and discharge the duties of his position.

13. Among all these things, our own welfare and the benefits which friendship bids us ask for others are things to be desired on their own account, but a competency of the necessaries of life is usually sought, if it be sought in the proper way, not on its own account, but for the sake of the two higher benefits. Welfare consists in the possession of life itself, and health and soundness of mind and body. The claims of friendship, moreover, are not to be con-

316. 1 Tm 6:6–10.   317. Prv 30:8, 9.

fined within *too* narrow range, for it embraces all to whom love and kindly affection are due, although the heart goes out to some of these more freely, to others more cautiously; yea, it even extends to our enemies, for whom also we are commanded to pray. There is accordingly no one in the whole human family to whom kindly affection is not due by reason of the bond of a common humanity, although it may not be due on the ground of reciprocal love;—but in those by whom we are requited with a holy and pure love, we find great and reasonable pleasure.

For these things, therefore, it becomes us to pray: if we have them, that we may keep them, if we have them not, that we may get them.

CHAPTER 7

14. Is this all? Are these the benefits in which exclusively the happy life is found? Or does truth teach us that something else is to be preferred to them all? We know that both the competency of things necessary and the well-being of ourselves and of our friends, so long as these concern this present world alone, are to be cast aside as dross in comparison with the obtaining of eternal life, for although the body may be in health, the mind cannot be regarded as sound which does not prefer eternal to temporal things; yea, the life which we live in time is wasted if it be not spent in obtaining that by which we may be worthy of eternal life. Therefore all things which are the objects of useful and becoming desire are unquestionably to be viewed with reference to that one life which is lived with God, and is derived from him. In so doing, we love ourselves if we love God; and we truly love our neighbors as ourselves, according to the second great commandment, if, so far as is in our power, we persuade them to a similar love of God. We love God, therefore, for what he is in himself, and ourselves and our neighbors for his sake. Even when living thus, let us not think that we are securely established in that happy life, as if there was nothing more for which we should still pray. For how could we be said to live a happy life now, while that which alone is the object of a well-directed life is still wanting to us?

CHAPTER 8

15. Why, then, are our desires scattered over many things, and why, through fear of not praying as we ought, do we ask what we should

pray for, and not rather say with the psalmist, "One thing have I desired of the Lord, that will I seek after: that I may dwell in the house of the Lord all the days of my life, to behold the beauty of the Lord, and to inquire in His temple"?[318] For in the house of the Lord "all the days of life" are not days distinguished by their successively coming and passing away: the beginning of one day is not the end of another, but they are all alike unending in that place where the life which is made up of them has itself no end. In order to our obtaining this true blessed life, he who is himself the True Blessed Life has taught us to pray, not with much speaking, as if our being heard depended upon the fluency with which we express ourselves, seeing that we are praying to One who, as the Lord tells us, "knoweth what things we have need of before we ask Him."[319] Whence it may seem surprising that, although he has forbidden "much speaking," he who knoweth before we ask him what things we need has nevertheless given us exhortation to prayer in such words as these: "Men ought always to pray and not to faint"; setting before us the case of a widow, who, desiring to have justice done to her against her adversary, did by her persevering entreaties persuade an unjust judge to listen to her, not moved by a regard either to justice or to mercy, but overcome by her wearisome importunity; in order that we might be admonished how much more certainly the Lord God, who is merciful and just, gives ear to us praying continually to him, when this widow, by her unremitting supplication, prevailed over the indifference of an unjust and wicked judge, and how willingly and benignantly he fulfills the good desires of those whom he knows to have forgiven others their trespasses, when this suppliant, though seeking vengeance upon her adversary, obtained her desire.[320] A similar lesson the Lord gives in the parable of the man to whom a friend in his journey had come, and who, having nothing to set before him, desired to borrow from another friend three loaves (in which, perhaps, there is a figure of the Trinity of persons of one substance), and finding him already along with his household asleep, succeeded by very urgent and importunate entreaties in rousing him up, so that he gave him as many as he needed, being moved rather by a wish to avoid further annoyance than by benevolent thoughts: from which the Lord would have us under-

318. Ps 27:4.   319. Mt 6:7, 8.   320. Lk 18:1–8.

stand that, if even one who was asleep is constrained to give, even in spite of himself, after being disturbed in his sleep by the person who asks of him, how much more kindly will he give who never sleeps, and who rouses us from sleep that we may ask from him.[321]

16. With the same design he added: "Ask, and ye shall receive; seek, and ye shall find; knock, and it shall be opened unto you: for every one that asketh receiveth; and he that seeketh findeth; and to him that knocketh it shall be opened. If a son shall ask bread of any of you that is a father, will he give him a stone? or if he ask a fish, will he for a fish give him a serpent? or if he shall ask an egg, will he offer him a scorpion? If ye then, being evil, know how to give good gifts unto your children, how much more shall your heavenly Father give good things to them that ask Him?"[322] We have here what corresponds to those three things which the apostle commends: *faith* is signified by the fish, either on account of the element of water used in baptism or because it remains unharmed amid the tempestuous waves of this world—contrasted with which is the serpent, that with poisonous deceit persuaded man to disbelieve God; *hope* is signified by the egg, because the life of the young bird is not yet in it, but is to be—is not seen, but hoped for, because "hope which is seen is not hope"[323]—contrasted with which is the scorpion, for the man who hopes for eternal life forgets the things which are behind, and reaches forth to the things which are before, for to him it is dangerous to look back; but the scorpion is to be guarded against on account of what it has in its tail, namely, a sharp and venomous sting; *charity* is signified by bread, for "the greatest of these is charity," and bread surpasses all other kinds of food in usefulness—contrasted with which is a stone, because hard hearts refuse to exercise charity. Whether this be the meaning of these symbols, or some other more suitable be found, it is at least certain that he who knoweth how to give good gifts to his children urges us to "ask and seek and knock."

17. Why this should be done by him who "before we ask Him knoweth what things we have need of," might perplex our minds, if we did not understand that the Lord our God requires us to ask not that thereby our wish may be intimated to him, for to him it cannot be unknown, but in order that by prayer there may be exercised in

321. Lk 11:5–8.   322. Lk 11:9–13; Mt 7:7–11.   323. Rom 8:24.

us by supplications that desire by which we may receive what he prepares to bestow. His gifts are very great, but we are small and straitened in our capacity of receiving. Wherefore it is said to us: "Be ye enlarged, not bearing the yoke along with unbelievers."[324] For, in proportion to the simplicity of our faith, the firmness of our hope, and the ardor of our desire, will we more largely receive of that which is immensely great; which "eye hath not seen," for it is not color; which "the ear hath not heard," for it is not sound; and which hath not ascended into the heart of man, for the heart of man must ascend to it.[325]

CHAPTER 9

18. When we cherish uninterrupted desire along with the exercise of faith and hope and charity, we "pray always." But at certain stated hours and seasons we also use words in prayer to God, that by these signs of things we may admonish ourselves, and may acquaint ourselves with the measure of progress which we have made in this desire, and may more warmly excite ourselves to obtain an increase of its strength. For the effect following upon prayer will be excellent in proportion to the fervor of the desire which precedes its utterance. And therefore, what else is intended by the words of the apostle: "Pray without ceasing,"[326] than, "Desire without intermission, from Him who alone can give it, a happy life, which no life can be but that which is eternal"? This, therefore, let us desire continually from the Lord our God, and thus let us pray continually. But at certain hours we recall our minds from other cares and business, in which desire itself somehow is cooled down, to the business of prayer, admonishing ourselves by the words of our prayer to fix attention upon that which we desire, lest what had begun to lose heat become altogether cold, and be finally extinguished, if the flame be not more frequently fanned. Whence, also, when the same apostle says, "Let your requests be made known unto God,"[327] this is not to be understood as if thereby they become known to God, who certainly knew them before they were uttered, but in this sense, that they are to be made known to ourselves in the presence of God by patient waiting upon him, not in the presence of men by ostentatious worship. Or perhaps that they may be made

324. 2 Cor 6:13, 14.   325. 1 Cor 2:9.   326. 1 Thes 5:17.   327. Phil 4:6.

known also to the angels that are in the presence of God, that these beings may in some way present them to God, and consult him concerning them, and may bring to us, either manifestly or secretly, that which, hearkening to his commandment, they may have learned to be his will, and which must be fulfilled by them according to that which they have there learned to be their duty; for the angel said to Tobit:[328] "Now, therefore, when thou didst pray, and Sara thy daughter-in-law, I did bring the remembrance of your prayers before the Holy One."

CHAPTER 10

19. Wherefore it is neither wrong nor unprofitable to spend much time in praying, if there be leisure for this without hindering other good and necessary works to which duty calls us, although even in the doing of these, as I have said, we ought by cherishing holy desire to pray without ceasing. For to spend a long time in prayer is not, as some think, the same thing as to pray "with much speaking." Multiplied words are one thing, long-continued warmth of desire is another. For even of the Lord himself it is written, that he continued all night in prayer,[329] and that his prayer was more prolonged when he was in an agony;[330] and in this is not an example given to us by him who is in time an Intercessor such as we need, and who is with the Father eternally the Hearer of prayer?

20. The brethren in Egypt are reported to have very frequent prayers, but these very brief, and, as it were, sudden and ejaculatory, lest the wakeful and aroused attention which is indispensable in prayer should by protracted exercises vanish or lose its keenness. And in this they themselves show plainly enough, that just as this attention is not to be allowed to become exhausted if it cannot continue long, so it is not to be suddenly suspended if it is sustained. Far be it from us either to use "much speaking" in prayer, or to refrain from prolonged prayer, if fervent attention of the soul continue. To use much speaking in prayer is to employ a superfluity of words in asking a necessary thing; but to prolong prayer is to have the heart throbbing with continued pious emotion toward him to whom we pray. For in most cases prayer consists more in groaning than in speaking, in tears rather than in words. But he setteth our

328. Tobit 12:12.   329. Lk 6:12.   330. Lk 22:43.

tears in his sight, and our groaning is not hidden from him who made all things by the Word, and does not need human words.

CHAPTER 11

21. To us, therefore, words are necessary, that by them we may be assisted in considering and observing what we ask, not as means by which we expect that God is to be either informed or moved to compliance. When, therefore, we say, "Hallowed be Thy name," we admonish ourselves to desire that his name, which is always holy, may be also among men esteemed holy, that is to say, not despised, which is an advantage not to God, but to men. When we say, "Thy kingdom come," which shall certainly come whether we wish it or not, we do by these words stir up our own desires for that kingdom, that it may come to us, and that we may be found worthy to reign in it. When we say, "Thy will be done on earth as it is in heaven," we pray for ourselves that he would give us the grace of obedience, that his will may be done by us in the same way as it is done in heavenly places by his angels. When we say, "Give us this day our daily bread," the words "this day" signify for the present time, in which we ask either for that competency of temporal blessings which I have spoken of before ("bread" being used to designate the whole of those blessings, because of its constituting so important a part of them), or the sacrament of believers, which is in this present time necessary, but necessary in order to obtain the felicity not of the present time, but of eternity. When we say, "Forgive us our debts as we forgive our debtors," we remind ourselves both what we should ask, and what we should do in order that we may be worthy to receive what we ask. When we say, "Lead us not into temptation," we admonish ourselves to seek that we may not, through being deprived of God's help, be either ensnared to consent or compelled to yield to temptation. When we say, "Deliver us from evil," we admonish ourselves to consider that we are not yet enjoying that good estate in which we shall experience no evil. And this petition, which stands last in the Lord's Prayer, is so comprehensive that a Christian, in whatsoever affliction he be placed, may in using it give utterance to his groans and find vent for his tears— may begin with this petition, go on with it, and with it conclude his prayer. For it was necessary that by the use of these words the things which they signify should be kept before our memory.

CHAPTER 12

22. For whatever other words we may say—whether the desire of the person praying go before the words, and employ them in order to give definite form to its requests, or come after them, and concentrate attention upon them, that it may increase in fervor—if we pray rightly, and as becomes our wants, we say nothing but what is already contained in the Lord's Prayer. And whoever says in prayer anything which cannot find its place in that Gospel prayer is praying in a way which, if it be not unlawful, is at least not spiritual, and I know not how carnal prayers can be lawful, since it becomes those who are born again by the Spirit to pray in no other way than spiritually. For example, when one prays, "Be Thou glorified among all nations as Thou art glorified among us," and "Let Thy prophets be found faithful,"[331] what else does he ask than, "Hallowed be Thy name"? When one says, "Turn us again, O Lord God of hosts, cause Thy face to shine, and we shall be saved,"[332] what else is he saying than, "Let Thy kingdom come"? When one says, "Order my steps in Thy word, and let not any iniquity have dominion over me,"[333] what else is he saying than, "Thy will be done on earth as it is in heaven"? When one says, "Give me neither poverty nor riches,"[334] what else is this than, "Give us this day our daily bread"? When one says, "Lord, remember David, and all his compassion,"[335] or, "O Lord, if I have done this, if there be iniquity in my hands, if I have rewarded evil to them that did evil to me,"[336] what else is this than, "Forgive us our debts as we forgive our debtors"? When one says, "Take away from me the lusts of the appetite, and let not sensual desire take hold on me,"[337] what else is this than, "Lead us not into temptation"? When one says, "Deliver me from mine enemies, O my God; defend me from them that rise up against me,"[338] what else is this than, "Deliver us from evil"? And if you go over all the words of holy prayers, you will, I believe, find nothing which cannot be comprised and summed up in the petitions of the Lord's Prayer. Wherefore, in praying, we are free to use different words to any extent, but we must ask the same things; in this we have no choice.

331. Ecclus 36:4, 18.   332. Ps 80:7, 19.   333. Ps 119:133.
334. Prv 30:8.   335. Ps 132:1 (Septuagint).   336. Ps 7:3, 4.
337. Ecclus 23:6.   338. Ps 59:1.

23. These things it is our duty to ask without hesitation for ourselves and for our friends, and for strangers—yea, even for enemies, although in the heart of the person praying, desire for one and for another may arise, differing in nature or in strength according to the more immediate or more remote relationship. But he who says in prayer such words as, "O Lord, multiply my riches"; or, "Give me as much wealth as Thou hast given to this or that man"; or, "Increase my honors, make me eminent for power and fame in this world," or something else of this sort, and who asks merely from a desire for these things, and not in order through them to benefit men agreeably to God's will, I do not think that he will find any part of the Lord's Prayer in connection with which he could fit in these requests. Wherefore let us be ashamed at least to ask these things, if we be not ashamed to desire them. If, however, we are ashamed of even desiring them, but feel ourselves overcome by the desire, how much better would it be to ask to be freed from this plague of desire by him to whom we say, "Deliver us from evil"!

CHAPTER 13

24. You have now, if I am not mistaken, an answer to two questions—what kind of person you ought to be if you would pray, and what things you should ask in prayer; and the answer has been given not by my teaching, but by his who has condescended to teach us all. A happy life is to be sought after, and this is to be asked from the Lord God. Many different answers have been given by many in discussing wherein true happiness consists, but why should we go to many teachers, or consider many answers to this question? It has been briefly and truly stated in the divine Scriptures, "Blessed is the people whose God is the Lord."[339] That we may be numbered among this people, and that we may attain to beholding him and dwelling forever with him, "the end of the commandment is, charity out of a pure heart, and of a good conscience, and of faith unfeigned."[340] In the same three, hope has been placed instead of a good conscience. Faith, hope, and charity, therefore, lead unto God the man who prays, i.e., who believes, hopes, and desires, and is guided as to what he should ask from the Lord by studying the Lord's Prayer. Fasting, and abstinence from gratifying carnal de-

339. Ps 144:15.　　　340. 1 Tm 1:5.

sire in other pleasures without injury to health, and especially frequent almsgiving, are a great assistance in prayer, so that we may be able to say, "In the day of my trouble I sought the Lord, with my hands in the night before Him, and I was not deceived."[341] For how can God, who is a Spirit, and who cannot be touched, be sought with hands in any other sense than by good works?

CHAPTER 14

25. Perhaps you may still ask why the apostle said, "We know not what to pray for as we ought,"[342] for it is wholly incredible that either he or those to whom he wrote were ignorant of the Lord's Prayer. He could not say this either rashly or falsely; what, then, do we suppose to be his reason for the statement? Is it not that vexations and troubles in this world are for the most part profitable either to heal the swelling of pride, or to prove and exercise patience, for which, after such probation and discipline, a greater reward is reserved, or to punish and eradicate some sins, but we, not knowing what beneficial purpose these may serve, desire to be freed from all tribulation? To this ignorance the apostle showed that even he himself was not a stranger (unless, perhaps, he did it notwithstanding his knowing what to pray for as he ought), when, lest he should be exalted above measure by the greatness of the revelations, there was given unto him a thorn in the flesh, a messenger of Satan to buffet him, for which thing, not knowing surely what he ought to pray for, he besought the Lord thrice that it might depart from him. At length he received the answer of God, declaring why that which so great a man prayed for was denied, and why it was expedient that it should not be done: "My grace is sufficient for thee; my strength is made perfect in weakness."[343]

26. Accordingly, we know not what to pray for as we ought in regard to tribulations, which may do us good or harm, and yet, because they are hard and painful, and against the natural feelings of our weak nature, we pray, with a desire which is common to mankind, that they may be removed from us. But we ought to exercise such submission to the will of the Lord our God, that if he does not remove those vexations, we do not suppose ourselves to be

341. Ps 77:2 (Septuagint).   342. Rom 8:26.

343. 2 Cor 12:7–9.

neglected by him, but rather, in patient endurance of evil, hope to be made partakers of greater good, for so his strength is perfected in our weakness. God has sometimes in anger granted the request of impatient petitioners, as in mercy he denied it to the apostle. For we read what the Israelites asked, and in what manner they asked and obtained their request; but while their desire was granted, their impatience was severely corrected.[344] Again, he gave them, in answer to their request, a king according to their heart, as it is written, not according to his own heart.[345] He granted also what the devil asked, namely, that his servant, who was to be proved, might be tempted.[346] He granted also the request of unclean spirits, when they besought him that their legion might be sent into the great herd of swine.[347] These things are written to prevent anyone from thinking too highly of himself if he has received an answer when he was urgently asking anything which it would be more advantageous for him not to receive, or to prevent him from being cast down and despairing of the divine compassion toward himself if he be not heard, when, perchance, he is asking something by the obtaining of which he might be more grievously afflicted, or might be by the corrupting influences of prosperity wholly destroyed. In regard to such things, therefore, we know not what to pray for as we ought. Accordingly, if anything is ordered in a way contrary to our prayer, we ought, patiently bearing the disappointment, and in everything giving thanks to God, to entertain no doubt whatever that it was right that the will of God and not our will should be done. For of this the Mediator has given us an example, inasmuch as, after he had said, "Father, if it be possible, let this cup pass from me," transforming the human will which was in him through his incarnation, he immediately added, "Nevertheless, O Father, not as I will but as Thou wilt."[348] Wherefore, not without reason are many made righteous by the obedience of One.[349]

27. But whoever desires from the Lord that "one thing," and seeks after it,[350] asks in certainty and in confidence, and has no fear lest when obtained it be injurious to him, seeing that, without it, anything else which he may have obtained by asking in a right way is of no advantage to him. The thing referred to is the one true and

344. Nm 11.   345. 1 Sm 8:6, 7.   346. Jb 1:12, 2:6.   347. Lk 8:32.

348. Mt 26:39.   349. Rom 5:19.   350. Ps 27:4.

only happy life, in which, immortal and incorruptible in body and spirit, we may contemplate the joy of the Lord forever. All other things are desired, and are without impropriety prayed for, with a view to this one thing. For whosoever has it shall have all that he wishes, and cannot possibly wish to have anything along with it which would be unbecoming. For in it is the fountain of life, which we must now thirst for in prayer so long as we live in hope, not yet seeing that which we hope for, trusting under the shadow of his wings before whom are all our desires, that we may be abundantly satisfied with the fatness of his house, and made to drink of the river of his pleasures, because with him is the fountain of life, and in his light we shall see light,[351] when our desire shall be satisfied with good things, and when there shall be nothing beyond to be sought after with groaning, but all things shall be possessed by us with rejoicing. At the same time, because this blessing is nothing else than the "peace which passeth all understanding,"[352] even when we are asking it in our prayers, we know not what to pray for as we ought. For inasmuch as we cannot present it to our minds as it really is, we do not know it, but whatever image of it may be presented to our minds we reject, disown, and condemn; we know it is not what we are seeking, although we do not yet know enough to be able to define what we seek.

CHAPTER 15

28. There is therefore in us a certain learned ignorance, so to speak—an ignorance which we learn from that Spirit of God who helps our infirmities. For after the apostle said, "If we hope for that we see not, then do we with patience wait for it," he added in the same passage, "Likewise the Spirit also helpeth our infirmities: for we know not what we should pray for as we ought, but the Spirit itself maketh intercession for us, with groanings which cannot be uttered. And He that searcheth the hearts knoweth what is in the mind of the Spirit, because He maketh intercession for the saints according to the will of God."[353] This is not to be understood as if it meant that the Holy Spirit of God, who is in the Trinity, God unchangeable, and is one God with the Father and the Son, intercedes for the saints like one who is not a divine person, for it is said, "He

351. Ps 36:8–10.   352. Phil 4:7.   353. Rom 8:25–27.

maketh intercession for the saints," because he enables the saints to make intercession, as in another place it is said, "The Lord your God proveth you, that He may know whether ye love Him,"[354] i.e., that he may make you know. He therefore makes the saints intercede with groanings which cannot be uttered, when he inspires them with longings for that great blessing, as yet unknown, for which we patiently wait. For how is that which is desired set forth in language if it be unknown, for if it were utterly unknown it would not be desired; and on the other hand, if it were seen, it would not be desired nor sought for with groanings?

CHAPTER 16

29. Considering all these things, and whatever else the Lord shall have made known to you in this matter, which either does not occur to me or would take too much time to state here, strive in prayer to overcome this world: pray in hope, pray in faith, pray in love, pray earnestly and patiently, pray as a widow belonging to Christ. For although prayer is, as he has taught, the duty of all his members, i.e., of all who believe in him and are united to his body, a more assiduous attention to prayer is found to be specially enjoined in Scripture upon those who are widows. Two women of the name of Anna are honorably named there—the one, Elkanah's wife, who was the mother of holy Samuel; the other, the widow who recognized the Most Holy One when he was yet a babe. The former, though married, prayed with sorrow of mind and brokenness of heart because she had no sons, and she obtained Samuel and dedicated him to the Lord, because she vowed to do so when she prayed for him.[355] It is not easy, however, to find to what petition of the Lord's Prayer her petition could be referred, unless it be to the last, "Deliver us from evil," because it was esteemed to be an evil to be married and not to have offspring as the fruit of marriage. Observe, however, what is written concerning the other Anna, the widow: she "departed not from the temple, but served God with fastings and prayers night and day."[356] In like manner, the apostle said in words already quoted, "She that is a widow indeed, and desolate, trusteth in God and continueth in supplications and prayers night and day";[357] and the Lord, when exhorting men to pray al-

354. Dt 12:3.   355. 1 Sm 1.   356. Lk 2:36, 37.   357. 1 Tm 5:5.

ways and not to faint, made mention of a widow, who, by persevering importunity, persuaded a judge to attend to her cause, though he was an unjust and wicked man, and one who neither feared God nor regarded man. How incumbent it is on widows to go beyond others in devoting time to prayer may be plainly enough seen from the fact that from among them are taken the examples set forth as an exhortation to all to earnestness in prayer.

30. Now what makes this work specially suitable to widows but their bereaved and desolate condition? Whosoever, then, understands that he is in this world bereaved and desolate as long as he is a pilgrim absent from his Lord, is careful to commit his widowhood, so to speak, to his God as his shield in continual and most fervent prayer. Pray, therefore, as a widow of Christ, not yet seeing him whose help you implore. And though you are very wealthy, pray as a poor person, for you have not yet the true riches of the world to come, in which you have no loss to fear. Though you have sons and grandchildren, and a large household, still pray, as I said already, as one who is desolate, for we have no certainty in regard to all temporal blessings that they shall abide for our consolation even to the end of this present life. If you seek and relish the things that are above, you desire things everlasting and sure; and as long as you do not yet possess them, you ought to regard yourself as desolate, even though all your family are spared to you, and live as you desire. And if you thus act, assuredly your example will be followed by your most devout daughter-in-law[358] and the other holy widows and virgins that are settled in peace under your care, for the more pious the manner in which you order your house, the more are you bound to persevere fervently in prayer, not engaging yourselves with the affairs of this world further than is demanded in the interests of religion.

31. By all means remember to pray earnestly for me. I would not have you yield such deference to the office fraught with perils which I bear, as to refrain from giving the assistance which I know myself to need. Prayer was made by the household of Christ for Peter and for Paul. I rejoice that you are in his household, and I need, incomparably more than Peter and Paul did, the help of the prayers of the brethren. Emulate each other in prayer with a holy

358. Juliana, the mother of Demetrias.

rivalry, with one heart, for you wrestle not against each other, but against the devil, who is the common enemy of all the saints. "By fasting, by vigils, and all mortification of the body, prayer is greatly helped."[359] Let each one do what she can; what one cannot herself do, she does by another who can do it, if she loves in another that which personal inability alone hinders her from doing; wherefore let her who can do less not keep back the one who can do more, and let her who can do more not urge unduly her who can do less. For your conscience is responsible to God; to each other owe nothing but mutual love. May the Lord, who is able to do above what we ask or think, give ear to your prayers.[360]

Letter 189
[418 A.D.]

To Boniface,[361] My Noble Lord and Justly Distinguished and Honorable Son, Augustine Sends Greeting in the Lord.

1. I had already written a reply to Your Charity, but while I was waiting for an opportunity of forwarding the letter, my beloved son Faustus arrived here on his way to Your Excellency. After he

---

359. Tb 12:8.   360. Eph 3:20.

361. Count Boniface was governor of the province of Africa under Placidia, who for twenty-five years ruled the empire in the name of her son Valentinian. By his perfidious rival Ætius, Boniface was persuaded to disobey the order of Placidia, when, under the instigation of Ætius himself, she recalled him from the government of Africa. The necessity of powerful allies in order to maintain his position led him to invite the Vandals to pass from Spain into Africa. They came, under Genseric, and the fertile provinces of Northern Africa fell an easy prey to their invading armies. When the treachery of Ætius was discovered, Placidia received Boniface again into favor, and he devoted all his military talents to the task of expelling the barbarians whom his own invitation had made masters of North Africa. But it was now too late to wrest this Roman province from the Vandals; defeated in a great battle, Boniface was compelled in 430 to retire into Hippo Regius, where he succeeded in resisting the besieging army for fourteen months. It was during this siege, and after it had continued three months, that Augustine died. Reinforced by troops from Constantinople, Boniface fought one more desperate but unsuccessful battle, after which he left Hippo in the hands of Genseric, and returned by order of Placidia to Italy. For fuller particulars of his history, see Edward Gibbon's *History of the Decline and Fall of the Roman Empire*, Chap. 33.

had received the letter which I had intended to be carried by him to
Your Benevolence, he stated to me that you were very desirous that
I should write you something which might build you up unto the
eternal salvation of which you have hope in Christ Jesus our Lord.
And, although I was busily occupied at the time, he insisted, with
an earnestness corresponding to the love which, as you know, he
bears to you, that I should do this without delay. To meet his conve-
nience, therefore, as he was in haste to depart, I thought it better to
write, though necessarily without much time for reflection, rather
than put off the gratification of your pious desire, my noble lord
and justly distinguished and honorable son.

2. All is contained in these brief sentences: "Love the Lord thy
God with all thy heart, and with all thy soul, and with all thy
strength: and love thy neighbor as thyself";[362] for these are the
words in which the Lord, when on earth, gave an epitome of religion, saying in the Gospel, "On these two commandments hang all
the law and the prophets." Daily advance, then, in this love, both
by praying and by well-doing, that through the help of him, who
enjoined it on you, and whose gift it is, it may be nourished and
increased, until, being perfected, it render you perfect. "For this is
the love which," as the apostle says, "is shed abroad in our hearts
by the Holy Ghost, which is given unto us."[363] This is "the fulfilling
of the law";[364] this is the same love by which faith works, of which
he says again, "Neither circumcision availeth anything, nor uncircumcision; but faith, which worketh by love."[365]

3. In this love, then, all our holy fathers, patriarchs, prophets,
and apostles pleased God. In this all true martyrs contended
against the devil even to the shedding of blood, and because in
them it neither waxed cold nor failed, they became conquerors. In
this all true believers daily make progress, seeking to acquire not
an earthly kingdom, but the kingdom of heaven; not a temporal,
but an eternal inheritance; not gold and silver, but the incorruptible
riches of the angels; not the good things of this life, which are enjoyed with trembling, and which no one can take with him when
he dies, but the vision of God, whose grace and power of imparting
felicity transcend all beauty of form in bodies not only on earth but
also in heaven, transcend all spiritual loveliness in men, however

362. Mt 22:37–40.   363. Rom 5:5.   364. Rom 13:10.   365. Gal 5:6.

just and holy, transcend all the glory of the angels and powers of the world above, transcend not only all that language can express, but all that thought can imagine concerning him. And let us not despair of the fulfillment of such a great promise because it is exceeding great, but rather believe that we shall receive it because he who has promised it is exceeding great, as the blessed Apostle John says, "Now are we the sons of God; and it doth not yet appear what we shall be: but we know that, when He shall appear, we shall be like Him; for we shall see Him as He is."[366]

4. Do not think that it is impossible for anyone to please God while engaged in active military service. Among such persons was the holy David, to whom God gave so great a testimony; among them also were many righteous men of that time; among them was also that centurion who said to the Lord, "I am not worthy that Thou shouldest come under my roof, but speak the word only, and my servant shall be healed: for I am a man under authority, having soldiers under me: and I say to this man, Go, and he goeth; and to another, Come, and he cometh; and to my servant, Do this, and he doeth it"; and concerning whom the Lord said, "Verily, I say unto you, I have not found so great faith, no, not in Israel."[367] Among them was that Cornelius to whom an angel said, "Cornelius, thine alms are accepted, and thy prayers are heard,"[368] when he directed him to send to the blessed Apostle Peter, and to hear from him what he ought to do, to which apostle he sent a devout soldier, requesting him to come to him. Among them were also the soldiers who, when they had come to be baptized by John—the sacred forerunner of the Lord, and the friend of the Bridegroom, of whom the Lord says, "Among them that are born of women there hath not arisen a greater than John the Baptist"[369]—and had inquired of him what they should do, received the answer, "Do violence to no man, neither accuse any falsely; and be content with your wages."[370] Certainly he did not prohibit them to serve as soldiers when he commanded them to be content with their pay for the service.

5. They occupy indeed a higher place before God who, abandoning all these secular employments, serve him with the strictest chastity, but "every one," as the apostle says, "hath his proper gift of

366. Jn 3:2.   367. Mt 8:8–10.   368. Acts 10:4.   369. Mt 11:11.
370. Lk 3:14.

God, one after this manner, and another after that."[371] Some, then, in praying for you, fight against your invisible enemies; you, in fighting for them, contend against the barbarians, their visible enemies. Would that one faith existed in all, for then there would be less weary struggling, and the devil with his angels would be more easily conquered, but since it is necessary in this life that the citizens of the kingdom of heaven should be subjected to temptations among erring and impious men, that they may be exercised, and "tried as gold in the furnace,"[372] we ought not before the appointed time to desire to live with those alone who are holy and righteous, so that, by patience, we may deserve to receive this blessedness in its proper time.

6. Think, then, of this first of all, when you are arming for the battle, that even your bodily strength is a gift of God, for, considering this, you will not employ the gift of God against God. For when faith is pledged, it is to be kept even with the enemy against whom the war is waged, how much more with the friend for whom the battle is fought! Peace should be the object of your desire; war should be waged only as a necessity, and waged only that God may by it deliver men from the necessity and preserve them in peace. For peace is not sought in order to aid the kindling of war, but war is waged in order that peace may be obtained. Therefore, even in waging war, cherish the spirit of a peacemaker, that by conquering those whom you attack, you may lead them back to the advantages of peace, for our Lord says, "Blessed are the peacemakers, for they shall be called the children of God."[373] If, however, peace among men be so sweet as procuring temporal safety, how much sweeter is that peace with God which procures for men the eternal felicity of the angels! Let necessity, therefore, and not your will, slay the enemy who fights against you. As violence is used toward him who rebels and resists, so mercy is due to the vanquished or the captive, especially in the case in which future troubling of the peace is not to be feared.

7. Let the manner of your life be adorned by chastity, sobriety, and moderation, for it is exceedingly disgraceful that lust should subdue him whom man finds invincible, and that wine should overpower him whom the sword assails in vain. As to worldly

371. 1 Cor 7:7.   372. Ws 3:6.   373. Mt 5:9.

riches, if you do not possess them, let them not be sought after on earth by doing evil; and if you possess them, let them by good works be laid up in heaven. The manly and Christian spirit ought neither to be elated by the accession, nor crushed by the loss of this world's treasures. Let us rather think of what the Lord says: "Where your treasure is, there will your heart be also";[374] and certainly, when we hear the exhortation to lift up our hearts, it is our duty to give unfeignedly the response which you know that we are accustomed to give.[375]

8. In these things, indeed, I know that you are very careful, and the good report which I hear of you fills me with great delight and moves me to congratulate you on account of it in the Lord. This letter, therefore, may serve rather as a mirror in which you may see what you are, than as a directory from which to learn what you ought to be: nevertheless, whatever you may discover, either from this letter or from the Holy Scriptures, to be still wanting to you in regard to a holy life, persevere in urgently seeking it both by effort and by prayer; and for the things which you have, give thanks to God as the Fountain of goodness, whence you have received them; in every good action let the glory be given to God, and humility be exercised by you, for, as it is written, "Every good gift and every perfect gift is from above, and cometh down from the Father of lights."[376] But however much you may advance in the love of God and of your neighbor, and in true piety, do not imagine, as long as you are in this life, that you are without sin, for concerning this we read in Holy Scripture: "Is not the life of man upon earth a life of temptation?"[377] Wherefore, since always, as long as you are in this body, it is necessary for you to say in prayer, as the Lord taught us: "Forgive us our debts, as we forgive our debtors,"[378] remember quickly to forgive, if anyone shall do you wrong and shall ask par-

374. Mt 6:21.

375. The allusion is evidently to the ancient formulary in public worship, first mentioned by Cyprian in his treatise on the Lord's Prayer. To the presbyter's exhortation, "Sursum corda!" the people responded, "Habemus ad Dominum." For an account of this formulary and a most beautiful exposition of it, quoted from Cyril of Jerusalem, see Riddle's *Christian Antiquities*, Book IV, chap. 1, sec. 2.

376. Jas 1:17.   377. Jb 7:1 (Septuagint).   378. Mt 6:12.

don from you, that you may be able to pray sincerely, and may prevail in seeking pardon for your own sins.

These things, my beloved friend, I have written to you in haste,
as the anxiety of the bearer to depart urged me not to detain him;
but I thank God that I have in some measure complied with your
pious wish. May the mercy of God ever protect you, my noble lord
and justly distinguished son.

From Expositions
of the Psalms

Psalm 16[379]

1. Our King in this psalm speaks in the character of the human nature He assumed, of whom the royal title at the time of His passion was eminently set forth.

2. Now He saith as follows: "Preserve me, O Lord, for in Thee have I hoped" (v. 1): "I have said to the Lord, Thou art my God, for Thou requirest not my goods" (v. 2): for with my goods Thou dost not look to be made blessed.

3. "To the saints who are on His earth" (v. 3): to the saints who have placed their hope in the land of the living, the citizens of the heavenly Jerusalem, whose spiritual conversation is, by the anchor of hope, fixed in that country, which is rightly called God's earth; although as yet in this earth too they be conversant in the flesh. "He hath wonderfully fulfilled all My wishes in them." To those saints then He hath wonderfully fulfilled all My wishes in their advancement, whereby they have perceived, how both the humanity of My divinity hath profited them that I might die, and the divinity of the humanity that I might rise again.

4. "Their infirmities have been multiplied"[380] (v. 4): their infirmities have been multiplied not for their destruction, but that they might long for the Physician. "Afterwards they made haste." Accordingly after infirmities multiplied they made haste, that they might be healed. "I will not gather together their assemblies by blood." For their assemblies shall not be carnal, nor will I gather them together as one propitiated by the blood of cattle.[381] "Nor will I be mindful of their names within My lips." But by a spiritual change what they have been shall be forgotten; nor by Me shall they be any more called either sinners, or enemies, or men; but righteous, and My brethren, and sons of God through My peace.

5. "The Lord is the portion of Mine inheritance, and of My cup" (v. 5). For together with Me they shall possess the inheritance, the Lord Himself. Let others choose for themselves portions, earthly

---

379. Latin Vulgate no. 15.   380. So Oxford mss.   381. Is 1:11, 12.

and temporal, to enjoy: the portion of the saints is the Lord eternal. Let others drink of deadly pleasures, the portion of My cup is the Lord. In that I say, "Mine," I include the Church: for where the Head is, there is the body also. For into the inheritance will I gather together their assemblies, and by the inebriation of the cup I will forget their old names. "Thou art He who will restore to Me My inheritance": that to these too, whom I free, may be known "the glory wherein I was with Thee before the world was made."[382] For Thou wilt not restore to Me that which I never lost, but Thou wilt restore to these, who have lost it, the knowledge of that glory: in whom because I am, Thou wilt restore to Me.

6. "The lines have fallen to me in glorious places" (v. 6). The boundaries of my possession have fallen in Thy glory as it were by lot, like as God is the possession of the priests and Levites.[383] "For Mine inheritance is glorious to Me." "For Mine inheritance is glorious," not to all, but to them that see; in whom because I am, "it is to Me."

7. "I will bless the Lord, who hath given Me understanding" (v. 7): whereby this inheritance may be seen and possessed. "Yea moreover too even unto night my reins have chastened Me." Yea besides understanding, even unto death, My inferior part, the assumption of flesh, hath instructed Me, that I might experience the darkness of mortality, which that understanding hath not.

8. "I foresaw the Lord in My sight always" (v. 8). But coming into things that pass away, I removed not Mine eye from Him who abideth ever, foreseeing this, that to Him I should return after passing through the things temporal. "For He is on My right hand, that I should not be moved." For He favoreth Me, that I should abide fixedly in Him.

9. "Wherefore My heart was glad, and My tongue exulted" (v. 9). Wherefore both in My thoughts is gladness, and in my words exultation. "Moreover too My flesh shall rest in hope." Moreover too My flesh shall not fail unto destruction, but shall sleep in hope of the resurrection.

10. "For Thou wilt not leave My soul in hell" (v. 10). For Thou wilt neither give My soul for a possession to those parts below. "Neither wilt Thou grant Thine Holy One to see corruption." Nei-

382. Jn 17:5.   383. Num 18:20.

ther wilt Thou suffer that sanctified body, whereby others are to be also sanctified, to see corruption. "Thou hast made known to Me the paths of life" (v. 11). Thou hast made known through Me the paths of humiliation, that[384] men might return to life, from whence they fell through pride; in whom because I am, "Thou hast made known to Me." "Thou wilt fill Me with joy with Thy countenance." Thou wilt fill them with joy, that they should seek nothing further, when they shall see Thee "face to face"; in whom because I am, "Thou wilt fill Me." "Pleasure is at Thy right hand even to the end." Pleasure is in Thy favor and mercy in this life's journey, leading on even to the end of the glory of Thy countenance.[385]

Psalm 18[386]

TO THE END, FOR THE SERVANT OF THE LORD, DAVID HIMSELF.

1. That is, for the strong of hand, Christ in His Manhood.[387] "The words of this song which he spoke to the Lord on the day when the Lord delivered him out of the hands of his enemies, and of the hand of Saul; and he said, On the day when the Lord delivered him out of the hands of his enemies and of the hand of Saul": namely, the king of the Jews, whom they had demanded for themselves.[388] For as "David" is said to be by interpretation, strong of hand, so "Saul" is said to be demanding. Now it is well known, how that People demanded for themselves a king, and received him for their king, not according to the will of God, but according to their own will.

2. Christ, then, and the Church, that is, whole Christ, the Head and the Body, saith here, "I will love Thee, O Lord, My strength" (v. 1). I will love Thee, O Lord, by whom I am strong.[389]

3. "O Lord, My stay, and My refuge, and My deliverer" (v. 2). O Lord, who hast stayed Me, because I sought refuge with Thee: and I sought refuge, because Thou hast delivered Me. "My God is My helper; and I will hope in Him." My God, who hast first

---

384. Oxford mss. "that by it."   385. Compare Acts 2:25 and 13:34.—C.

386. Lat. 17.   387. *Secundum hominem.*   388. 1 Sm 8:5.

389. 2 Sm 22.—C.

afforded me the help of Thy call, that I might be able to hope in Thee. "My defender, and the horn of My salvation, and My redeemer." My defender, because I have not leaned upon Myself, lifting up as it were the horn of pride against Thee; but have found Thee a horn indeed, that is, the sure height of salvation: and that I might find it, Thou redeemedst Me.

4. "With praise will I call upon the Lord, and I shall be safe from Mine enemies" (v. 3). Seeking not My own but the Lord's glory, I will call upon Him, and there shall be no means whereby the errors of ungodliness can hurt Me.

5. "The pains of death," that is, of the flesh, have "compassed Me about. And the overflowings of ungodliness have troubled Me" (v. 4). Ungodly troubles[390] stirred up for a time, like torrents of rain which will soon subside, have come on to trouble Me.

6. "The pains of hell compassed Me about" (v. 5). Among those that compassed Me about to destroy Me, were pains of envy, which work death, and lead on to the hell of sin. "The snares of death prevented Me." They prevented Me, so that they wished to hurt Me first, which shall afterward be recompensed unto them. Now they seize unto destruction such men as they have evilly persuaded by the boast of righteousness: in the name but not in the reality of which they glory against the Gentiles.

7. "And in Mine oppression I called upon the Lord, and cried unto My God. And He heard My voice from His holy temple" (v. 6). He heard from My heart, wherein He dwelleth, My voice. "And My cry in His sight entered into His ears"; and My cry, which I utter, not in the ears of men, but inwardly before Him Himself, "entered into His ears."

8. "And the earth was moved and trembled" (v. 7). When the Son of Man was thus glorified, sinners were moved and trembled. "And the foundations of the mountains were troubled." And the hopes of the proud, which were in this life, were troubled. "And were moved, for God was wroth with them." That is, that the hope of temporal goods might have now no more establishment in the hearts of men.

9. "There went up smoke in His wrath" (v. 8). The tearful supplication of penitents went up, when they came to know God's

---

390. Or, "crowds."

threatenings against the ungodly. "And fire burneth from His face." And the ardor of love after repentance burns by the knowledge of Him. "Coals were kindled from Him." They, who were already dead, abandoned by the fire of good desire and the light of righteousness, and who remained in coldness and darkness, re-enkindled and enlightened, have come to life again.

10. "And He bowed the heaven, and came down" (v. 9). And He humbled the just One, that He might descend to men's infirmity. "And darkness under His feet." And the ungodly, who savor of things earthly, in the darkness of their own malice, knew not Him: for the earth under His feet is as it were His footstool.

11. "And He mounted above the cherubim, and did fly" (v. 10). And He was exalted above the fullness of knowledge, that no man should come to Him but by love: for "love is the fulfilling of the law."[391] And full soon He showed to His lovers that He is incomprehensible, lest they should suppose that He is comprehended by corporeal imaginations. "He flew above the wings of the winds." But that swiftness, whereby He showed Himself to be incomprehensible, is above the powers of souls, whereon as upon wings they raise themselves from earthly fears into the air of liberty.

12. "And hath made darkness His hiding place" (v. 11). And hath settled the obscurity of the Sacraments, and the hidden hope in the heart of believers, where He may lie hid, and not abandon them. In this darkness too, wherein "we yet walk by faith, and not by sight,"[392] as long as "we hope for what we see not, and with patience wait for it."[393] "Round about Him is His tabernacle." Yet they that believe Him turn to Him and encircle Him; for that He is in the midst of them, since He is equally the friend of all, in whom as in a tabernacle He at this time dwells. "Dark water in clouds of air." Nor let any one on this account, if he understand the Scripture, imagine that he is already in that light, which will be when we shall have come out of faith into sight: for in the prophets and in all the preachers of the word of God there is obscure teaching.

13. "In respect of the brightness in His sight" (v. 12): in comparison with the brightness, which is in the sight of His manifestation. "His clouds have passed over." The preachers of His word are not now bounded by the confines of Judaea, but have passed over to the

391. Rom 13:10.   392. 2 Cor 5:7.   393. Rom 8:25.

Gentiles. "Hail and coals of fire." Reproofs are figured,[394] whereby, as by hail, the hard hearts are bruised: but if a cultivated and genial soil, that is, a godly mind, receive them, the hail's hardness dissolves into water, that is, the terror of the lightning-charged, and as it were frozen, reproof dissolves into satisfying doctrine; and hearts kindled by the fire of love revive. All these things in His clouds have passed over to the Gentiles.

14. "And the Lord hath thundered from heaven" (v. 13). And in confidence of the Gospel the Lord hath sounded forth from the heart of the just One. "And the Highest gave His voice"; that we might entertain it, and in the depth of human things, might hear things heavenly.

15. "And He sent out His arrows, and scattered them" (v. 14). And He sent out evangelists traversing straight paths on the wings of strength, not in their own power, but His by whom they were sent. And "He scattered them," to whom they were sent, that to some of them they should be "the savor of life unto life, to others the savor of death unto death."[395] "And He multiplied lightnings, and troubled them." And He multiplied miracles, and troubled them.

16. "And the fountains of water were seen. And the fountains of water springing up into everlasting life,"[396] which were made in the preachers, were seen. "And the foundations of the round world were revealed" (v. 15). And the prophets, who were not understood, and upon whom was to be built the world of believers in the Lord, were revealed. "At Thy chiding, O Lord"; crying out, "The kingdom of God is come nigh unto you."[397] "At the blasting of the breath of Thy displeasure"; saying, "Except ye repent, ye shall all likewise perish."[398]

17. "He hath sent down from on high, and hath fetched Me (v. 16): by calling out of the Gentiles for an inheritance "a glorious Church, not having spot, or wrinkle."[399] "He hath taken Me out of the multitude of waters." He hath taken Me out of the multitude of peoples.

18. "He hath delivered Me from My strongest enemies" (v. 17). He hath delivered Me from Mine enemies, who prevailed to the afflicting and overturning of this temporal life of Mine. "And from

---

394. Read "full lightning-charged reproofs."   395. 2 Cor 2:16.

396. Jn 4:14.   397. Lk 10:9.   398. Lk 13:5.   399. Eph 5:27.

them which hate Me; for they are too strong for Me": as long as I am under them knowing not God.

19. "They have prevented Me in the day of My affliction" (v. 18). They have first injured Me, in the time when I am bearing a mortal and toilsome body. "And the Lord hath become My stay." And since the stay of earthly pleasure was disturbed and torn up by the bitterness of misery, the Lord hath become My stay.

20. "And hath brought Me forth into a broad place" (v. 19). And since I was enduring the straits of the flesh, He brought Me forth into the spiritual breadth of faith. "He hath delivered Me, because He desired Me." Before that I desired Him, He delivered Me from My most powerful enemies (who were envious of Me when I once desired Him), and from them that hated Me, because I do desire Him.

21. "And the Lord shall reward Me according to My righteousness" (v. 20). And the Lord shall reward Me according to the righteousness of My good will, who first showed mercy, before that I had the good will. "And according to the cleanness of My hands He will recompense Me." And according to the cleanness of My deeds He will recompense Me, who hath given Me to do well by bringing Me forth into the broad place of faith.

22. "Because I have kept the ways of the Lord" (v. 21). That the breadth of good works, that are by faith, and the long-suffering of perseverance should follow after.

23. "Nor have I walked impiously apart from My God." "For all His judgments are[400] in My sight" (v. 22). "For" with persevering contemplation I weigh "all His judgments," that is, the rewards of the righteous, and the punishments of the ungodly, and the scourges of such as are to be chastened, and the trials of such as are to be proved. "And I have not cast out His righteousness from Me": as they do that faint under their burden of them, and return to their own vomit.

24. "And I shall be undefiled with Him, and I shall keep Myself from Mine iniquity" (v. 23).

25. "And the Lord shall reward Me according to My righteousness (v. 24). Accordingly not only for the breadth of faith, which worketh by love; but also for the length of perseverance, will the

---

400. Oxford mss. "are always."

Lord reward Me according to My righteousness. "And according to the cleanness of My hands in the sight of His eyes." Not as men see, but "in the sight of His eyes." For "the things that are seen are temporal; but the things that are not seen are eternal":[401] whereto the height of hope appertains.

26. "With the holy Thou shalt be holy" (v. 25). There is a hidden depth also, wherein Thou art known to be holy with the holy, for that Thou makest holy. "And with the harmless Thou shalt be harmless." For Thou harmest no man, but each one is bound by the bands of his own sins.[402]

27. "And with the chosen Thou shalt be chosen" (v. 26). And by him whom Thou choosest, Thou art chosen. "And with the froward Thou shalt be froward." And with the froward Thou seemest froward: for they say, "The way of the Lord is not right":[403] and their way is not right.

28. "For Thou wilt make whole the humble people" (v. 27). Now this seems froward to the froward, that Thou wilt make them whole that confess their sins. "And Thou wilt humble the eyes of the proud." But them that are "ignorant of God's righteousness, and seek to establish their own,"[404] Thou wilt humble.

29. "For thou wilt light My candle, O Lord" (v. 28). For our light is not from ourselves; but "Thou wilt light my candle, O Lord. O my God, Thou wilt enlighten my darkness." For we through our sins are darkness; but "Thou, O my God, wilt enlighten my darkness."

30. "For by Thee shall I be delivered from temptation" (v. 29). For not by myself, but by Thee, shall I be delivered from temptation. "And in my God shall I leap over the wall." And not in myself, but in my God shall I leap over the wall, which sin has raised between men and the heavenly Jerusalem.

31. "My God, His way is undefiled" (v. 30). My God cometh not unto men, except they shall have purified the way of faith, whereby He may come to them; for that "His way is undefiled." "The words of the Lord have been proved by fire." The words of the Lord are tried by the fire of tribulation. "He is the Protector of them that hope in Him." And all that hope not in themselves, but in Him, are not consumed by that same tribulation. For hope followeth faith.

32. "For who is God, but the Lord?" (v. 31) whom we serve.

---

401. 2 Cor 4:18.   402. Prv 5:22.   403. Ez 18:25.   404. Rom 10:3.

"And who God, but our God?" And who is God, but the Lord? whom after good service we sons shall possess as the hoped-for inheritance.

33. "God, who hath girded me with strength" (v. 32). God, who hath girded me that I might be strong, lest the loosely flowing folds of desire hinder my deeds and steps. "And hath made my way undefiled." And hath made the way of love, whereby I may come to Him, undefiled, as the way of faith is undefiled, whereby He comes to me.

34. "Who hath made my feet perfect like harts' feet" (v. 33). Who hath made my love perfect to surmount the thorny and dark entanglements of this world. "And will set me up on high." And will fix my aim on the heavenly habitation, that "I may be filled with all the fullness of God."[405]

35. "Who teacheth my hands for battle" (v. 34). Who teacheth me to work for the overthrow of mine enemies, who strive to shut the kingdom of heaven against us. "And Thou hast made mine arms as a bow of steel." And Thou hast made my earnest striving after good works unwearied.

36. "And Thou hast given me the defense of my salvation, and Thy right hand hath held me up" (v. 35). And the favor of Thy grace hath held me up. "And Thy discipline hath directed me to the end." And Thy correction, not suffering me to wander from the way, hath directed me that whatsoever I do, I refer to that end, whereby I may cleave to Thee. "And this Thy discipline, it shall teach me." And that same correction of Thine shall teach me to attain to that, whereunto it hath directed me.

37. "Thou hast enlarged my steps under me" (v. 36). Nor shall the straits of the flesh hinder me; for Thou hast enlarged my love, working in gladness even with these mortal things and members which are under me. "And my footsteps have not been weakened." And either my goings, or the marks which I have imprinted for the imitation of those that follow, have not been weakened.

38. "I will follow up mine enemies, and seize them" (v. 37). I will follow up my carnal affections, and will not be seized by them, but will seize them, so that they may be consumed. "And I will not turn, till they fail." And from this purpose I will not turn myself to rest, till they fail who make a tumult about me.

405. Eph 3:19.

39. "I will break them, and they shall not be able to stand" (v. 38): and they shall not hold out against me. "They shall fall under my feet." When they are cast down, I will place before me the loves whereby I walk forevermore.

40. "And Thou hast girded me with strength to the war" (v. 39). And the loose desires of my flesh hast Thou bound up with strength, that in such a fight I may not be encumbered. "Thou hast supplanted under me them that rose up against me." Thou hast caused them to be deceived, who followed upon me, that they should be brought under me, who desired to be over me.

41. "And thou hast given mine enemies the back to me" (v. 40). And thou hast turned mine enemies, and hast made them to be a back to me, that is, to follow me. "And Thou hast destroyed them that hate me." But such other of them as have persisted in hatred, Thou hast destroyed.

42. "They have cried out, and there was none to save them" (v. 41). For who can save them, whom Thou wouldest not save? "To the Lord, and He did not hear them." Nor did they cry out to any chance one, but to the Lord: and He did not judge them worthy of being heard, who depart not from their wickedness.

43. "And I will beat them as small as dust before the face of the wind" (v. 42). And I will beat them small; for dry they are, receiving not the shower of God's mercy; that borne aloft and puffed up with pride they may be hurried along from firm and unshaken hope, and as it were from the earth's solidity and stability. "As the clay of the streets I will destroy them." In their wanton and loose course along the broad ways of perdition, which many walk, will I destroy them.

44. "Thou wilt deliver Me from the contradictions of the people" (v. 43). Thou wilt deliver Me from the contradictions of them who said, "If we send Him away, all the world will go after Him."[406]

45. "Thou shalt make Me the head of the Gentiles. A people whom I have not known have served Me." The people of the Gentiles, whom in bodily presence I have not visited, have served Me. "At the hearing of the ear they have obeyed Me" (v. 44). They have not seen Me with the eye: but, receiving my preachers, at the hearing of the ear they have obeyed Me.

---

406. Jn 11:48, 12:19.

46. "The strange children have lied unto Me." Children, not to be called Mine, but rather strange children, to whom it is rightly said, "Ye are of your father the devil,"[407] have lied unto Me. "The strange children have waxen old" (v. 45). The strange children, to whom for their renovation I brought the new Testament, have remained in the old man. "And they have halted from their own paths." And like those that are weak in one foot, for holding the old they have rejected the new Testament, they have become halt, even in their old Law, rather following their own traditions than God's. For they brought frivolous charges of unwashen hands,[408] because such were the paths, which themselves had made and worn by long use, in wandering from the ways of God's commands.

47. "The Lord liveth, and blessed be my God." "But to be carnally minded is death":[409] for "the Lord liveth, and blessed be my God. And let the God of my salvation be exalted" (v. 46). And let me not think after an earthly fashion of the God of my salvation; nor look from Him for this earthly salvation, but that on high.

48. "O God, who givest Me vengeance, and subduest the people under Me" (v. 47). O God, who avengest Me by subduing the people under Me. "My Deliverer from My angry enemies": the Jews crying out, "Crucify Him, Crucify Him."[410]

49. "From them that rise up against Me Thou wilt exalt Me" (v. 48). From the Jews that rise up against Me in My passion, Thou wilt exalt Me in My resurrection. "From the unjust man Thou wilt deliver Me." From their unjust rule Thou wilt deliver Me.

50. "For this cause will I confess to Thee among the Gentiles, O Lord" (v. 49). For this cause shall the Gentiles confess to Thee through Me, O Lord. "And I will sing unto Thy Name." And Thou shalt be more widely known by My good deeds.

51. "Magnifying the salvation of His King" (v. 50). God, who magnifieth, so as to make wonderful the salvation, which His Son giveth to believers.[411] "And showing mercy to His Christ": God, who showeth mercy to His Christ: "To David and to His seed for evermore": to the Deliverer Himself strong of hand, who hath overcome this world; and to them whom, as believers in the Gospel,

---

407. Jn 8:44.   408. Mt 15:2.   409. Rom 8:6.   410. Jn 19:6.

411. The epigraph of this psalm in 2 Sm 23:1–5 seems to connect with Is 55:3, and so with Acts 13:34.—C.

He hath begotten for evermore. What things soever are spoken in this psalm which cannot apply to the Lord Himself personally, that is to the Head of the Church, must be referred to the Church. For whole Christ speaks here, in whom are all His members.

Psalm 23[412]

A PSALM OF DAVID HIMSELF.

1. The Church speaks to Christ: "The Lord feedeth me, and I shall lack nothing" (v. 1). The Lord Jesus Christ is my Shepherd, "and I shall lack nothing."

2. "In a place of pasture there hath He placed me" (v. 2). In a place of fresh pasture, leading me to faith, there hath He placed me to be nourished. "By the water of refreshing hath He brought me up." By the water of baptism, whereby they are refreshed who have lost health and strength, hath He brought me up.

3. "He hath converted my soul: He hath led me forth in the paths of righteousness, for His Name's sake" (v. 3). He hath brought me forth in the narrow ways, wherein few walk, of His righteousness; not for my merit's sake, but for His Name's sake.

4. "Yea, though I walk in the midst of the shadow of death" (v. 4). Yea, though I walk in the midst of this life, which is the shadow of death.[413] "I will fear no evil, for Thou art with me." I will fear no evil, for Thou dwellest in my heart by faith: and Thou art now with me, that after the shadow of death I too may be with Thee. "Thy rod and Thy staff, they have comforted me." Thy discipline, like a rod for a flock of sheep, and like a staff for children of some size, and growing out of the natural into spiritual life, they have not been grievous to me; rather have they comforted me: because Thou art mindful of me.

5. "Thou hast prepared a table in my sight, against them that trouble me" (v. 5). Now after the rod, whereby, while a little one, and living the natural life, I was brought up among the flock in the pastures; after that rod, I say, when I began to be under the staff,

412. Lat. 22.

413. Note this very comprehensive comment on the real meaning of the valley.—C.

Thou hast prepared a table in my sight, that I should no more be fed as a babe with milk,[414] but being older should take meat, strengthened against them that trouble me. "Thou hast fattened my head with oil." Thou hast gladdened my mind with spiritual joy. "And Thy inebriating cup, how excellent is it!" And Thy cup yielding forgetfulness of former vain delights, how excellent is it!

6. "And Thy mercy shall follow me all the days of my life"; that is, as long as I live in this mortal life, not Thine, but mine. "That I may dwell in the house of the Lord[415] for length of days" (v. 6). Now Thy mercy shall follow me not here only, but also that I may dwell in the house of the Lord forever.

Psalm 26[416]

OF DAVID HIMSELF.

1. It may be attributed to David himself, not the Mediator, the Man Christ Jesus, but the whole Church now perfectly established in Christ.

2. "Judge me, O Lord, for I have walked in my innocence" (v. 1). Judge me, O Lord, for, after the mercy which Thou first showedst me, I have some desert of my innocence, the way whereof I have kept. "And trusting in the Lord I shall not be moved." And yet not even so trusting in myself, but in the Lord, I shall abide in Him.

3. "Prove me, O Lord, and try me" (v. 2). Lest, however, any of my secret sins should be hid from me, prove me, O Lord, and try me, making me known, not to Thee from whom nothing is hid, but to myself, and to men. "Burn my reins and my heart." Apply a remedial purgation, as it were fire, to my pleasures and thoughts. "For Thy mercy is before mine eyes" (v. 3). For, that I be not consumed by that fire, not my merits, but Thy mercy, whereby Thou hast brought me on to such a life, is before my eyes. "And I have been pleasing in Thy truth." And since my own falsehood hath

414. 1 Cor 3:2.

415. He applies the figures of v. 5 and here to the Lord's Table, the chrism (i.e., confirmation), and the Church in time and eternity.—C.

416. Lat. 25.

been displeasing to me, but Thy truth pleasing, I have myself been pleasing also with it and in it.

4. "I have not sat with the council of vanity" (v. 4). I have not chosen to give my heart to them who endeavor to provide, what is impossible, how they may be blessed in the enjoyment of things transitory. "And I will not enter in with them that work wickedly." And since this is the very cause of all wickedness, therefore I will not have my conscience hid, with them that work wickedly.

5. "I have hated the congregation of evildoers." But to arrive at this council of vanity, congregations of evildoers are formed, which I have hated. "And I will not sit with the ungodly" (v. 5). And, therefore, with such a council, with the ungodly, I will not sit, that is, I will not place my consent. "And I will not sit with the ungodly."

6. "I will wash mine hands amid the innocent" (v. 6). I will make clean my works among the innocent: among the innocent will I wash mine hands, with which I shall embrace Thy glorious gifts. "And I will compass Thy altar, O Lord."

7. "That I may hear the voice of Thy praise." That I may learn how to praise Thee. "And that I may declare all Thy wondrous works" (v. 7). And after I have learned, I may set forth all Thy wondrous works.

8. "O Lord, I have loved the beauty of Thy house"; of Thy Church. "And the place of the habitation of Thy glory" (v. 8): where Thou dwellest, and art glorified.

9. "Destroy not my soul with the ungodly" (v. 9). Destroy not then, together with them that hate Thee, my soul, which hath loved the beauty of Thy house. "And my life with the men of blood." And with them that hate their neighbor. For Thy house is beautified with the two commandments.[417]

10. "In whose hands is wickedness." Destroy me not then with the ungodly and the men of blood, whose works are wicked. "Their right hand is full of gifts" (v. 10). And that which was given them to obtain eternal salvation, they have converted into the receiving this world's gifts, "supposing that godliness is a trade."[418]

11. "But I have walked in mine innocence: deliver me, and have mercy on me" (v. 11). Let so great a price of my Lord's Blood avail

417. Mt 22:40.—C.   418. 1 Tm 6:5.

for my complete deliverance: and in the dangers of this life let not Thy mercy leave me.

12. "My foot hath stood in uprightness." My Love hath not withdrawn from Thy righteousness. "In the Churches I will bless Thee, O Lord" (v. 12). I will not hide Thy blessing, O Lord, from those whom Thou hast called; for next to the love of Thee I join the love of my neighbor.

Psalm 27[419]

OF DAVID HIMSELF, BEFORE HE WAS ANOINTED.[420]

1. Christ's young soldier speaketh, on his coming to the faith. "The Lord is my light, and my salvation: whom shall I fear?" (v. 1). The Lord will give me both knowledge of Himself, and salvation: who shall take me from Him? "The Lord is the Protector of my life: of whom shall I be afraid?" The Lord will repel all the assaults and snares of mine enemy: of no man shall I be afraid.

2. "Whilst the guilty approach unto me to eat up my flesh" (v. 2). While the guilty come near to recognize and insult me, that they may exalt themselves above me in my change for the better; that with their reviling tooth they may consume not me, but rather my fleshly desires. "Mine enemies who trouble me." Not they only who trouble me, blaming me with a friendly intent, and wishing to recall me from my purpose, but mine enemies also. "They became weak, and fell."[421] While then they do this with the desire of defending their own opinion, they became weak to believe better things, and began to hate the word of salvation, whereby I do what displeases them.

3. "If camps stand together against me, my heart will not fear." But if the multitude of gainsayers conspire to stand together

419. Lat. 26.

420. In the Second Exposition he dwells on the spiritual *chrism*, from which the Son of David is called *Christ*; affirms that Christians partake of the same anointing; speaking of confirmation as their sacramental anointing and what it implies.—C.

421. A minute prophecy. Jn 18:6.—C.

against me, my heart will not fear, so as to go over to their side. "If war rise up against me, in this will I trust" (v. 3). If the persecution of this world arise against me, in this petition, which I am pondering, will I place my hope.

4. "One have I asked of the Lord, this will I require." For one petition have I asked the Lord, this will I require. "That I may dwell in the house of the Lord all the days of my life" (v. 4). That as long as I am in this life, no adversities may exclude me from the number of them who hold the unity and the truth of the Lord's faith throughout the world. "That I may contemplate the delight of the Lord." With this end, namely, that persevering in the faith, the delightsome vision may appear to me, which I may contemplate face to face. "And I shall be protected, His temple." And death being swallowed up in victory, I shall be clothed with immortality, being made His temple.[422]

5. "For He hath hidden me in His tabernacle in the day of my evils" (v. 5). For He hath hidden me in the dispensation of His Incarnate Word in the time of temptations, to which my mortal life is exposed. "He hath protected me in the secret place of His tabernacle." He hath protected me with the heart believing unto righteousness.

6. "On a rock hath He exalted me." And that what I believed might be made manifest for salvation, He hath made my confession to be conspicuous in His own strength. "And now, lo! He hath exalted mine head above mine enemies" (v. 6). What doth He reserve for me at the last, when even now the body is dead because of sin, lo! I feel that my mind serves the law of God, and is not led captive under the rebellious law of sin? "I have gone about, and have sacrificed in His tabernacle the sacrifice of rejoicing." I have considered the circuit of the world, believing on Christ; and in that for us God was humbled in time, I have praised Him with rejoicing: for with such sacrifice He is well pleased. "I will sing and give praises to the Lord." In heart and in deed I will be glad in the Lord.

7. "Hear my voice, O Lord, wherewith I have cried unto Thee" (v. 7). Hear, Lord, my interior voice, which with a strong intention I have addressed to Thy ears. "Have mercy upon me, and hear me." Have mercy upon me, and hear me therein.

---

422. The Old Latin of this charming verse seems to have read, "One hope have I desired," etc.—C.

8. "My heart hath said to Thee, I have sought Thy countenance" (v. 8). For I have not exhibited myself to men; but in secret, where Thou alone hearest, my heart hath said to Thee; I have not sought from Thee aught without Thee as a reward, but Thy countenance. "Thy countenance, O Lord, will I seek." In thus search will I perseveringly persist: for not aught that is common, but Thy countenance, O Lord, will I seek, that I may love Thee freely, since nothing more precious do I find.

9. "Turn not away Thy face from me" (v. 9): that I may find what I seek. "Turn not aside in anger from Thy servant": lest while seeking Thee, I fall in with somewhat else. For what is more grievous than this punishment to one who loveth and seeketh the truth of Thy countenance? "Be Thou my Helper." How shall I find it, if Thou help me not? "Leave me not, neither despise me, O God my Savior." Scorn not that a mortal dares to seek the Eternal; for Thou, God, dost heal the wound of my sin.

10. "For my father and my mother have left me" (v. 10). For the kingdom of this world and the city of this world, of which I was born in time and mortality, have left me seeking Thee, and despising what they promised, since they could not give what I seek. "But the Lord took me up." But the Lord, who can give me Himself, took me up.

11. "Appoint me a law, O Lord, in Thy way" (v. 11). For me then who am setting out toward Thee, and commenting so great a profession, of arriving at wisdom, from fear, appoint, O Lord, a law in Thy way, lest in my wandering Thy rule abandon me. "And direct me in the right path because of mine enemies." And direct me in the right way of its straits. For it is not enough to begin, since enemies cease not until the end is attained.

12. "Deliver me not up unto the souls of them that trouble me" (v. 12). Suffer not them that trouble me to be satiated with my evils. "For unrighteous witnesses have risen up against me." For there have risen up against me they that speak falsely of me, to remove and call me back from Thee, as if I seek glory of men. "And iniquity hath lied unto itself." Therefore iniquity hath been pleased with its own lie. For me it hath not moved, to whom because of this there hath been promised a greater reward in heaven.

13. "I believe to see the good things of the Lord in the land of the living" (v. 13). And since my Lord hath first suffered these things, if

I too despise the tongues of the dying ("for the mouth that lieth slayeth the soul"),[423] I believe to see the good things of the Lord in the land of the living, where there is no place for falsity.

14. "Wait on the Lord, quit thyself like a man: and let thy heart be strong, yea wait on the Lord" (v. 14). But when shall this be? It is arduous for a mortal, it is slow to a lover: but listen to the voice, that deceiveth not, of him that saith, "Wait on the Lord." Endure the burning of the reins manfully, and the burning of the heart stoutly. Think not that what thou dost not as yet receive is denied thee. That thou faint not in despair, see how it is said, "Wait on the Lord."

Psalm 30[424]

TO THE END, THE PSALM OF THE CANTICLE[425] OF THE DEDI-
CATION OF THE HOUSE, OF DAVID HIMSELF.

1. To the end, a psalm of the joy of the resurrection, and the change, the renewing of the body to an immortal state, and not only of the Lord, but also of the whole Church. For in the former psalm the tabernacle was finished, wherein we dwell in the time of war: but now the house is dedicated, which will abide in peace everlasting.

2. It is then whole Christ who speaketh. "I will exalt Thee, O Lord, for Thou hast taken Me up" (v. 1). I will praise Thy high Majesty, O Lord, for Thou hast taken Me up. "Thou hast not made Mine enemies to rejoice over Me." And those who have so often endeavored to oppress Me with various persecutions throughout the world, Thou hast not made to rejoice over Me.

3. "O Lord, My God, I have cried unto Thee, and Thou hast healed Me" (v. 2). O Lord, My God, I have cried unto Thee, and I no longer bear about a body enfeebled and sick by mortality.

4. "O Lord, Thou hast brought back My Soul from hell, and Thou hast saved Me from them that go down into the pit" (v. 3). Thou hast saved Me from the condition of profound darkness, and the lowest slough of corruptible flesh.

---

423. Ws 1:11.   424. Lat. 29.

425. A *shir*, or "song." So Psalm 18 = *shirah*, the only two instances in the first division of the Psalter, forty-one psalms.—C.

5. "Sing to the Lord, O ye saints of His." The prophet seeing these future things, rejoiceth, and saith, "Sing to the Lord, O ye saints of His. And make confession of the remembrance of His holiness" (v. 4). And make confession to Him, that He hath not forgotten the sanctification, wherewith He hath sanctified you, although all this intermediate period belong to your desires.

6. "For in His indignation is wrath" (v. 5). For He hath avenged against you the first sin, for which you have paid by death. "And life in His will." And life eternal, whereunto you could not return by any strength of your own, hath He given, because He so would. "In the evening weeping will tarry." Evening began, when the light of wisdom withdrew from sinful man, when he was condemned to death: from this evening weeping will tarry, as long as God's people are, amid labors and temptations, awaiting the day of the Lord. "And exultation in the morning." Even to the morning, when there will be the exultation of the resurrection, which hath shone forth by anticipation in the morning resurrection of the Lord.

7. "But I said in my abundance, I shall not be moved for ever" (v. 6). But I, that people which was speaking from the first, said in mine abundance, suffering now no more any want, "I shall not be moved for ever."

8. "O Lord, in Thy will Thou hast afforded strength unto my beauty" (v. 7). But that this my abundance, O Lord is not of myself, but that in Thy will Thou hast afforded strength unto my beauty, I have learned from this, "Thou turnedst away Thy Face from me, and I became troubled"; for Thou hast sometimes turned away Thy Face from the sinner, and I became troubled, when the illumination of Thy knowledge withdrew from me.

9. "Unto Thee, O Lord, will I cry, and unto my God will I pray" (v. 8). And bringing to mind that time of my trouble and misery, and as it were established therein, I hear the voice of Thy First-Begotten, my Head, about to die for me, and saying "Unto Thee, O Lord, will I cry, and unto My God will I pray."

10. "What profit" is there in the shedding of My blood, while I go down to corruption? "Shall dust confess unto Thee?" For if I shall not rise immediately, and My body shall become corrupt, "shall dust confess unto Thee?" that is, the crowd of the ungodly, whom I shall justify by My resurrection? "Or declare Thy truth?" Or for the salvation of the rest declare Thy truth?

11. "The Lord hath heard, and had mercy on Me, the Lord hath become My helper." Nor did "He suffer His Holy One to see corruption"[426] (v. 10).

12. "Thou hast turned My mourning into joy to Me" (v. 11). Whom I, the Church, having received, the First-Begotten from the dead,[427] now in the dedication of Thine house, say, "Thou hast turned my mourning into joy to me. Thou hast put off my sackcloth, and girded me with gladness." Thou hast torn off the veil of my sins, the sadness of my mortality; and hast girded me with the first robe, with immortal gladness.

13. "That my glory should sing unto Thee, and I should not be pricked" (v. 12). That now, not my humiliation, but my glory should not lament, but should sing unto Thee, for that now out of humiliation Thou hast exalted me; and that I should not be pricked with the consciousness of sin, with the fear of death, with the fear of judgment. "O Lord, my God, I will confess unto Thee for ever." And this is my glory, O Lord, my God, that I should confess unto Thee forever, that I have nothing of myself, but that all my good is of Thee, who art "God, All in all."[428]

Psalm 31[429]

TO THE END, A PSALM OF DAVID HIMSELF, AN ECSTASY.[430]

1. To the end, a psalm of David Himself, the Mediator strong of hand in persecutions. For the word ecstasy, which is added to the title, signifies a transport of the mind, which is produced either by a panic, or by some revelation. But in this psalm the panic of the people of God troubled by the persecution of all the heathen, and by the failing of faith throughout the world, is principally seen. But first the Mediator Himself speaks: then the People redeemed by His Blood gives thanks: at last in trouble it speaks at length, which

426. Ps 26:10.   427. Rv 1:5.

428. 1 Cor 15:28. This psalm was used at Easter and Pentecost.—C.

429. Lat. 30.

430. Borrowed from the Septuagint, where it is anticipated from v. 22.—C.

is what belongs to the ecstasy; but the Person of the Prophet himself is twice interposed, near the end, and at the end.

2. "In Thee, O Lord, have I trusted, let Me not be put to confusion for ever" (v. 1). In Thee, O Lord, have I trusted, let Me never be confounded, while they shall insult Me as one like other men. "In Thy righteousness rescue Me, and deliver Me." And in Thy righteousness rescue Me from the pit of death, and deliver Me out of their company.

3. "Bend down Thine ear unto Me" (v. 2). Hear Me in My humiliation, nigh at hand unto Me. "Make haste to deliver Me." Defer not to the end of the world, as with all who believe on Me, My separation from sinners. "Be unto Me a God who protecteth Me." Be unto Me God, and Protector. "And a house of refuge, that Thou mayest save Me." And as a house, wherein taking refuge I may be saved.

4. "For Thou art My strength, and My refuge" (v. 3). For Thou art unto Me My strength to bear My persecutors, and My refuge to escape them. "And for Thy Name's sake Thou shalt be My guide, and shalt nourish Me." And that by Me Thou mayest be known to all the Gentiles. I will in all things follow Thy will; and, by assembling, by degrees, Saints unto Me, Thou shalt fulfill My body, and My perfect stature.

5. "Thou shalt bring Me out of this trap, which they have hidden for Me" (v. 4). Thou shalt bring Me out of these snares, which they have hidden for Me. "For Thou art My Protector."

6. "Into Thy hands I commend My Spirit" (v. 5). To Thy power I commend My Spirit, soon to receive It back. "Thou hast redeemed Me, O Lord God of truth." Let the people too, redeemed by the Passion of their Lord, and joyful in the glorifying of their Head, say, "Thou hast redeemed me, O Lord God of truth."

7. "Thou hatest them that hold to vanity uselessly" (v. 6). Thou hatest them that hold to the false happiness of the world. "But I have trusted in the Lord."

8. "I will be glad, and rejoice in Thy mercy": which doth not deceive me. "For Thou hast regarded My humiliation": wherein Thou hast subjected me to vanity in hope.[431] "Thou hast saved my soul from necessities" (v. 7). Thou hast saved my soul from the necessities of fear, that with a free love it may serve Thee.

431. Rom 8:20.

9. "And hast not shut me up into the hands of the enemy" (v. 8). And hast not shut me up, that I should have no opening for recovering unto liberty, and be given over forever into the power of the devil, ensnaring me with the desire of this life, and terrifying me with death. "Thou hast set my feet in a large room." The resurrection of my Lord being known, and mine own being promised me, my love, having been brought out of the straits of fear, walks abroad in continuance, into the expanse of liberty.

10. "Have mercy on me, O Lord, for I am troubled" (v. 9). But what is this unlooked-for cruelty of the persecutors, striking such dread into me? "Have mercy on me, O Lord." For I am now no more alarmed for death, but for torments and tortures. "Mine eye hath been disordered by anger." I had mine eye upon Thee, that Thou shouldest not abandon me: Thou art angry, and hast disordered it. "My soul, and my belly." By the same anger my soul hath been disturbed, and my memory, whereby I retained what my God hath suffered for me, and what He hath promised me.

11. "For my life hath failed in pain" (v. 10). For my life is to confess Thee, but it failed in pain, when the enemy had said, Let them be tortured until they deny Him. "And my years in groanings." The time that I pass in this world is not taken away from me by death, but abides, and is spent in groanings. "My strength hath been weakened by want." I want the health of this body, and racking pains come on me: I want the dissolution of the body, and death forbears to come: and in this want my confidence hath been weakened. "And my bones have been disturbed." And my steadfastness hath been disturbed.

12. "I have been made a reproach above all mine enemies" (v. 11). All the wicked are my enemies; and nevertheless they for their wickednesses are tortured only till they confess: I then have over-passed their reproach, I, whose confession death doth not follow, but racking pains follow upon it. "And to my neighbors too much." This hath seemed too much to them, who were already drawing near to know Thee, and to hold the faith that I hold. "And a fear to mine acquaintance." And into my very acquaintance I struck fear by the example of my dreadful tribulation. "They that did see me, fled without from me." Because they did not understand my inward and invisible hope, they fled from me into things outward and visible.

13. "I have been forgotten, as one dead from the heart" (v. 12). And they have forgotten me, as if I were dead from their hearts. "I have become as a lost vessel." I have seemed to myself to be lost to all the Lord's service, living in this world, and gaining none, when all were afraid to join themselves unto me.

14. "For I have heard the rebuking of many dwelling by in a circuit" (v. 13). For I have heard many rebuking me, in the pilgrimage of this world near me, following the circuit of time, and refusing to return with me to the eternal country. "Whilst they were assembling themselves together against me, they conspired that they might take my soul." That my soul, which should by death easily escape from their power, might consent unto them, they imagined a device, whereby they would not suffer me even to die.

15. "But I have hoped in Thee, O Lord; I have said, Thou art my God" (v. 14). For Thou hast not changed, that Thou shouldest not save, Who dost correct.

16. "In Thy hands" are "my lots" (v. 15). In Thy power are my lots. For I see no desert for which out of the universal ungodliness of the human race Thou hast elected me particularly to salvation. And though there be with Thee some just and secret order in my election, yet I, from whom this is hid, have attained by lot unto my Lord's vesture.[432] "Deliver me from the hands of mine enemies, and from them that persecute me."

17. "Make Thy Face to shine upon Thy servant" (v. 16). Make it known to men, who do not think that I belong unto Thee, that Thy Face is bent upon me, and that I serve Thee. "Save me in Thy mercy."

18. "O Lord, let me not be confounded, for I have called upon Thee" (v. 17). O Lord, let me not be put to shame by those who insult me, for that I have called upon Thee. "Let the ungodly be ashamed, and be brought down to hell." Let them rather who call upon stones be ashamed, and made to dwell with darkness.

19. "Let the deceitful lips be made dumb" (v. 18). In making known to the peoples Thy mysteries wrought in me, strike with dumb amazement the lips of them that invent falsehood of me. "Which speak iniquity against the Righteous, in pride and contempt." Which speak iniquity against Christ, in their pride and contempt of Him as a crucified man.

432. Jn 19:24.

20. "How great" is "the multitude of Thy sweetness, O Lord" (v. 19). Here the Prophet exclaims, having sight of all this, and admiring how manifoldly plenteous is Thy sweetness, O Lord. "Which Thou hast hid for them that fear Thee." Even those, whom Thou correctest, Thou lovest much: but lest they should go on negligently from relaxed security, Thou hidest from them the sweetness of Thy love, for whom it is profitable to fear Thee. "Thou hast perfected it for them that hope in Thee." But Thou hast perfected this sweetness for them that hope in Thee. For Thou dost not withdraw from them what they look for perseveringly even unto the end. "In sight of the sons of men." For it does not escape the notice of the sons of men, who now live no more after Adam, but after the Son of Man. "Thou wilt hide them in the hidden place of Thy Countenance": which seat Thou shalt preserve for everlasting in the hidden place of the knowledge of Thee for them that hope in Thee. "From the troubling of men." So that now they suffer no more trouble from men.

21. "Thou wilt protect them in Thy tabernacle from the contradiction of tongues" (v. 20). But here meanwhile while evil tongues murmur against them, saying, Who hath come thence? Thou wilt protect them in the tabernacle, that of faith in those things, which the Lord wrought and endured for us in time.

22. "Blessed be the Lord; for He hath made His mercy marvelous, in the city of compassing" (v. 21). Blessed be the Lord, for after the correction of the sharpest persecutions He hath made His mercy marvelous to all throughout the world, in the circuit of human society.

23. "I said in my ecstasy"[433] (v. 22). Whence that people again speaking saith, I said in my fear, when the heathen were raging horribly against me. "I have been cast forth from the sight of Thine eyes." For if Thou hadst regard to me, Thou wouldest not suffer me to endure these things. "Therefore Thou heardest, O Lord, the voice of my prayer, when I cried unto Thee." Therefore putting a limit to correction, and showing that I have part in Thy care, Thou heardest, O Lord, the voice of my prayer, when I raised it high out of tribulation.

---

433. Elsewhere St. Augustine explains the word "ecstasy" as sometimes = transport, sometimes = panic.—C.

24. "Love the Lord, all ye His saints" (v. 23). The Prophet again exhorts, having sight of these things, and saith, "Love the Lord, all ye His saints; for the Lord will require truth." Since "if the righteous shall scarcely be saved, where shall the sinner and the ungodly appear?"[434] "And He will repay them that do exceeding proudly." And He will repay them who even when conquered are not converted, because they are very proud.

25. "Quit you like men, and let your heart be strengthened" (v. 24): working good without fainting, that ye may reap in due season. "All ye who trust in the Lord": that is, ye who duly fear and worship Him, trust ye in the Lord.

Psalm 36[435]

1. "The ungodly hath said in himself that he will sin: there is no fear of God before his eyes" (v. 1). Not of one man, but of a race of ungodly men he speaketh, who fight against their own selves, by not understanding, that so they may live well; not because they cannot, but because they will not. For it is one thing, when one endeavors to understand some thing, and through infirmity of flesh cannot; as saith the Scripture[436] in a certain place, "For the corruptible body presseth down the soul, and the earthly tabernacle weigheth down the mind that museth upon many things"; but another when the human heart acts mischievously against itself, so that what it could understand, if it had but good will thereto, it understandeth not, not because it is difficult, but because the will is contrary. But so it is when men love their own sins, and hate God's Commandments. For the Word of God is thy adversary, if thou be a friend to thy ungodliness; but if thou art an adversary to thy ungodliness, the Word of God is thy friend, as well as the adversary of thy ungodliness.

2. "For he hath wrought deceitfully in His sight" (v. 2). In whose sight? In His, whose fear was not before the eyes of him that did

---

434. Pt 4:18. 435. Lat. 35.

436. Ws 9:15. Here cited as Scripture, but only deuterocanonical (as St. Jerome testifies), illustrating the Law and the Prophets, but not of authority in itself.—C.

work deceitfully. "To find out his iniquity, and hate it." He wrought so as not to find it. For there are men who as it were endeavor to seek out the iniquity, and fear to find it; because if they should find it, it is said to them, Depart from it: this thou didst before thou knewest; thou didst iniquity being in ignorance; God giveth pardon: now thou hast discovered it, forsake it, that to thy ignorance pardon may easily be given; and that with a clear face thou mayest say to God, "Remember not the sins of my youth, and of my ignorance."[437] Thus he seeketh it, thus he feareth lest he find it; for he seeketh it deceitfully. When saith a man, I knew not that it was sin? When he hath seen that it is sin, and ceaseth to do the sin, which he did only because he was ignorant: such a one in truth would know his sin, to find it out, and hate it. But now many "work deceitfully to find out their iniquity": they work not from their heart to find it out and hate it. But because in the very search after iniquity, there is deceit, in the finding it there will be defense of it. For when one hath found his iniquity, lo, now it is manifest to him that it is iniquity. Do it not, thou sayest. And he who wrought deceitfully to find it out, now he hath found, hateth it not; for what saith he? How many do this! Who is there that doth it not? And will God destroy them all? Or at least he saith this: if God would not these things to be done, would men live who commit the same? Seest thou that thou didst work deceitfully to find out thy iniquity? For if not deceitfully but sincerely thou hadst wrought, thou wouldest now have found it out, and hated it; now thou hast found it out, and thou defendest it; therefore thou didst work deceitfully, when thou soughtest it.

3. "The words of his mouth are iniquity and deceit: he would not understand, that he might do good" (v. 3). Ye see that he attributeth that to the will: for there are men who would understand and cannot, and there are men who would not understand, and therefore understand not. "He would not understand, that he might do good."

4. "He hath meditated iniquity on his bed." What said He, "On his bed" (v. 4)? "The ungodly hath said in himself, that he will sin": what above he said, in himself, that here he said, "On his bed." Our bed is our heart: there we suffer the tossing of an evil conscience;

437. Ps 25:7.

and there we rest when our conscience is good. Whoso loveth the bed of his heart, let him do some good therein. There is our bed, where the Lord Jesus Christ commands us to pray. "Enter into thy chamber, and shut thy door."[438] What is, "Shut thy door"? Expect not from God such things as are without, but such as are within; "and thy Father which seeth in secret, shall reward thee openly." Who is he that shutteth not the door? He who asketh much from God such things, and in such wise directeth all his prayers, that he may receive the goods that are of this world. Thy door is open, the multitude seeth when thou prayest. What is it to shut thy door? To ask that of God, which God alone knoweth how He giveth. What is that for which thou prayest, when thou hast shut the door? What "eye hath not seen, nor ear heard, or hath entered into the heart of man."[439] And haply it hath not entered into thy very bed, that is, into thy heart. But God knoweth what He will give: but when shall it be? When the Lord shall be revealed, when the Judge shall appear.

5. "He hath set himself in every way that is not good." What is, "he hath set himself"? He hath sinned perseveringly. Whence also of a certain pious and good man it is said, "He hath not stood in the way of sinners."[440] As this "hath not stood," so that "hath set himself." "But wickedness hath he not hated." There is the end, there the fruit: if a man cannot but have wickedness, let him at least hate it. For when thou hatest it, it scarcely occurs to thee to do any wickedness. For sin is in our mortal body, but what saith the apostle? "Let not sin reign in your mortal body, that ye should obey it in the lusts thereof."[441] When beginneth it not to be therein? When that shall be fulfilled in us which he saith, "When this corruptible shall have put on incorruption, and this mortal shall have put on immortality."[442] Before this comes to pass, there is a delighting in sin in the body, but greater is the delighting and the pleasure in the Word of Wisdom, in the Commandment of God. Overcome sin and the lust thereof. Sin and iniquity do thou hate, that thou mayest join thyself to God, who hateth it as well as thou. Now being joined in mind unto the Law of God, in mind thou servest the Law of God. And if in the flesh thou therefore servest the law

438. Mt 6:6.   439. Is 64:4; 1 Cor 2:9.   440. Ps 1:1.   441. Rom 6:12.

442. 1 Cor 15:54.

of sin,[443] because there are in thee certain carnal delightings, then will there be none when thou shalt no longer fight. It is one thing not to fight, and to be in true and lasting peace; another to fight and overcome; another to fight and to be overcome; another not to fight at all, but to be carried away.

6. "Thy mercy, O Lord, is in the heavens, and Thy truth reacheth even unto the clouds" (v. 5). I know not what Mercy of Him he meaneth, which is in the heavens. For the Mercy of the Lord is also in the earth. Thou hast it written, "The earth is full of the Mercy of the Lord."[444] Of what Mercy then speaketh He, when He saith, "Thy Mercy, O Lord, is in the heavens"? The gifts of God are partly temporal and earthly, partly eternal and heavenly. Whoso for this worshippeth God, that he may receive those temporal and earthly goods, which are open to all, is still as it were like the brutes: he enjoyeth indeed the Mercy of God, but not that which is excepted, which shall not be given, save only to the righteous, to the holy, to the good. What are the gifts which abound to all? "He maketh His sun to rise on the evil and on the good, and sendeth rain on the just and on the unjust."[445] Who hath not this Mercy of God, first that he hath being, that he is distinguished from the brutes, that he is a rational animal, so as to understand God; second, that he enjoys this light, this air, rain, fruits, diversity of seasons, and all the earthly comforts, health of body, the affection of friends, the safety of his family? All these are good, and they are God's gifts.

7. But this man rightly understood what mercy he should pray for from God. "Thy Mercy, O Lord, is in the heavens; and Thy Truth reacheth even to the clouds." That is, the Mercy which Thou givest to Thy saints, is heavenly, not earthly; is eternal, not temporal. And how couldest Thou declare it unto men? Because "Thy Truth reacheth even unto the clouds." For who could know the heavenly Mercy of God, unless God should declare it unto men? How did He declare it? By sending His truth even unto the clouds. What are the clouds? The preachers of the Word of God. . . . Truth reached even to the clouds: therefore unto us could be de-

---

443. I.e., "art subject to it," not "obeyest it." He is not here speaking of actual willful sin, but of motions toward sin to which the man does not consent; Rom 7:25.

444. Ps 5.   445. Mt 5:45.

clared the Mercy of God, which is in heaven and not in earth. And truly, Brethren, the clouds are the preachers of the Word of Truth. When God threateneth through His preachers, He thunders through the clouds. When God worketh miracles through His preachers, He lightneth through the clouds, He terrifieth through the clouds, and watereth by the rain. Those preachers, then, by whom is preached the Gospel of God, are the clouds of God. Let us then hope for Mercy, but for that which is in the heavens.

8. "Thy Righteousness is like the mountains of God: Thy Judgments are a great deep" (v. 6). Who are the mountains of God? Those who are called clouds, the same are also the mountains of God. The great preachers are the mountains of God. And as when the sun riseth, he first clothes the mountains with light, and thence the light descends to the lowest parts of the earth: so our Lord Jesus Christ, when He came, first irradiated the height of the apostles, first enlightened the mountains, and so His Light descended to the valley of the world. And therefore saith He in a certain psalm, "I lifted up mine eyes unto the mountains, from whence cometh my help."[446] But think not that the mountains themselves will give thee help: for they receive what they may give, give not of their own. And if thou remain in the mountains, thy hope will not be strong: but in Him who enlighteneth the mountains, ought to be thy hope and presumption. Thy help indeed will come to thee through the mountains, because the Scriptures are administered to thee through the mountains, through the great preachers of the Truth: but fix not thy hope in them. Hear what He saith next following: "I lifted up mine eyes unto the mountains, from whence cometh my help." What then? Do the mountains give thee help? No; hear what follows, "My help cometh from the Lord, which made Heaven and earth."[447] Through the mountains cometh help, but not from the mountains. From whom then? "From the Lord, which made Heaven and earth."

9. "Thy Judgments are like the great abyss." The abyss he calleth the depth of sin, whither everyone cometh by despising God; as in a certain place it is said, "God gave them over to their own hearts' lusts, to do the things which are not convenient."[448] . . . Because then they were proud and ungrateful, they were held worthy to be

446. Ps 121:1.   447. Ps 121:2.   448. Rom 1:28.

delivered up to the lusts of their own hearts, and became a great abyss, so that they not only sinned, but also worked craftily, lest they should understand their iniquity, and hate it. That is the depth of wickedness, to be unwilling to find it out and to hate it. But how one cometh to that depth, see; "Thy Judgments are the great abyss." As the mountains are by the Righteousness of God,[449] who through His Grace become great: so also through His Judgments come they unto the depth, who sink lowest. By this then let the mountains delight thee, by this turn away from the abyss, and turn thyself unto that, of which it is said, "My help cometh from the Lord." But whereby? "I have lifted up mine eyes unto the mountains." What meaneth this? I will speak plainly. In the Church of God thou findest an abyss, thou findest also mountains; thou findest there but few good, because the mountains are few, the abyss broad; that is, thou findest many living ill after the wrath of God, because they have so worked that they are delivered up to the lusts of their own heart; so now they defend their sins and confess them not; but say, Why? What have I done? Such a one did this and such a one did that. Now will they even defend what the Divine Word reproves. This is the abyss. Therefore in a certain place[450] saith the Scripture (hear this abyss), "The sinner when he cometh unto the depth of sin despiseth." See, "Thy Judgments are like the great abyss." But yet not art thou a mountain; not yet art thou in the abyss; fly from the abyss, tend toward the mountains; but yet remain not on the mountains. "For thy help cometh from the Lord, which made Heaven and earth."

10. Because he said, Thy Mercy is in the heavens, that it may be known to be also on earth, he said, "O Lord, Thou savest man and beast,[451] as Thy Mercy is multiplied, O God" (v. 7). Great is Thy Mercy, and manifold is Thy Mercy, O God; and that showest Thou both to man and beast. For from whom is the saving of men? From God. Is not the saving of beasts also from God? For He who made man, made also beasts; He who made both, saveth both; but the saving of beasts is temporal. But there are who as a great thing ask

---

449. Alternatively, "The Righteousness of God is like the mountains."

450. Prv 18:3.

451. In Vulgate and Septuagint this is included in verse 6. The English version agrees with the text as here connected.—C.

this of God, which He hath given to beasts. "Thy Mercy, O God, is multiplied," so that not only unto men, but unto beasts also is given the same saving which is given to men, a carnal and temporal saving.

11. Have not men then somewhat reserved with God, which beasts deserve not, and whereunto beasts arrive not? They have evidently. And where is that which they have. "The children of men put their trust under the shadow of Thy wings." Attend, my Beloved, to this most pleasant sentence: "Thou savest man and beast." First, he spake of "man and beast," then of "the children of men"; as though "men" were one, "the children of men" other. Sometimes in Scripture children of men is said generally of all men, sometimes in some proper manner, with some proper signification, so that not all men are understood; chiefly when there is a distinction. For not without reason is it here put, "O Lord, Thou savest man and beast: but the children of men"; as though setting aside the first, he keepeth separate the children of men. Separate from whom? Not only from beasts, but also from men, who seek from God the saving of beasts, and desire this as a great thing. Who then are the children of men? Those who put their trust under the shadow of His wings. For those men together with beasts rejoice in possession, but the children of men rejoice in hope: those follow after present goods with beasts, these hope for future goods with Angels.

12. "They shall be satiated[452] with the fullness of Thy House" (v. 8). He promiseth us some great thing. He would speak it, and He speaketh it not. Can He not, or do not we receive it? I dare, my Brethren, to say, even of holy tongues and hearts, by which Truth is declared to us, that it can neither be spoken, which they declared, nor even thought of. For it is a great thing, and ineffable; and even they saw through a glass darkly, as saith the apostle, "For now we see through a glass darkly; but then face to face."[453] Lo, they who saw through a glass darkly, thus burst forth. What then shall we be, when we shall see face to face? That with which they travailed in heart, and could not with their tongue bring forth, that men might receive it. For what necessity was there that he should say, "They shall be satiated with the fullness of Thy House"? He sought a

452. I cannot but change the word "drunken" here for one more decent and equally faithful.—C.

453. 1 Cor 13:12.

word whereby to express from human things what he would say, and because he saw that men drowning themselves in drunkenness receive indeed wine without measure, but lose their senses, he saw what to say; for when shall have been received that ineffable joy, then shall be lost in a manner the human soul, it shall become Divine, and be satiated with the fullness of God's House. Wherefore also in another psalm it is said, "Thy cup inebriating, how excellent is it!"[454] With this cup were the martyrs satiated when going to their passion, they knew not their own. What so inebriated as not to know a wife weeping, not children, not parents? They knew them not, they thought not that they were before their eyes. Wonder not: they were inebriated. Wherewith were they so? Lo, they had received a cup wherewith they were satiated. Wherefore he also gives thanks to God, saying, "What shall I render unto the Lord for all His benefits toward me? I will take the cup of Salvation, and call upon the Name of the Lord."[455] Therefore, Brethren of men, let us be children and let us trust under the shadow of His wings and be satiated with the fullness of His House. As I could, I have spoken; and as far as I can I see, and how far I see, I cannot speak. "And of the torrent of Thy Pleasure shalt Thou give them to drink." A torrent we call water coming with a flood. There will be a flood of God's Mercy to overflow and inebriate those who now put their trust under the shadow of His wings. What is that Pleasure? As it were a torrent inebriating the thirsty. Let him then who thirsts now, lay up hope: whoso thirsts now, let him have hope; when inebriated, he shall have possession: before he have possession, let him thirst in hope. "Blessed are they which do hunger and thirst after righteousness, for they shall be filled."[456]

13. With what fountain then wilt thou be overflowed, and whence runneth such a torrent of His pleasure? "For with Thee," saith he, "is the fountain of Life." What is the fountain of Life, but Christ? He came to thee in the flesh, that He might bedew thy thirsty lips: He will satisfy thee trusting, who bedewed thee thirsting. "For with Thee is the fountain of Life; in Thy Light shall we see light" (v. 9). Here a fountain is one thing, light another: there not so. For that which is the Fountain, the same is also Light: and whatever thou wilt thou callest It, for It is not what thou callest It: for thou

454. Ps 23:5 (Septuagint).   455. Ps 116:12, 13.   456. Mt 5:6.

canst not find a fit name: for It remaineth not in one name. If thou shouldest say, that It is Light only, it would be said to thee, Then without cause am I told to hunger and thirst, for who is there that eateth light? It is said to me plainly, directly, "Blessed are the pure in heart: for they shall see God."[457] If It is Light, my eyes must I prepare. Prepare also lips; for That which is Light is also a Fountain: a Fountain, because It satisfieth the thirsty: Light, because It enlighteneth the blind. Here sometimes, light is in one place, a fountain in another. For sometimes fountains run even in darkness; and sometimes in the desert thou sufferest the sun, findest no fountain: here then can these two be separated: there thou shalt not be wearied, for there is a Fountain; there thou shalt not be darkened, for there is Light.

14. "Show forth Thy Mercy unto them that know Thee; Thy Righteousness to them that are of a right heart" (v. 10). As I have said, those are of a right heart who follow in this life the will of God. The will of God is sometimes that thou shouldest be whole, sometimes that thou shouldest be sick. If when thou art whole God's will be sweet, and when thou art sick God's will be bitter; thou art not of a right heart. Wherefore? Because thou wilt not make right thy will according to God's will, but wilt bend God's will to thine. That is right, but thou art crooked: thy will must be made right to that, not that made crooked to thee; and thou wilt have a right heart. It is well with thee in this world; be God blessed, who comforteth thee: it goeth hardly with thee in this world; be God blessed, because He[458] chasteneth and proveth thee; and so wilt thou be of a right heart, saying, "I will bless the Lord at all times: His Praise shall be ever in my mouth."[459]

15. "Let not the foot of pride come against me" (v. 11). But now he said, The children of men shall put their trust under the shadow of Thy wings: they shall be satiated with the fullness of Thy House. When one hath begun to be plentifully overflowed with that Fountain, let him take heed lest he grow proud. For the same was not wanting to Adam, the first man: but the foot of pride came against him, and the hand of the sinner removed him, that is, the proud hand of the devil. As he who seduced him, said of himself, "I will sit in the sides of the north";[460] so he persuaded him by saying,

457. Mt 5:6, 8.   458. Alternatively, "Who."   459. Ps 34:1.
460. Is 14:13.

"Taste, and ye shall be as gods."[461] By pride then have we so fallen as to arrive at this mortality. And because pride had wounded us, humility maketh us whole. God came humbly, that from such great wound of pride He might heal man. He came, for "The Word was made Flesh, and dwelt among us."[462] He was taken by the Jews; He was reviled of them. Ye heard when the Gospel was read, what they said, and to Whom they said, "Thou hast a devil";[463] and He said not, Ye have a devil, for ye are still in your sins, and the devil possesseth your hearts. He said not this, which if He had said, He had said truly: but it was not meet that He should say it, lest He should seem not to preach Truth, but to retort evil speaking. He let go what He heard as though He heard it not. For a Physician was He, and to cure the madman had He come. As a Physician careth not what he may hear from the madman; but how the madman may recover and become sane; nor even if he receive a blow from the madman, careth he; but while he to him giveth new wounds, he cureth his old fever: so also the Lord came to the sick man, to the madman came He, that whatever He might hear, whatever He might suffer, He should despise; by this very thing teaching us humility, that being taught by humility, we might be healed from pride: from which he here prayeth to be delivered, saying, "Let not the foot of pride come against me; neither let the hand of the sinner remove me." For if the foot of pride come, the hand of the sinner removeth. What is the hand of the sinner? The working of him that adviseth ill. Hast thou become proud? Quickly he corrupteth thee who adviseth ill. Humbly fix thyself in God, and care not much what is said to thee. Hence is that which is elsewhere spoken, "From my secret sins cleanse Thou me; and from others' sins also keep Thy servant."[464] What is, "From my secret sins"? "Let not the foot of pride come against me." What is, "From other men's sins also keep Thy servant"? "Let not the hand of the wicked remove me." Keep that which is within, and thou shalt not fear from without.

16. But wherefore so greatly fearest thou this? Because it is said, "Thereby have fallen all that work iniquity" (v. 12); so that they have come into that abyss of which it is said, "Thy judgments are

461. Gn 3:5.   462. Jn 1:34.

463. Jn 8:48. This was then the Gospel for the day, or one of the Lessons.—C.

464. Ps 19:12, 13.

like the great abyss": so that they have come even to that deep wherein sinners who despise have fallen. "Have fallen." Whereby did they first fall? By the foot of pride. Hear the foot of pride. "When they knew God, they glorified Him not as God." Therefore came against them the foot of pride, whereby they came into the depth. "God gave them over to their own hearts' lusts, to do those things which are not convenient."[465] The root of sin, and the head of sin feared he who said, "Let not the foot of pride come against me." Wherefore said he, "the foot"? Because by walking proudly man deserted God, and departed from Him. His foot, called he his affection. "Let not the foot of pride come against me: let not the hand of the wicked remove me": that is, let not the works of the wicked remove me from Thee, that I should wish to imitate them. But wherefore said he this against pride, "Thereby have fallen all that work iniquity"? Because those who now are ungodly, have fallen by pride. Therefore when the Lord would caution His Church, He said, "It shall watch thy head, and thou shalt watch[466] his heel."[467] The serpent watcheth when the foot of pride may come against thee, when thou mayest fall, that he may cast thee down. But watch thou his head: the beginning of all sin is pride.[468] Thereby have fallen all that work iniquity: they are driven out, and are not able to stand." He first, who in the Truth stood not, then, through him, they whom God sent out of paradise. Whence he, the humble, who said that he was not worthy to unloose His shoe's latchet, is not driven out, but standeth and heareth Him, and rejoiceth greatly because of the Bridegroom's voice;[469] not because of his own, lest the foot of pride come against him, and he be driven out, and be not able to stand.

Psalm 51 [470]

1. Neither must this multitude's throng be defrauded, nor their infirmity burdened. Silence we ask, and quiet, in order that our

---

465. Rom 1:21–24.   466. Lat. *observabit*.   467. Gn 3:15.

468. Ecclus 10:13.   469. Jn 1:27, 3:29.

470. From a sermon to the people of Carthage.

voice, after yesterday's labor, be able with some little vigor to last out. It must be believed that your love hath met together in greater numbers today for nothing else, but that ye may pray for those whom an alien and perverse inclination doth keep away. For we are speaking neither of heathens nor of Jews, but of Christians: nor of those that are yet catechumens, but of many that are even baptized, from the Laver of whom ye do no wise differ, and yet to their heart ye are unlike. For today how many brethren of ours we think of, and deplore their going unto vanities and lying insanities, to the neglect of that to which they have been called. Who, if in the very circus from any cause they chance to be startled, do immediately cross themselves, and stand bearing It on the forehead, in the very place, from whence they had withdrawn, if they had borne It in heart. God's mercy must be implored, that He may give understanding for condemning these things, inclination to flee them, and mercy to forgive. Opportunately, then, of Penitence a psalm today has been chanted. Speak we even with the absent: there will be to them for our voice your memory. Neglect not the wounded and feeble, but that ye may more easily make whole, whole ye ought to abide. Correct by reproving, comfort by addressing, set an example by living well, He will be with them that hath been with you. For now that ye have overpassed these dangers, the fountain of God's mercy is not closed. Where ye have come they will come; where ye have passed they will pass. A grievous thing it is indeed, and exceeding perilous, nay ruinous, and for certain a deadly thing, that witting they sin. For in one way to these vanities doth he run that despiseth the voice of Christ; in another way, he that knoweth from what he is fleeing. But that not even of such men we ought to despair, this psalm doth show.

2. For there is written over it the title thereof, "A Psalm of David himself, when there came to him Nathan the prophet, when he went in unto Bathsheba." Bathsheba was a woman, wife of another. With grief indeed we speak, and with trembling; but yet God would not have to be hushed what He hath willed to be written. I will say then not what I will, but what I am obliged; I will say not as one exhorting to imitation, but as one instructing you to fear. Captivated with this woman's beauty, the wife of another, the king and prophet David, from whose seed according to the flesh the Lord

was to come,[471] committed adultery with her. This thing in this
psalm is not read, but in the title thereof it appeareth; but in the
book of Kings[472] it is more fully read. Both Scriptures are canonical,
to both without any doubt by Christians credit must be given. The
sin was committed, and was written down. Moreover her husband
in war he caused to be killed: and after this deed there was sent to
him Nathan the prophet,[473] sent by the Lord, to reprove him for so
great an outrage.

3. What men should beware of, we have said; but what if they
shall have fallen they should imitate, let us hear. For many men
will to fall with David, and will not to rise with David. Not then
for falling is the example set forth, but if thou shalt have fallen for
rising again. Take heed lest thou fall. Not the delight of the
younger be the lapse of the elder, but be the fall of the elder the
dread of the younger. For this it was set forth, for this was written,
for this in the Church often read and chanted: let them hear that
have not fallen, lest they fall; let them hear that have fallen, that
they may rise. So great a man's sin is not hushed, is proclaimed in
the Church. There men hear that are ill hearers, and seek for themselves countenance for sinning: they look out for means whereby
they may defend what they have made ready to commit, not how
they may beware of what they have not committed, and they say to
themselves, If David, why not I too? Thence that soul is more unrighteous, which, forasmuch as it hath done it because David did,
therefore hath done worse than David. I will say this very thing, if I
shall be able, more plainly. David had set forth to himself none for
a precedent as thou hast: he had fallen by lapse of concupiscence,
not by the countenance of holiness; thou dost set before thine eyes
as it were a holy man, in order that thou mayest sin; thou dost not
copy his holiness, but dost copy his fall. Thou[474] dost love that in
David, which in himself David hated; thou makest thee ready to
sin, thou inclinest to sin; in order that thou mayest sin thou consult-
est the book of God; the Scriptures of God for this thou hearest,
that thou mayest do what displeaseth God. This did not David; he
was reproved by a prophet, he stumbled not over a prophet. But

471. Rom 1:3.   472. 2 Sm 11:2–17.   473. 2 Sm 12:1.

474. Alternatively, "Love this in David which in himself David hated not."

others hearing to their health, by the fall of a strong man measure their weakness, and desiring to avoid what God condemneth, from careless looking do restrain their eyes. Them they fix not upon the beauty of another's flesh, nor make themselves careless with perverse simpleness; they say not, "With good intent I have observed, of kindness I have observed, of charity I have long looked." For they set before themselves the fall of David, and they see that this great man for this purpose hath fallen, in order that little men may not be willing to look on that whereby they may fall. For they restrain their eyes from wantonness, not readily do they join themselves in company, they do not mingle with strange women, they raise not complying eyes to strange balconies, to strange terraces. For from afar David saw her with whom he was captivated.[475] Woman afar, lust near. What he saw was elsewhere, in himself that whereby he fell. This weakness of the flesh must be therefore minded, the words of the apostle recollected, "Let not sin therefore reign in your mortal body."[476] He hath not said, let there not be, but, "let there not reign." There is sin in thee, when thou takest pleasure; there reigneth, if thou shalt have consented. Carnal pleasure, especially if proceeding unto unlawful and strange objects, is to be bridled, not let loose: by government to be tamed, not to be set up for government. Look and be without care, if thou hast nothing whereby thou mayest be moved. But thou makest answer, "I contain with strong resolution." Art thou any wise stronger than David?

4. He admonisheth, moreover, by such an example, that no one ought to lift himself up in prosperous circumstances. For many fear adverse circumstances, fear not prosperous circumstances. Prosperity is more perilous to soul than adversity to body. First, prosperity doth corrupt, in order that adversity may find something to break. My brethren, stricter watch must be kept against felicity. Wherefore, see ye after what manner the saying of God amid our own felicity doth take from us security: "Serve ye," He saith, "the Lord in fear, and exult unto Him with trembling."[477] In exultation, in order that we may render thanks; in trembling, lest we fall. This sin did not David, when he was suffering Saul for persecutor.[478] When holy David was suffering Saul his enemy, when he was being vexed by his persecutions, when he was fleeing through

475. 2 Sm 11:2.   476. Rom 6:12.   477. Ps 2:11.   478. 1 Sm 24:5, 26:9.

divers places, in order that he might not fall into his hands, he lusted not for her that was another's, he slew not husband after committing adultery with wife. He was in the infirmity of his tribulation so much the more intimate with God as he seemed more miserable. Something useful is tribulation; useful the surgeon's lancet rather than the devil's temptation. He became secure when his enemies were overthrown, pressure was removed, swelling grew out. This example therefore doth avail to this end, that we should fear felicity. "Tribulation," he saith, "and grief I found, and on the name of the Lord I called."[479]

5. But it was done; I would say these words to those that have not done the like, in order that they should watch to keep their uncorruptness, and that while they take heed how a great one has fallen, they that be small should fear. But if any that hath already fallen heareth these words, and that hath in his conscience any evil thing; to the words of this psalm let him advert; let him heed the greatness of the wound, but not despair of the majesty of the Physician. Sin with despair is certain death. Let no one therefore say, If already any evil thing I have done, already I am to be condemned: God pardoneth not such evil things, why add I not sins to sins? I will enjoy this world in pleasure, in wantonness, in wicked cupidity: now hope of amendment having been lost, let me have even what I see, if I cannot have what I believe. This psalm then, while it maketh heedful those that have not believed, so doth not will them that have fallen to be despaired of. Whoever thou art that hast sinned, and hesitatest to exercise penitence[480] for thy sin, despairing of thy salvation, hear David groaning. To thee Nathan the prophet hath not been sent, David himself hath been sent to thee. Hear him crying, and with him cry: hear him groaning, and with him groan; hear him weeping, and mingle tears; hear him amended, and with him rejoice. If from thee sin could not be excluded, be not hope of pardon excluded. There was sent to that man Nathan the prophet; observe the king's humility.[481] He rejected not the words of him giving admonition, he said not, Darest thou speak to me, a king?

479. Ps 116:3, 4.

480. Here I have corrected the feeble translation, "do penance," which is unjust to the author's entire system of thought.—C.

481. Alternatively, "The pride of royalty."

An exalted king heard a prophet, let His humble people hear Christ.

6. Hear therefore these words, and say thou with him: "Have pity upon me, O God, after Thy great mercy" (v. 1). He that imploreth great mercy, confesseth great misery. Let them seek a little mercy of Thee, that have sinned in ignorance: "Have pity," he saith, "upon me, after Thy great mercy." Relieve a deep wound after Thy great healing. Deep is what I have, but in the Almighty I take refuge. Of my own so deadly wound I should despair, unless I could find so great a Physician. "Have pity upon me, O God, after Thy great mercy: and after the multitude of Thy pities, blot out my iniquity." What he saith, "Blot out my iniquity," is this, "Have pity upon me, O God." And what he saith, "After the multitude of Thy pities," is this, "After Thy great mercy." Because great is the mercy, many are the mercies; and of Thy great mercy, many are Thy pitying. Thou dost regard mockers to amend them, dost regard ignorant men to teach them, dost regard men confessing to pardon. Did he this in ignorance? A certain man had done some, aye many evil things he had done; "Mercy," he saith, "I obtained, because ignorant I did it in unbelief."[482] This David could not say, "Ignorant I did it." For he was not ignorant how very evil a thing was the touching of another's wife, and how very evil a thing was the killing of the husband, who knew not of it, and was not even angered. They obtain therefore the mercy of the Lord that have in ignorance done it; and they that have knowing done it, obtain not any mercy it may chance, but "great mercy."

7. "More and more wash me from mine unrighteousness" (v. 2). What is, "More and more wash"? One much stained. More and more wash the sins of one knowing. Thou that hast washed off the sins of one ignorant. Not even thus is it to be despaired of Thy mercy. "And from my delinquency purge Thou me." According to the manner in which He is physician, offer a recompense. He is God, offer sacrifice. What wilt thou give that thou mayest be purged? For see upon whom thou callest; upon a Just One thou callest. He hateth sins, if He is just; He taketh vengeance upon sins, if He is just; thou wilt not be able to take away from the Lord God

482. 1 Tm 1:13.

His justice: entreat mercy, but observe the justice: there is mercy to pardon the sinner, there is justice to punish the sin. What then? Thou askest mercy; shall sin unpunished abide? Let David answer, let those that have fallen answer, answer with David, and say, No, Lord, no sin of mine shall be unpunished; I know the justice of Him whose mercy I ask: it shall not be unpunished, but for this reason I will not that Thou punish me, because I punish my sin: for this reason I beg that Thou pardon, because I acknowledge.

8. "For mine iniquity I acknowledge, and my delinquency is before me ever" (v. 3). I have not put behind my back what I have done, I look not at others, forgetful of myself, I pretend not to pull out a straw from my brother's eye, when there is a beam in my eye;[483] my sin is before me, not behind me. For it was behind me when to me was sent the prophet, and set before me the parable of the poor man's sheep.[484] For saith Nathan the prophet to David, "There was a certain rich man having very many sheep; but a poor man his neighbor had one little ewe sheep, which in his bosom and of his own food he was feeding: there came a stranger to the rich man, nothing from his flock he took, for the lithe ewe sheep of the poor man his neighbor he lusted; her he slew for the stranger: what doth he deserve?" But the other being angry doth pronounce sentence: then the king, evidently knowing not wherein he had been taken,[485] declared the rich man deserving of death, and that the sheep be restored fourfold. Most sternly and most justly. But his sin was not yet before him, behind his back was what he had done: his own iniquity he did not yet acknowledge, and therefore another's he did not pardon. But the prophet, being for this purpose sent, took from his back the sin, and before his eyes placed it, so that he might see that sentence so stern to have been pronounced against himself. For cutting and healing his heart's wound, he made a lancet of his tongue.

9. "Against Thee alone have I sinned, and before Thee an evil thing have I done" (v. 4). What is this? For before men was not another's wife debauched and husband slain? Did not all men know

---

483. Mt 7:5.   484. 2 Sm 12:1, 2, etc.

485. Alternatively, "he was captive," or, "was held captive."

what David had done?[486] What is, "Against Thee alone have I
sinned, and before Thee an evil thing have I done"? Because Thou
alone art without sin. He is a just punisher that hath nothing in
Him to be punished; He is a just reprover that hath nothing in Him
to be reproved. "That thou mayest be justified in Thy sayings, and
conquer when Thou art judged." To whom he speaketh, brethren,
to whom he speaketh, is difficult to understand. To God surely he
speaketh, and it is evident that God the Father is not judged. What
is, "And conquer when Thou art judged"? He seeth the future
Judge to be judged, one just by sinners to be judged, and therein
conquering, because in Him was nothing to be judged. For alone
among men could truly say the God-Man, "If ye have found in Me
sin, say."[487] But perchance there was what escaped men, and they
found not what was really there, but was not manifest. In another
place[488] He saith, "Behold there cometh the Prince of the world,"
being an acute observer of all sins; "Behold," He saith, "there
cometh the Prince of this world," with death afflicting sinners, pre-
siding over death: for, "By the malice of the devil death came into
the world."[489] "Behold," He saith, "there cometh the Prince of the
world":—He said these words close upon His Passion:—"and in
Me he shall find nothing," nothing of sin, nothing worthy of death,
nothing worthy of condemnation. And as if it were said to Him,
Why then dost Thou die? He continueth and saith, "But that all
men may know that I do the will of My Father; arise, let us go
hence." I suffer, He saith, undeserving, for men deserving, in order
that them I may make deserving of My Life, for whom I undeservedly suffer their death. To Him then, having no sin, saith on
the present occasion the Prophet David, "Against Thee only have I
sinned, and before Thee an evil thing have I done, that Thou
mayest be justified in Thy sayings, and conquer when Thou art
judged." For Thou overcomest all men, all judges; and he that
deemeth himself just, before Thee is unjust: Thou alone justly
judgest, having been unjustly judged, That hast power to lay down
Thy life, and hast power again to take it.[490] Thou conquerest, then,
when Thou art judged. All men Thou overcomest, because Thou
art more than men, and by Thee were men made.

486. 2 Sm 11:4, 15.   487. Jn 8:46.   488. Jn 14:30.   489. Ws 2:24.
490. Jn 10:18.

10. "For, behold, in iniquities I was conceived" (v. 5). As though he were saying, They are conquered that have done what thou, David, hast done: for this is not a little evil and little sin, to wit, adultery and man-slaying. What of them that from the day that they were born of their mother's womb, have done no such thing? Even to them dost thou ascribe some sins, in order that He may conquer all men when He beginneth to be judged. David hath taken upon him the person of mankind, and hath heeded the bonds of all men, hath considered the offspring of death, hath adverted to the origin of iniquity, and he saith, "For, behold, in iniquities I was conceived." Was David born of adultery; being born of Jesse,[491] a righteous man, and his own wife? What is it that he saith himself to have been in iniquity conceived, except that iniquity is drawn from Adam? Even the very bond of death, with iniquity itself is in-grained? No man is born without bringing punishment, bringing desert of punishment. A prophet saith also in another place,[492] "No one is clean in Thy sight, not even an infant, whose life is of one day upon earth." For we know both by the baptism of Christ that sins are loosed, and that the baptism of Christ availeth the remission of sins. If infants are every way innocent, why do mothers run with them when sick to the Church? What by that baptism, what by that remission is put away? An innocent one I see that rather weeps than is angry. What doth baptism wash off? What doth that grace loose? There is loosed the offspring of sin. For if that infant could speak to thee, it would say, and if it had the understanding which David had, it would answer thee, Why heedest thou me, an infant? Thou dost not indeed see my actions: but I in iniquity have been conceived, "And in sins hath my mother nourished me in the womb."

Apart from this bond of mortal concupiscence was Christ born without a male, of a virgin conceiving by the Holy Ghost. He cannot be said to have been conceived in iniquity, it cannot be said, In sins His mother nourished Him in the womb, to whom was said, "The Holy Ghost shall come upon thee, and the Virtue of the Highest shall overshadow thee."[493] It is not therefore because it is sin to have to do with wives that men are conceived in iniquity, and in sins nourished in the womb by their mother; but because that

491. 1 Sm 16:18.   492. Jb 14:5 (Septuagint).   493. Lk 1:35.

which is made is surely made of flesh deserving punishment.[494] For the punishment of the flesh is death, and surely there is in it liability to death itself. Whence the apostle spoke not of the body as if to die, but as if dead: "The body indeed is dead," he saith, "because of sin, but the Spirit is life because of righteousness."[495] How then without bond of sin is born that which is conceived and sown of a body dead because of sin? This chaste operation in a married person hath not sin, but the origin of sin draweth with it condign punishment. For there is no husband that, because he is an husband, is not subject to death, or that is subject to death for any other reason but because of sin. For even the Lord was subject to death, but not on account of sin: He took upon Him our punishment, and so looseth our guilt. With reason then, "In Adam all die, but in Christ shall all be made alive."[496] For, "Through one man," saith the apostle, "sin hath entered into this world, and through sin death, and so hath passed unto all men, in that all have sinned."[497] Definite is the sentence: "In Adam," he saith, "all have sinned." Alone then could such an infant be innocent, as hath not been born of the work of Adam.

11. "For, behold, truth Thou hast loved: uncertain and hidden things of Thy wisdom, Thou hast manifested to me" (v. 6). That is, Thou hast not left unpunished even the sins of those whom Thou dost pardon. "Truth Thou hast loved": so mercy Thou hast granted first, as that Thou shouldest also preserve truth. Thou pardonest one confessing, pardonest, but only if he punisheth himself: so there are preserved mercy and truth: mercy because man is set free; truth, because sin is punished. "Uncertain and hidden things of Thy wisdom Thou hast manifested to me." What "hidden things"? What "uncertain things"? Because God pardoneth even such. Nothing is so hidden, nothing so uncertain.[498] For this uncertainty the Ninevites repented, for they said, though after the threatenings of the prophet, though after that cry, "Three days and Nineve shall be overthrown":[499] they said to themselves, mercy

---

494. The mother need not be conceived of as sinning in her passive relations to an act which is undefiled in itself (Heb 13:4); but she is a sinner like all mortals, and in that estate of sinfulness her offspring is begotten and nourished in the womb. So he argues.—C.

495. Rom 8:10.   496. 1 Cor 15:22.   497. Rom 5:12.

498. I.e., as His mercy is to us beforehand.   499. Jon 3:4.   500. Jon 3:9.

must be implored; they said in this sort reasoning among themselves, "Who knoweth whether God may turn for the better His
sentence, and have pity?"[500] It was "uncertain," when it is said,
"Who knoweth?" on an uncertainty they did repent,[501] certain
mercy they earned: they prostrated them in tears, in fastings, in
sackcloth and ashes they prostrated them, groaned, wept, God
spared. Nineve stood: was Nineve overthrown? One way indeed it
seemeth to men, and another way it seemed to God. But I think
that it was fulfilled that the prophet had foretold. Regard what
Nineve was, and see how it was overthrown; overthrown in evil,
builded in good; just as Saul the persecutor was overthrown, Paul
the preacher builded.[502] Who would not say that this city, in which
we now are, was happily overthrown, if all those madmen, leaving
their triflings, were to run together to the Church with contrite
heart, and were to call upon God's mercy for their past doings?
Should we not say, Where is that Carthage? Because there is not
what there was, it is overthrown: but if there is what there was not,
it is builded. So is said to Jeremiah, "Behold, I will give to thee to
root up, to dig under, to overthrow, to destroy," and again, "to
build, and to plant."[503] Thence is that voice of the Lord, "I will
smite and I will heal."[504] He smiteth the rottenness of the deed, He
healeth the pain of the wound. Physicians do thus when they cut;
they smite and heal; they arm themselves in order to strike, they
carry steel, and come to cure. But because great were the sins of the
Ninevites, they said, "Who knoweth?" This uncertainty had God
disclosed to His servant David. For when he had said, before the
prophet standing and convicting him, "I have sinned," straightway
he heard from the prophet, that is, from the Spirit of God which
was in the prophet, "Thy sin is put away from thee."[505] "Uncertain
and hidden things" of His wisdom He manifested to him.

12. "Thou shalt sprinkle me," he saith, "with hyssop, and I shall
be cleansed" (v. 7). Hyssop we know to be a herb humble but healing: to the rock it is said to adhere with roots. Thence in a mystery

---

500. Jon 3:9.

501. Here the translator has "did penance," which has no meaning at all apart
from ecclesiastical discipline, to which the men of Nineve were certainly not subjected.—C.

502. Acts 9:4.   503. Jer 1:10.   504. Dt 32:39.   505. 2 Sm 12:13.

the similitude of cleansing the heart has been taken. Do thou also take hold, with the root of thy love, on thy Rock: be humble in thy humble God, in order that thou mayest be exalted in thy glorified God. Thou shalt be sprinkled with hyssop, the humility of Christ shall cleanse thee. Despise not the herb, attend to the efficacy of the medicine. Something further I will say, which we are wont to hear from physicians, or to experience in sick persons. Hyssop, they say, is proper for purging the lungs. In the lung is wont to be noted pride: for there is inflation, there breathing. It was said of Saul the persecutor as of Saul the proud, that he was going to bind Christians, breathing slaughter:[506] he was breathing out slaughter, breathing out blood, his lung not yet cleansed. Hear also in this place one humbled, because with hyssop purged: "Thou shalt wash me," that is, shalt cleanse me: "and above snow I shall be whitened." "Although," He saith, "your sins shall have been like scarlet, like snow I will whiten."[507] Out of such men Christ doth present to Himself a vesture without spot and wrinkle.[508] Further, His vesture on the mount, which shone forth like whitened snow,[509] signified the Church cleansed from every spot of sin.

13. But where is humility from hyssop? Hear what followeth: "To my hearing Thou shall give exultation and gladness, and bones humbled shall exult" (v. 8). I will rejoice in hearing Thee, not in speaking against Thee. Thou hast sinned, why defendest thou thyself? Thou wilt speak: suffer thou; hear, yield to divine words, lest thou be put to confusion, and be still more wounded: sin hath been committed, be it not defended: to confession let it come, not to defense. Thou engagest thyself as defender of thy sin, thou art conquered: no innocent patron hast thou engaged, thy defense is not profitable to thee. For who art thou that defendest thyself? Thou art meet to accuse thyself. Say not, either, "I have done nothing"; or, "What great thing have I done?" or, "Other men as well have done." If in doing sin thou sayest thou hast done nothing, thou wilt be nothing, thou wilt receive nothing: God is ready to give indulgence, thou closest the door against thyself: He is ready to give, do not oppose the bar of defense, but open the bosom of confession. "To my hearing Thou shalt give exultation and gladness."

14. "Turn Thou away Thy face from my sins, and all mine iniq-

506. Acts 9:1.   507. Is 1:18.   508. Eph 5:27.   509. Mt 17:2.

uities blot out" (v. 9). For now bones humbled exult, now with hyssop cleansed, humble I have become. "Turn Thou away Thy face," not from me, but "from my sins." For in another place praying he saith, "Turn not away Thy face from me."[510] He that would not that God's face be turned away from himself, would that God's face be turned away from his sins. For to sin, when God turneth not Himself away, he adverteth: if he adverteth, he animadverteth. "And all mine iniquities blot out." He is busied with that capital sin: he reckoneth on more, he would have all his iniquities to be blotted out: he relieth on the Physician's hand, on that "great mercy," upon which he hath called in the beginning of the psalm: "All mine iniquities blot out." God turneth away His face, and so blotteth out; by "turning away" His face, sins He blotteth out. By "turning toward," He writeth them. Thou hast heard of Him blotting out by turning away, hear of Him by turning toward, doing what? "But the countenance of the Lord is upon men doing evil things, that He may destroy from the earth the remembrance of them":[511] He shall destroy the remembrance of them, not by "blotting out their sins." But here he doth ask what? "Turn away Thy face from my sins." Well he asketh. For he himself doth not turn away his face from his *own* sins, saying, "For my sin I acknowledge." With reason thou askest and well askest, that God turn away from thy sin, if thou from thence dost not turn away thy face: but if thou settest thy sin at thy back, God doth there set His face. Do thou turn sin before thy face, if thou wilt that God thence turn away His face; and then safely thou askest, and He heareth.

15. "A clean heart create in me, O God" (v. 10). "Create"—he meant to say, "as it were *begin* something new." But, because repentant he was praying (that had committed some sin, which before he had committed, he was more innocent), after what manner he hath said "create" he showeth. "And a right spirit renew in my inner parts." By my doing, he saith, the uprightness of my spirit hath been made old and bowed. For he saith in another psalm, "They have bowed my soul."[512] And when a man doth make himself stoop unto earthly lusts, he is "bowed" in a manner, but when he is made erect for things above, upright is his heart made, in order that God may be good to him. For, "How good is the God of Israel to the upright of heart!"[513] Moreover, brethren, listen. Sometimes God in this world

510. Ps 27:9.   511. Ps 34:16.   512. Ps 57:6.   513. Ps 73:1.

chastiseth for his sin him that He pardoneth in the world to come. For even to David himself, to whom it had been already said by the prophet, "Thy sin is put away,"[514] there happened certain things which God had threatened for that very sin.[515] For his son Abessalom against him waged bloody war, and many ways humbled his father.[516] He was walking in grief, in the tribulation of his humiliation, so resigned to God, that, ascribing to Him all that was just, he confessed that he was suffering nothing undeservedly, having now an heart upright, to which God was not displeasing. A slanderous person and one throwing in his teeth harsh curses[517] he patiently heard, one of the soldiers on the opposite side, that were with his unnatural son. And when he was heaping curses upon the king, one of the companions of David, enraged, would have gone and smitten him; but he is kept back by David. And he is kept back how? For that he said, God sent him to curse me. Acknowledging his guilt he embraced his penance, seeking glory not his own, praising the Lord in that good which he had, praising the Lord in that which he was suffering, "blessing the Lord always, ever His praise was in his mouth."[518] Such are all the upright in heart: not those crooked persons who think themselves upright and God crooked: who when they do any evil thing, rejoice; when they suffer any evil thing, blaspheme; nay, if set in tribulation and scourging, they say from their distorted heart, "O God, what have I done to Thee?" Truly it is because they have done nothing to God, for they have done all to themselves. "And an upright spirit, renew in my inner parts."

16. "Cast me not forth from Thy face" (v. 11). Turn away Thy face from my sins: and "cast me not forth from Thy face." Whose face he feareth, upon the face of the Same he calleth. "And Thy Holy Spirit take not away from me." For in one confessing there is the Holy Spirit. Even now, to the gift of the Holy Spirit it belongeth, that what thou hast done displeaseth thee. The unclean spirit sins do please; the Holy One they displease. Though then thou still implore pardon, yet thou art joined to God on the other part, because the evil thing that thou hast committed displeaseth thee: for the same thing displeaseth both thee and Him. Now, to assail thy fever, ye are two, thou and the Physician. For the reason that

514. 2 Sm 12:13.   515. Compare 2 Sm 11:10.—C.   516. 2 Sm 15:10.

517. 2 Sm 16:10.   518. Ps 34:1.

there cannot be confession of sin and punishment of sin in a man of himself: when one is angry with himself, and is displeasing to himself, then it is not without the gift of the Holy Spirit, nor doth he say, Thy Holy Spirit give to me, but, "Take not away from me."

17. "Give back to me the exultation of Thy salvation" (v. 12). "Give back" what I had; what by sinning I had lost: to wit, of Thy Christ. For who without Him can be made whole? Because even before that He was Son of Mary, "In the beginning He was the Word, and the Word was with God, and the Word was God";[519] and so, by the holy fathers a future dispensation of flesh taken upon Him was looked for; as is believed by us to have been done. Times are changed, not faith. "And with Principal Spirit confirm me." Some have here understood the Trinity in God, Itself God; the dispensation of Flesh being excepted therefrom: since it is written, "God is a Spirit."[520] For that which is not body, and yet is, seemeth to exist in such sort as that it is spirit. Therefore some understand here the Trinity spoken of: "In upright Spirit," the Son; in "Holy Spirit," Holy Ghost; in "Principal Spirit," Father.[521] It is not any heretical opinion, therefore, whether this be so, or whether "upright Spirit" He would have to be taken of man himself (when He saith, "An upright spirit renew in my inner parts"), which I have bowed and distorted by sinning, so that in that case the Holy Spirit be Himself the Principal Spirit: which also he would not have to be taken away from him, and thereby would have himself to be confirmed therein.

18. But see what he annexeth: "With Principal Spirit," he saith, "confirm Thou me." Wherein "confirm"? Because Thou hast pardoned me, because I am secure, that what Thou hast forgiven is not to be ascribed, on this being made secure and with this grace confirmed, therefore I am not ungrateful. But I shall do what? "I would teach unrighteous men Thy ways" (v. 13). Being *myself* of the unrighteous (that is, one that was myself an unrighteous man, now no longer unrighteous; the Holy Spirit not having been taken away from me, and I being confirmed with Principal Spirit). "I would teach unrighteous men Thy ways." What ways wilt thou teach unrighteous men? "And ungodly men to Thee shall be converted." If David's sin is counted for ungodliness, let not ungodly

519. Jn 1:1.   520. Jn 4:24.   521. Jerome on the Epistle to Gal 4:6.

men despair of themselves, forasmuch as God hath spared an ungodly man; but let them take heed that to Him they be converted,
that His ways they learn. But if David's deed is not counted for ungodliness, but this is properly called ungodliness, namely, to apos-
tatize from God, not to worship one God, or never to have
worshipped, or to have forsaken, Him whom one did worship,
then what he saith hath the force of superabundance, "And ungodly men shall to Thee be converted." So full art thou of the fatness of mercy, that for those converted to Thee, not only sinners of
any sort, but even ungodly, there is no cause for despair. Wherefore? That believing on Him that justifieth an ungodly man, their
faith may be counted for righteousness.[522]

19. "Deliver me from bloods, O God, God of my health" (v. 14).
The Latin translator hath expressed, though by a word not Latin,
yet an accuracy from the Greek. For we all know that in Latin, *san-
guines* (bloods) are not spoken of, nor yet *sanguina* (bloods in the
neuter), nevertheless because the Greek translator hath thus used
the plural number, not without reason, but because he found this in
the original language the Hebrew, a godly translator hath preferred to use a word not Latin, rather than one not exact. Wherefore then hath he said in the plural number, "From bloods"? In
many bloods, as in the origin of the sinful flesh, many sins he would
have to be understood. The apostle having regard to the very sins
which come of the corruption of flesh and blood, saith, "Flesh and
blood shall not possess the kingdom of God."[523] For doubtless, after
the true faith of the same apostle, that flesh shall rise again and
shall itself gain incorruption, as He saith Himself, "This corruptible must put on incorruption, and this mortal put on immortality."[524] Because then this corruption is of sin, by the name thereof
sins are called. In like manner as both that morsel of flesh and
member which playeth in the mouth when we articulate words is
called a tongue, and that is called a tongue which by the tongue
is made, so we call one tongue the Greek, another the Latin; for the
flesh is not diverse, but the sound. In the same manner, then, as
the speech which is made by the tongue is called a tongue; so
also the iniquity which is made by blood is called blood. Heeding,
then, his many iniquities, as in the expression above,[525] "And all my

522. Rom 4:5.   523. 1 Cor 15:50.   524. 1 Cor 15:53.   525. Ps 51:9.

iniquities blot out," and ascribing them to the corruption of flesh and blood, "Free me," he saith, "from bloods"; that is, free me from iniquities, cleanse me from all corruption. . . . Not yet is the substance, but certain hope. "And my tongue shall exult of Thy righteousness."

20. "O Lord, my lips Thou shalt open, and my mouth shall tell of Thy praise" (v. 15). "Thy praise," because[526] I have been created: "Thy praise," because sinning I have not been forsaken: "Thy praise," because I have been admonished to confess: "Thy praise," because in order that I might be secured I have been cleansed.

21. "Because if Thou hadst willed sacrifice, I would have given it surely" (v. 16). David was living at that time when sacrifices of victim animals were offered to God, and he saw these times that were to be. Do we not perceive ourselves in these words? Those sacrifices were figurative, foretelling the One Saving Sacrifice. Not even we have been left without a Sacrifice to offer to God. For hear what he saith, having a concern for his sin, and wishing the evil thing which he hath done to be forgiven him: "If Thou hadst willed," he saith, "sacrifice, I would have given it surely. With holocausts Thou wilt not be delighted." Nothing shall we therefore offer? So shall we come to God? And whence shall we propitiate Him? Offer; certainly in thyself thou hast what thou mayest offer. Do not from without fetch frankincense, but say, "In me are, O God, Thy vows, which I will render of praise to Thee."[527] Do not from without seek cattle to slay, thou hast in thyself what thou mayest kill. "Sacrifice to God is a spirit troubled, a heart contrite and humbled God despiseth not" (v. 17). Utterly he despiseth bull, he-goat, ram: now is not the time that these should be offered. They were offered when they indicated something, when they promised something; when the things promised come, the promises are taken away. "A heart contrite and humbled God despiseth not." Ye know that God is high: if thou shalt have made thyself high, He will be from thee; if thou shalt have humbled thyself, He will draw near to thee.

22. See who this is: David as one man was seeming to implore; see ye here our image and the type of the Church.

"Deal kindly, O Lord, in Thy good will with Sion" (v. 18). With this Sion deal kindly. What is Sion? A city holy. What is a city holy?

526. Most mss. "whereby" throughout.   527. Ps 56:12.

That which cannot be hidden, being upon a mountain established. Sion in prospect, because it hath prospect of something which it hopeth for. For Sion is interpreted "prospect," and Jerusalem, "vision of peace." Ye perceive then yourselves to be in Sion and in Jerusalem, if being sure ye look for hope that is to be, and if ye have peace with God. "And be the walls of Jerusalem builded." "Deal kindly, O Lord, in Thy good will with Sion, and be the walls of Jerusalem builded." For not to herself let Sion ascribe her merits: do Thou with her deal kindly, "Be the walls of Jerusalem builded": be the battlements of our immortality laid, in faith and hope and charity.

23. "Then Thou shalt accept the sacrifice of righteousness" (v. 19). But now sacrifice for iniquity, to wit, a spirit troubled, and a heart humbled; then the sacrifice of righteousness praises alone. For, "Blessed are they that dwell in Thy house, for ever and ever they shall praise Thee":[528] for this is the sacrifice of righteousness. "Oblations and holocausts." What are "holocausts"? A whole victim by fire consumed. When a whole beast was laid upon the altar with fire to be consumed, it was called a holocaust. May divine fire take us up whole, and that fervor catch us whole. What fervor? "Neither is there that hideth himself from the heat thereof."[529] What fervor? That whereof speaketh the apostle: "In spirit fervent."[530] Be not merely our soul taken up by that divine fire of wisdom, but also our body; that it may earn their immortality; so be it lifted up for a holocaust, that death be swallowed into victory. "Oblations and holocausts." "Then shall they lay upon thine altar calves." Whence "calves"? What shall He therein choose? Will it be the innocence of the new age, or necks freed from the yoke of the law?

Psalm 54[531]

1. The title of this psalm hath fruit in the prolixity thereof, if it be understood: and because the psalm is short, let us make up our not having to tarry over the psalm by tarrying over the title. For upon this dependeth every verse which is sung. If anyone, therefore, ob-

serve that which on the front of the house is fixed, secure he will enter; and, when he shall have entered, he will not err. For this on the post itself is prominently marked, namely, in what manner within he may not be in error. The title thereof standeth thus: "At the end, in hymns, understanding to David himself, when there came the Ziphites, and said to Saul, Behold, is not David hidden with us?" That Saul was persecutor of the holy man David, very well we know: that Saul was bearing the figure of a temporal kingdom, not to life but to death belonging, this also to your Love we remember to have imparted. And also that David himself was bearing the figure of Christ, or of the Body of Christ, ye ought both to know and to call to mind, ye that have already learned. What then of the Ziphites? There was a certain village, Ziph, whereof the inhabitants were Ziphites, in whose country David had hidden himself, when Saul would find and slay him. These Ziphites then, when they had learned this, betrayed him to the king his persecutor, saying, "Behold, is not David hidden with us?" Of no good to them indeed was their betrayal, and to David himself of no harm. For their evil disposition was shown: but Saul not even after their betrayal could seize David; but rather in a certain cave in that very country, when into his hands Saul had been given to slay, David spared him, and that which he had in his power he did not.[532] But the other was seeking to do that which he had not in his power. Let them that have been Ziphites take heed: let us see those whom to us the psalm presenteth to be understood by the occasion of those same men.

2. If we inquire then by what word is translated Ziphites, we find, "Men flourishing." Flourishing then were certain enemies to holy David, flourishing before him hiding. We may find them in mankind, if we are willing to understand the psalm. Let us find here at first David hiding, and we shall find his adversaries flourishing. Observe David hiding: "For ye are dead," saith the apostle to the members of Christ, "and your life is hid with Christ in God."[533] These men, therefore, that are hiding, when shall they be flourishing? "When Christ," he saith, "your life, shall have appeared, then ye also with Him shall appear in glory."[534] When these men shall be flourishing, then shall be those Ziphites withering.

532. 1 Sm 24:4.   533. Col 3:3.   534. Col 3:4.

For observe to what flower their glory is compared: "All flesh is grass, and the honor of flesh as the flower of grass."[535] What is the end? "The grass hath withered, and the flower hath fallen off." Where then shall be David? See what followeth: "But the Word of the Lord abideth for ever." . . .

3. These men sometimes are observed of the weak sons of light, and their feet totter, when they have seen evil men in felicity to flourish, and they say to themselves, "Of what profit to me is innocence? What doth it advantage me that I serve God, that I keep His commandments, that I oppress no one, from no one plunder anything, hurt no one, that what I can I bestow? Behold, all these things I do, and they flourish, I toil." But why? Wouldest thou also wish to be a Ziphite? They flourish in the world, wither in judgment, and after withering, into fire everlasting shall be cast: wouldest thou also choose this? Art thou ignorant of what He hath promised thee, who to thee hath come, what in Himself here He displayed? If the flower of the Ziphites were to be desired, would not Himself thy Lord also in this world have flourished? Or indeed was there wanting to Him the power to flourish? Nay but here He chose rather amid the Ziphites to hide, and to say to Pontius Pilate, as if to one being himself also a flower of the Ziphites, and in suspicion about His kingdom, "My kingdom is not of this world."[536] Therefore here He was hidden: and all good men are hidden here, because their good is within, it is concealed, in the heart it is, where is faith, where charity, where hope, where their treasure is. Do these good things appear in the world? Both these good things are hidden, and the reward of these good things is hidden.

4. "O God, in Thy name make me safe, and in Thy virtue judge me" (v. 1). Let the Church say this, hiding amid the Ziphites. Let the Christian body say this, keeping secret the good of its morals, expecting in secret the reward of its merits, let it say this: "In Thy virtue[537] judge me." Thou hast come, O Christ, humble Thou hast appeared, despised Thou hast been, scourged Thou hast been, crucified Thou hast been, slain Thou hast been; but, on the third day hast risen, on the fortieth day into heaven hast ascended: Thou sittest at the right hand of the Father, and no one seeth: Thy Spirit thence Thou hast sent, which men that were worthy have received; fulfilled with

535. Is 40:6.   536. Jn 18:36.   537. I.e., power or strength.—C.

Thy love, the praise of that very humility of Thine throughout the world and nations they have preached: Thy name I see to excel among mankind, but nevertheless as weak to us hast Thou been preached. For not even did that teacher of the Gentiles say, that among us he knew anything, "Save Christ Jesus, and Him crucified";[538] in order that of Him we might choose the reproach, rather than the glory of the flourishing Ziphites. Nevertheless, of Him he saith what? "Although He died of weakness, yet He liveth of the power[539] of God." He came then that He might die of weakness, He is to come that He may judge in the power of God: but through the weakness of the cross His name hath been illustrious. Whosoever shall not have believed upon the name made illustrious through weakness, shall stand in awe at the Judge, when He shall have come in power. But, lest He that once was weak, when He shall have come strong, with that fan send us to the left hand; may He "save us in His name, and judge us in His virtue." For who so rash as to have desired this, as to say to God, for instance "Judge me"? Is it not wont to be said to men for a curse, "God judge thee"? So evidently it is a curse, if He judge thee in His virtue; and shall not have saved thee in His name: but when in name precedent He shall have saved thee, to thy health in virtue consequent He shall judge. Be thou without care: that judgment shall not to thee be punishment, but dividing. For in a certain psalm[540] thus is said: "Judge me, O God, and divide my cause from the nation unholy."

5. "O God, hearken to my prayer, in Thy ears receive the words of my mouth" (v. 2). To Thee may my prayer attain, driven forth and darted out from the desire of Thy eternal blessings: to Thy ears I send it forth, aid it that it may reach, lest it fall short in the middle of the way, and fainting as it were it fall down. But even if there result not to me now the good things which I ask, I am secured nevertheless that hereafter they will come. For even in the case of transgressions a certain man is said to have asked of God, and not to have been hearkened to for his good. For privations of this world had inspired him to prayer, and being set in temporal tribulations he had wished that temporal tribulations should pass away, and there should return the flower of grass; and he saith, "My God, my God, why hast Thou forsaken me?"[541] The very voice of Christ it is,

538. 1 Cor 2:2.   539. *Virtute.*   540. Ps 43:1.   541. Ps 22:1.

but for His members' sake. "The words," he saith, "of my transgressions I have cried to Thee throughout the day, and Thou hast
not hearkened: and by night, and not for the sake of folly to me":
that is, "and by night I have cried, and Thou hast not hearkened;
and nevertheless in this very thing that Thou hast not hearkened, it
is not for the sake of folly to me that Thou hast not hearkened, but
rather for the sake of wisdom that Thou hast not hearkened, that I
might perceive what of Thee I ought to ask. For those things I was
asking which to my cost perchance I should have received." Thou
askest riches, O man; how many have been overset through their
riches? Whence knowest thou whether to thee riches may profit?
Have not many poor men more safely been in obscurity; having become rich men, so soon as they have begun to blaze forth, they have
been a prey to the stronger? How much better they would have
lain concealed, how much better they would have been unknown,
that have begun to be inquired after not for the sake of what they
were, but for the sake of what they had! In these temporal things
therefore, brethren, we admonish and exhort you in the Lord, that
ye ask not anything as if it were a thing settled, but that which God
knoweth to be expedient for you. For what is expedient for you, ye
know not at all. Sometimes that which ye think to be for you is
against you, and that which ye think to be against you is for you.
For sick ye are; do not dictate to the physician the medicines he
may choose to set beside you. If the teacher of the Gentiles, Paul the
apostle, saith, "For what we should pray for as we ought, we know
not,"[542] how much more we? Who nevertheless, when he seemed to
himself to pray wisely, namely, that from him should be taken
away the thorn of the flesh, the angel of Satan, that did buffet him,
in order that he might not in the greatness of the revelations be
lifted up, heard from the Lord what? Was that done which he
wished? Nay,[543] in order to that being done which was expedient,
he heard from the Lord, I say, what? "Thrice," he saith, "I besought the Lord that He would take it from me; and He said to me,
My Grace sufficeth for thee: for virtue in weakness is made perfect."[544] Salve to the wound I have applied; when I applied it I
know, when it should be taken away I know. Let not a sick man
draw back from the hands of the physician, let him not give advice

542. Rom 8:26.   543. "Nay" not in mss.   544. 2 Cor 12:8, 9.

to the physician. So it is with all these things temporal. There are tribulations; if well thou worshippest God, thou wilt know that He knoweth what is expedient for each man: there are prosperities; take the more heed, lest these same corrupt thy soul, so that it withdraw from Him that hath given these things.

6. "For aliens have risen up against me" (v. 3). What "aliens"? Was not David himself a Jew of the tribe of Judah? But the very place Ziph belonged to the tribe of Judah; it was of the Jews. How then "aliens"? Not in city, not in tribe, not in kindred, but in flower.[545] But see the Ziphites, see them for a time flourishing. With reason "alien" sons. Thou amid the Ziphites hiding saidst what? "Blessed the people whereof the Lord is its God." Out of this affection this prayer[546] is being sent forth into the ears of the Lord, when it is said, "for aliens have risen up against me."

7. "And mighty men have sought after my soul." For in a new manner, my brethren, they would destroy the race of holy men, and the race of them that abstain from hoping in this world, all they that have hope in this world. Certainly commingled they are, certainly together they live. Very much to one another are opposed these two sorts: the one of those that place no hope but in things secular, and in temporal felicity, and the other of those that do firmly place their hope in the Lord God. And though concordant are these Ziphites, do not much trust to their concord: temptations are wanting; when there shall have come any temptation, so as that a person may be reproved for the flower of the world, I say not to thee he will quarrel with the bishop, but not even to the Church Herself will he draw near, lest there fall any part of the grass. Wherefore have I said these words, brethren? Because now gladly ye all hear in the name of Christ, and according as ye understand, so ye shout out at the word; ye would not indeed shout at it unless ye understood.[547] This your understanding ought to be fruitful. But whether it is fruitful, temptation doth try; lest suddenly when ye are said to be ours, through temptation ye be found aliens, and it be said, "Aliens have risen up against me, and mighty men have

---

545. Jas 1:10, 11. He seems to bear this text in mind in these comments.—C.

546. I.e., this psalm.—C.

547. They seem to have applauded, or shouted *Amen*. So, also, often when Chrysostom preached.—C.

sought my soul." Be not that said which followeth, "They have not set forth God before their face." For when will he set God before his face, before whose eyes there is nought but the world? Namely, how he may have coin upon coin, how flocks may be increased, how barns may be filled, how it may be said to his soul, "Thou hast many good things, be merry, feast, take thy fill." Doth he set before his face Him, that unto one so boasting and so blooming with the flower of the Ziphites saith, "Fool" (that is, "man not understanding," "man unwise"), "this night shall be taken from thee thy soul; all these things which thou hast prepared, whose shall they be?"[548]

8. "For behold, God helpeth me" (v. 4). Even themselves know not themselves, amid whom I am hiding. But if they too were to set God before their face, they would find in what manner God helpeth me. For all holy men are helped by God, but within, where no one seeth. For in like manner as the conscience of ungodly men is a great punishment, so a great joy is the very conscience of godly men. "For our glory this is," saith the apostle, "the testimony of our conscience."[549] In this within, not in the flower of the Ziphites without, doth glory that man that now saith, "For behold God helpeth me." Surely though afar off are to be those things which He promiseth, this day have I a sweet and present help; today in my heart's joy I find that without cause certain say, "Who doth show to us good things? For there is signed upon us the light of Thy countenance, O Lord, Thou hast put pleasantness into my heart."[550] Not into my vineyard, not into my flock, not into my cask, not into my table, but "into my heart." "For behold God helpeth me." How doth He help thee? "And the Lord is the lifter up of my soul."

9. "Turn away evil things unto mine enemies" (v. 5). So however green they are, so however they flourish, for the fire they are being[551] reserved. "In Thy virtue destroy Thou them." Because to wit they flourish now, because to wit they spring up like grass:[552] do not thou be a man unwise and foolish, so that by giving thought to these things thou perish for ever and ever. For, "Turn Thou away evil things unto mine enemies." For if thou shalt have place in the body of David Himself, in His virtue He will destroy them. These men flourish in the felicity of the world, perish in the virtue of God.

548. Lk 12:20.   549. 2 Cor 1:12.   550. Ps 4:6, 7.

551. Alternatively, "let them be."   552. Ps 92:7.

Not in the same manner as they flourish, do they also perish: for they flourish for a time, perish for everlasting: flourish in unreal good things, perish in real torments. "In Thy strength destroy," whom in Thy weakness Thou hast endured.

10. "Voluntarily I will sacrifice to Thee" (v. 6). Who can even understand this good thing of the heart, at another's speaking thereof, unless in himself he hath tasted it? What is, "Voluntarily I will sacrifice to Thee"? . . . For what sacrifice here shall I take, brethren? Or what worthily shall I offer to the Lord for His mercy? Victims shall I seek from flock of sheep, ram shall I select, for any bull in the herds shall I look out, frankincense indeed from the land of the Sabaeans shall I bring? What shall I do? What offer; except that whereof He speaketh, "Sacrifice of praise shall honor Me"?[553] Wherefore then "voluntarily"? Because truly I love that which I praise. I praise God, and in the selfsame praise I rejoice: in the praise of Himself I rejoice, at whom being praised, I blush not. For He is not praised in the same manner as by those who love the theatrical follies is praised either by a charioteer, or a hunter, or actor of any kind, and by their praisers, other praisers are invited, are exhorted, to shout together: and when all have shouted, ofttimes, if their favorite is overcome, they are all put to the blush. Not so is our God: be He praised with the will, loved with charity: let it be gratuitous (or voluntary) that He is loved and that He is praised. What is "gratuitous"? Himself for the sake of Himself, not for the sake of something else. For if thou praisest God in order that He may give thee something else, no longer freely dost thou love God. Thou wouldest blush, if thy wife for the sake of riches were to love thee, and perchance if poverty should befall thee, should begin to think of adultery. Seeing that therefore thou wouldest be loved by thy partner freely, wilt thou for anything else love God? What reward art thou to receive of God, O covetous man? Not earth for thee, but Himself He keepeth, who made heaven and earth. "Voluntarily I will sacrifice to Thee": do it not of necessity. For if for the sake of anything else thou praisest God, out of necessity thou praisest. . . . These things also which He hath given, because of the Giver, are good things. For He giveth entirely, He giveth these temporal things: and to certain men to their good, to certain men to

553. Ps 1:23.

their harm, after the height and depth of His judgments. . . . "Voluntarily I will sacrifice to Thee." Wherefore "voluntarily"? Because *gratis*. What is *gratis*? "And I will confess to Thy name, O Lord, for it is a good thing": for nothing else, but because a "good thing" it is. Doth he say, "I will confess to Thy name, O Lord," because Thou givest me fruitful manors, because Thou givest me gold and silver, because Thou givest me extended riches, abundant money, most exalted dignity? Nay. But what? "For it is a good thing." Nothing I find better than Thy name.

11. "For out of all tribulation Thou hast delivered me" (v. 7). For this cause I have perceived how good a thing is Thy name: for if this I were able before tribulations to acknowledge, perchance for me there had been no need of them. But tribulation hath been applied for admonition, admonition hath redounded to Thy praise. For I should not have understood where I was, except of my weakness I had been admonished. "Out of all tribulations," therefore, "Thou hast delivered me. And upon mine enemies mine eye hath looked back": upon those Ziphites "mine eye hath looked back." Yea, their flower I have passed over in loftiness of heart, unto Thee I have come, and thence I have looked back upon them, and have seen that "All flesh is grass, and all the glory of man as the flower of grass":[554] as in a certain place is also said, "I have seen the ungodly man to be exalted and raised up like[555] the cedars of Lebanon: I passed by, and, lo! he was not."[556] Wherefore "he was not"? Because thou hast passed by. What is, "because thou hast passed by"? Because not to no purpose hast thou heard "Lift up thy heart"; because not on earth, where thou wouldest have rotted, thou hast remained; because thou hast lifted thy soul to God, and thou hast mounted beyond the cedars of Lebanon, and from that elevation hast observed: and "Lo! he was not"; and thou hast sought him, and there hath not been found place for him. No longer is labor before thee; because thou hast entered into the sanctuary of God, and hast understood for the last things.[557] So also here thus he concludeth. "And upon mine enemies mine eye hath looked back." This do ye therefore, brethren, with your souls; lift up your hearts, sharpen the edge of your mind, learn truly to love God, learn to de-

---

554. Is 40:6.   555. Oxford mss. "above."   556. Ps 37:35, 36.
557. Ps 73:16, 17.

spise the present world, learn voluntarily to sacrifice the offerings of praise; to the end that, mounting beyond the flower of the grass, ye may look back upon your enemies.

Psalm 67[558]

1. Your Love remembereth, that in two psalms,[559] which have been already treated of, we have stirred up our soul to bless the Lord, and with godly chant have said, "Bless thou, O my soul, the Lord." If therefore we have stirred up our soul in those psalms to bless the Lord, in this psalm is well said, "May God have pity on us, and bless us" (v. 1). Let our soul bless the Lord, and Let God bless us. When God blesseth us, we grow, and when we bless the Lord, we grow, to us both are profitable. He is not increased by our blessing, nor is He lessened by our cursing. He that curseth the Lord is himself lessened: he that blesseth the Lord is himself increased. First, there is in us the blessing of the Lord, and the consequence is that we also bless the Lord. That is the rain, this the fruit. Therefore there is rendered as it were fruit to God the Husbandman, raining upon and tilling us. Let us chant these words with no barren devotion, with no empty voice but with true heart. For most evidently God the Father hath been called a Husbandman.[560] The apostle saith, "God's husbandry ye are, God's building ye are."[561] In things visible of this world, the vine is not a building, and a building is not a vineyard, but we are the vineyard of the Lord, because He tilleth us for fruit; the building of God we are, since He who tilleth us, dwelleth in us. And what saith the same apostle? "I have planted, Apollos hath watered, but the increase God hath given. Therefore neither he that planteth is anything, nor he that watereth, but He that giveth the increase, even God."[562] He it is therefore that giveth the increase. Are those perchance the husbandmen? For a husbandman he is called that planteth, that watereth, but the apostle hath said, "I have planted, Apollos hath watered." Do we inquire whence himself hath done this? The apostle maketh answer, "Yet

558. Lat. 66. Sermon to the Commonalty.   559. Ps 103, 104.

560. Jn 15:1.   561. 1 Cor 3:9.   562. 1 Cor 3:6, 7.

not I, but the Grace of God with me."[563] Therefore whithersoever
thou turn thee, whether through angels, thou wilt find God thy
Husbandman; whether through prophets, the Same is thy Husbandman; whether through apostles, the very Same acknowledge
to be thy Husbandman. What then of us? Perchance we are the laborers of that Husbandman, and this too with powers imparted by
Himself, and by Grace granted by Himself. . . .

2. "Lighten His countenance upon us." Thou wast perchance
going to inquire, what is "bless us"? In many ways men would
have themselves to be blessed of God: one would have himself to be
blessed, so that he may have a house full of the necessary things of
this life; another desireth himself to be blessed, so that he may obtain soundness of body without flaw; another would have himself
to be blessed, if perchance he is sick, so that he may acquire soundness; another longing for sons, and perchance being sorrowful because none are born, would have himself to be blessed so that he
may have posterity. And who could number the divers wishes of
men desiring themselves to be blessed of the Lord God? But which
of us would say, that it was no blessing of God, if either husbandry
should bring him fruit, or if any man's house should abound in
plenty of things temporal, or if the very bodily health be either so
maintained that it be not lost, or, if lost, be regained?

3. "Every soul that is blessed is simple,"[564] not cleaving to things
earthly nor with glued wings groveling, but beaming with the
brightness of virtues, on the twin wings of twin love doth spring
into the free air; and seeth how from her is withdrawn that
whereon she was treading, not that whereon she was resting, and
she saith securely, "The Lord hath given, the Lord hath taken
away; as it hath pleased the Lord, so hath been done: be the name of
the Lord blessed." . . . But let not perchance any weak man say,
when shall I be of so great virtue, as was holy Job? The mightiness
of the tree thou wonderest at, because but now thou hast been born:
this great tree, whereat thou wonderest, under the branches and
shade whereof thou coolest thyself, hath been a switch. But dost
thou fear lest there be taken away from thee these things, when
such thou shalt have become? Observe that they are taken away
from evil men also. Why therefore dost thou delay conversion?

563. 1 Cor 15:10.   564. Prv 11:25 (Septuagint).

That which thou fearest when good to lose, perchance if evil thou wilt lose still. If being good thou shalt have lost them, there is by thee the Comforter that hath taken them away: the coffer is emptied of gold; the heart is full of faith: without, poor thou art, but within, rich thou art; thy riches with thee thou carriest, which thou wouldest not lose, even if naked from shipwreck thou shouldest escape. Why doth not the loss, that perchance, if evil, thou wilt lose, find thee good; forasmuch as thou seest evil men also suffer loss? But with greater loss they are stricken: empty is the house, more empty the conscience is. Whatsoever evil man shall have lost these things, hath nothing to hold by without, hath nothing within whereon he may rest. He fleeth when he hath suffered loss from the place where before the eyes of men with the display of riches he used to vaunt himself; now in the eyes of men to vaunt himself he is not able: to himself within he returneth not, because he hath nothing. He hath not imitated the ant, he hath not gathered to himself grains, while it was summer.[565] What have I meant by, while it was summer? While he had quietude of life, while he had this world's prosperity, when he had leisure, when happy he was being called by all men, his summer it was. He should have imitated the ant, he should have heard the Word of God, he should have gathered together grains, and he should have stored them within. There had come the trial of tribulation, there had come upon him a winter of numbness, tempest of fear, the cold of sorrow, whether it were loss, or any danger to his safety, or any bereavement of his family; or any dishonor and humiliation; it was winter; the ant falleth back upon that which in summer she hath gathered together; and within in her secret store, where no man seeth, she is recruited by her summer toils. When for herself she was gathering together these stores in summer, all men saw her: when on these she feedeth in winter, no one seeth. What is this? See the ant of God, he riseth day by day, he hasteneth to the Church of God, he prayeth, he heareth lection, he chanteth hymn, he digesteth that which he hath heard, with himself[566] he thinketh thereon, he storeth within grains gathered from the threshing-floor. They that providently hear those very things which even now are being spoken of, do thus, and by all men are seen to go forth to the Church, go back from Church, to

565. Prv 6:6, 3:25.   566. Or, "at home."

hear sermon, to hear lection, to choose a book, open and read it: all these things are seen, when they are done. That ant is treading his path, carrying and storing up in the sight of men seeing him. There cometh winter sometime, for to whom cometh it not? There chanceth loss, there chanceth bereavement: other men pity him perchance as being miserable, who know not what the ant hath within to eat, and they say, miserable he whom this hath befallen, or what spirits, dost thou think, hath he whom this hath befallen? How afflicted is he? He measureth by himself, hath compassion according to his own strength; and thus he is deceived: because the measure wherewith he measureth himself, he would apply to him whom he knoweth not. . . . O sluggard, gather in summer while thou art able; winter will not suffer thee to gather, but to eat that which thou shalt have gathered. For how many men so suffer tribulation, that there is no opportunity either to read anything, or to hear anything, and they obtain no admittance, perchance, to those that would comfort them. The ant hath remained in her nest; let her see if she hath gathered anything in summer, whereby she may recruit herself in winter.

4. There is a double interpretation; both must be given: "lighten," he saith, "Thy face upon us," show to us Thy countenance. For God doth not ever light His countenance, as if ever it had been without light: but He lighteth it upon us, so that what was hidden from us is opened to us, and that which was, but to us was hidden, is unveiled upon us, that is, is lightened. Or else surely it is, "Thy image lighten upon us," so that he said this, in "lighten Thy countenance upon us": Thou hast imprinted Thy countenance upon us; Thou hast made us after Thine image and Thy likeness;[567] Thou hast made us Thy coin; but Thine image ought not in darkness to remain. Send a ray of Thy wisdom, let it dispel our darkness, and let there shine in us Thy image; let us know ourselves to be Thine image, let us hear what hath been said in the Song of Songs, "If Thou shalt not have known Thyself, O Thou fair one among women."[568] For there is said to the Church, "If Thou shalt not have known Thyself." What is this? If Thou shalt not have known Thyself to have been made after the image of God. O Soul of the Church, precious, redeemed with the blood of the

567. Gn 1:26.   568. Sg 1:8.

Lamb immaculate, observe of how great value Thou art, think what hath been given for Thee. Let us say, therefore, and let us long that He "may lighten His face upon us." We wear His face: in like manner as the faces of emperors are spoken of, truly a kind of sacred face is that of God in His own image: but unrighteous men know not in themselves the image of God. In order that the countenance of God may be lightened upon them, they ought to say what? "Thou shalt light my candle, O Lord my God, Thou shalt light my darkness."[569] I am in the darkness of sins, but by the ray of Thy wisdom dispelled be my darkness, may Thy countenance appear; and if perchance through me it appeareth somewhat deformed, by Thee be there reformed that which by Thee hath been formed.

5. "That we may know on earth Thy way" (v. 2). "On earth," here, in this life, "we may know Thy way." What is, "Thy way"? That which leadeth to Thee. May we acknowledge whither we are going, acknowledge where we are as we go; neither in darkness we can do. Afar Thou art from men sojourning, a way to us Thou hast presented, through which we must return to Thee. "Let us acknowledge on earth Thy way." What is His way wherein we have desired, "That we may know on earth Thy way"? We are going to inquire this ourselves, not of ourselves to learn it. We can learn of it from the Gospel: "I am the Way,"[570] the Lord saith: Christ hath said, "I am the Way." But dost thou fear lest thou stray? He hath added, "And the Truth." Who strayeth in the Truth? He strayeth that hath departed from the Truth. The Truth is Christ, the Way is Christ: walk therein. Dost thou fear lest thou die before thou attain unto Him? "I am the Life: I am," He saith, "the Way and the Truth and the Life." As if He were saying, "What fearest thou? Through Me thou walkest, to Me thou walkest, in Me thou restest." What therefore meaneth, "We may know on earth Thy Way," but "we may know on earth Thy Christ"? But let the psalm itself reply: lest ye think that out of other Scriptures there must be adduced testimony, which perchance is here wanting; by repetition he hath shown what signified, "That we may know on earth Thy Way," and as if thou wast inquiring, "In what earth, what way?" "In all nations Thy Salvation." In what earth, thou art inquiring? Hear: "In all nations." What way art thou seeking? Hear: "Thy Salvation." Is

569. Ps 18:28.   570. Jn 14:6.

not perchance Christ his Salvation? And what is that which the old Symeon hath said, that old man, I say, in the Gospel, preserved full of years even unto the infancy of the Word?[571] For that old man took in his hands the Infant Word of God. Would He that in the womb deigned to be, disdain to be in the hands of an old man? The Same was in the womb of the virgin, as was in the hands of the old man, a weak infant both within the bowels, and in the old man's hand, to give us strength, by whom were made all things; and if all things, even His very mother. He came humble, He came weak, but clothed with a weakness to be changed into strength, because "though He was crucified of weakness, yet He liveth of the virtue of God,"[572] the apostle saith. He was then in the hands of an old man. And what saith that old man? Rejoicing that now he must be loosed from this world, seeing how in his own hand was held He by whom and in whom his Salvation was upheld; he saith what? "Now Thou lettest go," he saith, "O Lord, Thy servant in peace, for mine eyes have seen Thy Salvation."[573] Therefore, "May God bless us, and have pity on us; may He lighten His countenance upon us, that we may know on earth Thy Way!" In what earth? "In all nations." What Way? "Thy Salvation."

6. What followeth because the Salvation of God is known in all nations? "Let the peoples confess to Thee, O God" (v. 3); "confess to Thee," he saith, "all peoples." There standeth forth a heretic, and he saith, In Africa I[574] have peoples: and another from another quarter, And I in Galatia have peoples. Thou in Africa, he in Galatia: therefore I require one that hath them everywhere. Ye have indeed dared to exult at that voice, when ye heard, "Let the peoples confess to Thee, O God." Hear the following verse, how he speaketh not of a part: "Let there confess to Thee all peoples." Walk ye in the Way together with all nations; walk ye in the Way together with all peoples, O sons of peace, sons of the One Catholic Church,[575] walk ye in the Way, seeing as ye walk. Wayfarers do this to beguile their toil. Sing ye in this Way; I implore you by that

---

571. Lk 2:30.   572. 2 Cor 13:4.   573. Lk 2:29, 30.

574. Oxford mss. "I too."

575. I.e., the Nicene communion, in which Rome and Constantinople had coequal dignities—primacies of honor only, based on synodical concession to imperial capitals.—C.

Same Way, sing ye in this Way: a new song sing ye, let no one there sing old ones: sing ye the love songs of your fatherland, let no one sing old ones. New Way, new wayfarer, new song. Hear thou the apostle exhorting thee to a new song: "Whatever therefore is in Christ is a new creature; old things have passed away, behold they have been made new." A new song sing ye in the way, which ye have learned "on the earth." In what earth? "In all nations." Therefore even the new song doth not belong to a part. He that in a part singeth, singeth an old song: whatever he please to sing, he singeth an old song, the old man singeth: divided he is, carnal he is. Truly insofar as carnal he is, so far he is old; and insofar as he is spiritual, so far new. See what saith the apostle: "I could not speak to you as if to spiritual, but as if to carnal."[576] Whence proveth he them carnal? "For while one saith, I am of Paul; but another, I of Apollos: are ye not," he saith, "carnal?"[577] Therefore in the Spirit a new song sing thou in the safe way. Just as wayfarers sing, and ofttimes in the night sing. Awful round about all things do sound, or rather they sound not around, but are still around; and the more still the more awful; nevertheless, even they that fear robbers do sing. How much more safely thou singest in Christ! That way hath no robber, unless thou by forsaking the way fallest in the hands of a robber. . . . Why fear ye to confess, and in your confession to sing a new song together with all the earth; in all the earth, in Catholic peace, dost thou fear to confess to God, lest He condemn thee that hast confessed? If having not confessed thou liest concealed, having confessed thou wilt be condemned. Thou fearest to confess, that by not confessing canst not be concealed: thou wilt be condemned if thou hast held thy peace, that mightest have been delivered, by having confessed. "O God, confess to Thee all peoples."

7. And because this confession leadeth not to punishment, he continueth and saith, "Let the nations rejoice and exult" (v. 4). If robbers after confession made do wail before man, let the faithful after confessing before God rejoice. If a man be judge, the torturer and his fear exact from a robber a confession: yea sometimes fear wringeth out confession, pain extorteth it: and he that waileth in tortures, but feareth to be killed if he confess, supporteth tortures as far as he is able: and if he shall have been overcome by pain, he

576. 1 Cor 3:1.   577. 1 Cor 3:4.

giveth his voice for death. Nowise therefore is he joyful; nowise exulting: before he confesseth the claw teareth him; when he hath
confessed, the executioner leadeth him along a condemned felon:
wretched in every case. But "let the nations rejoice and exult."
Whence? Through that same confession. Why? Because good He is
to whom they confess: He exacteth confession, to the end that He
may deliver the humble; He condemneth one not confessing, to the
end that He may punish the proud. Therefore be thou sorrowful
before thou confessest; after having confessed exult, now thou wilt
be made whole. Thy conscience had gathered up evil humors, with
boil it had swollen, it was torturing thee, it suffered thee not to rest:
the Physician applieth the fomentations of words,[578] and sometimes
He lanceth it, He applieth the surgeon's knife by the chastisement
of tribulation: do thou acknowledge the Physician's hand, confess
thou, let every evil humor go forth and flow away in confession:
now exult, now rejoice, that which remaineth will be easy to be
made whole. . . . "Let the nations rejoice and exult, for Thou
judgest the peoples in equity." And that unrighteous men may not
fear, he hath added, "and the nations on the earth Thou directest."
Depraved were the nations and crooked were the nations, perverse
were the nations; for the ill desert of their depravity, and crooked-
ness and perverseness, the Judge's coming they feared: there
cometh the hand of the same, it is stretched out mercifully to the
peoples, they are guided in order that they may walk the straight
way; why should they fear the Judge to come, that have first acknowledged Him for a Corrector? To His hand let them give up
themselves, Himself guideth the nations on the earth. But guided
nations are walking in the Truth, are exulting in Him, are doing
good works; and if perchance there cometh in any water (for on sea
they are sailing) through the very small holes, through the crevices
into the hold, pumping it out by good works, lest by more and
more coming it accumulate, and sink the ship, pumping it out
daily, fasting, praying, doing alms-deeds, saying with pure heart,
"Forgive us our debts, as also we forgive our debtors"[579]—saying
such words walk thou secure, and exult in the way, sing in the way.
Do not fear the Judge: before thou wast a believer, thou didst find a

---

578. Oxford mss. *ferramenta verborum*, "the instruments of words."

579. Mt 6:12.

Savior. Thee ungodly He sought out that He might redeem, thee redeemed will He forsake so as to destroy? "And the nations on earth Thou directest."

8. He exulteth, rejoiceth, exhorteth, he repeateth those same verses in exhortation. "The earth hath given her fruit" (v. 6). What fruit? "Let all peoples confess to Thee." Earth it was, of thorns it was full; there came the hand of One rooting them up, there came a calling by His majesty and mercy, the earth began to confess; now the earth giveth her fruit. Would she give her fruit unless first she were rained on? Would she give her fruit, unless first the mercy of God had come from above? Let them read to me, thou sayest, how the earth being rained upon gave her fruit. Hear of the Lord raining upon her: "Repent, for the kingdom of heaven is at hand."[580] He raineth, and that same rain is thunder; it terrifieth: fear thou Him thundering, and receive Him raining. Behold, after that voice of a thundering and raining God, after that voice let us see something out of the Gospel itself. Behold that harlot of ill fame in the city burst into a strange house into which she had not been invited by the host, but by One invited she had been called;[581] called[582] not with tongue, but by Grace. The sick woman knew that she had there a place, where she was aware that her Physician was sitting at meat. She has gone in, that was a sinner; she dareth not draw near save to the feet: she weepeth at His feet, she washeth with tears, she wipeth with hair, she anointeth with ointment. Why wonderest thou? The earth hath given her fruit. This thing, I say, came to pass by the Lord raining there through His own mouth; there came to pass the things whereof we read in the Gospel; and by His raining through His clouds, by the sending of the apostles and by their preaching the truth, the earth more abundantly hath given her fruit, and that crop now hath filled the round world.

9. The fruit of the earth was first in Jerusalem. For from thence began the Church: there came there the Holy Spirit, and filled full the holy men gathered together in one place; miracles were done, with the tongues of all men they spake.[583] They were filled full of the Spirit of God, the people were converted that were in that place, fearing and receiving the divine shower, by confession they

580. Mt 3:2.   581. Lk 7:37.   582. Oxford mss. repeat *vocata*.

583. Acts 2:1, 4.

brought forth so much fruit, that all their goods they brought together into a common stock, making distribution to the poor, in
order that no one might call anything his own, but all things might
be to them in common, and they might have one soul and one heart
unto God.[584] For there had been forgiven[585] them the blood which
they had shed, it had been forgiven them by the Lord pardoning, in
order that now they might even learn to drink that which they had
shed. Great in that place is the fruit: the earth hath given her fruit,
both great fruit, and most excellent fruit. Ought by any means that
earth alone to give her fruit? "May there bless us God, our God,
may there bless us God" (v. 7). Still may He bless us: for blessing in
multiplication is wont most chiefly and properly to be perceived.
Let us prove this in Genesis; see the works of God: God made
light,[586] and God made a division between light and darkness: the
light He called day, and the darkness He called night. It is not said,
He blessed the light. For the same light returneth and changeth by
days and nights. He calleth the sky the firmament between waters
and waters: it is not said, He blessed the sky: He severed the sea
from the dry land, and named both, the dry land earth, and the
gathering together of the waters sea: neither here is it said, God
blessed. . . .

10. How should we will that *to us* He come? By living well, by
doing well. Let not things past please us; things present not hold us;
let us not "close the ear" as it were with tail, let us not press down
the ear on the ground; lest by things past we be kept back from
hearing, lest by things present we be entangled and prevented from
meditating on things future; let us reach forth unto those things
which are before, let us forget things past.[587] And that for which
now we toil, for which now we groan, for which now we sigh, of
which now we speak, which in part, however small soever, we perceive, and to receive are not able, we shall receive, we shall thoroughly enjoy in the resurrection of the just. Our youth shall be
renewed as an eagle's,[588] if only our old man we break[589] against the

584. Acts 4:32.   585. Or, "given."   586. Gn 1:3.   587. Phil 3:13.

588. Ps 103:5.

589. On Ps 103:5, he says that the eagle is said to break off an excessive growth of
the beak against a rock.

Rock of Christ. Whether those things be true, brethren, which are said of the serpent, or those which are said of the eagle, or whether it be rather a tale of men than truth, truth is nevertheless in the Scriptures, and not without reason the Scriptures have spoken of this: let us do whatever it signifieth, and not toil to discover how far that is true. Be thou such a one as that thy youth may be able to be renewed as an eagle's. And know thou that it cannot be renewed, except thine old man on the Rock shall have been broken off: that is, except by the aid of the Rock, except by the aid of Christ, thou wilt not be able to be renewed. Do not thou because of the pleasantness of the past life be deaf to the word of God: do not by things present be so held and entangled, as to say, I have no leisure to read, I have no leisure to hear. This is to press down the ear upon the ground. Do thou therefore not be such a one: but be such a one as on the other side thou findest, that is, so that thou forget things past, unto things before reach thyself out, in order that thine old man on the Rock thou mayest break off. And if any comparisons shall have been made for thee, if thou hast found them in the Scriptures, believe: if thou shalt not have found them spoken of except by report, do not very much believe them. The thing itself perchance is so, perchance is not so. Do thou profit by it, let that comparison avail for thy salvation. Thou art unwilling to profit by this comparison, by some other profit, it mattereth not provided thou do it: and, being secure, wait for the kingdom of God, lest thy prayer quarrel with thee. For, O Christian man, when thou sayest, Thy kingdom come, how sayest thou, "Thy kingdom come"?[590] Examine thy heart: see, behold, "Thy kingdom come." He crieth out to thee, "I come": dost thou not fear? Often we have told Your Love: both to preach the truth is nothing, if heart from tongue dissent: and to hear the truth is nothing, if fruit follow not hearing. From this place exalted as it were we are speaking to you: but how much we are beneath your feet in fear, God knoweth, who is gracious to the humble; for the voices of men praising do not give us so much pleasure as the devotion of men confessing, and the deeds of men now righteous. And how we have no pleasure but in your advances, but by those praises how much we are endangered, He

590. Mt 6:10.

knoweth, whom we pray to deliver us from all dangers, and to deign to know and crown us together with you, saved from every trial, in His kingdom.

Psalm 73 [591]

1. This psalm hath an inscription, that is, a title, "There have failed the hymns of David, the son of Jesse.[592] A Psalm[593] of Asaph himself." So many psalms we have on the titles whereof is written the name David, nowhere there is added, "son of Jesse," except in this alone. Which we must believe hath not been done to no purpose, nor capriciously. For everywhere God doth make intimations to us, and to the understanding thereof doth invite the godly study of love. What is, "there have failed the hymns of David, the son of Jesse"? Hymns are praises of God accompanied with singing: hymns are songs containing the praise of God. If there be praise, and it be not of God, it is no hymn: if there be praise, and God's praise, and it be not sung, it is no hymn. It must needs then, if it be a hymn, have these three things, both praise, and that of God, and singing. What is then, "there have failed the hymns"? There have failed the praises which are sung unto God. He seemeth to tell of a thing painful, and so to speak deplorable. For he that singeth praise, not only praiseth, but only praiseth with gladness: he that singeth praise, not only singeth, but also loveth him of whom he singeth. In praise, there is the speaking forth of one confessing; in singing, the affection of one loving. "There have failed" then "the hymns of David," he saith: and he hath added, "the son of Jesse." For David was king of Israel, son of Jesse,[594] at a certain time of the Old Testament, at which time the New Testament was therein hidden, like fruit in a root. For if thou seek fruit in a root, thou wilt not find, and yet dost thou not find any fruit in the branches, except

591. Lat. 72.

592. This sentence in our version and in the Vulgate stands at the end of the previous psalm, where it is more significant. David can prophesy no further concerning the glory that shall be revealed.—C.

593. Title of Psalm 73.   594. 1 Sm 16:19.

that which hath gone forth from the root. . . . And in like manner as Christ Himself to be born after the flesh was hidden in the root, that is in the seed of the patriarchs, and at a certain time must be revealed, as at the fruit appearing, according as it is written, "there hath flourished a shoot from the root of Jesse,"[595] so also the New Testament itself which is in Christ, in those former times was hidden, being known to the prophets alone, and to the very few godly men, not by the manifestation of things present, but by the revelation of things future. For what meaneth it, brethren (to mention but one thing), that Abraham sending his faithful servant to espouse a wife for his only son, maketh him swear to him, and in the oath saith to him, "Put thy hand under my thigh, and swear"?[596] What was there in the thigh of Abraham, where he put his hand in swearing? What was there there, except that which even then was promised to him, "In thy seed shall be blessed all nations"?[597] Under the name of thigh, flesh is signified. From the flesh of Abraham, through Isaac and Jacob, and not to mention many names, through Mary was our Lord Jesus Christ.

2. But that the root was in the patriarchs, how shall we show? Let us question Paul. The Gentiles now believing in Christ, and desiring as it were to boast over the Jews who crucified Christ; although also from that same people there came another wall, meeting in the corner, that is, in Christ Himself, the wall of uncircumcision, that is, of the Gentiles, coming from a different quarter: when, I say, the nations were lifting up themselves, he doth thus depress them. "For if thou," he saith, "being cut out of the natural wild olive, hast been grafted in among them, do not boast against the branches: for if thou boastest, thou dost not bear the root, but the root thee."[598] Therefore he speaketh of certain branches broken off from the root of the patriarchs because of unbelief, and the wild olive therein grafted in, that it might be partaker of the fatness of the olive, that is, the Church coming out of the Gentiles. And who doth graft the wild olive on the olive? The olive is wont to be grafted on the wild olive; the wild olive on the olive we never saw. For whosoever may have done so will find no berries but those of the wild olive. For that which is grafted in, the same groweth, and of that kind the fruit is found. There is not found the fruit of the

595. Is 11:1.   596. Gn 24:2.   597. Gn 22:18.   598. Rom 11:17, 18.

root but of the graft. The apostle showing that God did this thing by His Omnipotence, namely, that the wild olive should be grafted into the root of the olive, and should not bear wild berries, but olive—ascribing it to the Omnipotence of God, the apostle saith this, "If thou hast been cut out of the natural wild olive and against nature hast been grafted into a good[599] olive, do not boast," he saith, "against the branches."[600]

3. In the time then of the Old Testament, brethren, the promises from our God to that carnal people were earthly and temporal. There was promised an earthly kingdom, there was promised that land into which they were also led, after being delivered from Egypt: by Jesus[601] son of Nave they were led into the land of promise, where also earthly Jerusalem was built, where David reigned: they received the land, after being delivered from Egypt, by passing through the Red Sea. . . . Such were also those promises, which were not to endure, through which however were figured future promises which were to endure, so that all that course of temporal promises was a figure and a sort of prophecy of things future. Accordingly when that kingdom was failing, where reigned David, the son of Jesse, that is, one that was a man, though a prophet, though holy, because he saw and foresaw Christ to come, of whose seed also after the flesh He was to be born: nevertheless a man, nevertheless not yet Christ, nevertheless not yet our King Son of God, but King David son of Jesse: because then that kingdom was to fail, through the receiving of which kingdom at that time God was praised by carnal men; for this thing alone they esteemed a great matter, namely, that they were delivered temporally from those by whom they were being oppressed, and that they had escaped from persecuting enemies through the Red Sea, and had been led through the desert, and had found country and kingdom: for this alone they praised God, not yet perceiving the thing which God was designing beforehand and promising in these figures. In the failing therefore of those things for which the carnal people, over whom reigned that David, was praising God, "there failed the hymns of David," not the Son of God but the "son of Jesse."

599. The word "good" is not in the mss.; it is found at Oxford, and probably in mss. used for earlier editions.   600. Rom, 11:24, 18.

601. I.e., Joshua, the son of Nun.—C.

4. Whose voice is the psalm? "Of Asaph."[602] What is Asaph? As we find in interpretations from the Hebrew language into the Greek, and those again translated to us from the Greek into the Latin, Asaph is interpreted "synagogue." It is the voice therefore of the synagogue. But when thou hast heard "synagogue," do not forthwith abhor it, as if it were the murderer of the Lord. That synagogue was indeed the murderer of the Lord, no man doubteth it: but remember, that from the synagogue were the rams whereof we are the sons. Whence it is said in a psalm, "Bring ye to the Lord the sons of rams." What rams are thence? Peter, John, James, Andrew, Bartholomew, and the rest of the apostles. Hence also he too at first Saul, afterward Paul: that is, at first proud, afterward humble. . . . Therefore even Paul came to us from the synagogue, and Peter and the other apostles from the synagogue. Therefore when thou hast heard the voice of the synagogue, do not look to the deserving thereof, but observe the offspring. There is speaking therefore in this psalm, the synagogue, after the failing of the hymns of David, the son of Jesse that is, after the failing of things temporal, through which God was wont to be praised by the carnal people. But why did these fail, except in order that others might be sought for? That there might be sought for what? Was it things which were not there? No, but things which were there being hidden in figures: not which were not yet there,[603] but which there as it were in a sort were concealed in certain secret things of mysteries. What things? "These," saith the apostle himself, "were our figures."[604]

5. It was the synagogue therefore, that is, they that there worshipped God after a godly sort, but yet for the sake of earthly things, for the sake of these present things (for there are ungodly men who seek the blessings of present things from demons: but this people was on this account better than the Gentiles, because although it were blessings present and temporal, yet they sought them from the One God, who is the Creator of all things both spiritual and corporal). When therefore those godly men after the flesh were observing—that is that synagogue which was made up of good men, men for the time good, not spiritual men, such as were the prophets therein, such as were the few that understood the

---

602. See title of psalm above.   603. Oxford mss. add, "not which," etc.

604. 1 Cor 10:6.

kingdom heavenly, eternal—that synagogue, I say, observed what things it received from God, and what things God promised to that people, abundance of things earthly, land, peace, earthly felicity: but in all these things were figures, and they not perceiving what was there concealed in things figured, thought that God gave this for a great matter, and had nothing better to give to men loving Him and serving Him: they remarked and saw certain sinners, ungodly, blasphemers, servants of demons, sons of the devil, living in great naughtiness and pride, yet abounding in such things earthly, temporal, for which sort of things they were serving God themselves: and there sprang up a most evil thought in the heart, which made the feet to totter, and almost slip out of God's way. And behold this thought was in the people of the Old Testament: I would it be not in our carnal brethren, when now openly there is being proclaimed the felicity of the New Testament.

6. "How good is the God of Israel!" But to whom? "To men right in heart" (v. 1). To men perverse what? Perverse He seemeth. So also in another psalm He saith: "With a holy man holy Thou shalt be, and with the innocent man innocent Thou shalt be, and with the perverse man perverse Thou shalt be."[605] What is, perverse Thou shalt be with the perverse man? Perverse the perverse man shall think Thee. Not that by any means God is made perverse. Far be it: what He is, He is. But in like manner as the sun appeareth mild to one having clear, sound, healthy, strong eyes, but against weak eyes doth dart hard spears, so to say; the former looking at it, it doth invigorate, the latter it doth torture, though not being itself changed, but the man being changed: so when thou shalt have begun to be perverse, and to thee God shall seem to be perverse, thou art changed, not He. That therefore to thee will be punishment which to good men is joy. He calling to mind this thing, saith, "How good is the God of Israel to men right in heart!"

7. But what to thee? "But my feet were almost moved" (v. 2). When were the feet moved, except when the heart was not right? Whence was the heart not right? Hear: "My steps were well nigh overthrown." What he hath meant by "almost," the same he hath meant by "well nigh," and what he hath meant by "my feet were al-

605. Ps 18:25.

most moved," the same he hath meant by "my steps were over-thrown." Almost my feet were moved, almost my steps were over-thrown. Moved were the feet: but whence were the feet moved and the steps overthrown? Moved were the feet to going astray, over-thrown were the steps to falling: not entirely, but "almost." But what is this? Already I was going to stray, I had not gone: already I was falling, I had not fallen.

8. But why even this? "For I was jealous," he saith, "in the case of sinners, looking on the peace of sinners" (v. 3). I observed sinners, I saw them to have peace. What peace? Temporal, transient, falling, and earthly: but yet such as I also was desiring of God. I saw them that served not God to have that which I desired in order that I might serve God: and my feet were moved and my steps were al-most overthrown. But why sinners have this, he saith briefly: "Be-cause there is no avoidance of their death, and there is a firmament in their scourge" (v. 4). Now I have perceived, he saith, why they have peace, and flourish on the earth; because of their death there is no avoidance, because death sure and eternal doth await them, which neither doth avoid them, nor can they avoid it, "because there is no avoidance of their death, and there is a firmament in their scourge." And there is a firmament in their scourge. For their scourge is not temporal, but firm for everlasting. Because of these evil things then which are to be to them eternal, now what? "In the labors of men they are not, and with men they shall not be scourged" (v. 5). Doth not even the devil himself escape scourging with men, for whom nevertheless an eternal punishment is being prepared?

9. Wherefore on this account what do these men, while they are not scourged, while they labor not with men? "Therefore," he saith "there hath holden them pride" (v. 6). Observe these men, proud, undisciplined; observe the bull, devoted for a victim, suffered to stray at liberty; and to damage whatever he may, even up to the day of his slaughter. Now it is a good thing, brethren, that we should hear in the very words of a prophet of this bull as it were, whereof I have spoken. For thus of him the Scripture doth make mention in another place: he saith that they are, as it were, made ready as for a victim, and that they are spared for an evil liberty.[606] "Therefore,"

606. Prv 7:22.

he saith, "there hath holden them pride." What is, "there hath holden them pride"? "They have been clothed about with their iniquity and ungodliness." He hath not said, covered; but, "clothed about," on all sides covered up with their ungodliness. Deservedly miserable, they neither see nor are seen, because they are clothed about; and the inward parts of them are not seen. For whosoever could behold the inward parts of evil men, that are as it were happy for a time, whosoever could see their torturing consciences, whosoever could examine their souls racked with such mighty perturbations of desires and fears, would see them to be miserable even when they are called happy. But because "they are clothed about with their iniquity and ungodliness," they see not; but neither are they seen. The Spirit knew them, that saith these words concerning them: and we ought to examine such men with the same eye as that wherewith we know that we see, if there is taken from our eyes the covering of ungodliness.

10. At first these men are being described. "There shall go forth as if out of fat their iniquity" (v. 7). . . . A poor beggar committeth a theft; out of leanness hath gone forth the iniquity: but when a rich man aboundeth in so many things, why doth he plunder the things of others? Of the former the iniquity out of leanness, of the other out of fatness, hath gone forth. Therefore to the lean man when thou sayest, Why hast thou done this? Humbly afflicted and abject he replieth, Need hath compelled me. Why hast thou not feared God? Want was urgent. Say to a rich man, Why doest thou these things, and fearest not God?—supposing thee to be great enough to be able to say it—see if he even deigneth to hear; see if even against thyself there will not go forth iniquity out of his fatness. For now they declare war with their teachers and reprovers, and become enemies of them that speak the truth, having been long accustomed to be coaxed with the words of flatterers, being of tender ear, of unsound heart. Who would say to a rich man, Thou hast ill done in robbing other men's goods? Or perchance if any man shall have dared to speak, and he is such a man as he could not withstand, what doth he reply? All that he saith is in contempt of God. Why? Because he is proud. Why? Because he is fat. Why? Because he is devoted for a victim. "They have passed over unto purpose of heart." Here within they have passed over. What is, "they have passed over"? They have crossed over the way. What is, "they have

passed over"? They have exceeded the bounds of mankind, men
like the rest they think not themselves. They have passed over, I
say, the bounds of mankind. When thou sayest to such a man, Thy
brother this beggar is; when thou sayest to such a man, Thy
brother[607] this poor man is; the same parents ye have had, Adam
and Eve: do not heed thy haughtiness, do not heed the vapor unto
which thou hast been elevated; although an establishment waiteth
about thee, although countless gold and silver, although a marbled
house doth contain thee, although fretted ceilings cover thee, thou
and the poor man together have for covering that roof of the universe, the sky; but thou art different from the poor man in things
not thine own, added to thee from without: thyself see in them, not
them in thee. Observe thyself, how thou art in relation to the poor
man; thyself, not that which thou hast. For why dost thou despise
thy brother? In the bowels of your mothers ye were both naked.
Forsooth, even when ye shall have departed this life, and these bodies shall have rotted, when the soul hath been breathed forth, let
the bones of the rich and poor man be distinguished! I am speaking
of the equality of condition, of that very lot of mankind, wherein
all men are born: for both here doth a man become rich, and a poor
man will not alway be here, and as a rich man doth not come rich,
so neither doth he depart rich; the very same is the entrance of
both, and like is the departure. I add, that perchance ye will change
conditions. Now everywhere the Gospel is being preached: observe
a certain poor man full of sores, who was lying before the gate of a
rich man,[608] and was desiring to be filled with crumbs, which used
to fall from the table of the rich man; observe also that likeness[609] of
thine who was clothed with purple and fine linen, and fared sump-
tuously every day. It chanced, I say, for that poor man to die, and to
be borne by the angels into the bosom of Abraham: but the other died
and was buried; for the other's burial perchance no one cared. . . .
Brethren, how great was the toil of the poor man! Of how long du-
ration were the luxuries of the rich man! But the condition which
they have received in exchange is everlasting. . . . Deservedly too
late he will say, "Send Lazarus,"[610] "let him tell even my brethren,"
since to himself there is not granted the fruit of repentance. For it is

607. The words from "this beggar," added from Oxford mss.   608. Lk 16:19.
609. Alternatively, "father."   610. Lk 16:27.

not that repentance[611] is not given, but everlasting will be the repentance, and no salvation after repentance. Therefore these men "have passed over unto purpose of heart."

11. "They have thought and have spoken spitefulness" (v. 8). But men do speak spitefulness even with fear: but these men how? "Iniquity on high they have spoken." Not only they have spoken iniquity, but even openly, in the hearing of all, proudly: "I will do it"; "I will show you"; "thou shalt know with whom thou hast to do"; "I will not let thee live." Thou[612] mightest have but thought such things, not have given utterance to them! Within the chambers of thought at least the evil desire might have been confined, he might have at least restrained it within his thought. Why? Is he perchance lean? "There shall go forth as if out of fatness the iniquity of them." "Iniquity on high they have spoken."

12. "They have set against heaven their mouth, and their tongue hath passed over above the earth" (v. 9). For this, "hath passed over above the earth" is, they pass over all earthly things? What is it to pass over all earthly things? He doth not think of himself as a man that can die suddenly, when he is speaking; he doth menace as if he were always to live: his thought doth transcend earthly frailty, he knoweth not with what sort of vessel he is enwrapped; he knoweth not what hath been written in another place concerning such men: "His spirit shall go forth, and he shall return unto his earth, in that day shall perish all his thoughts."[613] But these men not thinking of their last day, speak pride,[614] and unto heaven they set their mouth, they transcend the earth. If a robber were not to think of his last day, that is, the last day of his trial, when sent to prison, nothing would be more monstrous than he: and yet he might escape. Whither dost thou flee to escape death? Certain will that day be. What is the long time which thou hast to live? How much is the long time which hath an end, even if it were a long time? To this there is added that it is nought: and the very thing which is called long time is not a long time, and is uncertain. Why doth he not think of this? Because he hath set against heaven his mouth, and

---

611. Used, of course, in the lower sense. [The sense, i.e., of mere *attrition*.—C.]

612. Oxford mss. "Thou proud man, thou," etc.   613. Ps 146:4.

614. Oxford and other mss. "proud things."

his tongue hath passed over above the earth. "And full days shall be found in them."

13. "Therefore there shall return hither My people" (v. 10). Now Asaph himself is returning hither. For he saw these things abound to unrighteous men, he saw them abound to proud men: he is returning to God and is beginning to inquire and discuss. But when? "When full days shall be found in them." What is "full days"? "But when there came the fullness of time, God sent His Son."[615] This is the very fullness of time, when He came to teach men that things temporal should be despised, that they should not esteem as a great matter whatever object evil men covet, that they should suffer whatever evil men fear. He became the way, He recalled us to inward thought, admonished us of what should be sought of God. And see from what thought reacting upon itself, and in a manner recalling the waves of its impulse, he doth pass over unto choosing true things.

14. "And they said, How hath God known, and is there knowledge in the Most High?" (v. 11). See through what thought they pass. Behold unjust men are happy, God doth not care for things human. Doth He indeed know what we do? See what things are being said. We are inquiring, brethren, "How hath God known," etc. (no longer let Christians say it). For how doth it appear to thee that God knoweth not, and that there is no knowledge in the Most High? He replieth, "Lo! themselves they are sinners, and in the world they have gotten abundant riches" (v. 12). Both sinners they are, and in the world they have gotten abundant riches. He confessed that he willed not to be a sinner in order that he might have riches. A carnal soul for things visible and earthly would have sold its justice. What sort of justice is that which is retained for the sake of gold, as if gold were a more precious thing than justice herself, or as if when a man denieth the deposit of another man's goods, he to whom he denied them should suffer a greater loss, than he that denieth them to him. The former doth lose a garment, the latter fidelity. "Lo! they are themselves sinners, and in the world they have gotten abundant riches." On this account therefore God knoweth not, and on this account there is no knowledge in the Most High.

15. "And I said, therefore[616] without cause I have justified my

615. Gal 4:4.   616. Mss. want "therefore."

heart" (v. 13). In that I serve God, and have not these things; they serve him not, and they abound in these things: "therefore without cause I have justified my heart, and have washed among the innocent my hands." This without cause I have done. Where is the reward of my good life? Where is the wage of my service? I live well and am in need; and the unjust man doth abound. "And I have washed among the innocent my hands. And I have been scourged all the day long" (v. 14). From me the scourges of God do not impart. I serve well, and I am scourged; he serveth not, and is honored. He hath proposed to himself a great question. The soul is disturbed, the soul doth pass over things which are to pass away unto despising things earthly and to desiring things eternal. There is a passage of the soul herself in this thought; where she doth toss in a sort of tempest she will reach the harbor. And it is with her as it is with sick persons, who are less violently sick, when recovery is far off: when recovery is at hand they are in higher fever; physicians call it the "critical accession" through which they pass to health: greater fever is there, but leading to health: greater heat, but recovery is at hand. So also is this man enfevered. For these are dangerous words, brethren, offensive, and almost blasphemous, "How hath God known?" This is why I say, "and almost"; He hath not said, God hath not known: he hath not said, there is no knowledge in the Most High: but as if inquiring, hesitating, doubting. This is the same as he said a little before, "My steps were almost overthrown."[617] He doth not affirm it, but the very doubt is dangerous. Through danger he is passing to health. Hear now the health: "Therefore in vain I have justified my heart, and have washed among the innocent my hands: and I have been scourged all the day long, and my chastening was in the morning." Chastening is correction. He that is being chastened is being corrected. What is, "in the morning"? It is not deferred. That of the ungodly is being deferred, mine is not deferred: the former is too late or is not at all; mine is in the morning.

16. "If I said, I shall declare thus; behold, the generation of Thy sons I have reprobated" (v. 15): that is, I will teach thus. How wilt thou teach that there is no knowledge in the Most High, that God doth not know? Wilt thou propound this opinion, that without

617. Ps 73:2.

cause men live justly who do live justly; that a just man hath lost his
service, because God doth more show favor to evil men, or else He
doth care for no one? Wilt thou tell this, declare this? He doth restrain himself by an authority repressing him. What authority? A
man wisheth some time to break out in this sentiment: but he is recalled by the Scriptures directing us always to live well, saying, that
God doth care for things human, that He maketh a distinction between a godly man and an ungodly man. Therefore this man also
wishing to put forth this sentiment, doth recollect himself. And
what saith he? "I have reprobated the generation of Thy sons." If I
shall declare thus, the generation of just men I shall reprobate. As
also some copies have it, "Behold, the generation of thy sons with
which I have been in concert": that is, with which consisting of Thy
sons I have been in concert; that is, with which I have agreed, to
which I have been conformed: I have been out of time with all, if so
I teach. For he doth sing in concert who giveth the tune together;
but he that giveth not the tune together doth not sing in concert.
Am I to say something different from that which Abraham said,
from that which Isaac said, from that which Jacob said, from that
which the prophets said? For all they said that God doth care for
things human, am I to say that He careth not? Is there greater wisdom in me than in them? Greater understanding in me than in
them? A most wholesome authority hath called back his thought
from ungodliness. And what followeth? That he might not reprobate, he did what? "And I undertook to know" (v. 16). May God be
with him in order that he may know. Meanwhile, brethren, from a
great fall he is being withheld, when he doth not presume that he
already knoweth, but hath undertaken to know that which he
knew not. For but now he was willing to appear as if knowing, and
to declare that God hath no care of things human. For this hath
come to be a most naughty and ungodly doctrine of unrighteous
men. Know, brethren, that many men dispute and say that God
careth not for things human, that by chances all things are ruled, or
that our wills have been made subject to the stars, that each one is
not dealt with according to his deserts, but by the necessity of his
stars—an evil doctrine, an impious doctrine. Unto these thoughts
was going that man whose feet were almost moved, and whose
steps were all but overthrown, into this error he was going; but because he was not in tune with the generation of the sons of God, he

undertook to know, and condemned the knowledge wherein with God's just men he agreed not. And what he saith let us hear; how that he undertook to know, and was helped, and learned something, and declared it to us. "And I undertook," he saith, "to know." "In this labor is before me." Truly a great labor; to know in what manner both God doth care for things human, and it is well with evil men, and good men labor. Great is the importance of the question; therefore, "and this labor is before me." As it were there is standing in my face a sort of wall, but thou hast the voice of a psalm, "In my God I shall pass over the wall."[618]

17. And he hath done this; for he saith how long labor is before him; "until I enter into the sanctuary of God, and understand upon the last things" (v. 17). A great thing it is, brethren: now for a long time I labor, he saith, and before my face I see a sort of insuperable labor, to know in what manner both God is just, and doth care for things human, and is not unjust because men sinning and doing wicked actions have happiness on this earth; but the godly and men serving God are wasted ofttimes in trials and in labors; a great difficulty it is to know this, but only "until I enter into the sanctuary of God." For in the sanctuary what is presented to thee, in order that thou mayest solve this question? "And I understand," he saith, "upon the last things," not present things. I, he saith, from the sanctuary of God stretch out mine eye unto the end, I pass over present things. All that which is called the human race, all that mass of mortality is to come to the balance, is to come to the scale, thereon will be weighed the works of men. All things now a cloud doth enfold: but to God are known the merits of each severally. "And I understand," he saith, "upon the last things": but not of myself; for before me there is labor. Whence "may I understand upon the last things"? Let me enter into the sanctuary of God. In that place then he understood also the reason why these men now are happy.

18. To wit, "because of deceitfulness Thou hast set upon them" (v. 18). Because deceitful they are, that is fraudulent; because deceitful they are, they suffer deceits. What is this, because fraudulent they are they suffer a fraud? They desire to play a fraud upon mankind in all their naughtinesses, they themselves also suffer a fraud, in choosing earthly good things, and in forsaking the eter-

nal. Therefore, brethren, in their very playing off a fraud they suffer a fraud. In that which but now I said, brethren, "What manner of wit[619] hath he who to gain a garment doth lose his fidelity"? Hath he whose garment he hath taken suffered a fraud, or he that is smitten with so great a loss? If a garment is more precious than fidelity, the former doth suffer the greater loss: but if incomparably good faith doth surpass the whole world, the latter shall seem to have sustained the loss of a garment; but to the former is said, "What doth it profit a man if he gain the whole world, but suffer the loss of his own soul?"[620] Therefore what hath befallen them? "Because of deceitfulness Thou hast set for them: Thou didst throw them down while they were being exalted." He hath not said, Thou didst throw them down because they were lifted up: not as it were after that they were lifted up Thou didst throw them down; but in their very lifting up they were thrown down. For thus to be lifted up is already to fall.

19. "How have they become a desolation suddenly?" (v. 19). He is wondering at them, understanding unto the last things. "They have vanished." Truly like smoke, which while it mounteth upward, doth vanish, so they have vanished. How doth he say, "They have vanished"? In the manner of one who understandeth the last things: "they have perished because of their iniquity." "Like as the dream of one rising up" (v. 20). How have they vanished? As vanisheth the dream of one rising up. Fancy a man in sleep to have seen himself find treasures; he is a rich man, but only until he awaketh. "Like as the dream of one rising up," so they have vanished, like the dream of one awaking. It is sought then and it is not: there is nothing in the hands, nothing in the bed. A poor man he went to sleep, a rich man in sleep he became: had he not awoke, he were a rich man: he woke up, he found the care which he had lost while sleeping. And these men shall find the misery which they had prepared for themselves. When they shall have awoke from this life, that thing doth pass away which was grasped as if in sleep. "Like as the dream of one rising up." And that there might not be said, "What then? A small thing doth their glory seem to thee, a small thing doth their state seem to thee, small things seem to thee inscriptions, images, statues, distinctions, troops of clients?" "O Lord," he

---

619. Uncertain whom Augustine is quoting. (Eds.)   620. Mt 16:26.

saith, "in Thy city their image[621] Thou shalt bring to nothing." . . .
He hath taken away the pride of rich men, he giveth counsel. As if
they[622] were saying, We are rich men, thou dost forbid us to be
proud, dost prohibit us from boasting of the parade of our riches:
what then are we to do with these riches? Is it come to this, that
there is nothing which they may do therewith? "Be they rich," he
saith, "in good works; let them readily distribute, communicate."[623]
And what doth this profit? "Let them treasure unto themselves a
good foundation for the future, that they may lay hold of true
life."[624] Where ought they to lay up treasure for themselves? In that
place whereunto he set his eye, when entering into the sanctuary of
God. Let there shudder all our rich brethren, abounding in money,
gold, silver, household, honors, let them shudder at that which but
now hath been said, "Thou shalt bring to nothing their image."
Are they not worthy to suffer these things, to wit that God bring to
nothing their image in His city, because also they have themselves
brought to nothing the image of God in their earthly city?

20. "Because my heart was delighted" (v. 21). He is saying with
what things he is tempted: "because my heart was delighted," he
saith, "my reins also were changed." When those temporal things
delighted me, my reins were changed. It may also be understood
thus: "because my heart was delighted" in God, "my reins also
were changed, that is, my lusts were changed, and I became wholly
chaste." "My reins were changed." And hear how. "And I was
brought unto nothing, and I knew not" (v. 22). I, the very man, who
now say these things of rich men, once longed for such things:
therefore "even I was brought to nothing" when my steps were almost overthrown. "And I was brought unto nothing, and I knew
not." We must not therefore despair even of them, against whom I
was saying such things.

21. What is, "I knew not"? "As it were a beast I became to Thee,
and I am alway with Thee" (v. 23). There is a great difference between this man and others. He became as it were a beast in longing
for earthly things, when being brought to nothing he knew not
things eternal: but he departed not from his God, because he did
not desire these things of demons, of the devil. For this I have al-

---

621. Oxford mss. "images."   622. Oxford mss. "the rich."   623. 1 Tm 6:18.
624. 1 Tm 6:19.

ready brought to your notice. The voice is from the synagogue, that is, from that people which served not idols. A beast indeed I became, when desiring from my God things earthly: but I never departed from That my God.

22. Because then, though having become a beast, I departed not from my God, there followeth, "Thou hast held the hand of my right hand." He hath not said my right hand, but "the hand of my right hand." If the hand of the right hand it is, a hand hath a hand. "The hand Thou hast held of my right hand," in order that Thou mightest conduct me. For what hath he put hand? For power. For we say that a man hath that in his hand which he hath in his power: just as the devil said to God concerning Job, "Lay to Thine hand, and take away the things which he hath."[625] What is, "lay to Thine hand"? Put[626] forth power. The hand of God he hath called the power of God: as hath been written in another place, "death and life are in the hands of the tongue."[627] Hath the tongue hands? But what is, "in the hands of the tongue"? In the power of the tongue. What is, "in the power of the tongue"? "Out of thy mouth thou shalt be justified, and out of thy mouth thou shalt be condemned."[628] "Thou hast held," therefore, "the hand of my right hand," the power of my right hand. What was my right hand? That I was always with Thee. Unto the left I was holding, because I became a beast, that is, because there was an earthly concupiscence in me: but the right was mine, because I was always with thee. Of this my right hand Thou hast held the hand, that is, hast directed the power. What power? "He gave them power to become sons of God."[629] He is beginning now to be among the sons of God, belonging to the New Testament. See in what manner the hand of his right hand was held. "In Thy will Thou hast conducted me." What is, "in thy will"? Not in my merits. What is, "in Thy will"? Hear the apostle, who was at first a beast longing for things earthly, and living after the Old Testament. He saith what? "I that at first was a blasphemer, and persecutor, and injurious: but mercy I obtained."[630] What is, "in Thy will"? "By the grace of God I am what I am."[631] "And in glory Thou hast taken me up." Now to what glory he was taken up, and in what glory, who can explain, who can say?

625. Jb 1:11.   626. Literally, "give."   627. Prv 18:21.   628. Mt 12:37.

629. Jn 1:12.   630. 1 Tm 1:13.   631. 1 Cor 15:10.

Let us await it, because in the resurrection it will be, in the last things it will be.

23. And he is beginning to think of that same heavenly felicity, and to reprove himself, because he hath been a beast and hath longed for things earthly. "For what have I in heaven, and from Thee what have I willed upon earth?" (v. 25). By your voice I see that ye have understood.[632] He compared with his earthly will the heavenly reward which he is to receive; he saw what was there being reserved for him; and while thinking and burning at the thought of some ineffable thing, which neither eye hath seen, nor ear heard, nor into the heart of man hath ascended,[633] he hath not said, this or that I have in heaven, but, "what have I in heaven?" What is that thing which I have in heaven? What is it? How great is it? Of what sort is it? "And," since that which I have in heaven doth not pass away, "from Thee what have I willed upon earth?"[634] . . . Thou reservest, he saith, for me in heaven riches immortal, even Thyself, and I have willed from Thee on earth that which even ungodly men have, which even evil men have, which even abandoned men have, money, gold, silver, jewels, households, which even many wicked men have: which even many profligate women have, many profligate men: these things as a great matter I have desired of my God upon earth: though my God reserveth Himself for me in heaven!

24. "My heart and my flesh hath failed, O God of my heart" (v. 26). This then for me in heaven hath been reserved, "God of my heart, and my portion is my God." What is it, brethren? Let us find out our riches, let mankind choose their parts. Let us see men torn with diversity of desires: let some choose war-service, some advocacy, some divers and sundry offices of teaching, some merchandise, some farming, let them take their portions in human affairs: let the people of God cry, "my portion is my God." Not for a time "my portion," but "my portion is my God for everlasting." Even if I always have gold, what have I? Even if I did not always have God, how great a good should I have? To this is added, that He

632. Here there were voluntary "amens," or the like, from the people.—C.

633. 1 Cor 2:9.

634. Here he interpolates: "I will speak as I am able, but forgive me; accept my endeavor, mine earnestness to attempt; for to explain it I have not power."—C.

promiseth Himself to me, and He promiseth that I shall have this for everlasting. So great a thing I have, and never have it not. Great felicity: "my portion is God!" How long? "For everlasting." For behold and see after what sort He hath loved him; He hath made his heart chaste: "God of my heart, and my portion is God for everlasting." His heart hath become chaste, for nought now God is loved, from Him is not sought any other reward. He that doth seek any other reward from God, and therefore is willing to serve God, more precious doth make that which he willeth to receive, than Him from whom he willeth to receive. What then, is there no reward belonging to God? None except Himself. The reward belonging to God is God Himself. This he loveth, this he esteemeth; if any other thing he shall have loved, the love will not be chaste. Thou art receding from the fire immortal, thou wilt grow cold, wilt be corrupted. Do not recede. Recede not, it will be thy corruption, it will be thy fornication. Now he is returning, now he is repenting, now he is choosing repentance, now he is saying, "my portion is God." And after what sort is he delighted with that Same, whom he hath chosen for his portion.

25. "Behold, they that put themselves afar from Thee shall perish" (v. 27). He therefore departed from God, but not far: for "I have become as it were a beast," he saith, and "I am always with Thee."[635] But they have departed afar, because not only things earthly they have desired, but have sought them from demons and the devil. "They that put themselves afar from Thee shall perish." And what is it, to become afar from God? "Thou hast destroyed every man that committeth fornication away from Thee." To this fornication is opposed chaste love. What is chaste love? Now the soul doth love her Bridegroom: what doth she require of Him, from her Bridegroom whom she loveth? Perchance in like manner as women choose for themselves men either as sons-in-law or as bridegrooms: she perchance chooseth riches, and loveth his gold, and estates, and silver and cattle and horses, and household, and the like. Far be it. He doth love Him alone, for nought he doth love Him: because in Him he hath all things, for "by Him were made all things."[636]

26. But thou doest what? "But for me to cleave to God is a good thing" (v. 28). This is whole good. Will ye have more? I grieve at

635. Ps 73:21.   636. Jn 1:3.

your willing. Brethren, what will ye have more? Than to cleave to God nothing is better, when we shall see Him face to face.[637] But now what? For yet as a stranger I am speaking: "to cleave," he saith, "to God is a good thing," but now in my sojourning (for not yet hath come the substance), I have "to put in God my hope." So long therefore as thou hast not yet cloven, therein put thy hope. Thou art wavering, cast forward an anchor to the land.[638] Not yet dost thou cleave by presence, cleave fast by hope. "To put in God my hope." And by doing what here wilt thou put in God thy hope? What will be thy business, but to praise Him whom thou lovest, and to make others to be fellow lovers of Him with thee? Lo, if thou shouldest love a charioteer, wouldest thou not carry along other men to love him with thee? A lover of a charioteer whithersoever he goeth doth speak of him, in order that as well as he, others also may love him. For nought are loved abandoned men, and from God is reward required in order that He may be loved? Love thou God for nought, grudge God to no one. . . . For what followeth? "In order that I may tell forth all Thy praises in the courts of the daughter of Sion." "In the courts," for the preaching of God beside the Church is vain. A small thing it is to praise God and to tell forth all His praise. In the courts of the daughter of Sion tell thou forth. Make for unity, do not divide the people; but draw them unto one, and make them one. I have forgotten how long I have been speaking. Now the psalm being ended, even judging by this closeness, I suppose I have held a long discourse: but it doth not suffice for your zeal; ye are too impetuous. O that with this impetuosity ye would seize upon the kingdom of heaven.

Psalm 90[639]

1. This psalm is entitled, "The prayer of Moses the man of God," through whom, His man, God gave the law to His people, through whom He freed them from the house of slavery, and led them forty

637. 1 Cor 13:12.
638. Oxford mss. "Wavering, from the earth cast an anchor before thee upward."
639. Lat. 89.

years through the wilderness. Moses was therefore the minister of the Old, and the prophet of the New Testament. For "all these things," saith the apostle, "happened unto them for examples: and they are written for our admonition, unto whom the ends of the world come."[640] In accordance therefore with this dispensation which was vouchsafed to Moses, this psalm is to be examined, as it has received its title from his prayer.

2. "Lord," he saith, "Thou hast been our refuge from one generation to another" (v. 1) either in every generation, or in two generations, the old and new: because, as I said, he was the minister of the Testament that related to the old generation, and the prophet of the Testament which appertained to the new. Jesus Himself, the Surety of that covenant, and the Bridegroom in the marriage which He entered into in that generation, saith, "Had ye believed Moses, ye would have believed Me: for he wrote of Me."[641] Now it is not to be believed that this psalm was entirely the composition of that Moses, as it is not distinguished by any of those of his expressions which are used in his songs: but the name of the great servant of God is used for the sake of some intimation, which should direct the attention of the reader or listener. "Lord," he saith, "Thou hast been our refuge from one generation to the other."

3. He adds how He became our refuge, since He began to be that, viz., a refuge, to us which He had not been before, not that He had not existed before He became our refuge: "Before the mountains were brought forth, or ever the earth and the world were made: and from age even unto age Thou art" (v. 2). Thou therefore who art forever, and before we were, and before the world was, hast become our refuge ever since we turned to Thee. But the expression, "before the mountains," etc., seems to me to contain a particular meaning; for mountains are the higher parts of the earth, and if God was before even the earth were formed (or, as some books have it, from the same Greek word, "framed"), since it was by Him that it was formed, what is the need of saying that He was before the mountains, or any certain parts of it, since God was not only before the earth, but before heaven and earth, and even the whole bodily and spiritual creation? But it may certainly be that the whole rational creation is marked by this distinction; that while

640. 1 Cor 10:11.   641. Jn 5:46.

the loftiness of angels is signified by the mountains, the lowliness of man is meant by the earth. And for this reason, although all the works of creation are not improperly said to be either made or formed; nevertheless, if there is any propriety in these words, the angels are "made"; for as they are enumerated among His heavenly works, the enumeration itself is thus concluded: "He spake the word, and they were made; He commanded, and they were created";[642] but the earth was "formed," that man might thence be created in the body. For the Scripture uses this word, where we read, God made, or "God formed man out of the dust of the ground."[643] Before then the noblest parts of the creation (for what is higher than the rational part of the heavenly creation) were made: before the earth was made, that Thou mightest have worshippers upon the earth; and even this is little, as all these had a beginning either in or with time; but "from age to age Thou art." It would have been better, from everlasting to everlasting: for God, who is before the ages, exists not from a certain age, nor to a certain age, which has an end, since He is without end. But it often happens in the Scripture, that the equivocal Greek word causes the Latin translator to put age for eternity and eternity for age. But he very rightly does not say, Thou wast from ages, and unto ages Thou shalt be: but puts the verb in the present, intimating that the substance of God is altogether immutable. It is not, He was, and Shall be, but only Is. Whence the expression, I Am that I Am; and, I Am "hath sent me unto you";[644] and, "Thou shalt change them, and they shall be changed: but Thou art the same, and Thy years shall not fail."[645] Behold then the eternity that is our refuge, that we may fly thither from the mutability of time, there to remain forevermore.

4. But as our life here is exposed to numerous and great temptations, and it is to be feared lest we may be turned aside by them from that refuge, let us see what in consequence of this the prayer of the man of God seeks for. "Turn not Thou man to lowness" (v. 3): that is, let not man, turned aside from Thy eternal and sublime things, lust for things of time, savor of earthly things. This prayer is what God has Himself enjoined us, in the Prayer, "Lead us not into temptation,"[646] He adds, "Again Thou sayest, Come

642. Ps 148:5.   643. Gn 2:7.   644. Ex 3:14.   645. Ps 102:26, 27.
646. Mt 6:13.

again, ye children of men." As if he said, I ask of Thee what Thou hast commanded me to ask: giving glory to His grace, that "he that glorieth, in the Lord he may glory,"[647] without whose help we cannot by an exertion of our own will overcome the temptations of this life. "Turn not Thou man to lowness: again thou sayest, Turn again, ye children of men." But grant what Thou has enjoined, by hearing the prayer of him who can at least pray, and aiding the faith of the willing soul.

5. "For a thousand years in Thy sight are but as yesterday, which is past by" (v. 4): hence we ought to turn to Thy refuge, where Thou art without any change, from the fleeting scenes around us; since however long a time may be wished for, for this life, "a thousand years in Thy sight are but as yesterday": not as tomorrow, which is to come, for all limited periods of time are reckoned as having already passed. Hence the apostle's choice is rather to aim at what is before,[648] that is, to desire things eternal, and to forget things behind, by which temporal matters should be understood. But that no one may imagine a thousand years are reckoned by God as one day, as if with God days were so long, when this is only said in contempt of the extent of time, he adds, "and as a watch in the night": which only lasts three hours. Nevertheless men have ventured to assert their knowledge of times, to the pretenders to which our Lord said, "It is not for you to know the times or seasons, which the Father hath put in His own power,"[649] and they allege that this period may be defined six thousand years, as of six days. Nor have they heeded the words, "are but as one day which is past by," for, when this was uttered, not a thousand years only had passed, and the expression, "as a watch in the night," ought to have warned them that they might not be deceived by the uncertainty of the seasons: for even if the six first days in which God finished His works seemed to give some plausibility to their opinion, six watches, which amount to eighteen hours, will not consist with that opinion.

6. Next, the man of God, or rather the prophetic spirit, seems to be reciting some law written in the secret wisdom of God, in which He has fixed a limit to the sinful life of mortals, and determined the troubles of mortality, in the following words: "Their years are as

647. 1 Cor 1:31.   648. Phil 3:13.   649. Acts 1:7.

things which are nothing worth: in the morning let it fade away like the grass" (v. 5). The happiness therefore of the heirs of the old covenant, which they asked of the Lord their God as a great boon, attained to receive this Law in His mysterious Providence. Moses seems to be reciting it: "Their years shall be things which are esteemed as nothing." Such are those things which are not before they are come: and when come, shall soon not be: for they do not come to be here, but to be gone. "In the morning," that is, before they come, "as a heat[650] let it pass by"; but "in the evening," it means after they come, "let it fall, and be dried up, and withered" (v. 6). It is "to fall" in death, be "dried up" in the corpse, "withered" in the dust. What is this but flesh, wherein is the accursed lust of fleshly things? "For all flesh is grass, and all the goodliness of man as the flower of the field; the grass withereth, the flower fadeth: but the word of the Lord abideth for ever."[651]

7. Making no secret that this fate is a penalty inflicted for sin, he adds at once, "For we consume away in Thy displeasure, and are troubled at Thy wrathful indignation" (v. 7): we consume away in our weakness, and are troubled from the fear of death; for we are become weak, and yet fearful to end that weakness. "Another," saith He, "shall gird thee, and carry thee whither thou wouldest not,"[652] although not to be punished, but to be crowned, by martyrdom; and the soul of our Lord, transforming us into Himself, was sorrowful even unto death: for "the Lord's going out" is no other than in "death."

8. "Thou hast set our misdeeds before Thee" (v. 8): that is, Thou hast not dissembled Thine anger: "and our age in the light of Thy countenance." "The light of Thy countenance" answers to "before Thee," and to "our misdeeds," as above.

9. "For all our days are failed, and in Thine anger we have failed" (v. 9). These words sufficiently prove that our subjection to death is a punishment. He speaks of our days failing, either because men fail in them from loving things that pass away, or because they are reduced to so small a number; which he asserts in the following lines: "our years are spent in thought like a spider." "The days of our age are threescore years and ten; and though men be so strong

---

650. Alternatively, "as an herb."—C.   651. Is 40:6, 8.   652. Jn 21:18.

that they come to fourscore years, yet is more of them but labor and sorrow" (v. 10). These words appear to express the shortness and misery of this life: since those who have reached their seventieth year are styled old men. Up to eighty, however, they appear to have some strength; but if they live beyond this, their existence is laborious through multiplied sorrows. Yet many even below the age of seventy experience an old age the most infirm and wretched: and old men have often been found to be wonderfully vigorous even beyond eighty years. It is therefore better to search for some spiritual meaning in these numbers. For the anger of God is not greater on the sins of Adam (through whom alone "sin entered into the world, and death by sin, and so death passed upon all men"),[653] because they live a much shorter time than the men of old; since even the length of their days is ridiculed in the comparison of a thousand years to yesterday that is past, and to three hours: especially since at the very time when they provoked the anger of God to send the deluge in which they perished, their life was at its longest span.

10. Moreover, seventy and eighty years equal a hundred and fifty; a number which the Psalms clearly insinuate to be a sacred one. One hundred and fifty have the same relative signification as fifteen, the latter number being composed of seven and eight together: the first of which points to the Old Testament through the observation of the Sabbath; the latter to the New, referring to the resurrection of our Lord. Hence the fifteen steps in the Temple. Hence in the Psalms, fifteen "songs of degrees." Hence the waters of the deluge overtopped the highest mountains by fifteen cubits:[654] and many other instances of the same nature. "Our years are passed in thought like a spider." We were laboring in things corruptible, corruptible works were we weaving together: which, as the Prophet Isaiah saith, by no means covered us.[655] "The days of our years are in themselves," etc. A distinction is here made between themselves and their strength: "in themselves," that is, in the years or days themselves, may mean in temporal things, which are promised in the Old Testament, signified by the number seventy; "but if" not in themselves, but "in their strength," refers not to temporal things, but to things eternal, "fourscore years," as the New Testament

653. Rom 5:12.   654. Gn 7:20.   655. Is 59:6.

contains the hope of a new life and resurrection forevermore: and what is added, that if they pass this latter period,[656] "their strength is labor and sorrow," intimates that such shall be the fate of him who goes beyond this faith, and seeks for more. It may also be understood thus: because although we are established in the New Testament, which the number eighty signifies, yet still our life is one of labor and sorrow, while "we groan within ourselves, awaiting the adoption, to wit, the redemption of our body; for we are saved by hope; and if we hope for that we see not, then do we with patience wait for it."[657] This relates to the mercy of God, of which he proceeds to say, "Since thy mercy cometh over us,[658] and we shall be chastened," for "the Lord chasteneth whom He loveth, and scourgeth every son whom He receiveth,"[659] and to some mighty ones He giveth a thorn in the flesh, to buffet them, that they may not be exalted above measure through the abundance of the revelations, so that strength be made perfect in weakness.[660] Some copies read, we shall be "taught," instead of "chastened," which is equally expressive of the Divine Mercy, for no man can be taught without labor and sorrow, since strength is made perfect in weakness.

11. "For who knoweth the power of Thy wrath: and for the fear of Thee to number Thine anger?" (v. 11). It belongs to very few men, he saith, to know the power of Thy wrath; for when Thou dost spare, Thy anger is so far heavier against most men; that we may know that labor and sorrow belong not to wrath, but rather to Thy mercy, when Thou chastenest and teachest those whom Thou lovest, to save them from the torments of eternal punishment: as it is said in another psalm,[661] "The sinner hath provoked the Lord: He will not require it of him according to the greatness of His wrath." With this also is understood, "Who knoweth?" Such is the difficulty of finding anyone who knoweth how to number Thine anger by Thy fear, that he adds this, meaning that it is to the purpose that Thou appearest to spare some, with whom Thou art more angry,

---

656. St. Augustine seems to refer the word *amplius* to a period beyond the eighty years. In the English version it clearly applies to the attainment of that age.

657. Rom 8:23–25.

658. *Quoniam supervenit super nos mansuetudo, et corripiemur*: the equivalent in the Prayer Book is, "so soon passeth it away, and we are gone."

659. Heb 12:6.   660. 2 Cor 12:7, 9.   661. Ps 10:3, Lat.

that the sinner may be prospered in his path, and receive a heavier doom at the last. For when the power of human wrath hath killed the body, it hath nothing more to do: but God hath power both to punish here, and after the death of the body to send into hell, and by the few who are thus taught, the vain and seductive prosperity of the wicked is judged to be greater wrath of God.[662]

12. "Make Thy right hand so well known" (v. 12). This is the reading of most of the Greek copies: not of some in Latin, which is thus, "Make Thy right hand well known to me." What is, "Thy right hand," but Thy Christ, of whom it is said, And to whom is the Arm of the Lord revealed?[663] Make Him so well known, that Thy faithful may learn in Him to ask and to hope for those things rather of Thee as rewards of their faith, which do not appear in the Old Testament, but are revealed in the New: that they may not imagine that the happiness derived from earthly and temporal blessings is to be highly esteemed, desired, or loved, and thus their feet slip,[664] when they see it in men who honor Thee not: that their steps may not give way, while they know not how to number Thine anger. Finally, in accordance with this prayer of the Man that is His, He has made His Christ so well known as to show by His sufferings that not these rewards which seem so highly prized in the Old Testament, where they are shadows of things to come, but things eternal, are to be desired. The right hand of God may also be understood in this sense, as that by which He will separate His saints from the wicked: because that hand becomes well known, when it scourgeth every son whom He receiveth, and suffers him not, in greater anger, to prosper in his sins, but in His mercy scourgeth him with the left,[665] that He may place him purified on His right hand.[666] The reading of most copies, "make Thy right hand well known to me," may be referred either to Christ or to eternal happiness: for God has not a right hand in bodily shape, as He has not that anger which is aroused into violent passion.

13. But what he addeth, "and those fettered in heart in wisdom," other copies read, "instructed," not "lettered," the Greek verb, expressing both senses, only differing by a single syllable. But since these also, as it is said, put their "feet in the fetters" of wisdom, are

---

662. Mt 10:28; Ps 73:2, 3, 7.   663. Is 53:1.   664. Ps 73:2.
665. Alternatively, "on the left."   666. Mt 25:33.

taught wisdom (he means the feet of the heart, not of the body), and bound by its golden chains[667] depart not from the path of God, and become not runaways from him; whichever reading we adopt, the truth in the meaning is safe. Them thus lettered, or instructed in heart in wisdom, God makes so well known in the New Testament, that they despised all things for the Faith which the impiety of Jews and Gentiles abhorred; and allowed themselves to be deprived of those things which in the Old Testament are thought high promises by those who judge after the flesh.

14. And as when they became so well known, as to despise these things, and by setting their affections on things eternal, gave a testimony through their sufferings (whence they are called witnesses or martyrs in the Greek), they endured for a long while many bitter temporal afflictions. This man of God giveth heed to this, and the prophetic spirit under the name of Moses continues thus, "Return, O Lord, how long? and be softened concerning Thy servants" (v. 13). These are the words of those, who, enduring many evils in that persecuting age, become known because their hearts are bound in the chain of wisdom so firmly, that not even such hardships can induce them to fly from their Lord to the good things of this world. "How long wilt Thou hide Thy face from me, O Lord?"[668] occurs in another psalm, in unison with this sentence, "Return, O Lord, how long?" And that they who, in a most carnal spirit, ascribe to God the form of a human body, may know that the "turning away" and "turning again" of His countenance is not like those motions of our own frame, let them recollect these words from above in the same psalm, "Thou hast set our misdeeds before Thee, and our secret sins in the light of Thy countenance." How then does he say in this passage, "Return," that God may be favorable, as if He had turned away His face in anger; when as in the former he speaks of God's anger in such a manner, as to insinuate that He had not turned away His countenance from the misdeeds and the course of life of those He was angry with, but rather had set them before Him, and in the light of His countenance? The word, "How long," belongs to righteousness beseeching, not indignant impatience. "Be softened," some have rendered by a verb, "soften." But "be soft-

667. Ecclus 6:24.   668. Ps 13:1.

ened" avoids an ambiguity, since to soften is a common verb, for he may be said to soften who pours out prayers, and he to whom they are poured out; for we say, I soften thee, and I soften toward thee.

15. Next, in anticipation of future blessings, of which he speaks as already vouchsafed, he says, "We are satisfied with Thy mercy in the morning" (v. 14). Prophecy has thus been kindled for us, in the midst of these toils and sorrows of the night, like a lamp in the darkness, until day dawn, and the Daystar arise in our hearts.[669] For blessed are the pure in heart, for they shall see God: then shall the righteous be filled with that blessing for which they hunger and thirst now,[670] while, walking in faith, they are absent from the Lord.[671] Hence are the words, "In Thy presence is fullness of joy";[672] and, "Early in the morning they shall stand by, and shall look up";[673] and as other translators have said it, "We shall be satisfied with Thy mercy in the morning"; then they shall be satisfied. As he says elsewhere, "I shall be satisfied, when Thy glory shall be revealed."[674] So it is said, "Lord, show us the Father, and it sufficeth us," and our Lord Himself answereth, "I will manifest Myself to Zion";[675] and until this promise is fulfilled, no blessing satisfies us, or ought to do so, lest our longings should be arrested in their course, when they ought to be increased until they gain their objects. "And we rejoiced and were glad all the days of our life." Those days are days without end; they all exist together. It is thus they satisfy us, for they give not way to days succeeding, since there is nothing there which exists not yet because it has not reached us, or ceases to exist because it has passed; all are together because there is one day only, which remains and passes not away: this is eternity itself. These are the days respecting which it is written, "What man is he that lusteth to live, and would fain see good days?"[676] These days in another passage are styled years: where unto God it is said, "But Thou art the same, and Thy years shall not fail,"[677] for these are not years that are accounted for nothing, or days that perish like a shadow, but they are days which have a real existence, the number of which he who thus spoke, "Lord, let me

669. 2 Pt 1:19.   670. Mt 5:8, 6.   671. 2 Cor 5:6.   672. Ps 16:11.

673. Ps 5:3.   674. Ps 17:15.   675. Jn 14:8, 21.   676. Ps 34:12.

677. Ps 102:27.

know mine end" (that is, after reaching what term I shall remain unchanged, and have no further blessing to crave), "and the number of my days, what it is" (what is, not what is not) prayed to know. He distinguishes them from the days of this life, of which he speaks as follows, "Behold, Thou hast made my days as it were a span long,"[678] which are not, because they stand not, remain not, but change in quick succession: nor is there a single hour in them in which our being is not such, but that one part of it has already passed, another is about to come, and none remains as it is. But those years and days, in which we too shall never fail, but evermore be refreshed, will never fail. Let our souls long earnestly for those days, let them thirst ardently for them, that there we may be filled, be satisfied, and say what we now say in anticipation, "We have been satisfied," etc. "We have been comforted again now, after the time that Thou hast brought us low, and for the years wherein we have seen evil" (v. 15).

16. But now in days that are as yet evil, let us speak as follows. "Look upon Thy servants, and upon Thy works" (v. 16). For Thy servants themselves are Thy works, not only inasmuch as they are men, but as Thy servants, that is, obedient to Thy commands. For we are His workmanship, created not merely in Adam, but in Christ Jesus, unto good works, which God hath before ordained that we should walk in them:[679] "for it is God which worketh in us both to will and to do of His good pleasure."[680] "And direct their sons," that they may be right in heart, for to such God is bountiful; for "God is bountiful to Israel, to those that are right in heart."

17. "And let the brightness of the Lord our God be upon us" (v. 17); whence the words, "O Lord, the light of Thy countenance is marked upon us."[681] And, "Make Thou straight the works of our hands upon us," that we may do them not for hope of earthly reward, for then they are not straight, but crooked. In many copies the psalm goes thus far, but in some there is found an additional verse at the end, as follows, "And make straight the work of our hands." To these words the learned have prefixed a star, called an asterisk, to show that they are found in the Hebrew, or in some other Greek translations, but not in the Septuagint. The meaning of this verse, if we are to expound it, appears to me this, that all our

678. Ps 39:4, 5.   679. Eph 2:10.   680. Phil 2.13.   681. Ps 4:6.

good works are one work of love, for love is the fulfilling of the Law.[682] For as in the former verse he had said, "And the works of our hands make Thou straight upon us," here he says "work," not works, as if anxious to show, in the last verse, that all our works are one, that is, are directed with a view to one work. For then are works righteous, when they are directed to this one end: "for the end of the commandment is charity out of a pure heart, and of a good conscience, and of faith unfeigned."[683] There is therefore one work, in which are all, "faith which worketh by love,"[684] whence our Lord's words in the Gospel, "This is the work of God, that ye believe in Him whom He hath sent."[685] Since, therefore, in this psalm, both old and new life, life both mortal and everlasting, years that are counted for nought, and years that have the fullness of loving-kindness and of true joy, that is, the penalty of the first and the reign of the Second Man, are marked so very clearly; I imagine, that the name of Moses, the man of God, became the title of the psalm, that pious and right-minded readers of the Scriptures might gain an intimation that the Mosaic laws, in which God appears to promise only, or nearly only, earthly rewards for good works, without doubt contains under a veil some such hopes as this psalm displays. But when anyone has passed over to Christ, the veil will be taken away,[686] and his eyes will be unveiled, that he may consider the wonderful things in the law of God, by the gift of Him, to whom we pray, "Open Thou mine eyes, and I shall see the wondrous things of Thy law.[687]

Psalm 96[688]

1. My lord and brother Severus[689] still defers the pleasure we shall feel in his discourse, which he oweth us, for he acknowledgeth that he is held a debtor. For all the churches through which he hath

---

682. Rom 13:10.   683. 1 Tm 1:5.   684. Gal 5:6.   685. Jn 6:29.

686. 2 Cor 3:15.   687. Ps 119:18.

688. Lat. 95. Delivered perhaps in the year 405.

689. Bishop of Milevis, mentioned in the discourse of a preceding day on Psalm 132.

passed, by his tongue the Lord hath gladdened: much more therefore ought that Church to be rejoiced, out of which the Lord hath
propagated his preaching among the rest. But what shall we do,
but obey his will? I said, however, brethren, that he deferred, not
that he defrauded us. Therefore let us keep him as a debtor bound,
and release him not until he hath paid. Attend therefore, beloved:
as far as the Lord alloweth, let us say somewhat of this psalm,
which indeed you already know; for the fresh mention of truth is
sweet. Possibly when its title was pronounced, some heard it with
wonder. For the psalm is inscribed: "When the house was being
built after the Captivity." This title having been prefixed, ye were
perhaps expecting in the text of the psalm to hear what stones were
hewn from the mountains, what masses were drawn to the spot,
what foundations were laid, what beams were placed on high,
what columns raised. Its song is of nothing of this kind. . . . It is no
such house that is in building; for behold where it is built, not in
one spot, not in any particular region. For thus he beginneth:

2. "O sing unto the Lord a new song; sing unto the Lord, all the
earth"[690] (v. 1). If all the earth singeth a new song, it is thus building while it singeth: the very act of singing is building, but only if
it singeth not the old song. The lust of the flesh singeth the old
song; the love of God singeth the new. . . . Hear why it is a new
song: the Lord saith, "A new commandment I give unto you, that
ye love one another."[691] The whole earth then singeth a new song:
there the house of God is built. All the earth is the house of God. If
all the earth is the house of God, he who clingeth not to all the earth
is a ruin, not a house; that old ruin whose shadow that ancient temple
represented. For there what was old was destroyed, that what was
new might be built up. . . . The apostle bindeth us together into
this very structure and fasteneth us when bound together in that
unity, saying, "Forbearing one another in love; endeavoring to
keep the unity of the Spirit in the bond of peace."[692] Where there is
this unity of Spirit, there is one stone; but one stone formed out of
many. How one formed out of many? By forbearing one another in
love. Therefore the house of the Lord our God is in building; it is
this that is being wrought, for this are these words, for this these
readings, for this the preaching of the Gospel over the whole

690. 1 Chr 16:23, etc.   691. Jn 15:12.   692. Eph 4:2, 3.

world; as yet it is in building. This house hath increased greatly and filled many nations. Nevertheless, it hath not yet prevailed through all nations; by its increase it hath held many and will prevail over all, and it is gainsaid by those who boast of their being of its household, and who say it hath already lost ground. It still increaseth, still all those nations which have not yet believed are destined to believe; that no man may say, will that tongue believe? Will the barbarians believe? What is the meaning of the Holy Spirit having appeared in the fiery tongues,[693] except that there is no tongue so hard that it cannot be softened by that fire? For we know that many barbarous nations have already believed in Christ: Christ already possesseth regions where the Roman Empire hath never yet reached; what is as yet closed to those who fight with the sword is not closed to Him who fighteth with wood. For "the Lord hath reigned from the wood."[694] Who is it who fighteth with wood? Christ. With His cross He hath vanquished kings, and fixed upon their forehead, when vanquished, that very cross; and they glory in it, for in it is their salvation. This is the work which is being wrought, thus the house increaseth, thus it is building: and that ye may know, hear the following verses of the psalm: see them laboring upon and constructing the house. "O sing unto the Lord all the earth."

3. "Sing unto the Lord, bless His Name: be telling good tidings of His salvation from day to day" (v. 2). How doth the building increase? "Be telling," he saith, "good tidings of His salvation from day to day." Let it be preached from day to day; from day to day, he saith, let it be built; let My house, saith God, increase. And as if it were said by the workmen, Where dost Thou command it to be built? Where dost Thou will Thy house to increase? Choose for us some level, spacious spot, if Thou wish an ample house built Thee. Where dost Thou bid us be telling good tidings from day to day? He showeth the place: "Declare His honor unto the heathen." His honor, not yours. O ye builders, "Declare His honor unto the heathen." Should ye choose to declare your own honor, ye shall fall: if His, ye shall be built up, while ye are building. Therefore they who choose to declare their own honor have refused to dwell in that house, and therefore they sing not a new song with all the earth.[695]

693. Acts 2:3.   694. Ps 96:11.   695. I.e., the Donatists.

For they do not share it with the whole round world, and hence they are not building in the house, but have erected a whited wall. How sternly doth God threaten the whited wall?[696] There are innumerable testimonies of the prophets, whence He curseth the whited wall. What is the whited wall, save hypocrisy, that is, pretense? Without it is bright, within it is dirt. . . . A certain person,[697] speaking of this whited wall, said thus: "as, if in a wall which standeth alone, and is not connected with any other walls, you make a door, whoever enters, is out of doors; so in that part which hath refused to sing the new song together with the house, but hath chosen to build a wall, and that a whited one, and not solid, what availeth it that it hath a door?" If thou enterest, thou art found to be without. For because they themselves did not enter by the door, their door also doth not admit them within. For the Lord saith, "I am the door: by Me they enter in."[698] "Declare His honor unto the heathen." What is, "unto the heathen"? Perhaps by nations but a few are meant: and that part which hath raised the whited wall hath still somewhat to say: why are not Getulia, Numidia, Mauritania, Byzacium, nations? Provinces are nations. Let the word of God take the word from hypocrisy, from the whited wall, building up the house over the whole world. It is not enough to say, "Declare His honor unto the heathen"; that thou mayest not think any nations excepted, he addeth, "and His wonders unto all people."

4. "For the Lord is great, and cannot worthily be praised" (v. 4). What Lord, except Jesus Christ, "is great, and cannot worthily be praised"? Ye know surely that He appeared as a Man: ye know surely that He was conceived in a woman's womb, ye know that He was born from the womb, that He was suckled, that He was carried in arms, circumcised, that a victim was offered for Him, that He grew; lastly, ye know that He was buffeted, spit upon, crowned with thorns, was crucified, died, was pierced with a spear; ye know that He suffered all these things: "He is great, and cannot worthily be praised." Despise not what is little, understand what is great. He became little, because ye were such: let Him be acknowledged great and in Him ye shall be great. . . . For what can a small tongue say toward the praise of the Great One? By saying, Beyond

696. Ez 13:10.   697. St. Optatus of Milevis.   698. Jn 10:9.

praise,[699] he hath spoken, and hath given to imagination what it may conceive: as if saying, What I cannot utter, do thou reflect on; and when thou shalt have reflected, it will not be enough. What no man's thought uttereth, doth any man's tongue utter? "The Lord is great, and cannot worthily be praised." Let Him be praised and preached: His honor declared, and His house built.

5. For the spot where he wished to build the house is itself woody, where it was said yesterday, "we found it in the wood."[700] For he was seeking that very house when he said, "in the wood." And why is that spot woody? Men used to worship images: it is not wonderful that they fed hogs. For that son who left his father and spent his all on harlots, living as a prodigal, used to feed hogs,[701] that is, to worship devils; and by this very superstition of the heathen, all the earth became a wood. But he who buildeth a house rooteth up the wood; and for this reason it was said, "While the house was being built, after the captivity." For men were held captive under the devil and served devils, but they were redeemed from captivity. They could sell, but they could not redeem themselves. The Redeemer came and gave a price; He poured forth His Blood, and bought the whole world. Ye ask what He bought? Ye see what He hath given; find out then what He bought. The Blood of Christ was the price. What is equal to this? What, but the whole world? What, but all nations? They are very ungrateful for their price, or very proud, who say that the price is so small that it bought the Africans only; or that they are so great, as that it was given for them alone. Let them not then exult, let them not be proud: He gave what He gave for the whole world. He knew what He bought, because He knew at what price He bought it. Thus because we are redeemed, the house is built after the captivity. And who are they who held us in captivity? Because they to whom it is said, "Declare His honor," are the clearers of the wood: that they may root out the wood, free the earth from captivity, and build, and raise up, by declaring the greatness of the Lord's house. How is the wood of devils cleared away, unless He who is above them all be preached? All nations then had devils for their gods: those whom they called gods

699. *Laudabilis nimis.*   700. Psalm 132:6. Hence it appears that Psalm 132 had been expounded the day before.   701. Lk 15:12–15.

were devils, as the apostle more openly saith, "The things which the Gentiles sacrifice, they sacrifice unto devils, and not to God."[702] Since therefore they were in captivity, because they sacrificed to devils, and on that account the whole earth had remained woody; He is declared to be great, and above all worldly praise.

6. For when he had said, "He is more to be feared than all gods," he added, "As for all the gods of the heathen, they are devils," because "all the gods of the heathen are devils." And is this all the praise of Him who cannot worthily be praised, that He is above all the gods of the heathen, which are devils? Wait, and hear what followeth: "It is the Lord that made the heavens." Not above all gods only therefore; but above all the heavens which He made, is the Lord. If he were to say, "above all gods, for the gods of the heathen are devils," and if the praise of our Lord stopped here, he had said less than we are accustomed to think of Christ, but when he said, "But it is the Lord that made the heavens," see what difference there is between the heavens and devils and what between the heavens and Him who made the heavens; behold how exalted is the Lord. He said not, "But the Lord sitteth above the heavens"; for perhaps someone else might be imagined to have made them, upon which He was enthroned, but, "It is the Lord that made the heavens." If He made the heavens, He made the angels also: Himself made the angels, Himself made the apostles. The devils yielded to the apostles, but the apostles themselves were heavens, who bore the Lord. . . . O heavens, which He made, declare His honor unto the heathen! Let His house be built throughout the earth, let all the earth sing a new song.

7. "Confession and beauty are before Him" (v. 6). Dost thou love beauty? Wishest thou to be beautiful? Confess! He said not, beauty and confession, but confession and beauty. Thou wast foul; confess, that thou mayest be fair: thou wast a sinner; confess, that thou mayest be righteous. Thou couldest deform thyself: thou canst not make thyself beautiful. But of what sort is our Betrothed, who hath loved one deformed, that He might make her fair? How, saith someone, loved He one deformed? "I came not," said He, "to call the righteous, but sinners."[703] Whom callest Thou? Sinners, that they may remain sinners? No, saith He. And by what means will

702. 1 Cor 10:20.   703. Mt 9:13.

they cease to be sinners? "Confession and beauty are before Him."
They honor Him by confession of their sins; they vomit the evils
which they had greedily devoured; they return not to their vomit,
like the unclean dog;[704] and there will then be confession and beauty:
we love beauty; let us first choose confession, that beauty may follow.
Again, there is one who loveth power and greatness: he wisheth to
be great as the angels are. There is a certain greatness in the angels,
and such power that if the angels exert it to the full, it cannot be
withstood. And every man desireth the power of the angels, but
their righteousness every man loveth not. First love righteousness,
and power shall follow thee. For what followeth here? "Holiness
and greatness are in His sanctification." Thou wast before seeking
for greatness: first love righteousness; when thou art righteous,
thou shall also be great. For if thou preposterously dost wish first to
be great, thou fallest before thou canst rise: for thou dost not rise,
thou art raised up. Thou risest better, if He raise thee who falleth
not. For He who falleth not descendeth unto thee; thou hadst
fallen. He descendeth, He hath stretched forth His hand unto thee;
thou canst not rise by thy own strength: embrace the hand of Him
who descendeth, that thou mayest be raised up by the Strong One.

8. What then? If "confession and beauty are before Him: holiness and greatness in His sanctification" (v. 7). This we declare,
when we are building the house; behold, it is already declared unto
the heathen; what ought the heathen to do, to whom those who
have cleared away the wood have declared the Lord's honor? He
now saith to the heathen themselves, "Ascribe unto the Lord, O ye
kindreds of the people: ascribe unto the Lord worship and honor."
Ascribe them not unto yourselves, because they also who have declared it unto you have not declared their own, but His honor. Do
ye then "ascribe unto the Lord worship and honor," and say, "Not
unto us, O Lord, not unto us: but unto Thy Name give the praise."[705]
Put not your trust in man. If each of you is baptized, let him say: He
baptizeth me, of whom the friend of the Bridegroom said, "He baptizeth with the Holy Ghost."[706] For when ye say this, ye ascribe unto
the Lord worship and honor: "Ascribe unto the Lord worship and
honor."

9. "Ascribe unto the Lord glory unto His Name" (v. 8). Not unto

704. 2 Pt 2:22.   705. Ps 115:1.   706. Jn 1:33, 3:29.

the name of man, not unto your own name, but unto His ascribe worship. . . . Confession is a present unto God. O heathen, if ye will enter into His courts, enter not empty. "Bring presents." What presents shall we bring with us? The sacrifice of God is a troubled spirit: a broken and a contrite heart, "O God, shalt not Thou despise."[707] Enter with an humble heart into the house of God, and thou hast entered with a present. But if thou art proud, thou enterest empty. For whence wouldest thou be proud, if thou wert not empty? For if thou wast full, thou wouldest not be puffed up. How couldest thou be full? If thou wert to bring a present, which thou shouldest carry to the courts of the Lord. Let us not retain you much longer: let us run over what remaineth. Behold the house increasing: behold the edifice pervade the whole world. Rejoice, because ye have entered into the courts; rejoice, because ye are being built into the temple of God. For those who enter are themselves built up; they themselves are the house of God: He is the inhabitor, for whom the house is built over the whole world, and this "after the captivity." "Bring presents, and come into His courts."

10. "O worship the Lord in His holy court" (v. 9): in the Catholic Church; this is His holy court. Let no man say, "Lo, here is Christ, or there. For there shall arise false prophets."[708] Say this unto them,[709] "There shall not be left here one stone upon another, that shall not be thrown down." Ye are calling me to the whited wall; I adore my God in His holy court. "Let the whole earth be moved before His face."

11. "Tell it out among the nations, that the Lord reigneth from the wood:[710] and that it is He who hath made the round world so fast that it cannot be moved" (v. 10). What testimonies of the building of the house of God! The clouds of heaven thunder out throughout the world that God's house is being built; and the frogs cry from the marsh,[711] We alone are Christians. What testimonies do I bring forward? That of the Psalter. I bring forward what thou singest as one deaf: open thine ears; thou singest this; thou singest with me, and thou agreest not with me; thy tongue soundeth what

707. Ps 51:17.   708. Mt 24:23, 24.   709. I.e., the Donatists.

710. The Church Father Justin Martyr claimed the Jewish scribes had omitted the phrase "from the wood" in their transcription of the Psalms.

711. I.e., so say the Donatists.—C.

mine doth, and yet thine heart disagreeth with mine. Dost thou not sing this? Behold the testimonies of the whole world: "Let the whole earth be moved before His face": and dost thou say, that thou art not moved? "Tell it out among the heathen, that the Lord hath reigned from the wood." Shall men perchance prevail here and say they reign by wood, because they reign by means of the clubs of their bandits? Reign by the cross of Christ, if thou art to reign by wood. For this wood of thine maketh thee wooden: the wood of Christ passeth thee across the sea. Thou hearest the psalm saying, "He hath set aright the round world, that it cannot be moved"; and thou sayest it hath not only been moved since it was made fast, but hath also decreased. Dost thou speak the truth, and the psalmist falsehood? Do the false prophets, when they cry out, "Lo, here is Christ, and there,"[712] speak truth, and doth this prophet lie? Brethren, against these most open words ye hear in the corners rumors like these; "such a one was a traditor," and, "such a one was a traditor."[713] What dost thou say? Are thy words, or the words of God, to be heard? For, "it is He who hath set aright the round world, that it cannot be moved." I show unto thee the round world built: bring thy present, and come into the courts of the Lord. Thou hast no presents: and on that account thou art not willing to enter. What is this? If God were to appoint unto thee a bull, goat, or ram, for a present, thou wouldest find one to bring: He hath appointed a humble heart, and thou wilt not enter; for thou findest not this in thyself, because thou art swollen with pride. "He hath set aright the round world, that it cannot be moved: and He shall judge the people righteously." Then shall they mourn, who now refuse to love righteousness.

12. "Let the heavens rejoice, and let the earth be glad" (v. 11). Let the heavens, which declare the glory of God, rejoice; let the heavens rejoice, which the Lord made; let the earth be glad, which the heavens rain upon. For the heavens are the preachers, the earth the listeners. "Let the sea be stirred up, and the fullness thereof." What sea? The world. The sea hath been stirred up, and the fullness thereof: the whole world was roused up against the Church, while

712. Mt 24:23.

713. Caecilianus and others, by communicating with whom they alleged the universal Church to have fallen.

it was being extended and built over all the earth. Concerning this stirring up, ye have heard in the Gospel, "They shall deliver you up to councils."[714] The sea was stirred up: but how should the sea ever conquer Him who made it?

13. "The plains shall be joyful, and all things that are in them" (v. 12). All the meek, all the gentle, all the righteous, are the "plains" of God. "Then shall all the trees of the woods rejoice." The trees of the woods are the heathen. Why do they rejoice? Because they were cut off from the wild olive, and engrafted into the good olive.[715] "Then shall all the trees of the woods rejoice": because huge cedars and cypresses have been cut down, and undecaying timbers have been bought for the building of the house. They were trees of the woods, but before they were sent to the building; they were trees of the woods, but before they produced the olive.

14. "Before the face of the Lord. For He cometh, for He cometh to judge the world" (v. 13). He came at first, and will come again. He first came in His Church in clouds. What are the clouds which bore Him? The apostles who preached, respecting whom ye have heard, when the Epistle was being read: "We are ambassadors," he saith, "for Christ: we pray you in Christ's stead, be ye reconciled to God."[716] These are the clouds in whom He cometh, excepting His last Advent, when He will come to judge the quick and the dead. He came first in the clouds. This was His first voice which sounded forth in the Gospel: "From this time shall they see the Son of Man coming in the clouds."[717] What is, "from this time"? Will not the Lord come in later times, when all the tribes of the earth shall mourn? He first came in His own preachers, and filled the whole round world. Let us not resist His first coming, that we may not tremble at His second. "But woe to them that are with child, and that give suck in those days!"[718] Ye have heard but now in the Gospel: "Take ye heed, for ye know not at what hour He cometh."[719] This is said figuratively. Who are those with child, and who give suck? Those who are with child are the souls whose hope is in the world, but those who have gained what they hoped for are meant by "they who give suck." For example, one wisheth to buy a country

714. Mk 13:9.   715. Rom 11:17.   716. 2 Cor 5:20.   717. Mk 13:26.
718. Mk 13:17.   719. Mk 13:33.

seat; he is with child, for his object is not gained as yet, the womb swelleth in hope; he buyeth it; he hath brought forth; he now giveth suck to what he hath bought. "Woe to them that are with child, and that give suck in those days!" Woe to those who put their hope in the world; woe to them that cling to those things which they brought forth through hope in the world. What then should the Christian do? He should use, not serve, the world.[720] What is this? Those that have as those that have not. . . . He who is without carefulness waiteth without fear for his Lord's coming. For what sort of love is it of Christ, to fear lest He come? Brethren, are we not ashamed? We love Him, and yet we fear lest He come. Are we sure that we love Him, or do we love our sins more? Therefore let us hate our sins for their own sake, and love Him who will come to punish our sins. He will come, whether we like or not, for because He cometh not just now, it is no reason that He will not come at all. He will come, and when thou knowest not; and if He shall find thee ready, thy ignorance is no hurt to thee. "Then shall all the trees of the wood rejoice before the Lord; for He cometh": at His first coming. And what afterward? "For He cometh to judge the earth. And all the trees of the woods shall rejoice." He came first: and later to judge the earth; He shall find those rejoicing who believed in His first coming, "for He cometh."

15. "For with righteousness shall He judge the world": not a part of it, for He bought not a part; He will judge the whole, for it was the whole of which He paid the price. Ye have heard the Gospel, where it saith that when He cometh, "He shall gather together His elect from the four winds."[721] He gathereth all His elect from the four winds: therefore from the whole world. For Adam himself (this I had said before) signifieth in Greek the whole world; for there are four letters, A, D, A, and M. But as the Greeks speak, the four quarters of the world have these initial letters, Ἀνατολὴ, they call the East; Δύσις, the West; Ἄρκτος, the North; Μεσημβρία, the South: thou hast the word Adam. Adam therefore hath been scattered over the whole world. He was in one place and fell, and as in a manner broken small, he filled the whole world: but the mercy of God gathered together the fragments from every side, and forged them by the fire of love, and made one what was broken.

720. 1 Cor 7:29–32.   721. Mk 13:27.

That Artist knew how to do this; let no one despair: it is indeed a great thing, but reflect who that Artist was. He who made, restored: He who formed, reformed. What are righteousness and truth? He will gather together His elect with Him to the judgment, but the rest He will separate one from another; for He will place some on the right, others on the left hand. But what is more just, what more true, than that they shall not expect mercy from their Judge, who have refused to act mercifully, before their Judge come? But those who chose to act with mercy, with mercy shall be judged.

Psalm 121[722]

1. Let them "lift up their eyes to the hills whence cometh their help" (v. 1). What meaneth, "The hills have been lightened"? The Son of righteousness hath already risen, the Gospel hath been already preached by the apostles, the Scriptures have been preached, all the mysteries have been laid open, the veil hath been rent, the secret place of the temple hath been revealed: let them now at length lift their eyes up to the hills, whence their help cometh . . . "Of His fullness have all we received,"[723] he saith. Thy help therefore is from Him, of whose fullness the hills received, not from the hills; toward which, nevertheless, save thou lift thine eyes through the Scriptures, thou wilt not approach, so as to be lighted by Him.

2. Sing therefore what followeth; if thou wish to hear how thou mayest most securely set thy feet on the steps, so that thou mayest not be fatigued in that ascent, nor stumble and fall: pray in these words: "Suffer not my foot to be moved!" (v. 3). Whereby are feet moved; whereby was the foot of him who was in paradise moved? But first consider whereby the feet of him who was among the angels were moved: who when his feet were moved fell, and from an angel became a devil, for when his feet were moved he fell. Seek whereby he fell: he fell through pride. Nothing then moveth the feet, save pride: nothing moveth the feet to a fall, save pride. Char-

722. Lat. 120. A sermon to the people on the day of St. Crispina.

723. Jn 1:16.

ity moveth them to walk and to improve and to ascend; pride moveth them to fall ... Rightly therefore the psalmist, hearing how he may ascend and may not fall, prayeth unto God that he may profit from the vale of misery, and may not fail in the swelling of pride, in these words, "Suffer not my feet to be moved!" And He replieth unto him, "Let him that keepeth thee not sleep." Attend, my beloved. It is as if one thought were expressed in two sentences; the man while ascending and singing "the song of degrees," saith, "Suffer not my foot to be moved," and it is as if God answered, Thou sayest unto Me, Let not my feet be moved: say also, "Let Him that keepeth thee not sleep," and thy foot shall not be moved.

3. Choose for thyself Him, who will neither sleep nor slumber, and thy foot shall not be moved. God is never asleep: if thou dost wish to have a keeper who never sleepeth, choose God for thy keeper. "Suffer not my feet to be moved," thou sayest: well, very well, but He also saith unto thee, "Let not him that keepeth thee slumber." Thou perhaps wast about to turn thyself unto men as thy keepers, and to say, whom shall I find who will not sleep? What man will not slumber? Whom do I find? Whither shall I go? Whither shall I return? The psalmist telleth thee: "He that keepeth Israel, shall neither slumber nor sleep" (v. 4). Dost thou wish to have a keeper who neither slumbereth nor sleepeth? Behold, "He that keepeth Israel shall neither slumber nor sleep," for Christ keepeth Israel. Be thou then Israel. What meaneth "Israel"? It is interpreted, "Seeing God." And how is God seen? First by faith, afterward by sight. If thou canst not as yet see Him by sight, see Him by faith ... Who is there, who will neither slumber nor sleep? When thou seekest among men, thou art deceived; thou wilt never find one. Trust not then in any man: every man slumbereth and will sleep. When doth he slumber? When he beareth the flesh of weakness. When will he sleep? When he is dead. Trust not then in man. A mortal may slumber; he sleepeth in death. Seek not a keeper among men.

4. And who, thou askest, shall help me, save He who slumbereth not, nor sleepeth? Hear what followeth: "The Lord Himself is thy keeper" (v. 5). It is not therefore man, that slumbereth and sleepeth, but the Lord, that keepeth thee. How doth He keep thee? "The Lord is thy defense upon the hand of thy right hand." ... It seemeth to me to have a hidden sense: otherwise he would have

simply said, without qualification, "The Lord will keep thee," without adding, "on thy right hand." For how? Doth God keep our right hand, and not our left? Did He not create the whole of us? Did not He who made our right hand make our left hand also? Finally, if it pleased Him to speak of the right hand alone, why said He, "on the hand of thy right hand," and not at once "upon thy right hand"? Why should He say this, unless He were keeping somewhat here hidden for us to arrive at by knocking? For He would either say, "The Lord shall keep thee," and add no more; or if He would add the right hand, "The Lord shall keep thee upon thy right hand"; or at least, as He added "hand," He would say, "The Lord shall keep thee upon thy hand, even thy right hand," not "upon the hand of thy right hand."

5. I ask you, how ye interpret what is said in the Gospel, "Let not your left hand know what your right hand doeth"?[724] For if ye understand this, ye will discover what is your right hand, and what is your left: at the same time ye will also understand that God made both hands, the left and the right; yet the left ought not to know what the right doeth. By our left hand is meant all that we have in a temporal way; by our right hand is meant, whatever our Lord promiseth us that is immutable and eternal. But if He who will give everlasting life, Himself also consoleth our present life by these temporal blessings, He hath Himself made our right hand and our left.

6. Let us now come to this verse of the psalm: "The Lord is thy defense upon the hand of thy right hand" (v. 5). By hand he meaneth power. How do we prove this? Because the power of God also is styled the hand of God . . . Whereof John saith, "He gave unto them power to become the sons of God."[725] Whence hast thou received this power? "To them," he saith, "that believe in His Name." If then thou believest, this very power is given thee, to be among the sons of God. But to be among the sons of God is to belong to the right hand. Thy faith therefore is the hand of thy right hand: that is, the power that is given thee, to be among the sons of God, is the hand of thy right hand.

7. "May the Lord shield thee upon the hand of thy right hand" (v. 6). I have said, and I believe ye have recognized it. For had ye

not recognized it, and that from the Scriptures, ye would not signify your understanding of it by your voices. Since then ye have understood, brethren, consider what followeth; wherefore the Lord shieldeth thee "upon the hand of thy right hand," that is, in thy faith, wherein we have received "power to become the sons of God," and to be on His right hand: wherefore should God shield us? On account of offenses. Whence come offenses? Offenses are to be feared from two quarters, for there are two precepts upon which the whole Law hangeth and the Prophets, the love of God and of our neighbor.[726] The Church is loved for the sake of our neighbor, but God for the sake of God. Of God, is understood the sun figuratively; of the Church, is understood the moon figuratively. Whoever can err, so as to think otherwise of God than he ought, believing not the Father and the Son and the Holy Ghost to be of one Substance, has been deceived by the cunning of heretics, chiefly of the Arians. If he hath believed anything less in the Son or in the Holy Spirit than in the Father, he hath suffered an offense in God; he is scorched by the sun. Whoever again believeth that the Church existeth in one province only,[727] and not that she is diffused over the whole world, and whoso believeth them that say, "Lo here," and "Lo there, is Christ,"[728] as ye but now heard when the Gospel was being read; since He who gave so great a price, purchased the whole world: he is offended, so to speak, in his neighbor, and is burnt by the moon. Whoever therefore erreth in the very Substance of Truth, is burnt by the sun, and is burnt through the day; because he erreth in Wisdom itself . . . God therefore hath made one sun, which riseth upon the good and the evil, that sun which the good and the evil see; but that Sun is another one, not created, not born, through whom all things were made;[729] where is the intelligence of the Immutable Truth: of this the ungodly say, "the Sun rose not upon us."[730] Whosoever erreth not in Wisdom itself is not burnt by the sun. Whosoever erreth not in the Church, and in the Lord's Flesh, and in those things which were done for us in time, is not burnt by the moon. But every man although he believeth in Christ erreth either in this or that respect, unless what is here prayed for, "The Lord is thy defense upon the hand of thy right

726. Mt 22:37–40.   727. I.e., the Donatists.   728. Mt 24:23.

729. Cf. the Nicene Creed.   730. Ws 5:6.

hand," is realized in him. He goeth on to say, "So that the sun shall not burn thee by day, nor the moon by night" (v. 6). Thy defense, therefore, is upon the hand of thy right hand for this reason, that the sun may not burn thee by day, nor the moon by night. Understand hence, brethren, that it is spoken figuratively. For, in truth, if we think of the visible sun, it burneth by day: doth the moon burn by night? But what is burning? Offense. Hear the apostle's words: "Who is weak, and I am not weak? who is offended, and I burn not?"[731]

8. "For the Lord shall preserve thee from all evil" (v. 7). From offenses in the sun, from offenses in the moon, from all evil shall He preserve thee, who is thy defense upon the hand of thy right hand, who will not sleep nor slumber. And for what reason? Because we are amid temptations: "The Lord shall preserve thee from all evil. The Lord preserve thy soul": even thy very soul. "The Lord preserve thy going out and thy coming in, from this time forth for evermore" (v. 8). Not thy body; for the martyrs were consumed in the body: but "the Lord preserve thy soul"; for the martyrs yielded not up their souls. The persecutors raged against Crispina,[732] whose birthday we are today celebrating; they were raging against a rich and delicate woman: but she was strong, for the Lord was her defense upon the hand of her right hand. He was her Keeper. Is there anyone in Africa, my brethren, who knoweth her not? For she was most illustrious, noble in birth, abounding in wealth: but all these things were in her left hand, beneath her head. An enemy advanced to strike her head, and the left hand was presented to him, which was under her head. Her head was above, the right hand embraced her from above.[733]

---

731. 2 Cor 11:29.   732. St. Crispina.

733. Sg 2:6. He thus concludes: "Although the psalm is short, yet our exposition and discourse on it hath been long. Imagine, my brethren, that owing to the birthday of the blessed Crispina I have invited you, and have been immoderate in protracting the banquet. Might not this have happened to you, if any military officer had invited you, and compel you to drink at his table without measure? May it be lawful for us to do this in a sacred exposition, that ye may be inebriated and satisfied to the full."—C.

Psalm 149[734]

1. Let us praise the Lord both in voice, and in understanding, and in good works; and, as this psalm exhorteth, let us sing unto Him a new song. It beginneth: "Sing ye to the Lord a new song. His praise is in the Church of the Saints" (v. 1). The old man hath an old song, the new man a new song. The Old Testament is an old song, the New Testament a new song. In the Old Testament are temporal and earthly promises. Whoso loveth earthly things singeth an old song: let him that desireth to sing a new song love the things of eternity. Love itself is new and eternal; therefore is it ever new, because it never groweth old. . . . And this song is of peace, this song is of charity. Whoso severeth himself from the union of the saints, singeth not a new song; for he hath followed old strife, not new charity. In new charity what is there? Peace, the bond of a holy society, a spiritual union, a building of living stones. Where is this? Not in one place, but throughout the whole world. This is said in another psalm, "Sing unto the Lord, all the earth."[735] From this is understood, that he who singeth not with the whole earth, singeth an old song, whatever words proceed out of his mouth. . . . We have already said, brethren, that all the earth singeth a new song. He who singeth not with the whole earth a new song, let him sing what he will, let his tongue sound forth Halleluia, let him utter it all day and all night, my ears are not so much bent to hear the voice of the singer, but I seek the deeds of the doer. For I ask, and say, "What is it that thou singest?" He answereth, "Halleluia." What is "Halleluia"? "Praise ye the Lord." Come, let us praise the Lord together. If thou praisest the Lord, and I praise the Lord, why are we at variance? Charity praiseth the Lord, discord blasphemeth the Lord."

2. The field of the Lord is the world, not Africa. It is not with the Lord's field, as it is without these fields of ours, where Getulia bears sixty or a hundredfold, Numidia only tenfold: everywhere fruit is borne to Him, both a hundredfold, and sixtyfold, and thirtyfold: only do thou choose what thou wilt be, if thou thinkest to belong to the Lord's cross. "The Church" then "of the saints" is the Catholic

---

734. Lat. 149. Sermon to the people.   735. Ps 96:1.

Church. The Church of the saints is not the Church of heretics. The Church of the saints is that which God first prefigured before it was seen, and then set forth that it might be seen. The Church of the saints was heretofore in writings, now it is in nations: the Church of the saints was heretofore only read of, now it is both read of and seen. When it was only read of, it was believed; now it is seen, and is spoken against. His praise is in the "children of the kingdom," that is, "the Church of the saints."

3. "Let Israel rejoice in Him who made Him" (v. 2). What is, "Israel"? "Seeing God." He who seeth God, rejoiceth in Him by whom he was made. What is it then, brethren? We have said that we belong to the Church of the saints: do we already see God? And how are we Israel, if we see not? There is one kind of sight belonging to this present time; there will be another belonging to the time hereafter: the sight which now is, is by faith; the sight which is to be will be in reality. If we believe, we see; if we love, we see: see what? God. Ask John: "God is love";[736] let us bless His holy Name, and rejoice in God by rejoicing in love. Whoso hath love, why send we him afar to see God? Let him regard his own conscience, and there he seeth God. . . . "And let the sons of Sion exult in their King." The sons of the Church are Israel. For Sion indeed was one city, which fell: amid its ruins certain saints dwelt after the flesh: but the true Sion, the true Jerusalem (for Sion and Jerusalem are one), is "eternal in the heavens,"[737] and is "our mother."[738] She it is that hath given us birth, she is the Church of the saints, she hath nourished us, she, who is in part a pilgrim, in part abiding in the heavens. In the part which abideth in heaven is the bliss of angels; in the part which wandereth in this world is the hope of the righteous. Of the former is said, "Glory to God in the highest"; of the latter, "and on earth peace to men of good will."[739] Let those then who, being in this life, groan, and long for their country, run by love, not by bodily feet; let them seek not ships but wings, let them lay hold on the two wings of love. What are the two wings of love? The love of God and of our neighbor. For now we are pilgrims, we sigh, we groan. There has come to us a letter from our country: we read it to you. "And the sons of Sion shall exult in their King." The Son of God, who made us, was made one of us: and He rules us as our

736. Jn 4:16.   737. 2 Cor 5:1.   738. Gal 4:26.   739. Lk 2:14.

King, because He is our Creator, who made us. But He by whom we were made is the same as He by whom we are ruled, and we are Christians because He is Christ. He is called Christ from Chrism, that is, Anointing. . . . Give to the Priest somewhat to offer. What could man find which he could give as a clean victim? What victim? What clean thing can a sinner offer? O unrighteous, O sinful man, whatever thou offerest is unclean, and somewhat that is clean must be offered for thee. . . . Let then the Priest that is clean offer Himself and cleanse thee. This is what Christ did. He found in man nothing clean for Him to offer for man: He offered Himself as a clean Victim. Happy Victim, true Victim, spotless Offering. He offered not then what we gave Him; yea rather, He offered what He took of us, and offered it clean. For of us He took flesh, and this He offered. But where took He it? In the womb of the Virgin Mary, that He might offer it clean for us unclean. He is our King, He is our Priest, in Him let us rejoice.

4. "Let them praise His Name in chorus" (v. 3). What meaneth "chorus"? Many know what a "chorus" is: nay, as we are speaking in a town, almost all know. A "chorus" is the union of singers. If we sing "in chorus," let us sing in concord. If anyone's voice is out of harmony in a chorus of singers, it offendeth the ear, and throweth the chorus into confusion. If the voice of one echoing discordantly troubleth the harmony of them who sing, how doth the discord of heresy throw into confusion the harmony of them who praise. The whole world is now the chorus of Christ. The chorus of Christ soundeth harmoniously from east to west.[740] "Let them sing a psalm unto Him with timbrel and psaltery." Wherefore taketh he to him the "timbrel and psaltery"? That not the voice alone may praise, but the works too. When timbrel and psaltery are taken, the hands harmonize with the voice. So too do thou, whensoever thou singest "Halleluia," deal forth thy bread to the hungry, clothe the naked, take in the stranger: then doth not only thy voice sound, but thy hand soundeth in harmony with it, for thy deeds agree with thy words. Thou hast taken to thee an instrument, and thy fingers agree with thy tongue. Nor must we keep back the mystical meaning of the "timbrel and psaltery." On the timbrel leather is stretched; on the psaltery gut is stretched; on either instrument the

740. Ps 113:3.

flesh is crucified. How well did he "sing a psalm on timbrel and psaltery," who said, "the world is crucified unto me, and I unto the world"?[741] This psaltery or timbrel He wishes thee to take up, who loveth a new song, who teacheth thee, saying to thee, "Whosoever willeth to be My disciple, let him deny himself, and take up his cross, and follow Me."[742] Let him not set down his psaltery, let him not set down his timbrel, let him stretch himself out on the wood, and be dried from the lust of the flesh. The more the strings are stretched, the more sharply do they sound. The Apostle Paul then, in order that his psaltery might sound sharply, what said he? "Stretching forth unto those things which are before," etc.[743] He stretched himself: Christ touched him, and the sweetness of truth sounded.

5. "For the Lord hath dealt kindly among His people" (v. 4). What dealing so kindly, as to die for the ungodly? What dealing so kindly, as with righteous Blood to blot out the handwriting against the sinner? What dealing so kindly, as to say, "I regard not what ye were, be ye now what ye were not"? He dealeth kindly in converting him that was turned away, in aiding him that is fighting, in crowning the conqueror. "And the meek He shall lift up in salvation." For the proud too are lifted up, but not in salvation: the meek are lifted in salvation, the proud in death: that is, the proud lift up themselves, and God humbleth them: the meek humble themselves; and God lifteth them up.

6. "The saints shall exult in glory" (v. 5). I would say somewhat important about the glory of the saints. For there is no one who loveth not glory. But the glory of fools, popular glory as it is called, hath snares to deceive, so that a man, influenced by the praises of vain men, shall be willing to live in such fashion as to be spoken of by men, whosoever they be, in whatsoever way. Hence it is that men, rendered mad, and puffed up with pride, empty within, without swollen, are willing ever to ruin their fortunes by bestowing them on stage-players, actors, men who fight with wild beasts, charioteers. What sums they give, what sums they spend! They lavish the powers not only of their patrimony, but of their minds too. They scorn the poor, because the people shouteth not that the poor should be given to, but the people do shout that the fighter with

wild beasts be given to. When then no shout is raised to them, they refuse to spend; when madmen shout to them, they are mad too: nay, all are mad, both performer, and spectator, and the giver. This mad glory is blamed by the Lord, is offensive in the eyes of the Almighty. . . . Thou choosest to clothe the fighter with wild beasts, who may be beaten, and make thee blush: Christ is never conquered; He hath conquered the devil, He hath conquered for thee, and to thee, and in thee; such a conqueror as this thou choosest not to clothe. Wherefore? Because there is less shouting, less madness about it. They then who delight in such glory have an empty conscience. Just as they drain their chests to send garments as presents, so do they empty their conscience, so as to have nothing precious therein.

7. But the saints who "exult in glory," no need is there for us to say how they exult: just hear the verse of the psalm which followeth: "The saints shall exult in glory, they shall rejoice in their beds"; not in theaters, or amphitheaters, or circuses, or follies, or marketplaces, but "in their chambers." What is, "in their chambers"? In their hearts.[744] Hear the Apostle Paul exulting in his closet: "For this is our glory, the testimony of our conscience."[745] On the other hand, there is reason to fear lest any be pleasing to himself, and so seem to be proud, and boast of his conscience. For everyone ought to exult with fear, for that wherein he exulteth is God's gift, not his own desert. For there be many that please themselves, and think themselves righteous; and there is another passage which goeth against them, which saith, "Who shall boast that he hath a clean heart, and that he is pure from sin?"[746] There is then, so to speak, a limit to glorying in our conscience, namely, to know that thy faith is sincere, thy hope sure, thy love without dissimulation. "The exultations of God are in their mouths" (v. 6). In such wise shall they "rejoice in their closets," as not to attribute to themselves that they are good, but praise Him from whom they have what they are, by whom they are called to attain to what they are not, and from whom they hope for perfection, to whom they give thanks, because He hath begun.

744. There is a play here on the word *cubile*, which was used of a box in the theater. *Cubile* often means a small apartment, and this is our author's idea. Mt 6:6. Elsewhere he speaks of the "closet" as the "heart." I vary the text accordingly.—C.

745. 2 Cor 1:12.   746. Prv 20:9.

8. "And swords sharpened on both sides in their hands." This sort of weapon contains a great mystical meaning, in that it is sharp on both sides. By "swords sharpened on both sides," we understand the Word of the Lord:[747] it is one sword, but therefore are they called many, because there are many mouths and many tongues of the saints. How is it two-edged? It speaks of things temporal, it speaks also of things eternal. In both cases it proveth what it saith, and him whom it strikes, it severeth from the world. Is not this the sword whereof the Lord said, "I am not come to send peace upon earth, but a sword"?[748] Observe how He came to divide, how He came to sever. He divideth the saints, He divideth the ungodly, He severeth from thee that which hindereth thee. The son willeth to serve God, the father willeth not: the sword cometh, the Word of God cometh, and severeth the son from the father. . . . Wherefore then is it in their hands, not in their tongues? "And swords," it saith, "sharpened on both sides in their hands." By "in their hands," he meaneth in power. They received then the word of God in power, to speak where they would, to whom they would, neither to fear power, nor to despise poverty. For they had in their hands a sword; where they would they brandished it, handled it, smote with it, and all this was in the power of the preachers. For if the Word be not in their hands, why is it written, "The Word of the Lord was put in the hand of the Prophet Haggai"?[749] Surely, brethren, God set not His Word in His fingers. What is meant by, "was put in his hand"? It was put into his power to preach the Word of the Lord. Lastly, we can understand these "hands" in another way also. For they who spake had the word of God in their tongues, they who wrote, in their hands.

9. Now, brethren, ye see the saints armed: observe the slaughter, observe their glorious battles. For if there be a commander, there must be soldiers; if soldiers, an enemy; if a warfare, a victory. What have these done who had in their hands swords sharpened on both sides? "To do vengeance on the nations." See whether vengeance have not been done on the nations. Daily is it done: we do it ourselves by speaking. Observe how the nations of Babylon are slain. She is repaid twofold: for so is it written of her, "repay her double for what she hath done."[750] How is she repaid double? The saints

---

747. Heb 4:12.   748. Mt 10:34.   749. Hg 1:1.   750. Rv 18:6.

wage war, they draw their "swords twice sharpened"; thence come defeats, slaughters, severances: how is she repaid double? When she had power to persecute the Christians, she slew the flesh indeed, but she crushed not God: now she is repaid double, for the pagans are extinguished and the idols are broken. . . . And lest thou shouldest think that men are really smitten with the sword, blood really shed, wounds made in the flesh, he goeth on and explaineth, "upbraidings among the peoples." What is "upbraidings"? Reproof. Let the "sword twice sharpened" go forth from you; delay not. Say to thy friend, if yet thou hast one[751] left to whom to say it, "What kind of man art thou, who hast abandoned Him by whom thou wast made, and worshippest what He made? Better is the Workman, than that which He worketh." When he beginneth to blush, when he beginneth to feel compunction, thou hast made a wound with thy sword, it hath reached the heart, he is about to die, that he may live.

10. "That they may bind their kings in fetters, and their nobles in bonds of iron" (v. 8). "To execute upon them the judgment written" (v. 9). The kings of the Gentiles are to be bound in fetters, "and their nobles in fetters," and that "of iron." . . . For these verses which we are beginning to explain are obscure. For this purpose God willed to set down some of His verses obscurely, not that anything new should be dug out of them, but that what was already well known might be made new by being obscurely set forth. We know that kings have been made Christians; we know that the nobles of the Gentiles have been made Christians. They are being made so at this day; they have been, they shall be; the "swords twice sharpened" are not idle in the hands of the saints. How then do we understand their being bound in fetters and chains of iron? Ye know, beloved and learned brethren (learned I call you, for ye have been nourished in the Church, and are accustomed to hear God's Word read), that "God hath chosen the weak things of the world to confound the strong, and the foolish things of the world hath God chosen to confound the wise, and things which are not, just as things which are, that the things which are may be brought to nought."[752] It is said by the Lord, "If thou wilt be perfect, go sell all that thou hast, and give to the poor, and come, follow Me, and thou shalt

751. I.e., a heathen one.—C.   752. 1 Cor 1:26, etc.

have treasure in heaven."[753] Many of the nobles did this, but they ceased to be nobles of the Gentiles, they chose rather to be poor in this world, noble in Christ. But many retain their former nobility, retain their royal powers, and yet are Christians. These are, as it were, "in fetters and in bonds of iron." How so? They received fetters, to keep them from going to things unlawful, the "fetters of wisdom,"[754] the fetters of the Word of God. Wherefore then are they bonds of iron and not bonds of gold? They are iron so long as they fear: let them love, and they shall be golden. Observe, beloved, what I say. Ye have heard just now the Apostle John, "There is no fear in love, but perfect love casteth out fear, because fear hath torment."[755] This is the bond of iron. And yet unless a man begin through fear to worship God, he will not attain to love. "The fear of the Lord is the beginning of wisdom."[756] The beginning then is bonds of iron, the end a collar of gold. For it is said of wisdom, "a collar of gold around thy neck."[757] There cometh to us a man powerful in this world, his wife offendeth him, and perhaps he hath desired another man's wife who is more beautiful, or another woman who is richer, he wisheth to put away the one he hath, yet he doeth it not. He heareth the words of the servant of God, he heareth the prophet, he heareth the apostle, and he doeth it not; he is told by one in whose hands is a "sword twice sharpened," "Thou shalt not do it: it is not lawful for thee; God alloweth thee not to put away thy wife, save for the cause of fornication."[758] He heareth this, he feareth, and doeth it not. . . . Listen, young men; the bonds are of iron, seek not to set your feet within them; if ye do, ye shall be bound more tightly with fetters. Such fetters the hands of the bishop make strong for you. Do not men who are thus fettered fly to the Church, and are here loosed? Men do fly hither, desiring to be rid of their wives; here they are more tightly bound: no man looseth these fetters. "What God joined together, let not man put asunder."[759] But these bonds are hard. Who but knows it? This hardness the apostles grieved at, and said, "If this be the case with a wife, it is not good to marry."[760] If the bonds be of iron, it is not good to set our feet within them. And the Lord said, "All men cannot re-

753. Mt 19:21.   754. Ecclus 6:25.   755. 1 Jn 4:18.   756. Ps 111:10.

757. Ecclus 6:24.   758. Mt 5:32.   759. Mt 19:6.   760. Mt 19:10.

ceive this saying, but let him that can receive it, receive it."[761] "Art thou bound unto a wife? seek not to be freed," for thou art bound with bonds of iron. "Art thou free from a wife, seek not a wife"; bind not thyself with bonds of iron.

11. "To do in them the judgment that is written." This is the judgment which the saints do throughout all nations. Wherefore "written"? Because these things were before written, and now are fulfilled. Behold now they are being done: erst they were read, and were not done. And he hath concluded thus, "this glory have all His saints." Throughout the whole world, throughout entire nations, this the saints do; thus are they glorified, thus do they "exalt God with their mouths," thus do they "rejoice in their beds," thus do they "exult in their glory," thus are they "lifted up in salvation," thus do they "sing a new song," thus in heart and voice and life they say Halleluia. Amen.

---

761. Mt 19:11, 12.

From The Trinity

Book VIII

Explains and proves that not only the Father is not greater than the Son, but neither are both together anything greater than the Holy Spirit, nor any two together in the same Trinity anything greater than one, nor all three together anything greater than each severally. It is then shown how the nature itself of God may be understood from our understanding of truth, and from our knowledge of the supreme good, and from the innate love of righteousness, whereby a righteous soul is loved even by a soul that is itself not yet righteous. But it is urged above all, that the knowledge of God is to be sought by love, which God is said to be in the Scriptures; and in this love is also pointed out the existence of some trace of a trinity.

Chapter 1   It Is Shown by Reason That in God Three Are Not Anything Greater Than One Person.

2. For we say that in this Trinity two or three persons are not anything greater than one of them; which carnal perception does not receive, for no other reason except because it perceives as it can the true things which are created, but cannot discern the truth itself by which they are created; for if it could, then the very corporeal light would in no way be more clear than this which we have said. For in respect to the substance of truth, since it alone truly is, nothing is greater, unless because it more truly is.[762] But in respect to whatsoever is intelligible and unchangeable, no one thing is more truly than another, since all alike are unchangeably eternal; and that which therein is called great is not great from any other source than from that by which it truly is. Wherefore, where magnitude itself is truth, whatsoever has more of magnitude must needs have more of truth; whatsoever therefore has not more of truth, has not also

762. In this and the following chapter, the meaning of Augustine will be clearer, if the Latin *"veritas," "vera,"* and *"vere,"* are rendered occasionally, by "reality," "real," and "really." He is endeavoring to prove the equality of the three persons, by the fact that they are equally real (true), and the degree of their reality (truth) is the same. Real being is true being; reality is truth. In common phraseology, truth and reality are synonymous.

more of magnitude. Further, whatsoever has more of truth is certainly more true, just as that is greater which has more of magnitude; therefore in respect to the substance of truth that is more great which is more true. But the Father and the Son together are not more truly than the Father singly, or the Son singly. Both together, therefore are not anything greater than each of them singly. And since also the Holy Spirit equally is truly, the Father and Son together are not anything greater than He, since neither are they more truly. The Father also and the Holy Spirit together, since they do not surpass the Son in truth (for they are not more truly), do not surpass him either in magnitude. And so the Son and the Holy Spirit together are just as great as the Father alone, since they are as truly. So also the Trinity itself is as great as each several person therein. For where truth itself is magnitude, that is not more great which is not more true: since in regard to the essence of truth, to be true is the same as to be, and to be is the same as to be great; therefore to be great is the same as to be true. And in regard to it, therefore, what is equally true must needs also be equally great.

Chapter 2   Every Corporeal Conception Must Be Rejected, in Order That It May Be Understood How God Is Truth.

3. But in respect to bodies, it may be the case that this gold and that gold may be equally true [real], but this may be greater than that, since magnitude is not the same thing in this case as truth; and it is one thing for it to be gold, another to be great. So also in the nature of the soul; a soul is not called great in the same respect in which it is called true. For he, too, has a true [real] soul who has not a great soul; since the essence of body and soul is not the essence of the truth [reality] itself; as is the Trinity, one God, alone, great, true, truthful, the truth. Of whom if we endeavor to think, so far as he himself permits and grants, let us not think of any touch or embrace in local space, as if of three bodies, or of any compactness of conjunction, as fables tell of three-bodied Geryon; but let whatsoever may occur to the mind, that is of such sort as to be greater in three than in each singly, and less in one than in two, be rejected without any doubt; for so everything corporeal is rejected. But also in spiritual things let nothing changeable that may have occurred to the mind be thought of God. For when we aspire from this

depth to that height, it is a step toward no small knowledge, if, before we can know what God is, we can already know what he is not. For certainly he is neither earth nor heaven; nor, as it were, earth and heaven; nor any such thing as we see in the heaven; nor any such thing as we do not see, but which perhaps is in heaven. Neither if you were to magnify in the imagination of your thought the light of the sun as much as you are able, either that it may be greater, or that it may be brighter, a thousand times as much, or times without number; neither is this God. Neither as we think of the pure angels as spirits animating celestial bodies, and changing and dealing with them after the will by which they serve God; not even if all, and there are "thousands of thousands,"[763] were brought together into one, and became one; neither is any such thing God. Neither if you were to think of the same spirits as without bodies— a thing indeed most difficult for carnal thought to do. Behold and see, if thou canst, O soul pressed down by the corruptible body, and weighed down by earthly thoughts, many and various; behold and see, if thou canst, that God is truth.[764] For it is written that "God is light";[765] not in such way as these eyes see, but in such way as the heart sees, when it is said, he is truth [reality]. Ask not what is truth [reality] for immediately the darkness of corporeal images and the clouds of phantasms will put themselves in the way, and will disturb that calm which at the first twinkling shone forth to thee, when I said truth [reality]. See that thou remainest, if thou canst, in that first twinkling with which thou art dazzled, as it were, by a flash, when it is said to thee, Truth [Reality]. But thou canst not; thou wilt glide back into those usual and earthly things. And what weight, pray, is it that will cause thee so to glide back, unless it be the bird-lime of the stains of appetite thou hast contracted, and the errors of thy wandering from the right path?

Chapter 3 How God May Be Known to Be the Chief Good. The Mind Does Not Become Good Unless by Turning to God.

4. Behold again, and see if thou canst. Thou certainly dost not love anything except what is good, since good is the earth, with the loftiness of its mountains, and the due measure of its hills, and the level

763. Apoc 5:11.   764. Ws 9:15.   765. 1 Jn 1:5.

surface of its plains; and good is an estate that is pleasant and fertile; and good is a house that is arranged in due proportions, and is spacious and bright; and good are animal and animate bodies; and good is air that is temperate, and salubrious; and good is food that is agreeable and fit for health; and good is health, without pains or lassitude; and good is the countenance of man that is disposed in fit proportions, and is cheerful in look, and bright in color; and good is the mind of a friend, with the sweetness of agreement, and with the confidence of love; and good is a righteous man; and good are riches, since they are readily useful; and good is the heaven, with its sun, and moon, and stars; and good are the angels, by their holy obedience; and good is discourse that sweetly teaches and suitably admonishes the hearer; and good is a poem that is harmonious in its numbers and weighty in its sense. And why add yet more and more? This thing is good and that good, but take away this and that, and regard good itself if thou canst; so wilt thou see God, not good by a good that is other than himself, but the good of all good. For in all these good things, whether those which I have mentioned, or any else that are to be discerned or thought, we could not say that one was better than another, when we judge truly, unless a conception of the good itself had been impressed upon us, such that according to it we might both approve some things as good, and prefer one good to another. So God is to be loved, not this and that good, but the good itself. For the good that must be sought for the soul is not one above which it is to fly by judging, but to which it is to cleave by loving; and what can this be except God? Not a good mind, or a good angel or the good heaven, but the good good. For perhaps what I wish to say may be more easily perceived in this way. For when, for instance, a mind is called good, as there are two words, so from these words I understand two things—one whereby it is mind, and another whereby it is good. And itself had no share in making itself a mind, for there was nothing as yet to make itself to be anything; but to make itself to be a good mind, I see, must be brought about by the will: not because that by which it is mind is not itself anything good—for how else is it already called, and most truly called, better than the body?—but it is not yet called a good mind, for this reason, that the action of the will still is wanted, by which it is to become more excellent; and if it has neglected this, then it is justly blamed, and is rightly called not a good mind. For it then differs from the mind which does perform this; and since the latter is praiseworthy, the former doubtless, which does not perform, it is blameable. But when it does this of set purpose and becomes a good mind, it yet cannot attain to being so unless it turn itself to something which itself is not. And to what can it turn itself that it may become a good mind, except to the good which it loves, and seeks, and obtains? And if it turns itself back again from this, and becomes not good, then by the very act of turning away from the good, unless that good remain in it from which it turns away, it cannot again turn itself back thither if it should wish to amend.

5. Wherefore there would be no changeable goods, unless there were the unchangeable good. Whenever then thou art told of this good thing and that good thing, which things can also in other respects be called not good, if thou canst put aside those things which are good by the participation of the good, and discern that good itself by the participation of which they are good (for when this or that good thing is spoken of, thou understandest together with them the good itself also): if, then, I say thou canst remove these things, and canst discern the good in itself, then thou wilt have discerned God. And if thou shalt cleave to him with love, thou shalt be forthwith blessed. But whereas other things are not loved, except because they are good, be ashamed, in cleaving to them, not to love the good itself whence they are good. That also, which is a mind, only because it is a mind, while it is not yet also good by the turning itself to the unchangeable good, but, as I said, is only a mind; whenever it so pleases us, as that we prefer it even, if we understand aright, to all corporeal light, does not please us in itself, but in that skill by which it was made. For it is thence approved as made, wherein it is seen to have been to be made. This is truth, and simple good, for it is nothing else than the good itself, and for this reason also the chief good. For no good can be diminished or increased, except that which is good from some other good. Therefore the mind turns itself, in order to be good, to that by which it comes to be a mind. Therefore the will is then in harmony with nature, so that the mind may be perfected in good, when that good is loved by the turning of the will to it, whence that other good also comes which is not lost by the turning away of the will from it. For by turning itself from the chief good, the mind loses the being a good mind; but it does not lose the being a mind. And this, too, is a good

already, and one better than the body. The will, therefore, loses that which the will obtains. For the mind already was, that could wish to be turned to that from which it was: but that as yet was not, that could wish to be before it was. And herein is our [supreme] good, when we see whether the thing ought to be or to have been, respecting which we comprehend that it ought to be or to have been, and when we see that the thing could not have been unless it ought to have been, of which we also do not comprehend in what manner it ought to have been. This good then is not far from every one of us: for in it we live, and move, and have our being.[766]

Chapter 4 God Must First Be Known by an Unerring Faith, That He May Be Loved.

6. But it is by love that we must stand firm to this and cleave to this, in order that we may enjoy the presence of that by which we are, and in the absence of which we could not be at all. For as "we walk as yet by faith, and not by sight,"[767] we certainly do not yet see God, as the same [apostle] saith, "face to face":[768] whom however we shall never see, unless now already we love. But who loves what he does not know? For it is possible something may be known and not loved: but I ask whether it is possible that what is not known can be loved; since if it cannot, then no one loves God before he knows him. And what is it to know God except to behold him and steadfastly perceive him with the mind? For he is not a body to be searched out by carnal eyes. But before also that we have power to behold and to perceive God, as he can be beheld and perceived, which is permitted to the pure in heart; for "blessed are the pure in heart, for they shall see God";[769] except he is loved by faith, it will not be possible for the heart to be cleansed, in order that it may be apt and meet to see him. For where are there those three, in order to build up which in the mind the whole apparatus of the divine Scriptures has been raised up, namely Faith, Hope, and Charity,[770] except in a mind believing what it does not yet see, and hoping and loving what it believes? Even he therefore who is not known, but yet is believed, can be loved. But indisputably we must take care,

766. Acts 17:27, 28.   767. 2 Cor 5:7.   768. 1 Cor 13:12.   769. Mt 5:8.
770. 1 Cor 13:13.

lest the mind believing that which it does not see, feign to itself something which is not, and hope for and love that which is false. For in that case, it will not be charity out of a pure heart, and of a good conscience, and of faith unfeigned, which is the end of the commandment, as the same apostle says.[771]

7. But it must needs be, that, when by reading or hearing of them we believe in any corporeal things which we have not seen, the mind frames for itself something under bodily features and forms, just as it may occur to our thoughts; which either is not true, or even if it be true, which can most rarely happen, yet this is of no benefit to us to believe in by faith, but it is useful for some other purpose, which is intimated by means of it. For who is there that reads or hears what the Apostle Paul has written, or what has been written of him, that does not imagine to himself the countenance both of the apostle himself and of all those whose names are there mentioned? And whereas, among such a multitude of men to whom these books are known, each imagines in a different way those bodily features and forms, it is assuredly uncertain which it is that imagines them more nearly and more like the reality. Nor, indeed, is our faith busied therein with the bodily countenance of those men; but only that by the grace of God they so lived and so acted as that Scripture witnesses: this it is which it is both useful to believe, and which must not be despaired of, and must be sought. For even the countenance of our Lord himself in the flesh is variously fancied by the diversity of countless imaginations, which yet was one, whatever it was. Nor in our faith which we have of our Lord Jesus Christ, is that wholesome which the mind imagines for itself, perhaps far other than the reality, but that which we think of man according to his kind: for we have a notion of human nature implanted in us, as it were by rule, according to which we know forthwith, that whatever such thing we see is a man or the form of a man.

Chapter 5 How the Trinity May Be Loved Though Unknown.

Our conception is framed according to this notion, when we believe that God was made man for us, as an example of humility, and to show the love of God toward us. For this it is which it is

771. 1 Tm 1:5.

good for us to believe, and to retain firmly and unshakenly in our heart, that the humility by which God was born of a woman, and was led to death through contumelies so great by mortal men, is the chiefest remedy by which the swelling of our pride may be cured, and the profound mystery by which the bond of sin may be loosed. So also because we know what omnipotence is, we believe concerning the omnipotent God in the power of his miracles and of his resurrection, and we frame conceptions respecting actions of this kind, according to the species and genera of things that are either ingrafted in us by nature, or gathered by experience, that our faith may not be feigned. For neither do we know the countenance of the Virgin Mary, from whom, untouched by a husband, nor tainted in the birth itself, he was wonderfully born. Neither have we seen what were the lineaments of the body of Lazarus; nor yet Bethany; nor the sepulchre, and that stone which he commanded to be removed when he raised him from the dead; nor the new tomb cut out in the rock, whence he himself arose; nor the Mount of Olives, from whence he ascended into heaven. And, in short, whoever of us have not seen these things, know not whether they are as we conceive them to be, nay judge them more probably not to be so. For when the aspect either of a place, or a man, or of any other body, which we happened to imagine before we saw it, turns out to be the same when it occurs to our sight as it was when it occurred to our mind, we are moved with no little wonder. So scarcely and hardly ever does it happen. And yet we believe those things most steadfastly, because we imagine them according to a special and general notion, of which we are certain. For we believe our Lord Jesus Christ to be born of a virgin who was called Mary. But what a virgin is, or what it is to be born, and what is a proper name, we do not believe, but certainly know. And whether that was the countenance of Mary which occurred to the mind in speaking of those things or recollecting them, we neither know at all, nor believe. It is allowable, then, in this case to say without violation of the faith, perhaps she had such or such a countenance, perhaps she had not: but no one could say without violation of the Christian faith, that perhaps Christ was born of a virgin.

8. Wherefore, since we desire to understand the eternity, and equality, and unity of the Trinity, as much as is permitted us, but

ought to believe before we understand; and since we must watch carefully, that our faith be not feigned; since we must have the fruition of the same Trinity, that we may live blessedly; but if we have believed anything false of it, our hope would be worthless, and our charity not pure: how then can we love, by believing, that Trinity which we do not know? Is it according to the special or general notion, according to which we love the Apostle Paul? In whose case, even if he was not of that countenance which occurs to us when we think of him (and this we do not know at all), yet we know what a man is. For not to go far away, this *we* are; and it is manifest he, too, was this, and that his soul joined to his body lived after the manner of mortals. Therefore we believe this of him, which we find in ourselves, according to the species or genus under which all human nature alike is comprised. What then do we know, whether specially or generally, of that most excellent Trinity, as if there were many such trinities, some of which we had learned by experience, so that we may believe that Trinity, too, to have been such as they, through the rule of similitude, impressed upon us, whether a special or a general notion; and thus love also that thing which we believe and do not yet know, from the parity of the thing which we do know? But this certainly is not so. Or is it that, as we love in our Lord Jesus Christ, that he rose from the dead, although we never saw anyone rise from thence, so we can believe in and love the Trinity which we do not see, and the like of which we never have seen? But we certainly know what it is to die, and what it is to live, because we both live, and from time to time have seen and experienced both dead and dying persons. And what else is it to rise again, except to live again, that is, to return to life from death? When, therefore, we say and believe that there is a Trinity, we know what a Trinity is, because we know what three are; but this is not what we love. For we can easily have this whenever we will, to pass over other things, by just holding up three fingers. Or do we indeed love, not every trinity, but *the* Trinity, that is God? We love then in the Trinity, that it is God, but we never saw or knew any other God, because God is One; he alone whom we have not yet seen, and whom we love by believing. But the question is, from what likeness or comparison of known things can we believe, in order that we may love God, whom we do not yet know?

Chapter 6   How the Man Not Yet Righteous Can Know the Righteous Man Whom He Loves.

9. Return then with me, and let us consider why we love the apostle. Is it at all on account of his human kind, which we know right well, in that we believe him to have been a man? Assuredly not; for if it were so, he now is not him whom we love, since he is no longer that man, for his soul is separated from his body. But we believe that which we love in him to be still living, for we love his righteous mind. From what general or special rule then, except that we know both what a mind is and what it is to be righteous? And we say, indeed, not unfitly, that we therefore know what a mind is, because we too have a mind. For neither did we ever see it with our eyes, and gather a special or general notion from the resemblance of more minds than one, which we had seen, but rather, as I have said before, because we too have it. For what is known so intimately, and so perceives itself to be itself, as that by which also all other things are perceived, that is, the mind itself? For we recognize the movements of bodies also, by which we perceive that others live besides ourselves, from the resemblance of ourselves; since we also so move our body in living as we observe those bodies to be moved. For even when a living body is moved, there is no way opened to our eyes to see the mind, a thing which cannot be seen by the eyes, but we perceive something to be contained in that bulk, such as is contained in ourselves, so as to move in like manner our own bulk, which is the life and the soul. Neither is this, as it were, the property of human foresight and reason, since brute animals also perceive that not only they themselves live, but also other brute animals interchangeably, and the one the other, and that we ourselves do so. Neither do they see our souls, save from the movements of the body, and that immediately and most easily by some natural agreement. Therefore we both know the mind of anyone from our own, and believe also from our own of him whom we do not know. For not only do we perceive that there is a mind, but we can also know what a mind is, by reflecting upon our own, for we have a mind. But whence do we know what a righteous man is? For we said above that we love the apostle for no other reason except that he is a righteous mind. We know, then, what a righteous man also is, just as we know what a mind is. But what a mind is, as

has been said, we know from ourselves, for there is a mind in us. But whence do we know what a righteous man is, if we are not righteous? But if no one but he who is righteous knows what is a righteous man, no one but a righteous man loves a righteous man; for one cannot love him whom one believes to be righteous, for this very reason that one does believe him to be righteous, if one does not know what it is to be righteous; according to that which we have shown above, that no one loves what he believes and does not see, except by some rule of a general or special notion. And if for this reason no one but a righteous man loves a righteous man, how will anyone wish to be a righteous man who is not yet so? For no one wishes to be that which he does not love. But, certainly, that he who is not righteous may be so, it is necessary that he should wish to be righteous; and in order that he may wish to be righteous, he loves the righteous man. Therefore, even he who is not yet righteous loves the righteous man.[772] But he cannot love the righteous man who is ignorant what a righteous man is. Accordingly, even he who is not yet righteous knows what a righteous man is. Whence then does he know this? Does he see it with his eyes? Is any corporeal thing righteous, as it is white, or black, or square, or round? Who could say this? Yet with one's eyes one has seen nothing except corporeal things. But there is nothing righteous in a man except the mind, and when a man is called a righteous man, he is called so from the mind, not from the body. For righteousness is in some sort the beauty of the mind, by which men are beautiful; very many too who are misshapen and deformed in body. And as the mind is not seen with the eyes, so neither is its beauty. From whence then does he who is not yet righteous know what a righteous man is, and love the righteous man that he may become righteous? Do certain signs shine forth by the motion of the body, by which this or that man is manifested to be righteous? But whence does anyone know that these are the signs of a righteous mind when he is wholly ignorant what it is to be righteous? Therefore he does

772. The "wish" and "love" which Augustine here attributes to the nonrighteous man is not true and spiritual, but selfish. In chapter 7, para. 10, he speaks of true love as distinct from that kind of desire which is a mere wish. The latter he calls *cupiditas*. "That is to be called love which is true, otherwise it is desire (*cupiditas*); and so those who desire (*cupidi*) are improperly said to love (*diligere*), just as they who love (*diligunt*) are said improperly to desire (*cupere*)."

know. But whence do we know what it is to be righteous, even when we are not yet righteous? If we know from without ourselves, we know it by some bodily thing. But this is not a thing of the body. Therefore we know in ourselves what it is to be righteous. For I find this nowhere else when I seek to utter it, except within myself; and if I ask another what it is to be righteous, he seeks within himself what to answer; and whosoever hence can answer truly, he has found within himself what to answer. And when indeed I wish to speak of Carthage, I seek within myself what to speak, and I find within myself a notion or image of Carthage, but I have received this through the body, that is, through the perception of the body, since I have been present in that city in the body, and I saw and perceived it, and retained it in my memory, that I might find within myself a word concerning it, whenever I might wish to speak of it. For its word is the image itself of it in my memory, not that sound of two syllables when Carthage is named, or even when that name itself is thought of silently from time to time, but that which I discern in my mind, when I utter that dissyllable with my voice, or even before I utter it. So also, when I wish to speak of Alexandria, which I never saw, an image of it is present with me. For whereas I had heard from many and had believed that city to be great, in such way as it could be told me, I formed an image of it in my mind as I was able, and this is with me its word when I wish to speak of it, before I utter with my voice the five syllables which make the name that almost everyone knows. And yet if I could bring forth that image from my mind to the eyes of men who know Alexandria, certainly all either would say, It is not it; or if they said, It is, I should greatly wonder; and as I gazed at it in my mind, that is, at the image which was as it were its picture, I should yet not know it to be it, but should believe those who retained an image they had seen. But I do not so ask what it is to be righteous, nor do I so find it, nor do I so gaze upon it, when I utter it; neither am I so approved when I am heard, nor do I so approve when I hear, as though I have seen such a thing with my eyes, or learned it by some perception of the body, or heard it from those who had so learned it. For when I say, and say knowingly, that mind is righteous which knowingly and of purpose assigns to everyone his due in life and behavior, I do not think of anything absent, as Carthage, or imagine it as I am able, as Alexandria, whether it be so or not, but I discern something present, and I discern it within myself, though I myself am not that which I discern; and many if they hear will approve it. And whoever hears me and knowingly approves, he too discerns this same thing within himself, even though he himself be not what he discerns. But when a righteous man says this, he discerns and says that which he himself is. And whence also does he discern it, except within himself? But this is not to be wondered at; for whence should he discern himself except within himself? The wonderful thing is, that the mind should see within itself that which it has seen nowhere else, and should see truly, and should see the very true righteous mind, and should itself be a mind, and yet not a righteous mind, which nevertheless it sees within itself. Is there another mind that is righteous in a mind that is not yet righteous? Or if there is not, what does it there see when it sees and says what is a righteous mind, nor sees it anywhere else but in itself, when itself is not a righteous mind? Is that which it sees an inner truth present to the mind which has power to behold it? Yet all have not that power; and they who have power to behold it are not all also that which they behold, that is, they are not also righteous minds themselves, just as they are able to see and to say what is a righteous mind. And whence will they be able to be so, except by cleaving to that very same form itself which they behold, so that from thence they may be formed and may be righteous minds; not only discerning and saying that the mind is righteous which knowingly and of purpose assigns to everyone that which is his due in life and behavior, but so likewise that they themselves may live righteously and be righteous in character, by assigning to everyone that which is his due, so as to owe no man anything, but to love one another.[773] And whence can anyone cleave to that form but by loving it? Why then do we love another whom we believe to be righteous and do not love that form itself wherein we see what is a righteous mind, that we also may be able to be righteous? Is it that unless we loved that also, we should not love him at all, whom through it we love, but while we are not righteous, we love that form too little to allow of our being able to be righteous? The man therefore who is believed to be righteous is loved through that form and truth which he who loves discerns and understands within himself, but that very form

773. Rom 13:8.

and truth itself cannot be loved from any other source than itself.
For we do not find any other such thing besides itself, so that by believing we might love it when it is unknown, in that we here already know another such thing. For whatsoever of such a kind one
may have seen, is itself; and there is not any other such thing, since
itself alone is such as itself is. He therefore who loves men ought to
love them either because they are righteous or that they may become righteous. For so also he ought to love himself, either because
he is righteous or that he may become righteous, for in this way he
loves his neighbor as himself without any risk. For he who loves
himself otherwise, loves himself wrongfully, since he loves himself
to this end that he may be unrighteous; therefore to this end that he
may be wicked; and hence it follows next that he does not love himself, for, "He who loveth iniquity, hateth his own soul."[774]

Chapter 7   Of True Love, by Which We Arrive at the Knowledge of the Trinity. God Is to Be Sought, Not Outwardly, by Seeking to Do Wonderful Things with the Angels, But Inwardly, by Imitating the Piety of Good Angels.

10. No other thing, then, is chiefly to be regarded in this inquiry,
which we make concerning the Trinity and concerning knowing
God, except what is true love, nay, rather what is love. For that is to
be called love which is true, otherwise it is desire, and so those who
desire are said improperly to love, just as they who love are said improperly to desire. But this is true love, that cleaving to the truth we
may live righteously, and so may despise all mortal things in comparison with the love of men, whereby we wish them to live righteously. For so we should be prepared also to die profitably for our
brethren, as our Lord Jesus Christ taught us by his example. For as
there are two commandments on which hang all the Law and the
Prophets, love of God and love of our neighbor;[775] not without
cause the Scripture mostly puts one for both: whether it be of God
only as is that text, "For we know that all things work together for
good to them that love God";[776] and again, "But if any man love
God, the same is known of Him";[777] and that, "Because the love of
God is shed abroad in our hearts by the Holy Ghost which is given

---

774. Ps 6:6.   775. Mt 22:37–40.   776. Rom 8:28.   777. 1 Cor 8:3.

unto us";[778] and many other passages; because he who loves God must both needs do what God has commanded, and loves Him just in such proportion as he does so; therefore he must needs also love his neighbor, because God has commanded it: or whether it be that Scripture only mentions the love of our neighbor, as in that text, "Bear ye one another's burdens, and so fulfill the law of Christ";[779] and again, "For all the law is fulfilled in one word, even in this, Thou shalt love thy neighbor as thyself";[780] and in the Gospel, "All things whatsoever ye would that men should do to you, do ye even so to them; for this is the Law and the Prophets."[781] And many other passages occur in the sacred writings, in which only the love of our neighbor seems to be commanded for perfection, while the love of God is passed over in silence; whereas the Law and the Prophets hang on both precepts. But this, too, is because he who loves his neighbor must needs also love above all else love itself. But "God is love; and he that dwelleth in love, dwelleth in God."[782] Therefore he must needs above all else love God.

11. Wherefore they who seek God through those Powers which rule over the world, or parts of the world, are removed and cast away far from him; not by intervals of space, but by difference of affections, for they endeavor to find a path outwardly and forsake their own inward things, within which is God. Therefore, even although they may either have heard some holy heavenly Power, or in some way or another may have thought of it, yet they rather covet its deeds at which human weakness marvels, but do not imitate the piety by which divine rest is acquired. For they prefer, through pride, to be able to do that which an angel does, more than, through devotion, to be that which an angel is. For no holy being rejoices in his own power, but in his from whom he has the power which he fitly can have, and he knows it to be more a mark of power to be united to the Omnipotent by a pious will, than to be able, by his own power and will, to do what they may tremble at who are not able to do such things. Therefore the Lord Jesus Christ himself, in doing such things, in order that he might teach better things to those who marveled at them, and might turn those who were intent and in doubt about unusual temporal things to eternal

778. Rom 5:5.   779. Gal 6:2.   780. Gal 5:14.   781. Mt 7:12.
782. 1 Jn 4:6.

and inner things, says, "Come unto me, all ye that labor and are heavy laden, and I will give you rest. Take my yoke upon you." And he does not say, Learn of me, because I raise those who have been dead four days; but he says, "Learn of me; for I am meek and lowly in heart." For humility, which is most solid, is more powerful and safer than pride, that is most inflated. And so he goes on to say, "And ye shall find rest unto your souls,"[783] for "Love is not puffed up";[784] and "God is Love";[785] and "such as be faithful in love shall rest in Him,"[786] called back from the din which is without to silent joys. Behold, "God is Love": why do we go forth and run to the heights of the heavens and the lowest parts of the earth, seeking him who is within us, if we wish to be with him?

Chapter 8   That He Who Loves His Brother, Loves God; Because He Loves Love Itself, Which Is of God, and Is God.

12. Let no one say, I do not know what I love. Let him love his brother, and he will love the same love. For he knows the love with which he loves, more than the brother whom he loves. So now he can know God more than he knows his brother: clearly known more, because more present; known more, because more within him; known more, because more certain. Embrace the love of God, and by love embrace God. That is love itself, which associates together all good angels and all the servants of God by the bond of sanctity, and joins together us and them mutually with ourselves, and joins us subordinately to himself. In proportion, therefore, as we are healed from the swelling of pride, in such proportion are we more filled with love, and with what is he full, who is full of love, except with God? Well, but you will say, I see love, and, as far as I am able, I gaze upon it with my mind, and I believe the Scripture, saying, that "God is love; and he that dwelleth in love, dwelleth in God";[787] but when I see love, I do not see in it the Trinity. Nay, but thou dost see the Trinity if thou seest love. But if I can I will put you in mind, that thou mayest see that thou seest it; only let itself be present, that we may be moved by love to something good. Since, when we love love, we love one who loves something, and that on

783. Mt 11:28, 29.   784. 1 Cor 13:4.   785. 1 Jn 4:8.   786. Ws 3:9.
787. 1 Jn 4:16.

account of this very thing, that he does love something; therefore what does love love, that love itself also may be loved? For that is not love which loves nothing. But if it loves itself it must love something, that it may love itself as love. For as a word indicates something, and indicates also itself, but does not indicate itself to be a word, unless it indicates that it does indicate something, so love also loves indeed itself, but except it love itself as loving something, it loves itself not as love. What therefore does love love, except that which we love with love? But this, to begin from that which is nearest to us, is our brother. And listen how greatly the Apostle John commends brotherly love; "He that loveth his brother abideth in the light, and there is none occasion of stumbling in him."[788] It is manifest that he placed the perfection of righteousness in the love of our brother, for he certainly is perfect in whom "there is no occasion of stumbling." And yet he seems to have passed by the love of God in silence, which he never would have done, unless because he intends God to be understood in brotherly love itself. For in this same Epistle, a little further on, he says most plainly thus: "Beloved, let us love one another: for love is of God; and everyone that loveth is born of God, and knoweth God. He that loveth not, knoweth not God; for God is love." And this passage declares sufficiently and plainly that this same brotherly love itself (for that is brotherly love by which we love each other) is set forth by so great authority, not only to be from God, but also to be God. When, therefore, we love our brother from love, we love our brother from God; neither can it be that we do not love above all else that same love by which we love our brother: whence it may be gathered that these two commandments cannot exist unless interchangeably. For since "God is love," he who loves love certainly loves God, but he must needs love love, who loves his brother. And so a little after he says, "For he that loveth not his brother whom he hath seen, how can he love God whom he hath not seen?"[789] because the reason that he does not see God is, that he does not love his brother. For he who does not love his brother abideth not in love, and he who abideth not in love, abideth not in God, because God is love. Further, he who abideth not in God, abideth not in light, for "God is light, and in Him is no darkness at all."[790] He therefore who abideth not in light, what

788. 1 Jn 2:10.   789. 1 Jn 4:7, 8, 20.   790. 1 Jn 1:5.

wonder is it if he does not see light, that is, does not see God, because he is in darkness? But he sees his brother with human sight, with which God cannot be seen. But if he loved with spiritual love him whom he sees with human sight, he would see God, who is love itself, with the inner sight by which he can be seen. Therefore he who does not love his brother whom he sees, how can he love God, whom on that account he does not see, because God is love, which he has not who does not love his brother? Neither let that further question disturb us, how much of love we ought to spend upon our brother, and how much upon God: incomparably more upon God than upon ourselves, but upon our brother as much as upon ourselves; and we love ourselves so much the more, the more we love God. Therefore we love God and our neighbor from one and the same love, but we love God for the sake of God and ourselves and our neighbors for the sake of God.

Chapter 9   Our Love of the Righteous Is Kindled from Love Itself of the Unchangeable Form of Righteousness.

13. For why is it, pray, that we burn when we hear and read, "Behold, now is the accepted time; behold, now is the day of salvation: giving no offense in anything, that the ministry be not blamed: but in all things approving ourselves as the ministers of God, in much patience, in afflictions, in necessities, in distresses, in stripes, in imprisonments, in tumults, in labors, in watchings, in fastings; by pureness, by knowledge, by long-suffering, by kindness, by the Holy Ghost, by love unfeigned, by the word of truth, by the power of God, by the armor of righteousness on the right hand and on the left, by honor and dishonor, by evil report and good report: as deceivers, and yet true; as unknown, and yet well known; as dying, and, behold, we live; as chastened, and not killed; as sorrowful, yet alway rejoicing; as poor, yet making many rich; as having nothing, and yet possessing all things"?[791] Why is it that we are inflamed with love of the Apostle Paul when we read these things, unless that we believe him so to have lived? But we do not believe that the ministers of God ought so to live because we have heard it from anyone, but because we behold it inwardly within ourselves, or

791. 2 Cor 6:2–10.

rather above ourselves, in the truth itself. Him, therefore, whom we believe to have so lived, we love for that which we see. And except we loved above all else that form which we discern as always steadfast and unchangeable, we should not for that reason love him, because we hold fast in our belief that his life, when he was living in the flesh, was adapted to, and in harmony with, this form. But somehow we are stirred up the more to the love of this form itself, through the belief by which we believe someone to have so lived, and to the hope by which we no more at all despair, that we, too, are able so to live; we who are men, from this fact itself, that some men have so lived, so that we both desire this more ardently and pray for it more confidently, So both the love of that form, according to which they are believed to have lived, makes the life of these men themselves to be loved by us, and their life thus believed stirs up a more burning love toward that same form, so that the more ardently we love God, the more certainly and the more calmly do we see him, because we behold in God the unchangeable form of righteousness, according to which we judge that man ought to live. Therefore faith avails to the knowledge and to the love of God, not as though of one altogether unknown or altogether not loved, but so that thereby he may be known more clearly and loved more steadfastly.

Chapter 10   There Are Three Things in Love, as It Were a Trace of the Trinity.

14. But what is love or charity, which divine Scripture so greatly praises and proclaims, except the love of good? But love is *of* someone that loves, and *with* love something *is* loved. Behold, then, there are three things: he that loves, and that which is loved, and love. What, then, is love, except certain life which couples or seeks to couple together some two things, namely, him that loves and that which is loved? And this is so even in outward and carnal loves. But that we may drink in something more pure and clear, let us tread down the flesh and ascend to the mind. What does the mind love in a friend except the mind? There, then, also are three things: he that loves, and that which is loved, and love. It remains to ascend also from hence and to seek those things which are above, as far as is given to man. But here for a little while let our purpose

rest, not that it may think itself to have found already what it seeks, but just as usually the place has first to be found where anything is to be sought, while the thing itself is not yet found, but we have only found already where to look for it; so let it suffice to have said thus much, that we may have, as it were, the hinge of some starting-point, whence to weave the rest of our discourse.

From Tractates on the Gospel of John

1. The Lord Jesus attests that he is giving a new commandment to his disciples, that they love one another. "A new commandment," he says, "I give to you, that you love one another." Was not this commandment already in the ancient Law of God, where it was written, "You shall love your neighbor as yourself"?[792] Why therefore is that called new by the Lord which is clearly shown to be old? Can it be therefore that it is a new commandment because the old has been stripped off and he has put on us the new man?[793] For love renews one who hears, or rather one who obeys, not every [love] but this love [in regard to] which the Lord, in order to distinguish it from carnal love, added; "As I have loved you." For husbands and wives, parents and children, love one another, and whatever other human bond has bound men together (to remain silent about the blameworthy and damnable love by which adulterers and adultresses, whoremongers and prostitutes, love one another, and whoever else are joined together not by a human tie, but by a culpable baseness of human life).

(2) Therefore, Christ has given a new commandment to us: that we love one another as he also has loved us. This love renews us that we may be new men, heirs of the New Testament, singers of a new song. This love, dearest brothers, renewed even then those just men of ancient times, then the patriarchs and the prophets, as it did the blessed apostles later; even now it also renews the nations, and from the whole human race, which is scattered over the whole world, it makes and gathers a new people, the body of the new spouse, the bride of the Son of God, the Only-Begotten, about whom it is said in the Song of Songs, "Who is this who comes up in white?"[794] In white, of course, because renewed. By what, except by the new commandment?

(3) Because of this the members in her are concerned for one another. And if one member suffers, all members suffer with it; and if

792. Lv 19:18.   793. See Col 3:9–10.   794. Sg 8:5 (Septuagint).

one member is glorified, all members rejoice with it.[795] For they hear and keep: "A new commandment I give you, that you love one another," not as those who are corrupt love one another, not as men love one another because they are men, but as they love one another because they are gods and all [of them], sons of the Most High,[796] so that they may be brothers to his only Son, loving each other with the love with which he himself loved them, who will lead them to that end which may suffice for them, where their desire may be sated in good things.[797] For when God will be all in all, then nothing will be lacking to their desire.[798]

(4) Such an end does not have an end. There no one dies, where no one comes unless he should die to this world, not by the death of all in which the body is abandoned by the soul, but by the death of the elect in which, even when one still remains in mortal flesh, the heart is set on high. About this kind of death the apostle said, "For you are dead, and your life is hidden with Christ in God."[799] Perhaps about this it was said, "Strong as death is love."[800] For by this love it comes to pass that, dwelling in this still corruptible body, we die to this world and our life is hidden with Christ in God, nay rather, love itself is our death to the world and our life with God. For if death occurs when the soul goes out of the body, how is it not death when our love goes out of the world? Therefore strong as death is love. What is stronger than that by which the world is conquered?

2. Do not therefore think, my brothers, that in this which the Lord says, "A new commandment I give you, that you love one another," that greater commandment has been left out, by which we are instructed to love the Lord our God with the whole heart, with the whole soul, with the whole mind,[801] as if in fact, with this left out, "that you love one another" seems to have been said as though this would not pertain to that other in which it was said, "You shall love your neighbor as yourself." For "on these two commandments," he said, "the whole Law is based and the Prophets." But to those who understand well, both are found in each. For he who loves God cannot despise him when he teaches him to love his neighbor; and he who loves his neighbor in a holy and spiritual

---

795. Cf. 1 Cor 12:25–26.　　796. See Ps 81 (82):6.

797. See Ps 102 (103):5 (Septuagint).　　798. Cf. 1 Cor 15:28.

799. Col 3:3.　　800. Sg 8:6.　　801. See Mt 22:34–40.

way, what does he love in him except God? This is the love, separated from every worldly love, for the distinguishing of which the
Lord added, "as I have loved you." For what did he love in us except God? Not because we had [God], but that we might have
[him], so that he may lead us, as I said a little before, where God is
all in all.

(2) So also a physician is rightly said to love the sick. And what
does he love in them except health, which he desires, of course, to
restore, not the disease, which he comes to drive out? So therefore
let us also love one another, so that, as far as possible by the concern
of our love, we may draw one another to having God in us. He
himself, who said, "As I have loved you, that you also love one another," gives this love to us. Therefore he loved us for this purpose,
that we also should love one another, conferring this on us by loving us, that we should be bound together with each other by mutual love and, with the members fastened together by so sweet a
chain, we may be the body of so great a Head.

3. "By this," he said, "all will know that you are my disciples, if
you have love for one another," as though he were to say, "Even
those who are not mine will have my other gifts together with you,
not only nature, life, sensation, reason, and that well-being which is
common to human beings and cattle,[802] but also tongues, sacraments, prophecy, knowledge, faith, the distribution of their property to the poor, and the handing over of their bodies to be
burned—but because they do not have love, they clang like cym-
bals, they are nothing; nothing profits them.[803]

(2) Not, therefore, in those gifts of mine, however good, which
even they who are not my disciples can have, but "by this all will
know that you are my disciples, if you have love for one another."
Oh, Bride of Christ, beautiful among women! Oh, you in white,
coming up and leaning upon your beloved![804] For by his light you
are illuminated that you may shine; by his help you are supported
that you may not fall! Oh, how well it is sung to you in that Song of

802. Cf. Ps 35 (36):7.

803. 1 Cor 13:1–3. Here Augustine uses *caritas* for love, as also in the quotation
from Song of Songs (Sg 7:6) below; elsewhere in this tractate he uses *dilectio* and
the verb *diligere*, in all instances in accord with the Scripture he has in mind.

804. Cf. Sg 8:5 (Septuagint).

Songs, your wedding song, as it were, that "There is love in your delights"![805] She does not lose her soul with the ungodly;[806] she discerns your cause[807] and is strong as death, as is in your delights. Of how wondrous a kind is the death for which it was insufficient not to be in afflictions unless, in addition, it were in delights! But here let this discourse now be closed; what follows ought to be discussed from another beginning.

---

805. Sg 7:6. The Septuagint treats this verse as a question; the Vulgate and English versions take it as an exclamation. Augustine turns what is in the other texts a vocative and a prepositional phrase into a declaration.

806. Cf. Ps 25 (26):9.   807. Cf. Ps 42 (43):1.

From Homilies on the First Epistle of Saint John

Prologue

As you know, my people, I have been giving you a course of sermons on the Gospel according to John. During the present holy festival, the Church gives us certain fixed Lessons to be read year by year, which we must not alter, so that there will have to be a short break in the course which we had begun, and which we shall afterward continue. I have considered what part of Scripture would be a fitting subject on which to speak to you, as the Lord may grant me ability, during this joyous week, and which could be completed in these seven or eight days, and I have chosen the Epistle of John. We shall then still be listening to him whose Gospel we have for a while put down. It is a book very sweet to every healthy Christian heart that savors the bread of God, and it should be constantly in the mind of God's Holy Church. But I choose it more particularly because what it specially commends to us is charity. The man who has in himself that of which he hears must rejoice at the hearing. To him this reading will be like oil on the flame: if there is matter in him for nourishment, it will be nourished, it will grow and abide. For some, the Epistle should be like flame to firewood: if it was not already burning, the touch of the word may kindle it. In some, then, what is present is to be nourished: in some, what may be lacking is to be kindled, so that we may all rejoice together in one single charity. Where there is charity, there is peace: where there is humility, there is charity. And now let us hear John himself, and let me speak for your better understanding whatever the Lord shall put into my mind as I read the apostle's words.

First Homily

1 John 1:1–2:11

1. "That which was from the beginning, which we have heard, and which we have seen with our eyes, and our hands have handled, of the word of life."

There could be no handling with hands of the word, had not the Word been made flesh and dwelt among us. This Word, made flesh to be handled with hands, took its beginning as flesh from the Virgin Mary; but it took not then its beginning as Word—for we read: "that which was from the beginning." Epistle is confirmed by Gospel, in which you have already heard: "In the beginning was the Word, and the Word was with God."[808] One might understand "the word of life" as a speaking about Christ, and not the actual body of Christ, handled with hands. But see what follows: "and the life itself was manifested." Christ, then, is the word of life. How "manifested"? He was from the beginning, but not manifested to man, though manifested to the sight of angels, feeding as it were upon their own Bread. But we read that "man did eat angels' food."[809] The Life itself has been manifested in flesh—set in manifestation, that what can be seen by the heart alone might be seen also by the eyes for the healing of hearts. Only by the heart is the Word seen: flesh is seen by the bodily eyes. We had the means of seeing the flesh, but not of seeing the Word: the Word was made flesh which we could see, that the heart, by which we should see the Word, might be healed.

2. "We have seen and are witnesses"—seen, that is, as manifested, and manifested by the light of this sun. The sun's Maker could only be seen by that sun's light, because he "set his tabernacle in the sun, going forth himself as a bridegroom out of his chamber, rejoicing as a giant to run his course."[810] He who was before the sun which he made, before the daystar and all stars, before all angels, the true Creator (for all things were made by him, and without him was nothing made),[811] that he might be seen by the eyes of flesh which see the sun, set his own tabernacle in the sun—showed his flesh in manifestation by this light: the Bridegroom's chamber was the virgin's womb, where Bridegroom and Bride, Word and flesh, were joined together. It is written: "And the two shall be in one flesh," or, as the Lord says in the Gospel, "therefore they are no longer two, but one flesh."[812] So finely does Isaiah make the two one, when he speaks in Christ's person, "He put a band upon my head as on a bridegroom, and adorned me as a bride with her orna-

808. Jn 1:1.   809. Ps 78:25.   810. Ps 19:5.   811. Jn 1:3.
812. Gn 2:24; Mt 19:6.

ments."[813] The one speaker makes himself both Bridegroom and Bride; for they are "not two, but one flesh," since "the Word was made flesh and dwelt among us." When to that flesh is joined the Church there is the whole Christ, Head and Body.[814]

3. And we have seen, and are witnesses; and we make known to you the eternal life, which was with the Father and has been manifested among us: that which we have seen and heard, we make known to you."

They saw the Lord himself present in the flesh, and they heard the words of his mouth, and made them known to us. We also then have heard, but we have not seen. Are we less happy than they, who both saw and heard? No, for it goes on: "that ye also may have fellowship with us." They have seen, and we have not; yet we are their fellows, because we hold a common faith. There was one of them who saw, yet believed not, but would feel before he believed, saying: "unless I put my fingers into the print of the nails, and touch his scars, I will not believe."[815] So he who ever gives himself to be seen of angels gave himself for a time to be felt by the hands of men; and that disciple felt him and exclaimed, "My Lord and my God." Because he had touched a man, he confessed his God. And the Lord, for the comfort of us who cannot handle him with our hands now that he sits in heaven, but can touch him by faith, says to Thomas: "Because thou hast seen, thou hast believed: blessed are they who see not and believe."

It is we who are so described and designated. Let us then receive the blessing which the Lord has promised: let us hold fast that which we see not, since they who saw have made it known to us.

"That ye also may have fellowship with us." You may think it no great matter to have fellowship with men. But see what follows: "and our fellowship be with God the Father and his Son Jesus Christ. These things we write to you that your joy may be full." That fullness of joy is in the fellowship, the charity, the unity itself.

4. "And this is the message which we have heard from him and make known to you . . . that God is light, and there is no darkness

---

813. Is 61:10.

814. Augustine's constant doctrine, that the incarnate Christ and his Church are a single "whole."

815. Jn 20:25ff.

in him." The light and darkness here spoken of have nothing to do with our bodily eyes. As God surpasses the creature, as the Maker the thing made, as Wisdom itself surpasses that to which Wisdom has given being; so that light must far transcend all others. Perhaps we shall come near that light, if we know what it is and set ourselves before it that we may have enlightenment from it. In ourselves we are darkness: enlightened by it, we may become light; it will not confound us, because we confound ourselves. To confound myself is to know myself a sinner: not to be confounded by the light is to be enlightened by it. The man who sees himself darkened by sin and longs to be enlightened by the light is drawing near to it. As the psalm says: "Draw near to him and be enlightened; and your faces shall not be ashamed."[816] The light will not shame you, if it shows you your own ugliness, and that ugliness so offends you that you perceive the beauty of the light.

5. Have we expounded our text too hastily? We shall see as we proceed. Remember the words that came before: "that ye may have fellowship with us, and our fellowship be with God the Father, and his Son Jesus Christ." God is light, and there is no darkness in him, and we should have fellowship with him. The darkness must be driven from us, that the light may be in us; for darkness can have no fellowship with light—as Paul says.[817] But what follows? "If we say that we have fellowship with him, and walk in darkness, we lie." A man may well say to himself, "What can I do, how can I become light? I live in sins and iniquities." A gloomy despair creeps over him. There is no salvation but in fellowship with God. God is light, and there is no darkness in him. Iniquities are darkness: our iniquities overwhelm us, so that we cannot have fellowship with God. What hope is there?

Am I failing to keep my promise that in these days I should have a message of joy to speak to you? Listen: there may be a word of comfort, encouragement, and hope, that we faint not by the way. We are travelers, traveling to our homeland, and if we despair of reaching it, in our despair we faint. But he whose will it is that we should reach the homeland where he will keep us, nourishes us upon our journey. Listen: "If we walk in the light as he is in the

816. Ps 34:5.   817. 2 Cor 6:14.

light, we have fellowship with one another." And what of our sins? "The blood of Jesus Christ his Son shall cleanse us from all transgression." Great is the confidence that God has given us. Well may we celebrate our Paschal sacrifice, in which the Lord's blood is shed to cleanse us from all transgression. Let us rest confident: the devil held against us a bond of slavery, but Christ's blood has wiped it out.

Think for a moment of those brothers of ours whom we call "infants":[818] but now, in the name of Christ whom they have confessed, all their sins have been washed away by his blood. They came, old, into the baptistery and went out new—came in aged and went out infants. Their old life was somnolent age: their new life is the infancy of regeneration. But remember that past sins have been forgiven not only to them but to us. After the forgiving and wiping away of all sins, our life amid the temptations of this world may not avoid all stain. Then let a man do what he can: let him confess what he is, that he may be healed by the one who never changes. For he alone ever was, and is: we were not, and we are.

6. "If we say that we have no sin, we deceive ourselves, and the truth is not in us."—If then you confess yourself a sinner, the truth is in you, for the truth itself is light. Your life is not yet perfect in brightness, for there are sins in it: yet your enlightenment has begun with your confession of sin. Read on: "but if we confess our transgressions, he is faithful and just to forgive us our transgressions and to cleanse us from all iniquity," Not only the transgressions that are past, but any that this life brings upon us; for so long as a man wears flesh, he cannot be without at least the lesser sins. But these that we call the lesser must not be made light of: if you make light of their gravity, you must tremble at their number. The many lesser make a large: many drops fill up a river, many grains make a lump. Where then is our hope? First of all, in confession; that none count himself righteous, man who was not, and is, lifting up his head before the eyes of God who sees what he is. First of all, then, confession, and next, love; for of charity it is said that it covers the multitude of sins.[819] Let us see whether charity itself is not commended to us on account of the transgressions that steal upon us; for charity alone can quench transgression. Pride quenches charity;

818. The baptism of catechumens took place on Easter Eve.   819. 1 Pt 4:8.

humility strengthens it; charity quenches transgression. Humility is part of our confession that we are sinners. But humility lies not in the spoken word, which might seek only to avoid the offense of arrogance in calling ourselves righteous. In wickedness and folly a man will say, I know that I am righteous, but I cannot say so openly, for folk will not suffer it: let my righteousness be known of God, and I will call myself a sinner—not because I am, but that I may not be set down as arrogant and offensive. No, say what you are, to man as well as to God. If you do not tell God what you are, he will condemn what he finds in you. If you would not have his condemnation, speak your own. If you would have his pardon, do you acknowledge your need of it: say to God, "Turn thy face from my sins"; say with the psalmist, "For I acknowledge my iniquity."[820]

"If we confess our transgressions, he is faithful and just to forgive us our transgressions and to cleanse us from all iniquity. If we say that we have not sinned, we make him a liar, and his word is not in us." If you say, I have not sinned, you make him a liar in seeking to maintain your own truth; but how can God be a liar, and man true, in the face of Scripture: "Let every man be a liar and God only true"?[821] God in himself is true, you in yourself are a liar: in God you can be true.

7. These words, "faithful and just to cleanse us from all iniquity," might seem to offer impunity to sin. Men might say to themselves, "We can sin, we can do freely what we will, for Christ cleanses us, he is faithful and just, he cleanses us from all iniquity." This evil confidence must be taken from you, and a wholesome fear put in its place: be careful, not confident. He is faithful and just to forgive us our transgressions, but only if you are never self-satisfied, if you are always being made perfect through change. "My little children, these things I write to you that ye sin not." What then will happen, if, human as we are, some sin overtake us? Must we then despair? "If any man sin, we have an advocate with the Father, Jesus Christ the righteous; and he is the propitiator of our sins."[822] Christ is the advocate. Strive yourself not to sin; but if human weakness suffers sin to overtake you, look to it instantly, let it

820. Ps 51:9, 3.   821. Rom 3:4.

822. Augustine's version of this text varies between *propitiator* and *propitiatio*.

instantly offend you, instantly condemn it; and having condemned it, you may come in confidence before the judge. For there is your advocate: do not fear to lose the cause in which you confess. If in the affairs of this life a man may commit himself to a clever speaker and so escape loss, shall you be lost if you commit yourself to the Word himself? Cry aloud, "We have an advocate with the Father."

8. See how John himself keeps humility. A righteous man, a great man, who from the Lord's breast drank deep mysteries, draughts of divinity from which he proclaimed: "In the beginning was the Word, and the Word was with God"—this John did not say, *You* have an advocate with the Father, but, If any man sin, *we* have an advocate. Neither, "you have," nor, "you have me": Christ, not himself, and "we" not "you." Rather would he set himself among sinners and have Christ for his advocate, than set himself as advocate in Christ's place and be found among the proud who face condemnation. My brothers, Jesus Christ the righteous is he whom we have as advocate with the Father: he is the propitiation of our sins. The man who held fast to this caused no heresy, no schism. Schisms arise when men say, *we* are righteous; when they say, *we* sanctify the unclean, *we* justify the wicked, *we* ask, *we* obtain.[823] But what said John? "If any man sin, we have an advocate with the Father, Jesus Christ the righteous." You will say, But may not holy men ask on our behalf? May not bishops and rulers ask on behalf of the people? Look at the Scripture, and you will find rulers commending themselves to the people's prayers. The apostle says to his people, "Praying also for us."[824] The apostle prays for the people and the people for the apostle. We pray for you, my brothers; but do you also pray for us. Let all the members pray for one another, and let the Head intercede for all. No wonder then that what follows here should shut the mouths of those who divide God's Church. John has said that we have Jesus Christ the righteous, himself the propitiation of our sins; but he knew that there would be some who would set themselves apart, saying, "Lo, here is Christ, or lo, there!"[825] trying to show that he who purchased the

---

823. Reference is to the Donatist principle that purity of conscience in the "giver" of the sacrament is needed for the cleansing of the conscience of the recipient.

824. Col 4:3.   825. Mt 24:23.

whole and possesses the whole is only in the part.[826] Therefore he adds at once: "not only of our sins, but of the sins of the whole world." Think, brethren, what that means. Surely we are pointed to the Church in all nations, the Church throughout the whole world. Be not led astray by those who pretend to justify but in fact mutilate. Abide in that mountain which has filled the world;[827] for Christ is "the propitiation of our sins, and not of ours only, but also of the whole world"—which he has won by his blood.

9. "And hereby we know him, if we keep his commandments." Which commandments? "Whosoever saith that he knows him, and keepeth not his commandments, is a liar, and the truth is not in him." You ask still, Which commandments? "Whosoever keepeth his word, truly in him is the love of God perfect." Maybe the commandment itself is named love. We asked, What commandments? and we are told that "whosoever keepeth his word, truly in him is the love of God perfect." Turn to the Gospel and see if this is not the commandment: "A new commandment give I unto you, that ye love one another."[828] "Hereby we know that we are in him, if we are made perfect in him." It speaks of the perfect in love: what is love's perfection? To love our enemies, and to love them to the end that they may be our brothers. Love your enemies, desiring them for brothers: love your enemies, calling them into your fellowship. For so loved he who as he hung upon the cross said, "Father, forgive them, for they know not what they do."[829] "Hereby we know that we are in him, if we are made perfect in him." It was of the perfection of love for enemies that the Lord said: "Be ye therefore perfect as your heavenly Father is perfect."[830] "He," therefore, "who says that he abides in him, ought himself to walk as he walked." And how is that, my brethren? What is "walking as Christ walked"? Walking upon the sea?[831] No, it is walking in the way of righteousness; and of that way I have already spoken. Nailed fast

826. Reference is to the Donatist assertion that the Catholic Church throughout the world has been polluted by communion with the polluted Church in Africa. Augustine constantly appealed against them (as here) to the scriptural promises of a worldwide extension of the Church, and he seems never to have considered the possibility that these promises may have to wait much longer for their fulfillment.

827. Dn 2:35.   828. Jn 13:34.   829. Lk 23:34.   830. Mt 5:48.

831. Mt 14:25ff.

upon the cross, he was walking in the way—the way of charity. "Father, forgive them, for they know not what they do." So then, when you have learned to pray for your enemy, you will walk the way of the Lord.

10. "Beloved, I write not unto you a new commandment, but the old commandment which ye had from the beginning. The old commandment is the word which ye have heard." Old, that is, because you have heard it before. But he shows it to be also new, when he says: "Again a new commandment I write unto you." Not another commandment, but the same one that he called old, is also new. Why is this? "Which is true in himself and in you." You have heard why it is old: because you knew it already; but why is it new? "Because the darkness is passed and the true light now shineth." That is what makes it new; for the darkness belongs to the old man, the light to the new. "Put off the old man," says Paul, "and put on the new";[832] and again: "Ye were sometime darkness, but now light in the Lord."[833]

11. "He that saith he is in the light"—now the whole meaning is to be made clear—"He that saith he is in the light, and hateth his brother, is still in darkness." Ah, my brothers, shall I continue saying to you, Love your enemies? Are you sure that you are not still hating your brothers—which is worse than failing to love enemies? If you loved your brothers only, you would not yet be perfect, but if you hate your brothers, what and where are you? Look each one into his own heart: cherish no hate against a brother for some hard word: in a quarrel for earth, turn not to earth. Whoever hates his brother may not say that he walks in the light—still less, that he walks in Christ. "He who saith he is in the light and hateth his brother, is in darkness until now."—Such and such a man, who was a pagan, has turned Christian. Think what has happened: a pagan, he was in darkness; now, he has become a Christian. All rejoice for him with thanks to God. We repeat the apostle's greeting: "Ye were sometime darkness, but now are light in the Lord." He worshipped idols, but now God; he worshipped the work of his own hands, but now the God who made him. He is changed: thanks be to God, all Christians rejoice for him. Why? Because now he is a worshipper of Father, Son, and Holy Spirit, and a hater

832. Col 3:9ff.   833. Eph 5:8.

of demons and idols. But still John is anxious for him: in the general rejoicing there is still mistrust. My brothers, let us take to our hearts that motherly anxiety. Not without reason is the mother anxious for us, when others rejoice—I mean the mother Charity, who dwelt in the heart of John when he thus spoke. For there is that in us which makes him fear even when men rejoice over us: and what is his fear? "He who saith that he is in the light"—says that he is now a Christian—"and hateth his brother, is in darkness still." There is nothing here to expound, but only that which must sadden if it comes to pass, and gladden if it be avoided.

12. "He that loveth his brother, abideth in the light, and there is no occasion of offense in him." Those who take or cause offense are those who are offended in Christ and his Church. If you keep hold of charity, you shall take offense neither in Christ nor in the Church; and you will desert neither Christ nor the Church. The deserter of the Church cannot be in Christ, since he is not among Christ's members: he cannot be in Christ, who is not in Christ's Body. It is they who desert either Christ or the Church who take offense. But we can see that in him who loves his brother there is no offense; for the lover of his brother endures all things for unity's sake. In the unity of charity brotherly love consists. You are offended by such and such a man, whether he be really evil, or evil only in your belief or only in your pretense; and you abandon all the many good. What sort of brotherly love has been shown in our Donatists? Because of their charge against Africans they have abandoned the world.[834] Were there no saints in the world at large? Was it right for you to condemn them unheard? No, if you loved your brothers, there would be no occasion of offense in you. What does the psalm say?—"Great peace have they which love thy law, and there is no offense for them."[835] So they who take offense lose their peace; and they who do not take or cause offense are the lovers of God's law, so that their dwelling is charity. If it be said that the psalm speaks of the lovers of God's law and not of brothers, then hear the Lord's words: "A new commandment give I unto you, that ye love one another." Law and commandment are one. And not taking offense is but forbearing one another, according to

834. Cf. above, chap. 8 note 826.   835. Ps 119:165.

Paul's saying: "forbearing one another in love, striving to keep the unity of the Spirit in the bond of peace."[836] And that this is the law of Christ is shown by the same apostle's enjoining of the law: "Bear ye one another's burdens, and so shall ye fulfill the law of Christ."[837]

13. "For he that hateth his brother is in darkness, and walketh in darkness, and knoweth not whither he goeth; because the darkness hath blinded his eyes." There is no blindness like that of those who hate their brothers. The proof is that they stumble on the mountain.[838] We know that the stone cut from the mountain without hands is Christ who came of the kingdom of Jewry without human father: the stone that shattered all the kingdoms of the earth, all the tyrannies of idols and devils; the stone that grew and became a great mountain and filled the whole world. We do not have to point out that mountain with the finger, as we sometimes point out the new moon to the short-sighted. This is a mountain that fills the whole face of the earth, the city of which it is written, "a city that is set on a hill cannot be hid."[839] And our Donatists stumble on the mountain, and when we tell them, "Go up!" they say, "There is no mountain there," and will sooner strike their face against it than seek a dwelling on it. Yesterday we read the text of Isaiah: "In the last days the mountain of the Lord's house shall be manifested, made ready on the summit of the mountains; and all nations shall come together unto it."[840] Who can go astray on that mountain? Who can break his head by stumbling upon it? Who cannot recognize the city set on a hill? No wonder that it is not recognized by those who hate their brothers, for they walk in darkness and know not whither they go; for the darkness hath blinded their eyes. That is the proof of their blindness: they hate their brothers. Because they find cause of stumbling in Africa, they cut themselves off from the world: to brethren whom they slander they refuse toleration for the sake of the peace of Christ; while to others, whom they condemn, they grant it for the sake of the party of Donatus.[841]

---

836. Eph 4:2ff.   837. Gal 6:2.   838. The allusion is to Dn 2:34ff.

839. Mt 5:14.   840. Is 2:2.

841. Augustine frequently taxed the Donatists with inconsistency in recognizing the sacraments of the Maximianists, a sect which had split off from the main body of their Church.

Second Homily

I JOHN 2:12–17

1. All that we read in Holy Scripture for our instruction and salvation demands an attentive ear. You have just heard how the eyes of those two disciples upon whom the Lord came in the way were held so that they did not know him.[842] He found them in despair of the redemption that was in Christ, supposing him now to have suffered and died as a man, not imagining him to live forever as the Son of God. And then he opened unto them the Scripture, and showed them that it behooved the Christ to suffer, and all things to be fulfilled that were written concerning him in the law of Moses and the Prophets and the Psalms—so embracing the whole of the Old Testament. Everything in those Scriptures speaks of Christ, but only to him that has ears. He opened their mind to understand the Scriptures, and so let us pray that he will open our own.

2. What was it then which the Lord showed as written concerning himself in Law, Prophets, and Psalms? The evangelist has set it down in few words, that we might know what in all that extent of Scripture we should believe and understand. There is many a page, many a book; but the content of all is in these few words of the Lord to his disciples: "that it behooved the Christ to suffer, and to rise again on the third day."[843] So much we learn of the Bridegroom; and what of the Bride? Wherefore must Christ suffer and rise again? Because "all the ends of the world shall remember and turn unto the Lord, and all the kindreds of the nations shall worship before him."[844] So here our minds are led on from Bridegroom to Bride; "and that in his name repentance and forgiveness of sins should be preached through all nations, beginning from Jerusalem."[845] Brethren, you hear: mark it well. Let none doubt that the Church is of all nations: let none doubt that it began from Jerusalem and filled all nations.

3. When we tell the Donatists that if they are Catholic Christians

---

842. In one of the special lessons for Eastertide to which Augustine refers in the Prologue: Lk 24:13ff.

843. Lk 24:46.   844. Ps 22:27.   845. Lk 24:47.

they must be in communion with that Church from which the Gospel has been spread throughout the world, they answer: "We have no communion with the city where our King was slain, our Lord was slain." But he loved that city and had compassion on it: therefore he said that the preaching of himself should begin from Jerusalem. You shrink in horror from the communion of that city which he made the starting-point for the preaching of his name. No wonder! The severed branch may hate the root. But he told his disciples: "tarry ye in the city, because I send my promise upon you."[846] He willed that his disciples should tarry there, and that there he should send them the Holy Spirit. The Church began in that place where the Holy Spirit came from heaven, and filled a hundred and twenty persons as they sat together. The number of the apostles was multiplied tenfold: there sat in that place a hundred and twenty persons, and the Holy Spirit came and filled all the place; there was a sound as of a rushing mighty wind, and cloven tongues as of fire. You have heard today the Lesson from the Acts: "They began to speak with tongues as the Spirit gave them utterance."[847] And all that were there, Jews coming from divers nations, heard each one his own tongue, and marveled how these unlearned and ignorant men should suddenly have learned, not one or two strange tongues, but the tongues of all peoples. That speaking in the beginning in all languages was a sign that men of every language should believe. But our Donatists, whose love for Christ is such that they refuse communion with the city that killed him, give to Christ the strange honor of confinement to two languages—the Latin and the Punic or African! Christ is to possess two tongues only; for these two alone, no more, are spoken by the followers of Donatus. Brethren, let us keep our minds awake! Let us see rather the gift of God's Spirit: let us believe what was foretold concerning him, and let us see the fulfillment of the psalmist's prophecy: "There is neither speech nor language, whose voices shall not be heard."[848] That this means, not the assembling of tongues in one place, but the coming of the gift of Christ to all tongues, is clear from what follows: "Their sound is gone out into all the earth, and their words unto the end of the world." And this, because "he hath set his tabernacle in the sun"—that is, where all

846. Lk 24:49.   847. Acts 2:4.   848. Ps 19:3ff.

may see it. His tabernacle is his flesh: his tabernacle is his Church—set in the sun, in the day, not in the night. Why then do they not acknowledge it? Turn again to where we ended yesterday's reading, and you will see the reason. "He that hateth his brother walketh in darkness, and knoweth not whither he goeth; because the darkness hath blinded his eyes." Let us then read on, and not be in darkness. We shall not be in darkness if we love the brethren; and the proof of love for the brotherhood lies in not rending our unity, in maintaining charity.

4. "I write unto you, little children because your sins are forgiven you through his name." "Little children," because newborn by the forgiveness of sins. But whose is the name through which sins are forgiven? Certainly not the name of Augustine; and therefore not the name of Donatus either. But no need to mention Augustine or Donatus: it is not even the name of Paul or the name of Peter. When the Corinthians were dividing their Church, and setting up parties instead of unity, mother Charity, travailing with her children in person of the apostle, opens her bosom and speaks as if tearing her breast: she weeps for the sons whom she sees borne out to burial, she recalls to the one Name those who would enroll themselves under many, she sends them back from the love of herself to the single love of Christ: "Was Paul crucified for you? or were ye baptized in the name of Paul?"[849] In other words: "If you would be with me, you must not be mine: be with me, and all of us are Christ's, who died for us, was crucified for us." And so in our text: "your sins are forgiven you through his name"—not through the name of any man.

5. "I write unto you, fathers." Why do "children" come first? "Because your sins are forgiven you through his name," and you are born again into a new life—which makes you children. And why "fathers"? "Because ye have known him who is from the beginning"; and there is a beginning in all fatherhood. Christ is new in the flesh, ancient in divinity; "before Abraham, I am."[850] And not before Abraham only: heaven and earth were made, before there was any man. Before them the Lord was, or rather is: most truly does he say, not "before Abraham I was," but "before Abraham, I am." That of which we say that it was, is not; and that of which we

say that it will be, is not yet. He knows only *being*: begotten of the eternal Father, begotten from eternity, in eternity; with no beginning, no end, no local extension; because he is that which is, because he is he who is. That is the name he told to Moses: "thou shalt say unto them, He who is hath sent me unto you."[851] Therefore, to say "before Abraham," "before Noah," "before Adam," is not enough. Hear the Scripture: "before the morning star I have begotten thee."[852] And the last word must be "before heaven and earth"; for "all things were made through him, and without him nothing was made."[853] Thus you may know who are fathers; for they become fathers by knowing that which is from the beginning.

6. "I write unto you, young men." There are children, fathers, and young men: children, because they are born, fathers because they know the beginning, and why "young men"? "Because ye have overcome the evil one." To children belongs birth, to fathers age, to young men strength. If the evil one is overcome by young men, he still fights with us—fights but vanquishes not. Is that because we are strong, or because he who was found weak in the hands of persecutors is strong in us? He who resisted not his persecutors has made us strong; for he was crucified in weakness, but lives in the power of God.[854]

7. "I write unto you, children"—children, "because ye have known the Father." "I write unto you, fathers"; and here he repeats, "because ye have known him who is from the beginning." Remember that you are fathers: if you forget him who is from the beginning, you have lost your fatherhood. "I write unto you, young men": once more, bear in mind your youth: fight, that you may overcome: overcome, that you may be crowned; be humble, lest you fall in the battle. "I write unto you, young men, because ye are strong, and the word of God abideth in you, and ye have overcome the evil one."

8. Brethren, all that is said here—that we have known that which is from the beginning, that we are strong, that we have known the Father—all this seems to commend knowledge; does it not also commend charity? If we have known, let us love; for knowledge without charity cannot save. "Knowledge puffeth up,

851. Ex 3:14.   852. Ps 110:3 (Septuagint and Vulgate).   853. Jn 1:3.
854. 2 Cor 13:4.

but charity edifieth."[855] If you would confess, but not love, you make yourselves like the demons: they confessed the Son of God; they said, "What have we to do with thee?"[856] and they were driven back. Do you confess, and embrace. They feared for their iniquities: do you love the forgiver of your iniquities. But we cannot love God, if we love the world: if we love the world, it will separate us from the love of God which is charity. The apostle makes us ready, then, to have charity dwelling in us. Two loves there are, of the world and of God: if the love of the world dwells in us, the love of God can find no entrance. The love of the world must depart, the love of God come in to dwell: make room for the better love. Once you loved the world, now cease to love it: empty your heart of earthly love and you shall drink of the love divine; charity will begin its dwelling in you, and from charity nothing evil can proceed. Hear then the words of the apostle who now would cleanse you. He sees men's hearts as a field, and in what condition? If he finds weeds, he roots them up; if he finds clean land, he plants—that tree which he would fain plant, which is charity. The weeds that he would root up are love of the world. Hear the rooter-up of weeds: "Love not the world, nor the things that are in the world. If a man love the world, the love of the Father is not in him."

9. You hear this. Brethren, let none say in his heart that this is not true. It is God's word spoken by the Holy Spirit through his apostle, and nothing can be truer: "if a man love the world, the love of the Father is not in him." Would you have the love of the Father, and be fellow heir with the Son? Love not the world. Shut out the evil love of the world, that you may be filled with the love of God. You are a vessel that was already full: you must pour away what you have, that you may take in what you have not. We know that these our brethren have been born again of water and the Spirit,[857] even as we were so many years ago. It is good for us not to love the world, lest there remain in us only sacraments for our condemnation, and not stays for our salvation. The stay of salvation is to have charity at the root, to have the virtue of godliness and not the form only. The form is good and holy; but it avails nothing apart from the root. The severed branch is cast into the fire. You should keep the form, but in union with the root; and there is no way to be

855. 1 Cor 8:1.   856. Mt 8:29.   857. Cf. First Homily, chap. 5.

firmly rooted, but by holding fast to charity, according to the words of the Apostle Paul: "rooted and grounded in charity."[858]

10. "Because all that is in the world is the desire of the flesh, and the desire of the eyes, and the pretensions of this life"—three things, "which are not of the Father but of the world. And the world passeth away, and the desires thereof; but he that doeth the will of God abideth for ever, as he abideth for ever."

Why may I not love what God has made? Make your choice: either to love things temporal and pass away with time's passing, or not to love the world, and to live forever with God. The river of time sweeps us on; but there, like a tree growing by the river, is our Lord Jesus Christ. He took flesh, died, rose again, ascended into heaven. He willed to plant himself as it were beside the river of things temporal. If you are drifting down to the rapids, lay hold of the tree: if you are caught up in the world's love, lay hold of Christ. He for your sake entered into time, that you might win eternity; for by his entering into time he did not cease himself to be eternal.

11. Let us not love the world, nor the things that are in the world. For the things that are in the world are "the desire of the flesh and the desire of the eyes and the pretensions of this life." The naming of these three forestalls objection. A man might say: "The things that are in the world are what God has made—heaven and earth, sea, sun, moon, stars, and all the furnishings of the heavens. Why should I not love what God has made?" Let God's Spirit indeed be in you to show you that all these things are good, but beware of loving things created and forsaking their Creator. You find them fair, but how much fairer is he that formed them! Think, my friends: you may learn by a parable, lest Satan get advantage of you, saying as he is wont: "Be happy in God's creation: he made it only for your happiness!" So men's wits are stolen, and they perish in forgetfulness of their Maker; they use the creature with lust instead of temperance, and the Creator is despised. Of such the apostle says: "They worshipped and served the creature rather than the Creator, who is blessed for ever."[859] God forbids you not to love them, but he will not have you seek your bliss in them: the end of your esteem for them should be the love of their Maker. Suppose, my brethren, a man should make for his betrothed a ring, and she should prefer

the ring given her to the betrothed who made it for her, would not her heart be convicted of infidelity in respect of the very gift of her betrothed, though what she loved were what he gave. Certainly let her love his gift; but if she should say "The ring is enough, I do not want to see his face again," what should we say of her? Should we not all abhor such frivolity and charge her with the mind of an adulteress? "Gold is more to you than a husband, a ring more than your betrothed: if it is in you to transfer your love from your betrothed to the ring and not to want the sight of him, he will have given you a pledge not for security but for divorce." Yet surely the pledge is given by the betrothed, just that in his pledge he himself may be loved. Even so, God has given you all these things: therefore, love him who made them. There is more that he would give you, even himself, their Maker. Though God has made these things, if you love them and are careless of their Creator—if you love the world, must not your love be set down for adulterous?

12. "World" is the name not only for this fabric that God has made, of heaven, earth and sea, of things visible and invisible. We use the word "world" also for the dwellers in it, just as we do the word "house" both for the structure and its occupants. Sometimes we approve the house while we condemn the occupants. Now just as men may dwell in heaven by lifting up their hearts, though in the flesh they walk on earth, so all lovers of the world are dwelling in the world by their love, and thus may themselves be called the world. And in them there is nothing but these three—the desire of the flesh, the desire of the eyes, and the pretensions of this life. They desire the pleasures of food, drink, and sex. But in such things there is a due limit. When you are told not to love them, it does not mean that you are forbidden to eat or drink or beget children; but for the Creator's sake there is a limit set, so that the love of all this does not make prisoner of you—lest your love of what you should possess for use become the love of final enjoyment. The test comes only when the choice between this and that is set before you: "Money or the right?" "I am without the wherewithal to live, the wherewithal to eat and drink." But what if you can only gain that wrongfully? Were it not better to set your love on what you cannot lose, than to commit a wrong? You have eyes for the gain of money, not for the loss of faith. Here then, he tells us, is the desire of the flesh, the desire, that is, of what belongs to the flesh, food and sex, and so forth.

13. "And the desire of the eyes." By this he means all that itch for marvels which I call curiosity. It has a very wide scope. The public spectacle, the theater, the devil's mysteries, the arts of magic and sorcery, all pander to curiosity. But sometimes it may try the servants of God, making them wish to be wonder-workers, to try whether God will hear them by a miracle. That is curiosity, the desire of the eyes: it is not of the Father. If God has given you such power, use it: he has offered it for your use; but the lack of it will prevent no one from belonging to the kingdom of God. When the apostles rejoiced because the devils were subject to them, what said the Lord to them? "Rejoice not in this: but rejoice, because your names are written in heaven."[860] He would have his apostles rejoice for the same cause as you too have for rejoicing. It will go hard with you, if your name is not written in heaven; but will it go hard if you have not raised the dead? if you have not walked upon the sea? if you have not cast out devils? If you have received the power to do such things, use it in humility and not in pride. For the Lord has said even of certain false prophets, that they should do signs and wonders. Therefore shun the "pretensions of this life." The pretensions of this life are pride. Men desire to vaunt themselves upon their honorable positions: they think themselves great because of their wealth or powerful standing.

14. Apart from these three things, you will find nothing that tempts human covetousness—nothing but desire of the flesh or desire of the eyes or pretensions of this life. By these three was the Lord tempted of the devil.[861] He was tempted by desire of the flesh, when it was said to him: "If thou art the Son of God, command these stones that they become bread"—when he was hungry from fasting. Remember how he repulsed the tempter, and taught his soldiers to fight, saying, "Man liveth not by bread alone, but by every word of God." He was tempted again by desire of the eyes, for a miracle, when the devil said, "Cast thyself down, for it is written, He hath charged his angels to bear thee up, that thou strike not thy foot against a stone." So did he resist the tempter; for if he had worked a miracle, he must have appeared either to have yielded or to have done it for "curiosity's" sake. He did indeed work miracles when he would, as God, but for the sake of healing the sick. If at

860. Lk 10:20.   861. Mt 4:1ff.

that time he had done so, it would have seemed as though his only purpose was to work a miracle. But, to avoid such misapprehension, observe how he answered; and if ever such temptation comes to you, do you answer as he did: "Get thee behind me, Satan; for it is written, Thou shalt not tempt the Lord thy God"—meaning "if I do this, I shall be tempting God." Our Lord spoke as he would have you speak. If the Enemy should whisper to you: "A poor sort of man, a poor sort of Christian must you be! Have you worked a single miracle, have the dead arisen at your prayer, have you healed the fever-stricken? Were there really anything in you, you would do some mighty work!"—answer him and say, "It is written, Thou shalt not tempt the Lord thy God; I will not tempt God, as though I should belong to him if I wrought a miracle, but not otherwise. How then should he have said, Rejoice that your names are written in heaven?" And lastly, our Lord was tempted with the pretensions of this life: when the devil raised him up on the height, and said to him, "All these things will I give thee, if thou wilt fall down and worship me." He would have tempted the King of ages with the exaltation of an earthly kingdom; but the Lord that made heaven and earth trod the tempter underfoot. No wonder, indeed, that the Lord should vanquish the devil; but his answer to the devil was to teach you your own: "It is written, Thou shalt worship the Lord thy God, and him only shalt thou serve."

Hold to the Lord's answers, and you will be free from all lusting after the world: in that freedom, you will be enslaved neither by desire of the flesh nor by desire of the eyes nor by the pretensions of this life; and you will make room for the coming of charity, which is the love of God. If your heart is occupied by love of the world, the love of God will not be in it. Hold to the love of God, that you may stand fast forever as God stands: for the being of every man is according to his love. Dost thou love the earth? To earth thou shalt turn. Dost thou love God? I would not dare to say, A god thou shalt be; yet we have the word of Scripture, "I have said, Ye are gods, and ye are all the sons of the Most High."[862] If then you would be gods and sons of the most high, "love not the world, nor the things that are in the world. If any man loveth the world, the love of the Fa-

---

862. Ps 82:6. Augustine is chary in use of the characteristically Greek idea of the "divinization" of the Christian by grace.

ther (which is charity) is not in him. For all that is in the world is the desire of the flesh and the desire of the eyes and the pretensions of this life: which are not of the Father but of the world (that is, of men who love the world). And the world passeth away, and the desires thereof; but whosoever doeth the will of God abideth for ever, even as God abideth for ever."

Fifth Homily

1 JOHN 3:9–18

1. I ask today for your closest attention, since we have no light matter for our considering. Indeed the interest with which you listened to yesterday's sermon assures me that it will be even keener today. For the question to be raised is a very difficult one. We are asking what is meant by this text in our Epistle: "He that is born of God sinneth not"—in view of that earlier saying in the same Epistle: "If we say that we have no sin, we deceive ourselves and the truth is not in us."

2. Now give your minds to these words. I want you to face the difficulty, so that your earnest attention may be a prayer on my behalf as well as yours, and God may grant us enlargement and open the way out: that none may find occasion of falling away in his word, the word that is neither preached nor written but for healing and salvation.

"Every one that is born of God committeth no sin, because his seed remaineth in him; and he cannot sin, because he is born of God." This is put very strongly. But maybe the words "sinneth not" refer, not to any sin, but to some particular sin. Then by the saying, "He that is born of God sinneth not," we may understand some special kind of sin, which a man that is born of God cannot commit—a sin of such a kind that its commission binds all other sins upon us, whereas if it be not committed the others may be absolved. What is that sin? Transgression of the commandment. And what commandment? "A new commandment give I unto you, that ye love one another."[863] Consider. This commandment of Christ has the name of love; and through that love are sins absolved. If it be not kept, not only is the sin grave but it is the root of all sins.

863. Jn 13:34.

3. Consider this, my brethren. The suggestion we have made is one that may give the key to our problem when rightly understood. There is a sin that cannot be committed by him who is born of God. If that sin be not committed, others are absolved: if it be committed, others are bound fast. And this sin is the transgression of Christ's command, the new covenant: "A new commandment give I unto you, that ye love one another." The man that acts contrary to charity, contrary to brotherly love, may not dare to boast that he is born of God. But for him who is established in brotherly love, there are certain sins that he cannot commit, above all the hating of a brother. And as for all other sins, of which it is said that "if we say that we have no sin we deceive ourselves, and the truth is not in us"—for them he may take confidence from another text of Scripture: "Charity covereth the multitude of sins."[864]

4. Charity, then, is the theme of our exhortation, as it is the theme of this Epistle. The Lord after his resurrection put no other question to Peter but "Lovest thou me?"[865] Once was not enough: a second time he asked the same, a third time the same. And though at the third questioning Peter was distressed, as though the Lord did not believe him, as one ignorant of what was passing in his heart; yet the question was asked once, twice, and thrice. Fear had three times denied, love three times confessed. Peter loves his Lord; and what shall he offer him? His own trouble had found utterance in those words of the psalm: "What shall I return unto the Lord for all that he hath returned to me?"[866] For the psalmist's mind was set upon the great things that God had done for him: he sought for what he might do in return, and could not find it. For there is nothing that one would return which one has not received from him for the return of it. And so we see that what he found to return was what he had received from God. "I will receive the cup of salvation, and call upon the name of the Lord." None had given him that saving cup but he to whom he would make the return. But to receive the saving cup, and to call upon the name of the Lord, is to be filled full with charity—so full that not only will you not hate your brother, but you will be ready to die for him. That is the perfection of charity—to be ready to die for your brother; and this our Lord displayed in himself, by dying for all, and praying for those by

864. 1 Pt 4:8.   865. Jn 21:15ff.   866. Ps 116:12ff.

whom he was crucified, with the words: "Father, forgive them; for they know not what they do."[867] But if he were the only one so to act, he had been no teacher, as having no disciples. Disciples there were who followed him and did the same. As Stephen was stoned, he fell upon his knee and prayed: "Lord, lay not this sin to their charge."[868] He showed his love for his murderers, in that he died for them. So we find Paul saying, "I would myself be spent in behalf of your souls";[869] for among those souls were some for whom Stephen prayed when he was dying at their hands.

That is the perfection of charity. Charity is perfect in him whom it makes ready to die for his brethren; but it is never perfect as soon as it is born. It is born that it may be perfected. Born, it is nourished: nourished, it is strengthened; strengthened, it is made perfect. And when it has reached perfection, how does it speak? "To me to live is Christ, and to die is gain. My desire was to be set free and to be with Christ; for that is by far the best. But to abide in the flesh is needful for your sake."[870] He was willing to live for their sakes, for whom he was ready to die.

5. To teach us that this is the perfect charity, which he that is born of God cannot violate or sin against, the Lord says to Peter: "Peter, lovest thou me?" And Peter answers, "I love thee." What return could Peter make to him that loved him? This: "Feed my sheep." That is, "Do for thy brethren what I have done for thee. I have redeemed all by my blood. Do not shrink from dying for the confession of the truth, that others may follow your example."

6. But this, my brothers, as I have said, is perfect charity, possessed by him that is born of God. Think, my dear people, and understand what I am saying. The person that is baptized has received the sacrament of birth. He possesses the sacrament—a sacrament great, divine, holy, unspeakable. Consider its purport: to make a new man through the remission of all his sins. Yet he must look well into his heart and see whether that which has been done in his body is made perfect there. Let him see whether he has charity, and then say, "I am born of God." If he has not charity, the Master's mark is on him, but he is a deserter straying from the ranks. Let him have charity, or else let him not say that he is born of God. He may say, "But I have the mystery of the sacrament." The apostle

will answer him: "If I know all mysteries, and have all faith, so as to remove mountains, and have not charity, I am nothing."[871]

7. You will remember that when we were beginning the reading of this Epistle I asked you to bear in mind that charity is what above all else it enjoins upon us. The writer may appear to pass from one subject to another, but to this always he returns: he means all that he says to be brought into relation with charity. So let us see whether he does so here. Listen: "Every man that is born of God, doth not commit sin." If we take this to mean *any* sin, it will conflict with that other saying, "If we say that we have no sin, we deceive ourselves and the truth is not in us." And so we ask, What sin? and look for some pointing from the writer himself; lest I may have been overhasty in suggesting that this sin is the violation of charity, because of his saying above: "He that hateth his brother is in darkness, and walketh in darkness, and knoweth not whither he goeth, because the darkness hath blinded his eyes." But perhaps in the words which follow here we shall find express mention of charity. You will see that indeed the turning of the sentence leads us to that very conclusion. "Every one that is born of God, sinneth not, because his seed abideth in him." (The seed of God is God's word; as the apostle puts it: "I have begotten you through the gospel."[872]) "And he cannot sin, because he is born of God." We look now to be told *wherein* he cannot sin. "In this are manifested the children of God and the children of the devil. Everyone that is not righteous, is not of God; and he that loveth not his brother."

He that loveth not his brother: the reference of these last words is clear. Love is the only final distinction between the sons of God and the sons of the devil. All may sign themselves with the sign of Christ's cross: all may answer Amen, and sing Alleluia: all may be baptized, all may come to church and line the walls of our places of meeting. But there is nothing to distinguish the sons of God from the sons of the devil, save charity. They that have charity are born of God: they that have not charity are not. There is the great token, the great dividing mark. Have what else you will; if this one thing you have not, all is to no purpose. If you lack all the rest, have this, and you have fulfilled the law. "For he that loveth another," says the apostle, "hath fulfilled the law"; and "charity is the fullness of

---

871. 1 Cor 13:2.   872. 1 Cor 4:15.

the law."[873] This, I would say, is the pearl which the merchantman in the Gospel went seeking: who found one pearl, and sold all that he had, and bought it.[874] Charity is that precious pearl, without which all that you have profits you nothing, and which suffices you if you have nothing else. Now your vision is by faith, then it will be by sight; and if we love while we do not see, with what ardor shall we embrace when we have seen! But how are our hearts to be trained? Through love of the brethren. You may say, "I have never seen God"; you cannot say, "I have never seen a man." Love your brother; in loving the brother whom you see, you will see God at the same time. For you will see charity itself, and there within is God dwelling.

8. "He that is not righteous, is not of God; and he that loveth not his brother. For this is the message"—note how proof is given!—"this is the message that we have heard from the beginning, that we should love one another." The writer points clearly to his authority: whoever transgresses that commandment is involved in that abominable sin into which they must fall who are not born of God. "Not as Cain, who was of the evil one, and slew his brother; and wherefore slew he him? Because his works were evil, and his brother's righteous." Thus where envy is, there cannot be brotherly love. Consider this, my people. Envy and love exclude one another. In the envious is the devil's sin; for it was by envy that the devil cast man down: he fell, and envied him that stood upright. He sought to cast down, not that he himself might stand, but that he might not be alone in his fall. Keep in your minds what the apostle's commandment teaches, that in charity there can be no envying. You have the express saying, in the praise of charity: "Charity envieth not."[875] There was no charity in Cain, and had there not been charity in Abel, God would not have accepted his sacrifice. When both brought their offering, the one from the fruits of the earth, and the other from the young of sheep, it is not to be thought that God cared not for the fruits of the earth and loved the lambs. God looked not at that which was in their hands, but saw what was in their heart; and seeing the one offer in charity had respect unto his sacrifice: seeing the other offer in envy, from his sacrifice turned away his eyes. The "good works" of Abel mean nothing but char-

873. Rom 13:8, 10.   874. Mt 13:46.   875. 1 Cor 13:4.

ity: the "evil works" of Cain mean nothing but hatred of a brother. More than hating his brother, he envied his good works; and because he would not follow his example, he resolved to slay him. Herein he showed himself a son of the devil, as Abel showed himself a righteous man of God. Herein, therefore, my brethren, is the proving of men. We are to observe not what men say, but their deeds and their heart. A man that will not do his brethren good, shows what he has in him: by temptation men are tested.

9. "Marvel not, my brethren, if the world hateth us." I should not need to keep telling you what "the world" means. It is not heaven or earth, or the works of God's making, but the lovers of the world. I know that some of you must find such repetition tedious, but it is not for nothing, if some cannot tell, when they are asked, whether the preacher said it! So let me try by hammering it in to leave something sticking in my hearers' minds![876] The world, in its good sense, is heaven and earth and God's works in them, as when it is said: "the world was made by him."[877] Again, the world may mean the fullness of the earth, as in John's own words: "he is the propitiator not only of our sins but of the sins of the whole world."[878] Here "world" means all the faithful, scattered in all parts of the earth. But in its bad sense, the world is the world's lovers; and those who love the world cannot love their brother.

10. ". . . if the world hateth us: we know"—and what is it that we know?—"that we have passed from death unto life"—and how do we know that?—"because we love the brethren." Let there be no questioning of another. Let each man turn to his own heart, and if there he finds charity toward his brother, let him be sure that he has passed from death unto life. His place already is on the right hand; he need not be concerned that his glory is at present hidden; when the Lord comes, then he will appear in glory. He has the vigor of life, though it is still winter; his root is vigorous, though the branches be dry; there is life in the pith, the leaves and fruit are ready there within, waiting for the summer. Therefore "we know that we have passed from death unto life, because we love the brethren. He that loveth not, remaineth in death." And lest you suppose it a light thing, my brothers, to hate or not to love, hear the

---

876. A pleasant example of the preacher's knowledge of his congregation.

877. Jn 1:10.   878. 1 Jn 2:2.

warning that follows: "Every one that hateth his brother is a murderer." If there were any that made light of hatred for brothers, can
he in his heart make light of murder? He may not lift his hand to
kill, yet already he is counted by the Lord a murderer. The brother
may live, but he is already judged as the shedder of blood. "Every
one that hateth his brother is a murderer, and ye know that no
murderer hath eternal life abiding in him."

11. "Hereby we know love." He speaks now of love's perfection,
that perfection on which we have dwelt. "Hereby we know love, in
that he laid down his life for us; and we ought to lay down our lives
for the brethren." Here is the bearing of the Lord's words: "Peter,
lovest thou me? Feed my sheep." Peter's feeding of his sheep was to
mean the laying down of his life for them: as we may learn from
the saying that followed. "When thou wast young, thou girdedst
thyself, and went whither thou wouldest; but when thou shalt be
old, another shall gird thee, and carry thee whither thou wilt not.
And this he said," adds the evangelist, "signifying by what death he
should glorify God"—teaching the man he had charged to feed his
sheep to lay down his life for the sheep.

12. Brethren, how does charity begin? Wait a moment. You have
heard how it is made perfect: the end of it and the form of it has
been enjoined by the Lord in the Gospel: "greater charity hath no
man than this, that he lay down his life for his friends."[879] Thus is
the perfection of charity shown in the Gospel, and thus commended here. But you will be asking among yourselves, When
shall we be able to possess such charity? Do not too soon despair of
yourself. Perhaps it is already born, but not yet grown to perfection: cherish it, so that it be not stifled. You may say, But how am I
to know? We have been told how it is perfected, but we would hear
how it begins. This is what John goes on to say: "He that hath this
world's goods, and seeth his brother an-hungered, and shutteth up
his bowels of compassion from him, how shall the love of God be
able to dwell in him?" There is where charity begins. If you are not
yet capable of dying for your brother, show now your capacity to
give him of your goods. Let charity even now be stirring your inmost heart to do it, not for display but out of the very marrow of
compassion, thinking only of the man and his need. If you cannot

879. Jn 15:13.

give of your superfluity to your brother, are you going to be able to lay down your life for him? In your purse lies money, of which thieves may rob you; and if they do not, still you must part from it when you die, though it part not from you while you live. What are you going to do with it? Your brother is hungry, in want: maybe he is in trouble, hard-pressed by some creditor. He has not what he needs, you have. He is your brother, he and you were purchased together, one price was paid for both of you, both were redeemed by the blood of Christ. Is there pity in you for him, if you have this world's goods? Do you ask, What concern is it of mine? Am I to give my money to save him from inconvenience? If that is the answer your heart gives you, the love of the Father dwells not in you, and if the love of the Father dwells not in you, you are not born of God. How can you boast of being a Christian? You have the name and not the deeds. If the work goes with the name, call you pagan who will, you prove yourself Christian by your deeds. For if your deeds prove not your Christianity, then though all may call you Christian, the name without the reality can avail you nothing. "He that hath this world's goods, and seeth his brother have need, and shutteth up his bowels of compassion from him, how can the love of God dwell in him?" And then it goes on: "Little children, let us not love in word only and in tongue, but in work and in truth."

Sixth Homily

I JOHN 3:19–4:3

1. You remember, my brothers, that we ended our sermon of yesterday with that sentence, which, as it was the last you heard, should certainly have stayed and still remain in your mind: "Little children, let us not love in word only and in tongue, but in work and in truth."

2. We ask. What is this work and this truth? Can there be a work more apparent than giving to the poor? Yet many do it for display and not for love. Can there be a greater work than dying for the brethren? Yet even of this many seek only the reputation, ambitious of acquiring the name, and not in truly heartfelt love. The true lover of his brother is he who before God assures his own

heart, wherein God alone sees, who puts to his heart the question whether what he does is indeed for love of the brethren; and has witness borne him by that eye that penetrates the heart, which no man can observe. So the Apostle Paul, ready as he was to die for his brethren, saying, "I will myself be spent for your souls,"[880] yet because that motion of his heart was visible to God only and not to the man to whom he spoke, he tells them: "To me indeed it is a very small thing to be judged of you, or by any day of man."[881] And in another place the same Paul shows that such things may be done for empty display, not in the solid strength of charity. In his commending of charity itself he says: "If I give all my goods to the poor, or give my body to burn, and have not charity, it profiteth me nothing."[882] Can anyone so act without charity? It is indeed possible. Look among those who for lack of charity have brought division upon our unity: You will see many who give much to the poor; you will see others so ready to face death that when the persecutor stays his hand they hurl themselves to destruction. Such men, certainly, do this without charity. Back, then, to the voice of conscience, of which the apostle says: "For this is our glory, the testimony of our conscience."[883] Back to the voice of conscience, of which the apostle says again: "Let each man prove his own work, and then shall he have glorying in himself and not in another."[884] Let each one of us prove his own work, whether it issues from the pulse of charity, whether the branches of good works spring forth from the root of love. "Let each man prove his own work," says Paul, "and then shall he have glorying in himself and not in another"—when witness is borne him not by another's tongue but by his own conscience.

3. This, then, is what our Epistle here teaches us. "Hereby we know that we are of the truth"—when we love in work and in truth, not in words and tongue only—"and assure our heart before him." "Before him"—that is, where God sees him. So says the Lord himself in the Gospel: "Take heed that ye do not your righteousness before men; to be seen of them: else ye shall have no reward with your Father who is in heaven." What else is the meaning of the saying: "Let not thy left hand know what thy right hand

880. 2 Cor 12:15.   881. 1 Cor 4:3.   882. 1 Cor 13:3.   883. 2 Cor 1:12.
884. Gal 6:4.

doeth,"[885] but that the right hand is a pure conscience, and the left the desire of the world? From desire of the world, many perform many a wonder: but it is the work of the left hand, not the right. The right hand must do the work, and without the left hand knowing it, lest worldly desire intrude itself when we do a thing in the love of what is good. And how can we be sure of this? You stand before God: ask your own heart, look at what you have done and what was your purpose in it—your own salvation, or the empty praise of man. Look within; for a man cannot judge one whom he cannot see.

If we assure our heart, let us do so in God's presence. "For if our heart feel evil," that is, charges us inwardly of not acting with the right intention, "God is greater than our heart and knoweth all things." You may hide your heart from man: hide it from God if you can. How shall you hide it from him to whom a sinner of old time spoke in trembling confession: "Whither shall I go from thy spirit? and whither shall I flee from thy presence?"[886] He sought a place of escape from God's judgment, and found none: for where is God not? "If I climb up into heaven, thou art there; if I go down into hell, thou art with me." Whither are you to go, whither can you flee? If you will hear counsel, flee to God himself if you would flee from him: flee to him by confessing, not by hiding; for hide you cannot, but confess you can. Say unto him, "Thou art my refuge,"[887] and let the love which alone opens the way to life be nourished in you. Let witness be borne you by your conscience, for it is of God; and if it is of God, desire not to display it before men; for neither can their praises exalt you to heaven nor their censures pull you down from thence. Let his eyes be on you, who gives the crown, let him be the witness by whose judgment you receive it. "God is greater than our heart, and knoweth all things."

4. "Beloved, if our heart feel no evil, we have confidence unto God." "Feel no evil"—that is, tells us truly that we love, and that the love in us is true love, sincere, not feigned, seeking our brother's good, looking for no profit from our brother but his own well-being. "We have confidence unto God, and whatsoever we ask, we shall receive from him, because we keep his commandments." Our confidence then is not in the sight of men, but where God himself

885. Mt 6:1, 3.   886. Ps 139:7ff.   887. Ps 32:7.

sees, in the heart, and we shall receive from him whatsoever we ask, only because we keep his commandments. What are his commandments? Need we always be repeating it?—"A new commandment give I unto you, that ye love one another."[888] The duty of which our text speaks is charity, charity is what it enjoins. Whoever has charity for the brethren and has it before God, in the place where God sees, and whoever's heart, when honestly examined, gives to his questioning no answer but that it holds the true root of charity, whence good fruits proceed—he has confidence with God, and whatever he asks he shall receive from him, because he keeps his commandments.

5. But there is a difficulty here. Of you or me, or of any man of our time, who may ask something of the Lord our God and not receive it, it is easy to say, "He has not charity." One man may think as he will of another. But a more serious question arises, when we consider those men whom all acknowledge to have written as saints and now to be with God.

6. You and I are nothing but the Church of God, known to all: if God will, we belong to his Church, and if we abide in her by love, we must so persevere if we would show the love we have. But how are we to think evil of the Apostle Paul? Did he not love his brethren? Did he not have the witness of his conscience in the sight of God? Was there not in Paul that root of charity whence all good fruits proceeded? It would be madness to deny it. Yet we find him asking and not receiving. "Lest I be exalted by the greatness of the revelations, there was given unto me a pricking of my flesh, a messenger of Satan to buffet me. Concerning which I besought the Lord three times that he would take it away from me; and he said unto me, My grace is sufficient for thee; for strength is made perfect in weakness."[889] You see, his prayer that the messenger of Satan might be taken away from him was not heard. But why? Because it was not for his good. Thus he was heard unto his own good, though not heard according to his desire. This is a great mystery, which I would have you, my people, understand and always remember in your temptations. The prayers of the saints are heard unto their good in all things, always heard unto their eternal good. And that is what they desire: to that end they are always heard.

888. Jn 13:34.   889. 2 Cor 12:7ff.

8. So we should understand that though God gives not what we wish, he gives what is for our good. When you are ill, you may ask for something that is bad for you, which the physician knows to be so. Suppose you ask for cold water: if it is good for you, the doctor will give it at once; if it is not, he will refuse it, but that does not mean that he does not hearken. In denying you your wish, he has hearkened to you for your health. So let charity, brethren, be in you: let charity be in you, and you need have no care. Even when your request is not granted, you are heard, though you know it not. Many are left to themselves, to their hurt, of whom the apostle says: "God gave them over to the desires of their heart."[890] A man that has asked for great wealth may have received it to his own hurt. While he was without it, he had little to fear; as soon as he has possession of it he has become a prey to the stronger. His wish to own what brings the robber's hand upon him, when in his poverty none attacked him, has indeed been granted to his hurt. Learn so to make your requests to God, as trusting the physician to do what he knows best. Confess your sickness, and let him apply the remedy: only hold fast yourself to charity. Let him use knife or cautery as he wills: if under the cutting, the burning, and the pain your cry is not heard, he knows how far the gangrene goes. You want him to withdraw his hand, while he searches the wound: he knows how deep he must press to reach the end. He does not hear you as you would, but as your cure demands. Be sure, then, my brethren, that the apostle's words are true: "For we know not what to pray for as we ought; but the Spirit himself maketh intercession for us with groanings that cannot be uttered, because it is he that intercedeth for the saints."[891] The Spirit that intercedes is nothing but the same charity which the Spirit has wrought in you: as the same apostle says, "The charity of God is shed abroad in our hearts through the Holy Spirit that is given to us."[892] Charity itself groans in prayer, and he who gave it cannot shut his ears to its voice. Cast away care, let charity make request, and the ears of God are ready to listen. The answer comes, not what you want, but what is to your advantage. Therefore, "Whatsoever we shall ask, we shall receive from him." Here, as I have said, there is no difficulty, if we understand that the receiving is for our good: otherwise the difficulty is

890. Rom 1:24.   891. Rom 8:26ff.   892. Rom 5.5.

so great as to lead you into calumny of the Apostle Paul. "Whatsoever we shall ask, we shall receive from him; because we keep his commandments, and do what is pleasing to him in his sight."—"In his sight"—that is, in the inward place where he sees us.

9. And what are these commandments? "This is his commandment, that we should believe the name of his Son Jesus Christ, and love one another." You see what the commandment is, and you see that its transgressor commits the sin from which every man that is born of God must be free. "As he gave us commandment"—namely, to love one another. "And he that keepeth his commandment"—remember that it enjoins upon us nothing but love of one another—"he that keepeth his commandment shall abide in him, and he in him. And hereby we know that he abideth in us, from the Spirit which he hath given us." Is it not plain that the Holy Spirit's work in man is to cause love and charity to be in him? Is it not plain that, in the words of the Apostle Paul, "the charity of God is shed abroad in our hearts through the Holy Spirit that is given to us"? John was speaking of charity, and saying that we ought to question our own heart in the sight of God. "But if our heart feel no evil"—that means, if the heart confess that any good work is wholly performed from love of brother. And if that were not enough, he adds when speaking of the commandment: "This is his commandment, that we should believe the name of his Son Jesus Christ, and love one another. And he that doeth his commandment abideth in him, and he in him. Hereby we know that he abideth in us, from the Spirit which he hath given us." If you find charity in yourself, you have the Spirit of God to give you understanding; and that is a thing most necessary.

10. At the Church's beginning the Holy Spirit fell upon the believers, and they spoke with tongues unlearned, as the Spirit gave them utterance. It was a sign, fitted to the time: all the world's tongues were a fitting signification of the Holy Spirit, because the Gospel of God was to have its course through every tongue in all parts of the earth. The sign was given, and then passed away. We no longer expect that those upon whom the hand is laid, that they may receive the Holy Spirit, will speak with tongues. When we laid our hand upon these "infants,"[893] the Church's newborn members, none

893. Cf. First Homily, chap. 5.

of you (I think) looked to see if they would speak with tongues, or, seeing that they did not, had the perversity to argue that they had not received the Holy Spirit, for if they had received, they would have spoken with tongues as happened at the first. If then the Holy Spirit's presence is no longer testified by such marvels, on what is anyone to ground assurance that he has received the Holy Spirit? Let him inquire of his own heart: if he loves his brother, the Spirit of God abides in him. Let him see himself, examine himself before the eye of God: let him see if there is in him the love of peace and unity, love of the Church that is spread throughout all the world. Let him look for love, not only of the brother present at his door. We have many brothers whom we do not see, yet are we linked to them in the unity of the Spirit. That not all are here with us is natural, but all of us are in one Body, and have one Head in heaven. My brothers, our eyes cannot see themselves; they are as it were unknown to themselves, but we cannot say that they know not themselves in the charity of a single bodily organism. That they know themselves in charity's union is plain from the fact that when both are open, the right eye cannot mark anything unmarked by the left. You cannot turn one upon its object without the other: they go together, and turn together; they have one direction, though their positions are separate. If then all who love God with you share with you a single direction, do not think of your bodily separation from them in space: together you have set your heart's eye upon the light of truth. And so, if you would know that you have received the Spirit, ask your own heart: it may be that the sacrament is yours without the virtue of the sacrament.[894] Ask your heart; and if the love of brother is there, your mind may be at rest. There can be no love without the Spirit of God. Paul cries aloud: "The charity of God is shed abroad in our hearts through the Holy Spirit which is given to us."

11. "Beloved, believe not every Spirit." This is because he had said: "Hereby we know that he abideth in us, from the Spirit which he hath given to us." Now you are to observe how the Spirit himself is recognized: "Beloved, believe not every spirit, but test the spirits, if they be of God." And who is to be the tester of the spirits?

---

894. In schism the sacrament *must* be without its "virtue": within the Church it *may* be.

The task set before us is a hard one, my brethren, and it were good for us to be taught by the apostle how we are to discern the truth. He will teach us, no fear; but first observe with attention, and see how the chicaneries of idle heretics have their source here exposed. Observe: "Beloved, believe not every spirit; but test the spirits if they be of God." The Holy Spirit is described in the Gospel under the symbol of water, when the Lord cried, saying: "If any man thirst, let him come to me and drink: he that believeth on me, from his belly shall flow rivers of living water." And the evangelist expounds the meaning of the saying, in the next verse: "this he spake of the Spirit which they that should believe on him were to receive."[895] There were not many baptized by our Lord: it says, "the Spirit was not yet given, because Jesus was not yet glorified." Some were already baptized, but they had not yet received the Holy Spirit, whom the Lord sent from heaven on the day of Pentecost. For the giving of the Spirit, the Lord's glorifying was waited for. Yet before he was glorified and sent the Spirit, he was calling men to prepare themselves to receive that water of which he said: "Let him that thirsts come unto me and drink"; and, "He that believeth on me, from his belly shall flow rivers of living water." What are "rivers of living water"? What is this "water"? No need to ask me: the Gospel tells you. "This he spake of the Spirit, which they that should believe on him were to receive." There is a difference, then, between the water of the sacrament and the water that signifies the Spirit of God. The water of the sacrament is visible: the water of the Spirit is invisible. The former washes the body, and signifies what happens in the soul: by the Spirit the soul itself is cleansed and nourished. This is the Spirit of God that cannot be possessed by heretics, or any that sever themselves from the Church. Moreover, all they who are so severed, not by their own express act but by reason of their wickedness, and thus become chaff, tossed about within the threshing-floor, and not grain, all these possess not the Spirit—that Spirit signified by our Lord with the name of water.

12. It still remains for us to discover how the presence of God's Spirit is to be tested. We are given an indication, though not perhaps a simple one, but let us see. We shall be brought back to charity, the charity which instructs us, because it is our anointing. But

what is said here? "Test the spirits, if they be of God; for many false prophets have gone out into the world." There we are pointed to all that is heresy or schism. And the means of testing is now to be given. "Hereby is known the Spirit of God." Open your heart's ear! We have been asking in our perplexity, who can know or discern? Now we are to receive a sign. "Hereby is known the Spirit of God. Every spirit that confesseth that Jesus Christ is come in the flesh, is of God. And every spirit that confesseth not that Jesus Christ is come in the flesh, is not of God; and this is Antichrist, of whom ye have heard that he is to come: and now is he in the world." We are listening eagerly for the discernment of spirits, and what we have heard seems to give us no help in discerning them. What are we told? "Every spirit that confesseth that Jesus Christ is come in the flesh, is of God." But then the spirit that is in heretics will be of God; for many of them confess that Jesus Christ is come in the flesh.

13. Ah, my brethren, but we must pay heed to men's actions and not to the noise of their words! Let us ask why Christ came in the flesh; then we may find who are they that deny his coming so. If you pay heed to words, you will hear many a heresy confessing that Christ has come in the flesh, but truth convicts them. Why did Christ come in the flesh? Was he not God? Is it not written of him: "In the beginning was the Word, and the Word was with God, and the Word was God"?[896] Was he not then, as he is now, the food of angels? Did he not come to this world without leaving heaven, and again ascend without leaving us alone? Why then did he come in the flesh? Because it needed that we should be shown the hope of resurrection. He was God, and he came in the flesh. Death was not possible for God: for the flesh it was; and he came in the flesh in order that he might die for us. And how came he to die for us? "Greater charity hath no man than this, that a man lay down his life for his friends."[897] Charity therefore it was that brought him to death; and it follows that whoever has not charity, denies Christ's coming in the flesh.

Now put the question to every heretic.[898] "Did Christ come in the flesh?" "He did: so I believe and confess." "Nay, but you deny it." "How so? You hear me assert it." "Nay, I convict you of your de-

896. Jn 1:1.   897. Jn 15:13.

898. But, of course, Augustine is thinking of Donatists.

nial: you assert it with the voice and deny it with the heart; you assert it in words, but deny it in deed." "In what way do I deny it in deed?" "Because Christ came in the flesh in order that he should die for us, and he died for us because he taught the height of charity: 'Greater charity hath no man than this, that he lay down his life for his friends.' You have not charity, because you break up unity to do yourself honor."

Hence, then, you may know the Spirit that is of God. Tap with your finger on the vessel of earthenware, and see whether the sound it gives be cracked or false. See if it sounds true and whole: see if charity is there. You are removing yourself from the world's unity, you are dividing the Church by schisms, you are rending the Body of Christ. He came in the flesh to gather men together: you cry aloud to scatter them abroad. Therefore the Spirit of God is he that maintains Christ's coming in the flesh, not in word but in deed, not by loud noises but by love. He is not the Spirit of God who denies Jesus Christ's coming in the flesh, whose denial also is not by his tongue but by his life, not in words but in deeds. So it is clear how we are to know the brethren. Many are within the Church that are within in seeming only; but none are without that are not without in reality.[899]

Ninth Homily

I JOHN 4:17-21

1. You will remember, my dear people, that we have still to treat and expound to you, as the Lord shall enable us, the last part of John's Epistle. I have not forgotten my debt, and you should not forget to demand it of me. For that same charity which is the chief, if not the sole theme, of this Epistle, will make me most faithful in acknowledging my debt, and you most welcome in demanding it. Most welcome in demanding: for demands are unpleasant, where there is not charity, but where there is, they are welcome; and for him on whom they are made, though they involve labor, yet the

---

899. Augustine would, however, have added that some of those who are "without" are nevertheless predestinate members of the Church.

labor is lightened or even nullified by charity itself. Can we not see, even in dumb, unreasoning creatures, where there is no spiritual charity but only one that belongs to the fleshly nature, with what eager insistence the mother's milk is demanded by her little ones? Yet however rough be the suckling's onset upon the udder, the mother likes it better than if there were no sucking, no demanding of the debt that charity admits. Indeed we often see the bigger calf butting with its head at the cow's udders, and the mother's body forced upward by the pressure; yet she will never kick her calf away, but if the young one be not there to suck, she will low for him to come to it. Of spiritual charity, the apostle says: "I have become little among you, like a nurse cherishing her children."[900] If such charity be in us, we cannot but love you when you press your demand upon us. Backwardness in you we do not love: it makes us afraid of the failing of your strength.

The occurrence of certain set Lessons for the festal days, which we were obliged to read and discourse upon, has compelled us to leave for a time the text of our Epistle; but now we are to return to the course which was broken, and I ask your devout attention to what remains.

2. "Herein is love made perfect in us, that we may have confidence in the day of judgment; because, as he is, so are we in this world." This tells us how every man may test the progress of charity in him—or rather his own progress in charity: for if charity is God, in God there can be neither progress nor regress, and charity is only said to make progress in you inasmuch as you make progress in charity. Ask therefore how far you have progressed in charity, and listen to the answer of your heart, that you may know the measure of your progress. John has promised to show us how we may know it, saying, "Herein is love made perfect in us." Herein—"that we may have confidence in the day of judgment." In every man that has confidence in the day of judgment, charity is made perfect. To have confidence in the day of judgment is not to fear its coming. There are men who do not believe in a day of judgment, and they cannot have confidence in a day which they do not believe will come. We can leave them aside: may God awaken them into life, but of the dead we will say nothing. They do not be-

900. 1 Thes 2:7.

lieve in a coming day of judgment, and neither fear nor desire that in which they do not believe. But for any man that has begun to believe in a day of judgment, the beginning of belief is the beginning of fear. So long as he fears, he cannot have confidence in the day of judgment, and not yet is charity made perfect in him. Yet there is no cause for despair: where you see a beginning, why despair of the end? And fear itself is a beginning—as Scripture says: "The fear of the Lord is the beginning of wisdom."[901] A man has begun to fear the day of judgment: let fear make him amend himself; let him keep watch against the sins that are his enemies; let him begin to renew the life within him, and as the apostle says, to "mortify his members that are upon the earth."[902] The "members upon the earth" mean the spiritual things of wickedness, the "greediness and uncleanness" and the rest, which the text proceeds to recount. In the measure in which he that has begun to fear the day of judgment mortifies his members upon the earth, the heavenly members arise and gain strength. These heavenly members are all kinds of good works; and as they arise, the man begins to desire that which he was fearing. He feared lest Christ should come and find in him godlessness for condemnation: now he desires Christ's coming, because he is to find godliness ready to be crowned. When the soul has begun to long for Christ's coming, the chaste soul that longs for the husband's embrace, she forswears the adulterer, becoming inwardly virgin in the power of faith, hope, and charity; and now she has confidence in the day of judgment: there is no inner conflict in her prayer, "Thy kingdom come." He who fears the coming of God's kingdom must fear lest this prayer be heard; and it is a strange sort of prayer that fears to be heard. But he who prays in the confidence of charity, truly desires that the kingdom may come. And so, my brothers, do all that you can to train yourselves to long for the day of judgment. For the perfection of charity is attested only when a longing for that day has begun to arise. To long for it is to have confidence in it, and to have confidence in it is to have no alarm of conscience, in the charity that is perfect and pure.

3. "Herein is his love made perfect in us, that we may have confidence in the day of judgment." Wherefore shall we have confidence? "Because, as he is, so are we in this world." The meaning of this is

901. Ps 11:10.   902. Col 3:3ff.

to be understood in reference to charity itself. The Lord says in the Gospel: "If ye love them that love you, what reward have you? Do not the publicans the same?"[903] Then he tells us what he would have us do. "But I say unto you, Love your enemies, and pray for them that persecute you." And for the command to love our enemies, he gives us our pattern in God himself, saying, "that ye may be sons of your Father which is in heaven." God loves his enemies, for God is he "who maketh his sun to rise on the good and the evil, and raineth upon the just and the unjust." Thus the perfection to which God calls us is that of loving our enemies as he has loved his own; and so our confidence in the day of judgment is because, as he is, even so are we in this world. As he loves his enemies, making his sun to rise on the good and the evil, and raining upon the just and the unjust; so we, though we cannot give sun and rain to our enemies, may give them our tears when we pray for them.

4. And now observe what the Epistle says about this very confidence. How are we to recognize the perfection of charity? "There is no fear in charity." What then of the man who has begun to fear the day of judgment? If charity were perfect in him, he would not fear; for perfect charity would make perfect righteousness, and he would have no cause for fear: rather he would have cause for longing that wickedness pass away and God's kingdom come. Therefore, "there is no fear in charity." But this is true, not of charity's beginnings: "perfect charity," he continues, "casteth out fear." Fear, then, may be a starting-point; for "the fear of the Lord is the beginning of wisdom." Fear, as it were, prepares the place for charity; but when charity has taken up its dwelling, the fear that prepared the place for it is expelled. As one grows, the other diminishes: as charity moves to the center, fear is driven outside. The greater the charity, the lesser the fear: the lesser the charity, the greater the fear. But if there has been no fear, there is no way for charity to enter. When we sew a seam, the thread must be let in by the needle: the needle goes in first, but it must come out if the thread is to follow. So fear takes first hold upon the mind, but does not stay there, because the purpose of its entry was to let charity in. And once the quiet of fearlessness is established in the soul, what joy is ours, whether in this world or in the world to come! Even in this world,

903. Mt 5:44ff.

who shall harm us if we are filled with charity? Hear the apostle's triumphant cry: "Who shall separate us from the charity of Christ? Shall tribulation, or distress, or persecution, or hunger, or nakedness, or peril, or sword?"[904] And again, in the words of Peter: "And who is he that can harm you, if ye be followers of that which is good?"[905]

"There is no fear in love: but perfect love casteth out fear; because fear hath torment." The heart is tormented by consciousness of sins: justification has not yet come, there is that within which pricks and stings. So in the verses of the psalm which speak of the perfecting of righteousness: "Thou hast turned for me my mourning into joy: thou hast stripped off my sackcloth, and girded me with gladness, so that my glory may sing unto thee, and my pricking is ended."[906] Pricking is ended, when the goad of conscience is stilled. Fear is a goad; but you are not to fear, for charity enters, with healing for the wound of fear. The fear of God wounds like the surgeon's knife: it cuts out the festering part, and seems to enlarge the wound. When there was festering in the body, the wound was smaller, but it was dangerous. The pain was not so sharp as now at the touch of the surgeon's knife. The treating of it may hurt more than if it had no treatment; but the added pain in the application of the cure serves to end pain for good by the recovery of health. Therefore let fear take hold of your heart, that it may give an entry to charity: let the surgeon's knife make way for the healing scar. Such is our Surgeon's skill, that not even a scar may show: you have only to submit yourself to his hand. For if you are without fear, you will not be able to be justified. That is the word of Scripture: "He that is without fear shall not be able to be justified."[907] So there must needs first enter fear, by means of which charity can come in. Fear is the remedy, charity is health. "He that feareth is not made perfect in love." And that is because "fear hath torment," like the surgeon's incision.

5. There is indeed another text which may seem to contradict this, if it be not rightly understood. We read in a certain passage of

904. Rom 8:35.   905. 1 Pt 3:13.   906. Ps 30:11ff.

907. Eccl 1:22. The text has: "Unrighteous anger shall not be able to be justified." Augustine may be quoting from memory as often: the context in Ecclesiasticus is "the fear of the Lord."

the Psalms: "the fear of the Lord is pure, enduring for ever and ever."[908] That points us to an everlasting fear, that yet is pure. But if so, is there a contradiction to it in the words of our Epistle: "there is no fear in charity, but perfect charity casteth out fear"? Let us inquire of both these oracles of God. The Spirit that speaks is one, though there be two books, two mouths, two tongues. One and the same breath may blow two flutes, and cannot one and the same Spirit fill two hearts and set two tongues in motion? But if two flutes, filled by one spirit, one breathing, may sound in harmony, is it possible that two tongues, moved by the Spirit of God, should be discordant? There must then here be some harmony, some concord, that demands a sympathetic ear. The Spirit of God has filled by his inspiration two hearts and two mouths, has moved two tongues: of one tongue we hear, "there is no fear in charity, but perfect charity casteth out fear"; of the other we hear, "the fear of the Lord is pure, enduring for ever and ever." Well! Is there a discord between the sounds? No: you must listen with care and observe the melody. Not for nothing does the word "pure" come in the one saying, and not in the other: there must be one kind of fear that is called pure, and another kind that is not. Let us distinguish these two fears, and then we may grasp the harmony of the flutes. How shall we do this? Listen, my people. There are men who fear God because they fear to be cast into hell, to burn with the devil in everlasting fire. This is the fear that makes an opening for charity; but it enters only to go out again. If as yet it is the thought of punishment that makes you fear God, not yet do you love him whom so you fear: you are not longing for good things, you are but apprehensive of evil. But that very apprehension leads you to amend yourself, and so to begin to long for the good things; and when you begin to do that, the pure fear will arise in you—the fear of losing what is good. It is one thing, you see, to fear God, lest he send you to hell with the devil: it is another to fear God, lest he depart from you. The first fear is not yet pure, for it comes not of the love of god but of the fear of punishment. But when you fear God lest his presence leave you, you are embracing him, and longing to enjoy him.

6. The difference between these two fears—the one which charity casts out, and the other pure and enduring forever—may best

be shown by thinking of two married women, differing in character. Suppose one of these two to be drawn toward adultery, to take pleasure in the wicked desire, but to fear the judgment of her husband. She fears her husband, but this fear comes of her still loving wickedness; to her the husband's presence is not welcome but burdensome; and if she does live in sin, she fears her husband's coming. (Of such are they who fear the coming of the day of judgment.) Suppose the other to love her husband, to own her duty to him in pure embraces, never admitting a stain of infidelity upon her thoughts. This one will long for her husband's presence; yet there will be fear in her no less than in the other. How are the two fears to be distinguished? You may put the same question to both of them: "Do you fear for your husband?" Both will answer: "I do"—the same words, but with a different meaning: for if you go on to ask "Why?" the one will say, "I am afraid of his coming," and the other, "I am afraid of his going away." One says, "I fear to be found guilty," the other, "I fear to be left alone." Now apply this to the mind of the Christian, and you will find the fear that charity casts out, and the other pure fear that endures forever and ever.

7. Let us then address ourselves first to those who fear God with the fear of the woman who finds pleasure in wickedness, fearing her husband's judgment on her guilt. "Soul," we will say, "thou that fearest God for his judgment, as the woman who finds pleasure in wickedness fears her husband: if such a woman be misliking to thee, mislike thyself. Would you have your own wife fear you for that reason? Would you not rather she were chaste for love of you and not for fear? Then show yourself to God as you would that your wife should be to you. Pray God to look upon you, and turn his face from your sins. There is only one way of deserving that God's face be turned from your sins, and that is never to turn your own face from them. You have the very words in the psalm: "For I confess my wickedness, and my sin is ever before me."[909] Do you make confession, and God will pardon.

8. Such is our address to that soul in which is still the fear that does not endure forever and ever, but is shut out and banished by charity. Let us speak now to that other soul which possesses already the pure fear, enduring forever and ever. Can we suppose that this

909. Ps 51:3.

soul is to be found and addressed? Is there such, do you think, among our people? In this church? In this whole earth? Such there must be, though unseen. It is winter, but within there is freshness and vigor at the root. Maybe our words will reach that soul's ears; but wherever it be, I would fain come upon it, and rather than have it listen to me, lend it my own ears. It should teach me rather than learn of me. A holy soul, all aflame with longing for God's kingdom, it shall hear not me but God himself speaking to it, and comforting its patient sojourn on this earth with words like these: "Already thou wouldest I should come, and I know that thou wouldest it: I know what thou art, that thou mayest await my coming with confidence. I know that the waiting is irksome to thee: yet wait the rather, and be patient; I come, and I come quickly." Yet to the lover it seems slow. You may hear that soul's yearning song, like a lily among the thorns—hear her sighs: "I will make music with understanding in the unspotted way: when wilt thou come unto me?"[910] But in the unspotted way there is no need for fearing; because perfect charity casteth out fear. Yet even when she has reached the embrace of her beloved, she will fear, though without anxiety. She will take heed and watch against her iniquity, lest she fall again into sin: fearing, not to be cast into hellfire, but to be left by him alone. So there will be in her the "pure fear that endureth for ever and ever."

Such is the music, the harmonious music, of our two flutes. Both tell of a kind of fear; but one tells of the soul's fear of judgment, the other of the soul's fear of desertion. One is the fear which charity excludes; the other is the fear that endures forever and ever.

9. "We are to love, because he first loved us." How indeed should we love, had he not first loved us? Through loving we have become friends; but it was as enemies that he loved us, in order that we might be made friends. He first loved us, and bestowed on us the power to love him. As yet we loved him not: through loving we are made fair. An ugly and misshapen man may love a beautiful woman, or an ugly and misshapen woman of dull complexion may love a handsome man; but love can make beautiful neither the man nor the woman. The man loves a fair woman and when he looks on himself in the glass, he is ashamed to raise his face to the beauty of

910. Ps 101:1ff.

her whom he loves. He can do nothing to make himself beautiful: if he waits for beauty to come to him, waiting will make him old and his face plainer. There is nothing he can do, no advice you can give him but to restrain his passion and venture no more to set his love upon an unequal match: if he loves and would marry a wife, he must desire modesty in her and not physical charm. But our soul, my brethren, is ugly through its iniquity: through loving God it is made fair. What manner of love is this, that transforms the lover into beauty! God is ever beautiful, never ugly, never changing. He that is ever beautiful, he first loved us—and loved none that were not ugly and misshapen. Yet the end of his love was not to leave us ugly, but to transform us, creating beauty in place of deformity. And how shall we win this beauty, but through loving him who is ever beautiful? Beauty grows in you with the growth of love; for charity itself is the soul's beauty. "We are to love, because he first loved us."

10. "If any man say, I love God" . . . Ask anyone you will to tell you if he loves God: he will make loud profession, "I do love God, God knows it!" But there is another matter on which he may be questioned. "If any man says, I love God, and hateth his brother, he is a liar." Why is he a liar? Because "he that loves not his brother whom he sees, how can he love God whom he sees not?" Does it then follow that he who loves his brother loves God also? Of necessity he must love God: of necessity he must love love itself. He cannot love his brother and not love love: he cannot help loving love. And if he loves love, he needs must love God: in loving love, he is loving God. You cannot have forgotten the words that came a little earlier: "God is love." If God is love, whoever loves love, loves God. Therefore love your brother, and have no other care. You cannot say, I love my brother, but not God. Just as to say, "I love God," when you do not love your brother, is to lie; so when you say, "I love my brother," you are deceived, if you imagine that you do not love God. You love your brother, and must needs love love itself; but love is God; therefore whoever Loves his brother must needs be loving God.

If you do not love the brother whom you see, how can you love God whom you do not see? Why does a man not see God? Because he has not love. He has not love because he does not love his brother; and it follows that the reason for his not seeing God is that he has not love. If he had love, he must see God; for God is love. By love the heart's eye must continually be cleansed and strengthened for the sight of that changeless Being, in whose presence the lover may ever delight, and enjoy it in the society of angels unto all eternity. But now he must run his course, so that one day he may rejoice in his true fatherland. He may not love his pilgrimage or the way along it. Nothing may be sweet to him save the God who calls us, until the day that we cleave fast to him, saying with the psalmist: "Thou hast destroyed all them that commit fornication against thee."[911] The fornicators against him are they that turn aside and love the world. Your part is told you in the verse that follows: "for me it is good to cleave fast unto God." That is my whole good, to cleave unto God, looking for nought else. If you ask, "Why cleave to God?" and a man should say "For that which he will give me," ask him again what God will give him. God made the heaven, God made the earth: what is there for him to give you? If already you cleave fast to him, what better thing can you find? If you could, he would give it.

11. "He that loves not his brother whom he sees, how can he love God whom he sees not? And this commandment we have from him, that he who loves God, love his brother also." Proudly you spoke the word, "I love God"—and you hate your brother! Murderer that you are, how can you love God? Did you not hear earlier in the Epistle, that "he that hateth his brother is a murderer"? "Indeed, indeed," you say, "I love God, though I hate my brother." Indeed, indeed, if you hate your brother you do not love God. Let me prove it by another text: again we read that "He gave us a commandment that we should love one another."[912] Can you love him whose commandment you hate? Can anyone say, "I love the emperor, but I hate his laws"? It is by the observation of his laws, published through his empire, that the emperor is aware of your love for him. Our emperor's law is this: "A new commandment give I unto you, that ye love one another."[913] You say you love Christ: then keep his commandment and love your brother. If you do not love your brother, how can you love him whose commandment you despise?

My brothers, I can never tire of speaking in Christ's name of charity. The more you covet possession of it, the more (I hope) will

911. Ps 73:27ff.   912. 1 Jn 3:23.   913. Jn 13:34.

charity itself grow within you, casting out fear, so that there remain the pure fear that endures forever and ever. Let us bear this world, bear all its afflictions, bear the offenses of our temptations. Let us never go back on our journeying; let us hold to the Church's unity, hold to Christ, hold to charity. Let us not be sundered from the members of his Bride, nor sundered from the faith, that we may make our boast in his presence; and so we shall abide safe in him— in this present time by faith, and in the time to come by sight, whereof in the gift of the Holy Spirit we have so sure a pledge.

Tenth Homily

I JOHN 5:1–3

1. Those of you who were present yesterday will remember, no doubt, the place our exposition has reached in the course of this Epistle. "He that loveth not his brother whom he sees, how can he love God whom he does not see? And this commandment we have from him, that he who loves God, love his brother also." That was the verse at which we ended: now let us see what comes next.

"Every one that believeth that Jesus is the Christ, is born of God." Who is the man that does not believe that Jesus is the Christ? He that does not live as Christ commanded. There are many that say, "I believe," but faith without works cannot save. The work of faith is love, according to the Apostle Paul's saying: "Faith which worketh through love."[914] That is the faith that Jesus is the Christ, as it is believed by Christians who are such not in name only but in deed and in life. It is not as the devils believe: they believe, as Scripture says, and tremble.[915] One might suppose that devils' faith could go no further than the confession: "We know who thou art, the Son of God."[916] What the devils said was what Peter said. When the Lord asked who he was and what men called him, the disciples answered: "Some call thee John the Baptist, others Elias, others Jeremias or one of the prophets."[917] And when he asked again, "And whom say ye that I am?" Peter answered and said, "Thou art the Christ, the Son of the living God." Then came the Lord's saying to him: "Blessed art thou,

914. Gal 5:26.   915. Jas 2:19.   916. Mt 8:19.   917. Mt 16:13ff.

Simon Bar-Jona; for flesh and blood hath not revealed it unto thee, but my Father which is in heaven." See what commendation is given to this faith of Peter's: "Thou art Peter, and upon this rock will I build my church." "Upon this rock" means "Upon this faith," upon the saying: "Thou art the Christ, the Son of the living God." "Upon this rock," says the Lord, "I will build my church." A high commendation indeed! Thus Peter says, "Thou art the Christ, the Son of the living God"; and the devils say, "We know who thou art, the Son of God, the Holy One of God." What Peter says, the devils say also: the words are the same, but not the thought. Peter's words, we may be sure, were spoken with love; for love goes with the Christian's faith, but not with the devils'. For Peter's words were meant to embrace the Christ, the devils' were meant to make him depart from them. For before saying, "We know who thou art, thou art the Son of God," they had said: "What have we to do with thee? Why art thou come before the time to destroy us?" It is one thing to confess Christ in order that you may hold to him: another thing to confess Christ in order that you may thrust him from you. You see then that the words of our text, "He that believeth," denote a faith of a special kind, not the faith that may be held by many. Therefore, my brothers, let no heretic say to you, "We also believe." I have given you the example of the devils, that you may examine the deeds of men's lives before rejoicing at the words of their belief.

2. Let us see then what is meant by belief in Christ, by belief that Jesus is the Christ. Our text goes on: "Every one that believeth that Jesus is the Christ, is born of God." But what does this belief mean? "And every one that loveth him that begat him, loveth him that is begotten of him." With faith the apostle straightway conjoins love; for without love faith is vain. The Christian's faith has love together with it: the devils' faith is loveless. Those who do not believe at all are in worse state than the devils, falling behind them in apprehension. The man who will not believe in Christ has not come so far as to do what the devils do. He may reach the point of believing, yet still hate him in whom he believes: the confession of his faith being through fear of punishment, not love for the offered prize; and now he is like the devils who dreaded the punishment in store for them. To such faith love must be added, so that it becomes the faith that Paul describes, the "faith that worketh through love"; and then you will have the Christian, the citizen of Jerusalem and

fellow citizen of angels, the pilgrim toiling eagerly on his way. Join him, for he is your good comrade; travel with him—if only you be what he is.

3. "Every one that loveth him that begat him, loveth him that is begotten of him. Hereby we know that we love the sons of God." What does this mean, my brothers? The apostle has just spoken of the Son of God, not of sons: the one Christ was set forth for our contemplation in the words, "Every one that believeth that Jesus is the Christ is born of God; and every one that loveth him that begat"—that is, the Father—"loveth him that is begotten of him"—that is, his Son our Lord Jesus Christ. And he goes on: "hereby we know that we love the sons of God." We should have expected: "Hereby we know that we love the Son of God." But John, having just spoken of the Son of God, now speaks of God's sons. It is because the sons of God are the Body of God's only Son; because he is Head, and we are members, the Son of God is still one. Therefore to love the sons of God is to love the Son of God; to love the Son of God is to love the Father; none can love the Father unless he love the Son; and he that loves the Son, loves also the sons of God. These sons of God are the members of God's Son; and he that loves them, by loving becomes himself a member: through love he becomes a part of the structure of Christ's Body. And thus the end will be the one Christ, loving himself, for the love of the members for one another is the love of the Body for itself.[918] "If one member suffer, all the members suffer with it; and if one member have glorying, all the members rejoice with it."[919] On which the apostle concludes, "Now ye are the body of Christ, and members of him." So John, speaking a little earlier of brotherly love, has said, "He that loveth not his brother whom he sees, how can he love God whom he sees not?" If you love your brother, can it be said that you do so and yet do not love Christ? Impossible—when it is Christ's members that you love. Loving the members of Christ, you are loving Christ; loving Christ, you are loving the Son of God; loving the Son of God, you are loving the Father. There can be no separation of love: you may choose for yourself what you will love, and all the

918. This celebrated passage is the crown of Augustine's doctrine of the unity of Christ and his Church.

919. 1 Cor 12:26ff.

rest will follow. You may say, "I love God only, God the Father."
That is not true. If you love him, you cannot love him only: if you
love the Father, you are loving the Son also. Suppose you grant
that, and say, "I love the Father and I love the Son, but nothing
more: God the Father, and God the Son, our Lord Jesus Christ,
who has ascended into heaven and sits on the right hand of the Father, the Word through whom all things were made, the Word that
was made flesh and dwelt among us: I love nothing more." That is
not true. If you love the Head, you love the members: if you do not
love the members, neither do you love the Head. How can you not
tremble at the voice of the Head, crying from heaven on the members' behalf: "Saul, Saul, why persecutest thou me"?[920] The persecutor of his members he called the persecutor of himself: that was
to call the lover of his members the lover of himself. And who are
his members, my brethren, you know—they are none other than
the Church of God.

"Hereby we know that we love the sons of God, because we love
God." How so? Are not the sons of God a different thing from
God? Yes, but he who loves God, loves his commandments; and
what are they? "A new commandment give I unto you, that ye love
one another." None may make one love an excuse from another.
Christian love is altogether of one piece, and as itself is compacted
into a unity, so it makes into one all that are linked to it, like a flame
fusing them together. The lump of gold is fused in the furnace, and
a single object is made of it, but unless the fire of charity is kindled,
there can be no fusing of the many into one.

4. We are told, then, how we may know that we love the sons of
God. It is "because we love God, and keep his commandments."
We are troubled and wearied by the difficulty of keeping God's
commandment. But listen! Friend, you go through toil and labor,
for the love of what? Of avarice. That love must bring toil to the
lover: there is no toil in the love of God. Avarice will enjoin upon
you the endurance of labors, dangers, wear and tear, and troubles;
and you will obey, but to what purpose? To gain the wherewithal
to fill your purse, and to lose your peace of mind. Peace of mind, I
dare say, you had more before you were rich than after you began
to be wealthy. See what avarice has charged you with: a houseful of

920. Acts 9:4.

goods and the fear of thieves; gain of money, and loss of sleep. There is what avarice bade you do, and you have done it. And what is God's charge? "Love me! You may love money and go after it, yet maybe not find it. Whoever seeks me, I am with him. You may love place and position: maybe you will never attain to them. No man has ever loved me and failed of my attaining. You would have a patron or a powerful friend, and you must go about to approach him by way of some inferior. Love me (God says to you); I have not to be approached through any go-between: love itself sets you in my presence." My brothers, there can be no sweetness greater than such love. Much to the point are the words of the psalm you have just heard: "The unrighteous have spoken to me of delights; but not as thy law, O Lord."[921] The law of God is God's commandment, and God's commandment is that new commandment, called new because it gives renewal: "A new commandment give I unto you, that ye love one another." That this is indeed the law of God is confirmed by the apostle's saying: "Bear ye one another's burdens, and so shall ye fulfill the law of Christ."[922] That is the consummation of all our works—love. There is the end, for which and unto which we run our course: when we reach it we shall have rest.

7. "For this is the love of God, that we keep his commandments." You have heard the saying: "On these two commandments hang all the Law and the Prophets."[923]—You are spared the turning from one Scripture page to another. "On these two commandments": and they are: "Thou shalt love the Lord thy God with all thy heart and all thy soul and all thy mind," and "Thou shalt love thy neighbor as thyself." These are the commandments of which the whole of our Epistle speaks. Hold fast then to love, and set your minds at rest. You need not fear doing ill to anyone; for who can do any ill to the person whom he loves? Love, and you cannot but do well. You may rebuke, but that will be the act of love, not of harshness: you may use the rod, but it will only be for discipline, for the love of love itself will not suffer you to pass over the lack of discipline in another. Sometimes there is a kind of contrariness apparent in the products of hatred and of love: hatred may use fair words and love may sound harshly. A man may hate his enemy and pretend friendship toward him: he may commend him when he sees

921. Ps 119:85.   922. Gal 6:2.   923. Mt 22

him do wrong, for he welcomes his thoughtlessness; he is glad to see him rush headlong in pursuit of his desires, where he may fall beyond hope of recovery. He will, in the words of the psalm, "commend the sinner in the desires of his soul";[924] he will smooth his going with the oil of flattery—hating, yet commending. Another, seeing his friend do the like, will call him back; and if the friend will not hear, he may use the language of reproof, he may denounce, he may even prosecute, for sometimes things may come to the point where there is no avoiding an action at law.[925] Thus we may see hatred speaking softly, and charity prosecuting, but neither soft speeches nor harsh reproofs are what you have to consider. Look for the spring, search out the root from which they proceed. The fair words of the one are designed for deceiving, the prosecution of the other is aimed at reformation.

My brothers, it is not for my preaching to work the enlargement of your hearts. Ask God that you may love one another, and he will grant it. You are to love all men, even your enemies—not because they *are* your brothers, but in order that they may be, so that brotherly love may ever burn within you, whether for him who is already a brother, or for your enemy, that love may turn him into one. Wherever you love a brother, you love a friend. Perhaps he stands already with you, linked to you already in the catholic unity of the Church: if his life accords with it, he whom you love is already a brother and not an enemy. Or if your love is given to one who has not yet believed in Christ, or who has believed only as the devils believe, you will reprove his folly: you will love him, and with a brotherly love, for though he is not yet a brother, the aim of your love is that he may be made one. Thus all our brotherly love is love for Christian people, for all the members of Christ. The learning of charity, my brothers, its vigor, its flowers, its fruit, its beauty, its pleasantness, its sustenance, its drink, its food, its loving embraces—all these can never cloy. And if God grants us such delights upon our pilgrimage, what joys await us in our homeland!

8. So, my brothers, let us make haste: let us make haste, and love the Christ. That Christ is Jesus; and who is he? The Word of God. The manner of his coming to our sick world is that "the word was

924. Ps 10:3.   925. Augustine has the Donatists in mind.

made flesh, and dwelt among us."[926] Thus has the prophecy of Scripture been fulfilled: "it behooved Christ to suffer, and to rise again the third day from the dead."[927] Where is the place of his Body? Where do his members carry on their laboring, and where must you be, to have over you the Head? ". . . and that repentance and remission of sins should be preached in his name throughout all nations, beginning at Jerusalem." There must your charity spread itself abroad. The word of Christ, the word of the psalm, that is, of God's Spirit, proclaims: "Thy commandment is exceeding broad." And there are men who set the boundary of charity in Africa![928] If you would love Christ, stretch out your charity over all the world: for Christ's members are spread the world over. If your love is for a part only, you are sundered: if sundered, you are not in the Body; if not in the Body, you are not under the Head. There is no profit in the faith of a blasphemer: you would worship him in the Head and you blaspheme him in the Body. He loves his Body: you may sever yourself from the Body of Christ, but the Head cannot be severed from his own Body. "In vain do you honor me," cries the Head from above you, "in vain do you honor me." Imagine one that would kiss your head and trample on your feet—crushing your feet with nailed boots, yet seeking to embrace your head and kiss it. Would you not break through the speech of pretended honor with the cry, "What are you about, sir? You are trampling on me!" You would not say, "You trample on my head," for honor was being done to your head; but that head would make protest more for the trampled members, than acknowledge the honor done to itself. Would not the head itself cry out, "I want none of your honoring! Cease to trample on me!" You may answer if you will, "Where is the trampling?": you may tell the head you sought to kiss it, to embrace it. But have you not sense to see that what you seek to embrace is all of a piece in structural unity with that on which you trample? You honor me above, you trample me below! And the pain of this exceeds the pleasure of that, for the honored head suffers for the trampled feet. The tongue will exclaim, "That hurts me!"—not "That hurts my foot," but "That hurts me." No use to ask the tongue who touched it, who struck it, pricked it, or stabbed

926. Jn 1:14.   927. Lk 24:46ff.   928. Donatists.

it. The answer is, No one: but it is linked to those parts that suffer trampling, and how should it not suffer pain, when there is no separation between it and them?

9. Our Lord Jesus Christ, at his ascension into heaven on the fortieth day, commended his body to lie on the earth where he had worn it; and he did so, because he saw that many would pay him honor for his ascension, and that their honoring must be vain if they tread underfoot his members upon earth. And to forestall the misprision of worshipping the Head in heaven while trampling the feet upon earth, he declared where his members should be found. Before his ascension he spoke his last words—the last he was to speak on earth. The Head, ready to ascend into heaven, commended his members upon earth, and then departed. From that time you will not find Christ speaking on earth; he will speak indeed, but it will be from heaven. And then, what will be the cause of his so speaking? It will be because his members were being trod down upon earth. To Saul the persecutor he spoke from on high: "Saul, Saul, why persecutest thou me?"[929] "I have ascended into heaven but still I lie upon earth. Here I sit on the Father's right hand; but there still I hunger and thirst, and go a stranger." In what way, then, did he before ascending commend his Body to us? When the disciples asked him, "Lord, wilt thou show thyself at this time, and when shall be the kingdom of Israel?"[930] he answered, on the point of his departure, "It is not yours to know the time which the Father hath set in his own power; but ye shall receive the virtue of the Holy Spirit, coming down upon you, and ye shall be my witnesses" . . . (see now the spreading abroad of his Body, the region wherein he will not have men trample on him) . . . "ye shall be my witnesses in Jerusalem, and into all Judaea, and Samaria, and to the ends of the whole earth": "This is where I who now ascend shall yet lie. I ascend because I am the Head: my Body yet lies here below. And where? Even through the whole earth." Take heed, then, lest you strike that Body, lest you do despite to it, lest you trample upon it: for those are Christ's last words on the eve of his going into heaven. Have in your mind's eye a sick man, lying at home in his bed, wasted with illness, near to death, breathing hard, his soul at his very lips. Suppose it chances that the thought of something dear

929. Acts 9:4.   930. Acts 1:6ff.

to him, greatly beloved, comes into his mind; and he calls for his heirs and says to them, "Do this, I pray you." He struggles to keep the soul within him until those words are clearly spoken and confirmed, and when he has so spoken his last, he breathes away his life, and his body is borne to the grave. Will not his heirs hold fast the memory of the dying man's last words? If any man should come and say to them, "Don't do it!"—what will they answer? "Not do that which my father charged me with his last breath— the thing that last sounded in my ears as my father left this world? However it be with any other words of his, those last words bind me in a special degree; for after them I never saw him or heard him speak again."

My brothers, think, as you have Christian hearts: if the words of a man on his way to the grave are so sweet, so welcome, of such weighty moment, to his heirs, what must be to the heirs of Christ the last words of him who was leaving them, not to return to the grave but to ascend into heaven! For the man who has lived and died, his soul is carried elsewhere while his body is laid in the earth: it matters not to him whether those last words of his are performed or not; quite other now are his doings, or his sufferings. Either he rejoices in Abraham's bosom, or in eternal fire he longs for a drop of water; and his dead body lies unfeeling in the grave. Yet his last dying words are faithfully observed. For what then can men look, who pay no observance to the last words of him who sits in heaven, looking from above to see whether they be contemned, or not contemned—the words of him who said: "Saul, Saul, why persecutest thou me?", who lays up for judgment all that he sees his members suffer?

10. And yet such men say, "What have we done? It is we who have suffered persecution, not inflicted it." Unhappy men, you are the persecutors—persecutors above all because you have divided the Church! The sword of the tongue is more powerful than any blade of steel. Hagar, Sarah's maid, was proud; and because of her pride she was afflicted by her mistress. That was discipline, not punishment. And so when she had gone away from her mistress, what did the angel bid her? "Return unto thy mistress."[931] Even so you, carnal souls like that proud maidservant, have no cause for

931. Gn 16:4ff.

your fury, though you may for discipline's sake have suffered some vexation. Return to your mistress, keep the Lord's peace. The Gospels are set out, we read of where the Church extends: you argue against us and call us "betrayers."[932] What then have we betrayed? Christ commends to you his Church, and you will not believe him: am I to believe your maligning of my forefathers? If you would have me believe your story of "betrayers," do you first believe the Christ. Which is the chiefer authority? Christ is God, you are men: which most deserves belief? Christ has spread his Church over the whole world: if it were I that said so, you might disregard it; but when the Gospel speaks, you should take heed. And what says the Gospel? "It behoved Christ to suffer and rise again the third day from the dead, and that repentance and forgiveness of sins should be preached in his name."[933] Where there is forgiveness of sins, there is the Church. If you ask why, it was to the Church that the word was spoken: "I will give unto thee the keys of the kingdom of heaven; and whatsoever thou shalt loose on earth shall be loosed in heaven, and whatsoever thou shalt loose on earth shall be loosed in heaven, and whatsoever thou shalt bind on earth shall be bound in heaven."[934] Where then is this forgiveness of sins extended? "Throughout all nations, beginning at Jerusalem." There is Christ's word for you to believe. But you know well that if you believed Christ, you could have nothing to say about the "betrayers"; and so you would have me believe your slanderings of my fathers rather than yourself believe the promises of Christ.

932. The Donatist charge against the Catholics as all tainted with *traditio*, the surrendering of the Scriptures.

933. Lk 24:47.   934. Mt 16:19.

Selected Sermons

Sermon 33

On What Is Written In the Psalm: "O God, I Will Sing You a New Song"   [405–11 A.D.]

CHARITY SINGS THE NEW SONG

1. As it is written, "O God, I will sing you a new song, on a harp of ten strings I will play to you,"[935] we take the harp of ten strings to be the Ten Commandments of the law. Now to sing and play is usually the occupation of lovers. The old man, you see, is in fear, the new is in love.[936] In this way also we distinguish the two testaments or covenants, the old and the new, which the apostle says are allegorically represented by the sons of Abraham, one born of the slave woman, the other of the free; *"which,"* he says, *"are two covenants."*[937] Slavery, surely, goes with fear, freedom with love, seeing that the apostle says, "You have not received the spirit of slavery again in fear, but you have received the spirit of sonship by adoption, in which we cry out, Abba, Father."[938] And Johns says, "There is no fear in charity, but perfect charity throws out fear."[939] So it is charity that sings the new song.

True, that slavish fear embodied in the old man can indeed have the harp of ten strings, because that law of the Ten Commandments was also given to the Jews according to the flesh, but it cannot sing to its accompaniment the new song. It is under the law and cannot fulfill the law. It carries the instrument but doesn't manage to play it; it is burdened, not embellished, with the harp. But any under grace, not under law, they are the ones who fulfill the law, because for them it is not a weight to shoulder but an honor to wear; it is not a rack for their fears, but a frame for their love. Fired by the spirit of love, they are already singing the new song on the harp of ten strings.

935. Ps 114:9.   936. See Col 3:9. Note the characteristic contrast between fear and love. He has a number of variations on this theme. He will sometimes say that these are the two basic passions, or emotions or drives, neither being good or bad in itself; it all depends on what you fear and what you love. Here he is treating fear as something to be outgrown and ousted by love.

937. Gal 4:22–23.   938. Rom 8:15.   939. 1 Jn 4:18.

THE FULLNESS OF THE LAW IS CHARITY

2. That, you see, is precisely what the apostle says: "For whoever loves the other has fulfilled the law. For, 'You shall not commit adultery, you shall not commit murder, you shall not steal, you shall not covet,' and any other commandment there is, are summed up in this saying: 'You shall love your neighbor as yourself.' Love of neighbor works no evil. Now the fullness of the law is charity."[940] Again, it is because the Lord had said, "I did not come to undo the law, but to fulfill it,"[941] that he gave his disciples the kind of commandment which would enable the law to be fulfilled by them: "A new commandment," he said, "I give to you, that you should love one another."[942]

So it's not surprising if the new commandment sings the new song, because as we have said, the Ten Commandments of the law are the harp of ten strings, and the fullness of the law is love. The apostle, though, only wanted to mention a few of the strings, the others to be taken as read, when he said, "You shall not commit adultery, you shall not commit murder," etc. Because just as there are two commandments of love, on which depend, as the Lord says, the whole Law and the Prophets,[943] and thereby he shows clearly enough that love is the fullness of the law, so too those Ten Commandments were given on two tables;[944] three, that is, are said to have been inscribed on the table and seven on the other. Just as the three first belong to love of God, so the seven others are assigned to love of neighbor.

THE FIRST THREE COMMANDMENTS

3. The first of the three is: *"Hear, Israel: the Lord your God is one Lord."*[945] *"You shall not make yourself an idol, or a likeness of anything, neither things in heaven above nor things on earth beneath,"*[946] and the other points by which it binds us to the worship of one God, after fornication with idols has been given up. The second commandment is: *"You shall not take the name of the Lord your God in vain."*[947] The third is about keeping the Sabbath.

---

940. Rom 13:8–10.   941. Mt 5:17.   942. Jn 13:34.   943. Mt 22:40.

944. Ex 31:18.   945. Dt 6:4.

946. Dt 5:8. Augustine, quoting from memory, is mixing up two texts, or rather conflating them. He substitutes the first clause of the famous Shema, Dt 6:4, for the first two clauses of the Decalogue, Dt 5:6–7.   947. Dt 5:11.

I think it's because of the Trinity that there are three commandments belonging to love of God. The unity of the Godhead has its
basis from the Father, and that is why the first commandment
speaks above all about the one God. Then the second commandment warns us against thinking of the Son of God as creature, by
taking him to be less than equal to the Father. *"For every creature,"*
as the apostle says, *"is subject to vanity."*[948] And here we are commanded not to take the name of the Lord our God in vain. Finally,
the Gift of God, which is the Holy Spirit, promises everlasting rest,
which is represented by the Sabbath.

So we keep the Sabbath spiritually if we do not perform servile
works. These, of course, were forbidden to the Jews on the Sabbath
even in the literal sense. But if you wish to understand the spiritual
sense of servile works, listen to the Lord saying *"Everyone who commits sin is the slave of sin."*[949] Now sin is not only something that
people easily recognize as such in some shameful or unjust deed,
but also what has the appearance of a good work, but is done for a
temporal reward and not for the sake of everlasting rest. You see,
whatever people do, if they do it simply with a view to obtaining an
earthly advantage, they do it in a servile or slavish fashion, and
thereby they are failing to keep the Sabbath.[950]

For God, surely, is to be loved freely and for nothing, and the

948. Rom 8:20.   949. Jn 8:34.

950. The point Augustine is making here is that "sin" does not consist just of
breaking laws or breaking rules, that is to say, doing things that are "obviously
wrong." Sin consists essentially of turning away from God, and consequently of
ignoring God or not taking him and our relations with him into account. It is not,
therefore, simply a moral or ethical, let alone a legal concept, but is strictly speaking
a theological concept. So here: doing good simply for the sake of furthering one's
career, for example, is to be acting and living in a context in which God doesn't
figure at all—an unreal context, therefore, in Augustine's view, a context of vanity,
of nothingness, of godlessness, of sin. But if you do good, without any explicitly
conscious thought of God, or his reward, simply because it is good, because it is
right, whether or not it furthers your career or brings you any other temporal benefit, then implicitly you are doing it in a context that includes God, because he is
the good of all goods. And if you do good explicitly "for the sake of everlasting
rest" and to earn a heavenly reward—there is just a little caution that Augustine
doesn't mention here, but is perhaps necessary for the devout: beware of thinking
of that heavenly reward as just being a temporal advantage, a furthering of your
career or feathering of your nest to the *n*th degree. What it is, is God. We should
do good for God's sake, and that is the same as doing it simply because it is good.

soul can only find rest in what it loves. But eternal rest can only be given it in loving God, who alone is eternal. And that is perfect sanctification and the spiritual Sabbath of Sabbaths. Since therefore we are sanctified in the Holy Spirit, surely the fact that of the three commandments referring to God the third is the commandment about the Sabbath should prompt anyone to suspect a profound mysterious meaning here.[951] And among all the things that Scripture in the book of Genesis records God having made, nothing is there said to have been sanctified but the seventh day, which signifies the Sabbath.[952]

SEVEN COMMANDMENTS ALLOTTED TO LOVE OF NEIGHBOR

4. Of the seven commandments that are allotted to love of neighbor the first is: *"Honor your father and your mother"*; the second: *"You shall not kill"*; the third: *"You shall not commit adultery"*; the fourth: *"You shall not steal"*; the fifth: *"You shall not utter false witness"*; the sixth: *"You shall not covet your neighbor's wife"*; the seventh: *"You shall not covet your neighbor's goods"*[953] This division is clearly supported by the apostle, where he says, *"Honor your father and your mother, which is the first commandment."*[954] You look it up, and you discover that it isn't the first in the whole Decalogue, because the first of the Ten Commandments is the one which instructs us about worshipping the one God. And there the one about honoring parents is written on the other table, and is the first because from it begin the commandments which refer to love of neighbor.

THE DONATISTS DO NOT SING THE NEW SONG

5. So let us sing the new song, playing on the ten-stringed harp. This is the new song, the grace of the new covenant, which distinguishes us from the old man, who was the first to be made, of the earth earthy.[955] He was made from the mire,[956] and on losing his happy state was rightly cast forth into wretchedness, because he

---

951. *Magnum sacramentum*. Presumably the great sacrament or mystery is the Holy Spirit represented in the Sabbath commandment.

952. And "Sabbath," he assumes we know, signifies "rest."

953. Dt 5:17–21.   954. Eph 6:2.   955. See 1 Cor 15:47.

956. See Gn 2:7.

had emerged as a transgressor of the commandment. But what does he say through the prophet, who gives thanks to God for the grace of God that reconciles us to God by the forgiveness of sins, and renews us when we have shed that oldness? *"He brought me out,"* he says, *"from the bog of wretchedness and from the mud of the mire, and set my feet upon the rock, and guided my steps, and put into my mouth a new song, a hymn to our God."*[957] That is the new song, which he plays on the harp of ten strings. For none can praise God, that is utter a hymn, unless they tune their deeds to their words by loving God and neighbor.

The rebaptizing Donatists should not think they belong to the new song.[958] They cannot sing the new song, seeing that with insufferable impiety they have cut themselves off from the Church which God willed to exist in every land. After all, the same

---

957. Ps. 40:2–3.

958. It is no doubt because of this mention of the Donatists that the scholars propose a date for the sermon before 411, the year in which a great colloquy between the Catholics and Donatists was held in Carthage, the victory going, with full state support, to the Catholics. The reasoning, however, is not absolutely conclusive, since the Donatists did not just disappear after this as at the waving of a magic wand, nor did Augustine stop disputing with them, though he did become more preoccupied with the Pelagians from this time on. The Donatists rebaptized Catholics and other Christians who joined them because they denied the validity of all sacraments conferred by *traditores* (handers-over, those who had betrayed the faith in the last great persecution instituted by Diocletian from 303 to 313), and their heirs and successors. They took very literally Saint Cyprian's maxim, "Outside the Church no salvation," and hence no sacraments of salvation—as had Cyprian himself. They also carried the idea to its logical conclusion, and held that any who communicated with the heirs of the *traditores* became accessories after the fact to their sin and so put themselves outside the true Church. This existed, in their view, only among themselves, and thus only in the provinces of North Africa (though there was a small Donatist congregation in Rome). This is what Augustine means by saying that they had "cut themselves off from the Church which God willed to exist in every land." By so cutting themselves off from the other churches they had sinned against charity. It was his controversy with the Donatists that led Augustine to emphasize that what essentially constitutes a Christian community or church, and what binds local churches together in unity all over the world is not common customs, or law, or liturgy, or language—but *love*. It is a point in his doctrine of the Church in which he has not, perhaps, had as many *practical* followers among the theologians and the rulers of the Catholic Church as one could have wished.

prophet⁹⁵⁹ says somewhere else, *"Sing to the Lord a new song, sing to the Lord every land."*⁹⁶⁰ So anyone who refuses to sing with every land, and doesn't withdraw from the old man, doesn't sing the new song, and doesn't play on the ten-stringed harp, because he is an enemy of charity, which alone is the fullness of the law, and which we say is contained in the Ten Commandments that pertain to love of God and of neighbor.

Sermon 34

Sermon Preached in Carthage at the Ancestors
[420 A.D.]⁹⁶¹

1. We have been urged to sing to the Lord a new song.⁹⁶² It's the new person who sings the new song. A song is a matter of cheerfulness, and if we think about it more thoroughly, it's a matter of love. So anyone who knows how to love the new life knows how to sing the new song. So for the sake of the new song we need to be reminded what the new life is. All these things, you see, belong to the one kingdom—the new person, the new song, the new testament or new covenant. So the new person will both sing the new song and belong to the new covenant.

WE LOVE BECAUSE WE ARE LOVED

2. There is no one of course who doesn't love, but the question is, what do they love? So we are not urged not to love, but to choose

959. He means David, both texts being from the Psalms. It was common form for the Fathers to call David a prophet, though in the traditional arrangement of the biblical books the Psalms are not numbered among the Prophets.

960. Ps 96:1.

961. No date has been suggested for it. But the beginning of section 6 makes it clear that the congregation contained a number of newly baptized Christians, no doubt in a prominent position in the front. So it is likely that it was preached shortly after Easter or Pentecost. I would be inclined to put it rather late—about 420. It has all the characteristic technique, but there is a distinct lack of concentration that perhaps indicates the onset of old age.

962. See Ps 149:1.

what we love. But what choice can we make unless we are first chosen, since we cannot even love unless we are first loved? Listen to the Apostle John. He is the apostle who lay back on the Lord's breast and drank in heavenly secrets during that supper.[963] Drunk with that draught, in that state of happy drunkenness he belched out the words, *"In the beginning was the Word."*[964] What exalted humility and sober drunkenness.[965] So that great belcher—that is, of course, preacher—among all the other things he drank in from the Lord's breast, also said this: *"We ourselves love because he first loved us."*[966] Seeing that he was talking about God, he had given a great deal to humanity by saying *"We ourselves love."* Who love whom? People love God, mortals the immortal, frail fragile beings the unchanging one, artifacts the artificer.

We ourselves have loved. And where did we get this from? *"Because he has first loved us."* Inquire where a person gets the ability to love God from, and absolutely the only discovery you will make is that it is because God has first loved him. He has given us himself, the one we have loved; he has given us what to love with. You can hear more plainly from the Apostle Paul what he has given us to love with. *"The love of God,"* he says, *"has been poured into our hearts."* Where from? From us, perhaps? No. So where from" *"Through the Holy Spirit which has been given to us."*[967]

LET US LOVE GOD WITH GOD

3. Having therefore such a great assurance, let us love God with God. Yes indeed, since the Holy Spirit is God, let us love God with God. Now why should I say more than once, "Let us love God with God"? Certainly, because I have said *"the love of God has been poured into our hearts through the Holy Spirit which has been given to us,"* it follows that since the Holy Spirit is God and we cannot love God except through the Holy Spirit, we can only love God with God. So that's the line the argument follows.

963. See Jn 13:23.   964. Jn 1:1.

965. It is not quite clear how humility comes in here. It is probable that belching did not carry the stigma of coarse vulgarity in those days that it does among us in respectable circles; the word was used quite normally in a metaphorical sense of springs, for example, where we would use the word "gushing."

966. 1 Jn 4:10.   967. Rom 5:5.

Now listen to John saying it even more plainly: *"God is love, and whoever abides in love abides in God and God abides in him."*[968] It isn't enough to say "Love is from God." Which of us would dare to say what is said here, *"God is love?"* The one who said it knew what he had. So why does human imagination with its flights of fancy fashion God for itself and manufacture an idol in the mind, composing it as best its thoughts may, and not as its objective search ought? "Is God like this? No, he's like that." Why sketch an outline, why arrange limbs, why provide him with an acceptable stature, why imagine a beautiful body? *"God is love."* What color has love, what outline, what shape? We see none of these things in it, and yet we love.

LOVE IS LOVED, THOUGH NOT SEEN

4. At the risk of shocking your charity, I am going to say, "Let us observe at the lower level what we may expect to find at the higher." The lowest kind of earthly love, the sordid love which sets its sights on bodily charms, can teach us something useful which we can apply at the higher and purer level. Some shameless lecher loves a very beautiful woman. He is of course roused by her beautiful body, but he also looks inwardly for some return of love. If he hears that she hates him, doesn't all that hot, urgent passion roused by her beautiful figure grow cold, and in some fashion or other shrink back from what he had intended? Isn't he put off, offended, doesn't he even begin to hate what he had previously loved? Has her figure altered? Isn't everything still there that had previously allured him? Yes, there it all is still. And yet while he was on fire for what he could see, he was demanding from her heart what he could not see. Should he perceive, on the other hand, that he is loved in return, how much more impetuous and ardent becomes his desire! She sees him, he sees her, no one sees love. And yet love is loved, though it is not seen.

5. Now raise yourselves from this muddy kind of lust, and so re- main in the most radiant kind of love. You don't see God. Love, and you have him. How many things are loved in our reprehensi- ble desires, and are not had! They are greedily sought, but are not for all that immediately possessed. Loving gold is hardly the same

968. 1 Jn 4:16.

thing as having gold, is it? Many people love it and don't have it. Is it the same as having broad and beautiful acres, which many people love and don't have? Is loving honors the same as having honors? Many who have none are on fire to receive them. They make every effort to get them, and most often die before they get what they were aiming at.

God, on the other hand, offers himself to us at a bargain price. He calls out to us, "Love me and you will have me because you can't even love me unless you already have me."

BE YOURSELVES WHAT YOU SING

6. My brothers and sisters, my children, O seedlings of the Catholic Church, O holy and heavenly seed, O you that have been born again in Christ and been born from above,[969] listen to me—or rather, listen to God through me: *"Sing to the Lord a new song."*[970] "Well, I am singing," you say. Yes, you are singing, of course you're singing, I can hear you. But don't let your life give evidence against your tongue. Sing with your voices, sing also with your hearts; sing with your mouths, sing also with your conduct.

"Sing to the Lord a new song." You ask what you should sing about the one you love? For of course you do want to sing about the one you love. You are asking for praises of his to sing. You have been told, *"Sing to the Lord a new song."* You are looking for praise songs, are you? *"His praise is in the Church of the saints."*[971] The praise of the one to be sung about is the singer himself. Do you want to sing God his praises? Be yourselves what you sing. You are his praise if you lead good lives.

His praise, you see, is not to be found in the synagogues of the Jews, nor in the madness of the pagans, nor in the errors of the heretics, nor in the applause of the theaters. You ask where it is to be found? Look at yourselves, you be it. *"His praise is in the Church of the saints."* You ask what to rejoice about when you are singing? *"Let Israel rejoice in the one who made him,"*[972] and all he can find to rejoice about is God.

---

969. See Jn 3:3, where the word usually translated "again" can also mean "from above." It is this passage that indicates the presence of a whole section of newly baptized Christians in the congregation.

970. Ps 149:1.   971. Ibid.   972. Ps 149:2.

IF YOU WANT TO ACQUIRE CHARITY, LOOK INTO YOURSELF

7. Submit yourselves, my dear brothers, to a thorough interrogation, turn out your innermost closets and cupboards. Take careful
stock of how much you have of charity, and increase the stock you
find. Pay attention to that sort of treasure, so that you may be rich
within. Other things that carry a high price tag are said to be dear,
aren't they—and quite rightly. Look at the way you normally talk:
"This is dearer than that." What do you mean by "it's dearer" but
that it has a higher price—it's more precious. Now if whatever is
more precious is said to be dearer, what can be dearer, my brothers,
than dearness itself, which is what charity means?

What do we suppose its price is? How can we work out its
price? The price of corn is your coppers; the price of a farm, your
silver; the price of a pearl, your gold; the price of charity, yourself.
So you ask yourself how you are going to get possession of a farm,
or a jewel, or a mule; you look around for what you may buy a farm
with, and you look into your assets. But if you want to acquire
charity, look into yourself, and find yourself.

After all, why are you afraid to give yourself, as though you may
waste yourself? Rather, it's if you don't give yourself that you will
lose yourself. Charity herself speaks through wisdom, and tells you
something to save you from panicking at being told, "Give yourself." If anyone wanted to sell you a farm he would say to you,
"Give me your gold," and if it was something else, "Give me your
coppers, give me your silver." Now listen to what charity says to
you, speaking through the mouth of wisdom: *"Give me your heart,
son."*[973] *"Give me,"* she says. Give her what? *"Your heart, son."* It was
ill when it was with you, when you kept it to yourself. You were
being pulled this way and that by toys and trifles and wanton, destructive loves. Take your heart away from all that. Where are you
to drag it to, where are you to put it? "Give me your heart," she
says; "let it be mine and it won't be lost to you."

See, in any case, if he wanted to leave anything at all in you by
which you might love even yourself—he who said to you, *"You
shall love the Lord your God with all your heart and with all your soul*

---

973. Prv 23:26.

and with all your mind."[974] What is left of your heart to love yourself with? What is left of your soul? Of your mind? "With all," he says. He who made you requires it all of you, the whole of it. But don't get depressed, as though there is nothing left in you to rejoice with. *"Let Israel rejoice,"* not in himself but *"in the one who made him."*[975]

WHEN YOU LOVE, IT IS YOU WHO PROFIT BY IT

8. You, of course, will answer, "If nothing is left in me to love myself with, because I am ordered to love him who made me with my whole heart and my whole soul and my whole mind, how can I be ordered in the second commandment to love my neighbor as myself?" Well, in actual fact, this is saying how you do owe love to your neighbor with all your heart and all your soul and all your mind. "How?" *"You shall love your neighbor as yourself."*[976] God with all of me, with my whole self, my neighbor as myself. "But myself what with and you what with?" Do you want to hear what you are to love yourself with? You love yourself precisely with the fact that you love God with your whole self.

Do you really imagine it profits God that you love God? That because you love God some benefit accrues to God? And if you don't love God, that he will have less? When you love, it's you who profit by it. It will deposit you where you cannot get lost.

But you will answer, "When did I not love myself?" You may be quite sure you weren't loving yourself when you weren't loving the God who made you. When in fact you were hating yourself, you imagined you were loving yourself. *"Whoever loves iniquity,"* you see, *"hates his own soul."*[977]

974. Mt 22:37.   975. Ps 149:2.   976. Mt 22:39.   977. Ps 11:5.

Sermon 344

On Love of God and Love of the World
[428 A.D.]⁹⁷⁸

TWO LOVES FIGHTING EACH OTHER IN THIS LIFE, LOVE OF
GOD AND LOVE OF THE WORLD

1. In this life there are two loves wrestling with each other in every trial and temptation: love of the world and love of God. And whichever of these two wins, that's where it pulls the lover as by the force of gravity. It isn't, you see, on wings or on foot that we come to God, but on the power of our desires. And again, it isn't with knots and chains that we find ourselves stuck to the earth, but with contrary desires. Christ came to change our love, and to make lovers of the heavenly life out of earthly lovers; he was made man on our account, having made us men in the first place; he was God taking on a human being, in order to make human beings into gods.

This is the combat we are challenged to, this the struggle with the flesh, this the struggle with the devil, this the struggle with the world. But let us have confidence, because the one who instituted this contest does not watch his own champions without helping them, nor does he encourage us to rely on our own strength. Anyone relying on his own strength, you see, is relying, being clearly a man, on the strength of a man; and *"accursed is everyone who rests his hope in man."*⁹⁷⁹ The martyrs caught fire from the flame of this pious and holy love, and indeed burned up the straw of the flesh with the steadily burning oak logs of the mind; while they themselves came through whole and entire to the one who had set them alight. However, on the flesh that despises these things due honor

978. This date is suggested by the Italian edition, but with no authorities quoted. The sermon does ramble rather, and shows a certain incoherence; qualities that do perhaps reveal the old man of seventy-four or so. The high probability is that it was preached in Hippo Regius; just possibly in Carthage. But if the date is correct, Augustine was not traveling anymore.

979. Jer 17:5.

will be bestowed in the resurrection of the dead. It is sown, you see, in disgrace, precisely in order to rise again in glory.[980]

THE RIGHT ORDER OF CHARITY; GOD TO BE LOVED MORE THAN ONE'S PARENTS

2. To those set alight by this love, or rather that they may be set alight, this is what he says: *"Whoever loves father or mother above me is not worthy of me; and whoever does not take up his cross and follow me is not worthy of me."*[981] He didn't abolish love of parents, wife, children, but put them in their right order. He didn't say "Whoever loves," but *"Whoever loves above me."* That's what the Church is saying in the Song of Songs: *"He put charity in order for me."*[982] Love your father, but not above your Lord; love the one who begot you, but not above the one who created you. Your father begot you, but didn't himself fashion you; because who or what would be born to him, when he sowed the seed, he himself did not know. Your father reared you, but when you were hungry he didn't provide bread for you from his own body. Finally, whatever your father is keeping for you on earth, he has to pass away for you to succeed to it; he will leave space for your life by his death. But what God your Father is keeping for you, he is keeping with himself, so that you may possess the inheritance with your Father, and not, as his successor, be waiting for his demise, but rather may cleave to him who is always going to abide, and may always abide yourself in him. So love your father, but not above your God.

Love your mother, but not above the Church, who bore you to eternal life. Finally, from the love you have for your parents weigh up how much you ought to love God and the Church. After all, if those who bore you, only to die in due course, are to be loved so much, with how much charity are those to be loved who have borne you in order to enter eternity, in order to remain in eternity? Love your wife, love your children after God, in such a way that you take care they too worship God with you; when you're joined to him, you will fear no separation. The reason you ought not to love them more than God is that you love them in a totally bad way if you neglect to bring them to God together with you. Perhaps the time for martyrdom will come. You, for your part, wish to confess

980. See 1 Cor 15:43.   981. Mt 10:37–38.   982. Sg 2:4.

Christ. When you've confessed him you will perhaps have some temporal punishment, some temporal death to endure. Father or wife or son is coaxing you not to die, and by coaxing you is insuring that you do die. If they are not to ensure that, it's because those words will come into your mind, *"Whoever loves father, or mother, or wife, or children above me is not worthy of me."*[983]

CHRIST IN GETHSEMANE GIVES US AN EXAMPLE OF FEELING, AND OVERCOMING, HUMAN FEARS

3. But feelings of carnal affection are easily played on by the coaxings of one's own kin. Gather in the folds of your flowing garments, gird yourself with strength. Is love of the flesh crucifying you? Pick up your cross and follow the Lord. He too, your savior, though God in the flesh, though God with flesh, still gave you a demonstration of purely human feelings, when he said, *"Father, if it is possible, let this cup pass from me."*[984] He knew that this cup could not pass from him, that it had come to him in order to be drunk. That cup was to be drunk willingly, not out of necessity. He was almighty; if he wished, it would most certainly pass from him, because he was God with the Father, and he and God the Father were one God. But in the form of a servant,[985] in the form he took from you for you, he uttered those words in the voice of a man, in the voice of the flesh. He stooped to transposing you into himself, so that you in him might utter words of weakness, so that you in him might take a grip on decisive strength. He showed you the will through which you could be tempted; and straightaway he taught you which will you should prefer to which. *"Father,"* he said, *"if it can be so, let this cup pass from me."* This is a human wish; I am wearing a man, I am speaking from the form of a servant. *"Father, if it can be so, let this cup pass."* It's the voice of the flesh, not the spirit,[986] the voice of infirmity, not of divinity. *"If it can be so, let this cup pass."*

This is the wish about which Peter is told, *"But when you get old, another will gird you, and take you away, and bring you where you do not wish."*[987] So how did the martyrs too overcome? Because they

---

983. See Mt 10:37, influenced by Lk 14:26.   984. Mt 26:39.

985. See Phil 2:7.   986. See Mk 14:38.   987. Jn 21:18.

put the wishes of the spirit before the wishes of the flesh. They loved this life, and they weighed it up and played it down. From it they considered how much eternal life should be loved, if this perishable life is loved like that. The man about to die doesn't want to die; and yet he will of necessity be dying sometime, even though he is reluctant to die immediately. You can do nothing by just not wanting to die, achieve nothing, extort nothing, you have no power or authority to eliminate the necessity of death. It will come, what you are afraid of, even though you don't want it; it will present itself, what you are putting off, even though you refuse it. Yes, you can take steps to put death off; you can't take any, can you, to eliminate it? So if such efforts are made by the lovers of this life to delay death, how great the pains that should be taken to eliminate it! Certainly, you don't want to die. Change your kind of love, and you will be shown, not a death that will present itself to you against your will, but a death which will, if you so will, absent itself altogether.

WHY FEAR THE FIRST DEATH, CHRISTIAN? WHAT IS REALLY NEEDED IS TO BE REDEEMED FROM THE SECOND DEATH

4. Observe then, if love has woken up just a little bit in your heart, if just a spark has been struck from the ashes of the flesh, if some solid oak chippings in your heart have caught it and burst into flames, which not only are not put out by the wind of trial and temptation, but are even fanned by it into a bigger blaze than ever; if you are burning, not like a wick which is put out by one light breath, but burning like oak chippings, burning like coal, so that you are on the contrary stirred up by a breath of wind; observe two sorts of death, one temporal, and that's the first; the other everlasting, and that's the second. The first death is ready and waiting for all; the second only for the bad, the godless, unbelievers, blasphemers, and whatever else is opposed to sound teaching.[988] Look closely, set these two sorts of death before your eyes. If it can be avoided, you don't want to suffer both of them.

I know, you love being alive, you don't want to die; and you would like to pass from this life to the other life in such a way that you don't rise again dead, but are changed, alive, into something

988. See Ti 2:1.

better. That's what you would like, that's what ordinary human feelings desire, that's what the soul itself has, in I don't know what kind of way, engraved in its deepest will and desire. Since in loving life it hates death, and since it doesn't hate its own flesh, it doesn't want what it hates to happen even to that. *"For nobody ever hated his own flesh."*[989] The apostle shows us these feelings, where he says, *"We have a dwelling from God, a house not made with hands, eternal in the heavens. Indeed, we groan in this one, longing to have our dwelling from heaven put on over us, in which,"* he says, *"we do not wish to be stripped, but to be clothed over and above, so that what is mortal may be swallowed up by life."*[990] You don't want to be stripped, but stripped you have to be. What you should do your best to ensure, though, is that when you have been stripped of your shirt of flesh by death, you may be found clothed with the armor of faith. That, you see, is what he goes on to add: *"provided, that is, that we may be found to be clothed, not naked."*[991]

The first death, I mean, is going to strip you of the flesh, to be set aside for a while, and received back again at its own proper time. This, whether you like it or not; it's not because you want to, after all, that you will rise again; or, if you don't want to, that you won't; or, if you don't believe in the resurrection, that that will be a reason for your not rising again. What's needed is that you, who are going to rise again willy-nilly, should rather do your best to ensure that you rise again in such a way that you have what you would like to have. The Lord Jesus himself, in fact, said, *"The moment is coming when all who are in the tombs will hear his voice and come forth,"* whether they're good, whether they're bad; *"all who are in the tombs will hear his voice and come forth"*; and they will be turned out of their hidden recesses. No creature will hold any of the dead against the voice of the living creator. *"All,"* he says, who are in the tombs will hear his voice and come forth. In saying *all*, he seems to have created some confusion, and mixed them all up. But listen to the distinction, listen to the separation: *"those who have done good,"* he says, *"to the resurrection of life; those who have committed evil to the resurrection of judgment."*[992]

This judgment, which the godless are going to rise again to un-

989. Eph 5:29.   990. 2 Cor 5:1–4.   991. 2 Cor 5:3.   992. Jn 5:28–29.

dergo, is called *"the second death."*[993] So, Christian, why be afraid of this first one? It will come even though you don't want it to, and it will be there waiting for you, even though you reject it. You can, perhaps, ransom yourself from the barbarians and so save yourself from being killed; you can ransom yourself for a vast sum, not sparing any of your property at all, and stripping your children of their inheritance; and on being ransomed, you die the next day! It's from the devil you need to be redeemed, who is dragging you off with him to the second death, where the wicked placed on the left hand will hear, *"Go, you accursed, into the eternal fire, which has been got ready for the devil and his angels."*[994] It's from this second death you need to be ransomed.

"What with?" you will answer.

Don't go looking for goats and bulls. Don't, as a last resort, go turning out your strongbox, and saying to yourself, "To ransom myself from the barbarians I had money." To ransom yourself from the second death, have justice.

It would be quite possible for the barbarian first to take your money himself, and then later on lead you away captive, so that there would be nothing with which to redeem yourself, seeing that the one who had possession of you also had possession of all your property. Justice, though, you cannot lose against your will. It's locked up in the innermost strongbox of your heart. Hold on to that, keep possession of that, that's what you can ransom yourself with from the second death. This, if you don't want it to, will not be waiting for you there, for the good reason that what you can use to redeem yourself from this death will be there if you want it to be. It is the will that obtains justice from the Lord, drinking it there as from its own proper source or spring. This is a spring nobody is forbidden to approach, if that person is worthy to do so.

Finally, consider the means you are helped by. What ransomed you from the barbarians was your silver, what redeemed you from the first death was your money; what has ransomed you from the second death is the blood of your Lord. He had the blood to redeem us with; and that's why he accepted to have blood, so that there would be something for him to shed for our redemption. The

993. Rv 20:6, 14.   994. Mt 25:41.

blood of your Lord, if you wish it so, was given for you; if you don't wish it so, it wasn't given for you.[995]

Yes, but perhaps you're saying, "My God had the blood to redeem me with; but he has already given it all, when he suffered. What is there left for him to give for me?"

That's the great thing about it, that he gave it once only, and gave it for all. The blood of Christ is salvation for the one who wishes it so, torment for the one who refuses it. So why hesitate, you there who don't want to die, to be delivered rather from the second death? From it you are indeed delivered, if you are ready to take up your cross and follow the Lord;[996] because he took up his cross, and sought the slave.

THE WAY PEOPLE LOVE THIS LIFE SHOULD CONVINCE US HOW MUCH WE SHOULD LOVE ETERNAL LIFE

5. Isn't it absolutely true, my brothers and sisters, that the ones who above all others encourage you to love eternal life, are the people who are so in love with temporal life? How many things people do, just to live a few more days! Who could count the efforts and exertions of all those who are so eager to live, and die a little while later? The things they do for the sake of those few days! What, on the same scale, are we doing for the sake of eternal life?

What do I mean by those few days they feel must be paid a ransom for, and that on this earth? By a few days, you see, I mean if the person grows old after being saved from death; I call it a few days, if a person is saved as a child and lives to a decrepit old age.[997] I don't mean that ransomed today, he may perhaps die tomorrow. Just look, with life so uncertain, merely for the sake of those few uncertain days, just look at the things people do, the things they think up! If they come, through some disease of the body, into the hands of a doctor, and every chance of recovery is despaired of by those

995. A theologically careless way of putting it; Christ shed his blood for all, without exception. It was the later error of the Jansenists, relying on some of Augustine's more careless statements, to say that Christ died only for the elect. No, his blood was shed for you, whether you wish it or not. But if you don't wish it, you don't profit from its having been shed for you; you refuse to be ransomed or redeemed.

996. See Lk 14:27.

997. Something that had happened to Augustine himself. See *Confessions*, I, 11.

who examine the case and give their opinion; and if there is a prospect of some other doctor who is capable of saving even desperate cases, what rewards are promised him! How much is given on a totally uncertain chance! For the sake of just a little more life, even what is needed to live on is given up. Now again, if he falls into the hands of an enemy or a brigand, to save him from being killed, even to get him ransomed if it's a father who has been taken, the sons run hither and thither and spend what would have been left to them, in order to redeem the one whom they could soon be carrying out to the grave. What expedients, what prayers, what efforts! Can anybody satisfactorily explain it?

And yet I want to tell you about something even more serious, and even more incredible, if it didn't actually happen. What am I saying, after all? That people give away all their money in order to live, that they leave themselves nothing to live on? In order to live a few days more, and those entirely uncertain, to live them in fear, live them in toil and trouble, how much they are prepared to spend! How much they give away! Alas for the human race! I've said that in order to go on living they spend what they have to live on; listen to something worse, something much more serious, something much more abominable, something quite incredible, as I said, unless it actually happened. To enable them to live a little longer, they give away even that on which they could live forever. Hear what I've said, and understand it. It's still a closed book, you see, and yet it worries many people, for whom the Lord had already opened it up when it was closed. Leave aside those people who, in order to be granted a little longer life, give away and let go what they have to live on. Pay attention to those who, in order to be granted a little longer life, let go of what they could live on forever. What is that? It's called faith, it's called loyalty. This is all like the money, by which eternal life is acquired.

The enemy will cut obliquely across your bows to terrify you, and he won't say to you, "Give me money, in order to go on living"; what he'll say is, "Deny Christ, in order to go on living." If you, in fact, do do that, in order to be permitted to live a little longer, you will be letting go of what would enable you to live always. Is that loving life, you there who were so afraid of death? My good man, why were you afraid of death, if not because you loved life? Christ is life. Why seek a small life, and forfeit a sure and certain one? Or perhaps you haven't let go of faith, but didn't have anything to let go of? So hold onto what will enable you to live always. Look a your neighbor, and how much he does in order to go on living a little while. Look, too, at the person who has denied Christ, and see what an evil thing he has done for the sake of a few more days of life. And you, now, are not willing to despise a few days of life, in order to die on no day, and to live out the everlasting day, to be protected by your redeemer, to be made the equal of the angels in the eternal kingdom? What have you been in love with? What have you been letting go of and losing? You have never taken up your cross in order to follow the Lord.

LOSING ONE'S LIFE IN ORDER TO FIND IT — AND FINDING IT IN ORDER TO LOSE IT

6. See how wise and thoughtful he wants you to be, the one who said to you, *"Take up your cross and follow me."*[998] *"Whoever finds his life,"* he said, *"will lose it; and whoever loses it on my account will find it."*[999] Whoever finds will lose it; whoever loses will find it. In order to lose it, the first thing is to find it; and when you've lost it, the final thing is to find it again. There are two findings; in between there is one losing, by which you pass across. None of us can lose our life for Christ's sake unless we have first found it; and none of us can find our life in Christ unless we have first lost it. Find, in order to lose; lose, in order to find.

How are you going to find it, in order to have something you can lose? When you think of yourself as being in part mortal, when you think of the one who made you and created you by breathing life into you,[1000] and realize that you owe it to the one who gave it; that it's to be paid back to the one who lent it; that it is to be kept safe by the one who provided it; then you have found your life, finding it in faith. I mean, you have believed this, and found your soul, your life.[1001] After all, you were lost, before you came to believe. You have

---

998. Mk 8:34.   999. Mt 10:39.   1000. See Gn 2:7.

1001. The same word, *anima*, meaning soul, and hence life. Jesus is talking about finding and losing one's soul. But to translate it so, given what English Christianity and language have done to the word "soul," would be to give an entirely wrong impression.

found your life, you had been dead, that is, in your unbelief; you have come back to life in faith. You are just like the one about whom it can be said, *"He was dead, and has come to life again; he was lost and is found."*[1002]

So you have found your life in the true faith, if you have come back to life from the death of unbelief. That is, you have found your soul. Lose it, and your soul becomes seed for you. I mean the farmer too by threshing and winnowing finds the wheat, and again by sowing it he loses the wheat. What had been lost in the sowing is found on the threshing floor. What is found in the harvest is lost in the sowing. So, *"whoever finds his life will lose it."* You work so hard at gathering; why be so slow in the sowing?

THERE IS A LIFE TO BE FOUND WHICH IT IS ABSOLUTELY IMPOSSIBLE TO LOSE

7. Notice carefully, however, how you are to find it, and why you are to lose it. What would you find it with, after all, unless a light were struck for you by the one to whom it is said, *"You will light up my lamp, Lord"*?[1003] So you have already found it, with him lighting a lamp for you. Notice why you are to lose it. It's not, you see, to be lost anywhere and everywhere, something that has been found with such diligence. He didn't say, "Whoever loses it will find it," but *"Whoever loses it on my account."* When you've taken a look, perhaps, at the body of a shipwrecked trader on the shore,[1004] you're moved to pity and you pay him his due of tears, and say, "Alas for this man! It was for the sake of gold that he lost his life." You are right to mourn him, right to feel sorry for him. Give him his due of weeping, since you can't also give him any help. For the sake of gold, you see, he was able to lose his life, but not able, for the sake of gold, to find it. He was quite capable of suffering the loss of his life and soul, but turned out to be less capable of gaining it.

We should reflect, you see, not on what he lost but on why he lost it. If it was on account of avarice, look, that's where the flesh lies;

1002. Lk 15:32.   1003. Ps 18:28.

1004. This remark indicates that he was preaching in a seaside town—and where more likely than in his home port of Hippo Regius? But it could have been Carthage, if the sermon was preached several years earlier than we are supposing.

where is what was so dear to him?[1005] And yet avarice gave the command, and for the sake of gold the soul was lost, and for the sake of Christ the soul does not perish, nor can it. You fool, don't hesitate; listen to the creator's advice. He's the one who fashioned you to use your wits, the one who made you before you were there to have any wits. Listen, don't hesitate to lose your life for Christ's sake. You are in fact entrusting to a trustworthy creator what you are said to be losing. You, indeed, will lose it; but he will receive it, and for him nothing perishes and is lost. If you love life, lose it in order to find it; because when you find it, it won't any longer be the sort of thing you can lose, there won't be any reason why you should lose it. The life in fact that will be found is one that will be found to be such that it cannot ever perish or be lost at all. Because Christ too, who by his birth, death and resurrection has given himself to you as a model *"arising from the dead dies no more, and death will no longer lord it over him."*[1006]

Sermon 349

On Charity
[412 A.D.]

THREE SORTS OF CHARITY: DIVINE, LAWFUL HUMAN, UN-
LAWFUL HUMAN LOVE OR CHARITY

1. A moment or two ago the apostle was talking to us about charity, while his Epistle was being read;[1007] and he was commending it to us in such a way that we should understand that all other things, great gifts of God though they be, do us no good at all without it. But where charity itself is, it cannot be alone. Let me too, then, give your graces a sermon on the grace of charity. One kind of charity is

---

1005. An untranslatable pun: *ecce ubi jacet caro; ubi est quod erat carum?* The pronunciation of *caro* [flesh], and *carum* [dear], was probably almost identical. The question is about the gold he died for—but can also be about his soul, his "dear one"; Ps 22:20.

1006. Rom 6:9.   1007. Evidently 1 Cor 13.

divine, another human; one human kind is lawful, another unlawful. So about these three kinds of charity or love—what is called *agape* in Greek has these two names with us English speakers[1008]—let me say whatever the Lord may grant me.

So my first division, as I said, is into a human and a divine kind of charity; and the human sort I again divided into two, suggesting that there is both a lawful and an unlawful sort. So first of all I will talk about the lawful human kind, with which no fault is to be found; then of the unlawful human kind, which is to be condemned; third, of the divine sort, which conducts us through to the kingdom.

ON THE CHARITY WITH WHICH WIVES, CHILDREN, PARENTS, AND SO ON ARE LOVED

2. So, to give a quick instance, the human charity by which one's wife is loved is lawful; by which a prostitute, or someone else's wife is loved, unlawful. Even in the streets and marketplace[1009] the lawful kind of charity is preferred to the prostitute variety; while in the house of God, in the temple of God, in the city of Christ, in the body of Christ, the love of a prostitute leads the lover straight to hell. So have the lawful kind of charity; it's human, but as I said, it's lawful. It's not only lawful, though, in the sense that it's permitted; but also lawful in the sense that if it's lacking, you are very much at fault. It's absolutely right for you to love your wives, to love your children, to love your friends, to love your fellow citizens with human charity. All these names, you see, imply a bond of relationship, and the glue, so to say, of charity.

But you will observe that this sort of charity can be found also among the godless, that is, among pagans, Jews, heretics. Which of them, after all, does not naturally love wife, children, brothers, neighbors, relations, friends, etc.? So this kind of charity is human. So if anyone is affected by such hardness of heart that he loses even

1008. *Apud Latinos*, of course; the two Latin words being *caritas* and *dilectio*, not *amor*, though that will be used here and there in the course of the sermon. We should remind ourselves that *caritas* is the noun from the adjective *carus*, "dear." It means "holding dear." So we have to try to import that notion into the English "charity."

1009. That is, in secular public life.

the human feeling of love, and doesn't love his children, doesn't love his wife, he isn't fit even to be counted among human beings. A man who loves his children is not thereby particularly praiseworthy; but one who does not love his children is certainly blameworthy, I mean, he should observe with whom he ought to have this kind of love in common; even wild beasts love their children; adders love their children; tigers love their children; lions love their children. There is no wild creature, surely, that doesn't gently coo or purr over its young. I mean, while it may terrify human beings, it cherishes its young. The lion roars in the forest, so that nobody dare walk through it; it goes into its den, where it has its young, it lays aside all its rabid ferocity. It puts it down outside, it doesn't step inside with it. So a man who doesn't love his children is worse than a lion. These are human sentiments, but they are lawful.

UNLAWFUL HUMAN LOVE

3. Be on your guard against unlawful love. You are the members of Christ, and you are the body of Christ. Listen to the apostle, and shake in your shoes. He couldn't, after all, have said it more seriously, said it more forcefully, couldn't have frightened Christians more sharply off the love of fornication, than when he said, *"So taking the members of Christ, shall I make them into the members of a harlot?"* Now to prepare the way for this question, he had just said above, *"Do you not know that one who cleaves to a harlot is made into one body?"* And he quoted the scriptural evidence, where it says, *"They shall be two in one flesh."*[1010] This, you see, was said by God; but about a man and wife where it is lawful, where it is allowed, where it is honorable; not where it is disgraceful, not where it is unlawful, not where it is damnable by every reasonable consideration.

Now just as one flesh is effected in the lawful congress of man and wife, so too one flesh is effected in the unlawful congress of harlot and lover. So since one flesh is effected, you should be shaken to the core, you should be horrified by what he added: *"So taking the members of Christ"*; pay attention, you Christian there, to the members of Christ; don't turn your attention to the members of Christ in someone else, pay attention to the members of Christ in yourself, seeing that you have been bought by the blood of Christ.

1010. 1 Cor 6:15–16; Gn 2:24.

"So taking the members of Christ, shall I make them into the members of a harlot?" Anyone who isn't horrified at this idea will find himself horrified by God.[1011]

UNLAWFUL HUMAN LOVE ABSOLUTELY INCOMPATIBLE WITH DIVINE LOVE

4. Again and again I beg you, my brothers—look; let's suppose, what is not the case, that God had promised such people impunity, and had said, "Those who do such things, well, I will take pity on them, I will not damn them." Let's pretend God has said that. Even with such a promise of impunity, is anyone going to take the members of Christ and make them into the members of a harlot? Nobody will do so, if there is present there the third, divine, kind of love. Remember I listed three kinds of love; I promised I would say about the three of them what God might grant me to say; about the lawful human sort, the unlawful human sort, about that surpassing and divine sort of love.

Let us question divine charity, and let us set before her the two human kinds of charity, and let us say to her, "Here is lawful human charity, with which wives are loved, and daughters, and other secular relations. Here on the other side is the unlawful sort, by which harlots are loved, by which one's maidservants are loved, by which another man's daughter is loved, when she has been neither asked for nor promised in marriage, by which another man's wife is loved. In front of you are two sorts of charity; with which of the two do you wish to stay?"

The man who chooses to stay with that lawful human love doesn't stay with the unlawful variety. You should none of you say to yourselves, "I have them both." If you have them both by admitting into yourself the love of a harlot, you are doing wrong to divine charity, who is living there as the lady of the house. I rather think, you see, that if you are a married man, and are in love with a

1011. *Deo horret*; a rather difficult phrase. But here the more material sense of *horreo* [I shudder], is in play. At the judgment the sinners will shudder at the presence of the divine judge. Throughout this passage it seems clear that by the phrase *membra Christi* he is referring not to the Christian as a person, but to his genital organs, which now belong to Christ. That indeed is probably the intention of Paul in the first half of 1 Cor 6:15: "Do you not know that your bodies are the members of Christ?"

harlot, you don't bring the harlot into your house, to live with your lady wife. You aren't quite as advanced as all that. You look for the cover of darkness, you look for out-of-the-way corners, you don't parade your shameful behavior. But even those who don't have wives, and are the lovers of harlots slightly less unlawfully, as it were (the reason I said "as it were," is that they too stand condemned, if they are already believers);[1012] I rather imagine that even a young man who hasn't yet got a wife will not, if he loves a harlot, bring her to live with his sister, will not bring her to live with his mother, for fear of insulting ordinary human decency, for fear of offending against the honor of his blood.[1013] So if you don't bring along the harlot you are in love with to live with your mother, with your sister, for fear, as I said, of offending against the honor of your blood, are you going to bring the love of a harlot along to live in your heart together with the love of God and offend against the honor of the blood of Christ?

LET US LOVE GOD, AND PRAY TO BE GIVEN THE LOVE OF GOD AS STRENUOUSLY AS THE BLIND MAN PRAYED TO BE GIVEN HIS SIGHT

5. Love God; you can't find anything better to love. You love silver, because it's better than iron or brass; you love gold more, because it's better than silver; you love precious stones more, because they exceed even the value of gold; finally, you love this light of day, which everyone who is afraid of death dreads leaving behind. You love, I repeat, this light of day, just as the man who cried out after Jesus, *"Have mercy on me, son of David,"*[1014] longed for it with such a huge love. The blind man was crying out as Jesus was passing by. And how much did he cry out? So much that he wouldn't keep quiet, even when the crowd tried to stop him. He overcame the opposer, caught hold of the savior. With the whole crowd shouting

1012. The implication is that they don't stand condemned by the civil law or by secular custom and mores.

1013. He is clearly addressing the men of the upper classes, who had a strong sense of family honor and pride of ancestry—indeed even men of the modest middle classes such as himself; the reason that he never married the concubine of his youth was almost certainly that she did not have enough "class."

1014. Lk 18:38.

the man down and trying to prevent him crying out, Jesus stopped, called him and said to him, *"What do you wish done for you? Lord, he said, that I may see. Look up, your faith has saved you."*[1015]

Love Christ; long for the light which Christ is. If that man longed for the light of the body, how much more ought you all to long for the light of the heart? Let us cry out to him, not with our voices, but with our behavior. Let us lead good lives, let us scorn the world; for us, let everything that passes away be as nothing. When we live that kind of life, we are going to be taken to task by worldly people who are, so it seems, fond of us; people who love the earth, smack of the dust, think nothing of heaven, breathe in the free air, not with their hearts, but only with their nostrils. They are undoubtedly going to take us to task, and to say, if they see us scorning these human, these earthly things, "What's wrong with you? why are you so crazy?" They are that crowd, trying to stop the blind man crying out. And a considerable number of them are Christians, who forbid us to live in a Christian way; because that crowd too was walking along with Christ, and yet when that man started yelling loudly to Christ and longing for the light, they were trying to bar him from Christ's favor. There are such Christians; but let us defeat their efforts by leading good lives, and let our lives be our voices crying out to Christ. He will stop for us, because he has already stopped and is standing still.

CHRIST'S PASSING BY AND HIS STOPPING AND STANDING STILL

6. Here too, you see, there is a great mystery, with a hidden meaning. He was passing by when that man started crying out; when he cured him, he stopped. Christ's passing by should make us intent on crying out. What is Christ's passing by? Everything he underwent for us in time is his passing by. He was born, he passed by; he isn't still being born, is he? He grew, he passed by; he isn't still growing, is he? He sucked the breast; is he still sucking? He was tired, and slept; is he still sleeping? He ate and drank; he isn't still doing that, is he? Finally, he was arrested, bound, scourged, crowned with thorns, beaten and slapped about, smeared with spittle, hanged on the cross, slain, struck with the lance, buried, rose

1015. Lk 18:39–42.

again; he's still passing by. He ascended into heaven, he is seated at the Father's right hand; he has stopped. Cry out as loudly as you can; now he is restoring your sight.

Because in the very fact that he *"was the Word with God,"* he was of course standing still, because he wasn't changing in any way. *"And the Word was God"*;[1016] *"and the Word became flesh."* The flesh by its passing died and suffered many things; the Word stood still. It's by the Word that the heart is enlightened and receives its sight; because it's through the Word that the flesh, which he took on, is treated with honor. Take away the Word, and what is the flesh? Just what yours is. But that the flesh of Christ might be treated with honor, *"the Word became flesh and dwelt amongst us."*[1017] So let us cry out, and lead good lives.

WE MUST, OF COURSE, LOVE OUR NEAREST AND DEAREST, BUT WE MUST LOVE CHRIST MORE

7. Love your children, love your wives, even if it's only in worldly matters and a worldly way. Because of course you ought to love them with reference to Christ, and take thought for them with reference to God, and in them love nothing but Christ, and hate it in your nearest and dearest if they don't want to have anything to do with Christ. Such, you see, is that divine sort of charity. What good, after all, would be done them by your fleeting and mortal charity? Still, when you do love them in a human way, love Christ more. I'm not saying you shouldn't love your wife; but love Christ more. I'm not saying you shouldn't love your father, not saying you shouldn't love your children; but love Christ more. Listen to him saying it himself, in case you should suppose these are just my words: *"Whoever loves father or mother more than me, is not worthy of me."*[1018]

When you hear *"is not worthy of me,"* aren't you afraid? The one about whom Christ says *"he is not worthy of me"* is not with him; where will the one be, who is not with him? If you don't love being with him, you should be afraid of being without him. Why be afraid of being without him? Because you will be with the devil, if you aren't with Christ. And where will the devil be? Listen to Christ himself: *"Go into the eternal fire, which has been prepared for*

1016. Jn 1:1.   1017. Jn 1:14.   1018. Mt 10:37.

the devil and his angels."[1019] If you aren't kindled with the fire of heaven, be afraid of the fire of Gehenna. If you don't love the idea of being among the angels of God, be afraid of being found among the angels of the devil. If you don't love the idea of being in the kingdom, be afraid of being in the burning furnace of inextinguishable, everlasting fire. Let fear first win the day in you, and then there will be love. Let fear be the nursemaid;[1020] don't let it stay in you, but let it lead you on to charity, as to the schoolmaster.

Sermon 350

On Charity
[427 A.D.]

THE WHOLE TEACHING OF THE SCRIPTURES CONTAINED IN THIS ONE WORD, CHARITY

1. All the varied plenty and wide-ranging teaching of the divine Scriptures is grasped, my brothers and sisters, and kept without any difficulty by the person whose heart is full of charity. It's what the apostle says: *"Now the fullness of the law is charity"*;[1021] and in another place, *"Now the end of the commandment is charity from a pure heart, and a good conscience, and unfeigned faith."*[1022] But what can the end of the commandment be, but the fulfillment of the commandment? And what is the fulfillment of the commandment but the fullness of the law? So what he said there, *"the fullness of the law is charity,"* is what he also said here, *"the end of the commandment is charity."*

Nor can there be the slightest doubt that the temple of God is the person in whom charity is dwelling. John, too, you see, says, *"God is charity."*[1023] Now when the apostles said these things and urged upon us the absolute primacy of charity, they could only be belching forth what they had themselves eaten. The Lord himself, in

---

1019. Mt 25:41.

1020. Paedagogus, the family slave who took the little boys to school.

1021. Rom 13:10.   1022. 1 Tm 1:5.   1023. 1 Jn 4:8, 16.

fact, feeding them on the word of truth, the word of charity, which he is himself, the living bread which came down from heaven,[1024] said, *"A new commandment I give you, that you should love one another."* And again, *"By this shall everybody know that you are my disciples, if you love one another."*[1025]

He came, you see, to put an end to the corruption of the flesh by the mockery he endured on the cross, and to unfasten the old chain of our death by the newness of his death; and so he made the new man with a new commandment. It was, after all, an old matter, stale news, that man should die. To prevent this prevailing over man forever, a new thing was done, that God should die. But because he died in the flesh, not in his divinity, through the everlasting life of his divinity he did not permit the destruction of the flesh to be everlasting. And so, as the apostle says, *"He died on account of our transgressions, he rose again on account of our justification."*[1026] So because he has brought the newness of life into action against the oldness of death, he himself sets a new commandment against the old sin. Any of you, then, who wish to extinguish the old sin, douse cupidity with the new commandment, and embrace charity. Just as cupidity, you see, is the root of all evil,[1027] so in the same way is charity the root of all good things.

CHARITY POSSESSES THE WHOLE LENGTH AND BREADTH OF SCRIPTURE

2. Charity is in secure possession of the whole length and breadth of the divine utterances, the charity with which we love God and neighbor. After all, the one and only heavenly master teaches us, *"You shall love the Lord your God with your whole heart and your whole soul and your whole mind; and you shall love your neighbor as yourself. On these two commandments depend the whole Law and the Prophets."*[1028] So if there's no time or leisure to pore over all the sacred pages, to leaf through all the volumes of the words they contain, to penetrate all the secrets of the Scriptures, hold onto charity, on which they all depend. In this way you will hold onto what you have learned there; you will also get hold of what you haven't yet learned. I mean, if you know charity, you know something from

---

1024. See Jn 6:48–49.   1025. Jn 13:34–35.   1026. Rom 4:25.

1027. See 1 Tim 6:10.   1028. Mt 22:37, 39–40.

which that also depends which perhaps you don't yet know; and in whatever you do understand in the Scriptures, charity is revealed; while in the parts you don't understand, charity is concealed. And so it is that those who keep a grip on charity in their behavior have a grasp both of what is revealed and of what is concealed in the divine writings.

DIFFERENT MANIFESTATIONS OF CHARITY

3. Therefore, brothers and sisters, pursue after charity, the sweet and salutary bond of our minds,[1029] without which the rich man is poor, and with which the poor man is rich. This it is that endures in adversity, is moderate in prosperity; brave under harsh sufferings, cheerful in good works; utterly reliable in temptation, utterly openhanded in hospitality; as happy as can be among true brothers and sisters, as patient as you can get among the false ones. Acceptable in Abel through his sacrifice, safe in Noah through the flood, absolutely faithful in the wanderings of Abraham, as meek as meek can be in Moses amid insults,[1030] so mild and gentle in David's trials and tribulations.[1031] In the three young men it innocently awaits the kindly fires; in the Maccabees it bravely endures the ferocious fires.[1032] Chaste in Susanna toward her husband, in Anna after her husband, in Mary apart from her husband. Free in Paul for rebuking, humble in Peter for listening and yielding.[1033] Human in Christians for confessing, divine in Christ for pardoning.

But what can I say in praise of charity that surpasses in grandeur what the Lord thunders forth through the mouth of his apostle, as he *"shows us a more excellent way,"* and says *"If I speak with the tongues of men and of angels, but do not have charity, I have become booming bronze, or a clashing cymbal. And if I have prophecy, and know all sacraments, and have all knowledge, and if I have all faith, such that I transfer mountains, but do not have charity, I am nothing. And if I give away all my property, and if I distribute all that is mine to the poor, and if I hand over my body so that I burn, but do not have charity, it profits me nothing. Charity is magnanimous, charity is kind.*

1029. See Eph 4:3, Col 3:14.   1030. See Num 12:3.

1031. A somewhat idealized David, one may think; but the allusion is to David's response to the unrelenting hostility of Saul; 1 Sm 21–27.

1032. See Dn 3:21–25: 1 Mc 7.   1033. See Gal 2:11.

Charity is not jealous, does not act boastfully, is not conceited, does not behave shamelessly, does not seek its own advantage, is not irritable, does not think evil, does not rejoice over iniquity, but rejoices together with the truth. It tolerates all things, believes all things, hopes all things, endures all things. Charity never falls away."[1034]

What a great thing this charity is! The soul of the Scriptures, the force of prophecy, the saving power of the sacraments,[1035] the fruit of faith, the wealth of the poor, the life of the dying. What could be more magnanimous than to die for the godless,[1036] what more kindly than to love one's enemies?[1037] It is the one thing that is not cast down by another's good fortune, because it is not jealous. It is the one thing that its own good fortune does not puff up, because it is not conceited. It is the one thing that is not pricked by a bad conscience, because it does not act boastfully. It is steady and unshaken amid reproaches, it is well-disposed in the face of hatred; calm in the face of anger, innocent in the midst of intrigues, groaning in the midst of iniquity, breathing again in the presence of truth. What could be braver than charity, not for paying back insults, but for not caring about them? What could be more faithful, not for vanity, but for eternity?

You see, the reason it endures all things in the present life is that it believes all things about the future life, and it endures everything that is inflicted on it here, because it hopes for everything that is promised it there. Rightly does it never fall away. So pursue after charity, and by thinking holy thoughts about it bring forth the fruits of justice. And whatever you can find in the praises of charity that is grander than what I have been able to say, let it appear in your behavior. It is right, after all, that an old man's sermon should be not only weighty, but brief.

1034. 1 Cor 12:31–13:8.

1035. "Sacraments" in the quotation of 1 Cor 13:2 rendered the Greek *mysteria*; and of course he understood the word in a much wider sense than we do nowadays. But here, by *salus sacramentorum* he is perhaps thinking of the sacraments as we understand the term—above all of the Eucharist.

1036. See Rom 5:6–8.   1037. See Mt 5:44.

Sermon 350A

On Charity and on Loving God Alone
[399 A.D.]

EVERY PAGE OF SCRIPTURE TELLS OF CHARITY

1. I am certainly aware that the hearts of Your Graces are well and truly fed every day on the exhortations of the divine readings and the nourishment of the word of God; all the same, on account of the mutual concern and longing that we have for each other, something should be said to Your Charity about charity. It's the one topic, you see, for which, if anyone wishes to speak about it, he doesn't have to choose a special reading to provide him with an opportunity for his sermon; every page of the Scriptures, after all, wherever you open them, rings of this subject. On this point the Lord himself is a witness, and we are reminded of it from the Gospel; because when he was asked which are the greatest commandments of the law, he answered, *"You shall love the Lord your God with your whole heart, and with your whole soul, and with your whole mind,"* and *"you shall love your neighbor as yourself"*; and in case you should look for anything else in the sacred pages he went on to say, *"On these two commandments depend the whole Law and the Prophets."*[1038]

If the whole Law and the Prophets depend on these two commandments, how much more the Gospel! It is charity, after all, that renews man; because just as cupidity makes a man old, so charity makes him new. That's why he says, as he grunts and groans in his struggle with cupidity or greed, *"I have grown old among all my enemies."*[1039] But that charity or love belongs to the new man is indicated by the Lord himself in this way: *"A new commandment do I give you, that you should love one another."*[1040] So if the Law and the Prophets depend on charity, though it is the old covenant that is obviously presented to us in the Law and the Prophets, how much more must the Gospel, which is so plainly called the new covenant,

1038. Mt 22:37, 39–40.   1039. Ps 6:7.   1040. Jn 13:34.

belong only to charity, seeing that the Lord didn't call anything his own commandment, except that you should love one another? He both called this commandment new, and he came here to renew us, and he made us into new men, and he promised us a new, and what's more eternal, inheritance.

THE CHARITY OF THE NEW TESTAMENT PREFIGURED IN THE OLD, AND UNDERSTOOD PLAINLY EVEN THEN BY CERTAIN GREAT LOVERS OF GOD

2. Because if you are wondering, perhaps, how the law is both called the Old Testament or covenant, and also depends on charity, though charity renews man, and belongs to the new man, here is the reason. It is an old covenant that is there drawn up, because it makes an earthly promise, and it is an earthly kingdom that the Lord there offers to his worshippers. But even then there were to be found lovers of God who loved him freely for his own sake, and cleansed their hearts by chastely sighing for him. They peeled off the outer shells of the old promises, and came upon the prefiguration of the new covenant that was to come, and they grasped that all the things that are commandments or promises in the old covenant with respect to the old man, are figures or symbols of the new covenant, which the Lord was going to fulfill in the last times, as the apostle says so plainly: *"Now these things happened to them as symbols; but they were written for our sake, upon whom the end of the ages has come."*[1041] So the new covenant was being foretold in a hidden way, and being foretold in those figures or symbols.

But when the time for the new covenant came, the new covenant began to be proclaimed openly, and those figures and symbols to be interpreted, and explanations to be given of how the new was to be understood even there, where it was the old that was promised. So the promulgator of the old covenant was Moses; but while he was the one who promulgated the old, he was also one who understood the new.[1042] He was promulgating the old to a fleshly, material-

---

1041. 1 Cor 10:11.

1042. It was, to our way of thinking, a strange commonplace among all the Fathers, and the scholastics after them, that the great, or spiritual, persons of the Old Testament were fully aware of the new covenant, which it prefigured and prepared the way for.

minded people, while he himself, being spiritual, was fully aware of the new. The apostles, however, were both promulgators and administrators of the new covenant; but this doesn't mean that what was later made publicly known through the apostles was not there at that earlier time. So charity is there in the old, charity here in the new. But there charity is more hidden away, fear more out in the open; while here charity is more publicly manifest, fear altogether less. To the extent, you see, that charity grows, fear diminishes. As charity grows, that is, the soul's sense of security increases; and where there is complete security there is no fear, with John the apostle saying, *"Consummate charity casts out fear."*[1043]

THE PSALM VERSE, "DO NOT BE ENVIOUS OF THE WICKED,"
INTERPRETED AS AN EXHORTATION TO THE LOVE OF THE
AGE TO COME

3. Thus in talking to Your Holinesses about this charity, I have also taken this present psalm[1044] as a point of departure—because, as I said, whichever of the Lord's pages you read, it admonishes us about nothing else but charity. See for yourselves whether the divine utterances have any other effect but that we should love; see whether they work toward anything else but to set us on fire, to inflame us, to kindle our desire, to get us sighing and groaning until we finally arrive. Human beings having a difficult time here on earth, and finding themselves beset by the greatest trials and temptations, frequently remark with their mortal thoughts and feeble reflections how the wicked usually have the best of it here for a time, and grow proud in their fleeting prosperity—indeed such thoughts often occur as a temptation to the servants of God,[1045] as though they were devoting themselves to God to no purpose at all, if they notice that they lack what they observe the godless to have in abundance. So with humanity in that sort of situation, the Holy Spirit foresaw that we would be tempted like this and wished to change the direction of our love, and prevent us from thinking that we should imitate godless and villainous men the more we see how

1043. 1 Jn 4:18.

1044. Ps 37—than which there are few Old Testament texts more redolent of the old covenant and its earthly, this-worldly promises.

1045. Monks, or religious men.

well they do in the world, simply out of love for the sort of things that their abundant possession of had them strutting about like turkey cocks. And so he said, *"Do not be envious of the evil-minded"*—it's the beginning of the psalm—*"nor jealous of those who work iniquity; since they shall soon wither like grass, and soon fall like the herbs of the meadow."*[1046]

Does the grass never grow and flourish? But it's only for a short time that it flourishes, it will soon dry up; and it's the cold weather that makes it flourish. The coming of the Lord Jesus Christ will be like the hot weather of the year; this present time is like the cold weather of the year. But let us be on our guard against our charity growing cold[1047] in the cold weather of the year. Our blossom time has not yet appeared; it is so cold on the outside, but there should be heat in the roots. That's the way, after all, that trees put out leaves in the summer, and are beautiful and fruitful, though they looked so dried up and withered in the winter. Was everything you see on the branches in summer also there throughout the winter? Yes, it was, but it was hiding in the roots. So our time to blossom, which has been promised us, is not yet; may our summer come; it isn't here yet, it's hidden away. We can say more correctly that it isn't apparent, than that it isn't here yet. The apostle, you see, says plainly, *"For you are dead."* It's as though he were speaking to trees during the winter. But to show you that while the surface seemed dead, the trees were still alive inside, he immediately went on to say, *"and your life is hidden with Christ in God."*[1048] We seem to be living on this earth; just consider where we have taken root. The root of our love is with Christ, it's in God. That's where our blossoming in all its glory is to be found; but it isn't apparent just now.

IF THE APOSTLE TOLD THE RICH NOT TO PLACE THEIR HOPES IN THIS WORLD, BUT TO HOPE FOR THE FUTURE, HOW MUCH MORE OUGHT THOSE TO DO SO, WHO HAVE VOWED TO HAVE NOTHING ON THIS EARTH!

4. But what did he go on to say? *"When Christ appears, your life, then you also will appear with him in glory."*[1049] So now is the time for groaning, then it will be for rejoicing; now for desiring, then for embracing. What we desire now is not present; but let us not falter

---

1046. Ps 37:1–2.   1047. See Mt 24:12.   1048. Col 3:3.   1049. Col 3:4.

in desire; let long, continuous desire be our daily exercise, because the one who made the promise doesn't cheat us. I'm not saying, brothers, that nobody should grow cold; nobody should even grow tepid. True, the lovers of the world may well jeer at the servants of God, saying, "Look what we've got, and what we enjoy; where are your good times, your fun?" But you, while you haven't got the things you can see, do have the things you believe in; they for their part don't believe in things that can't be demonstrated. Rejoice then because you have come to believe; you will rejoice more than ever, when eventually you see. And if you sigh and groan because you cannot point to what you believe, your groans of sorrow will profit you not only for salvation, but also for everlasting glory.

There's nothing they can show us of any great value; their good times are visibly present, ours are in the future. Though it would be truer for us to say that theirs are neither present nor future; I mean, because they love false good times in the present, they won't come to the true ones in the future. If, however, they would turn their backs on the false good times of the present, and find what they can do with what they actually have, and discover what they can acquire with it, they should listen to the advice of the blessed apostle, which he authorizes Timothy to pass on to the rich. He says, you see, *"Command the rich of this world not to have proud ideas, nor to place their hopes in the uncertainty of riches, but in the living God, who grants us all things abundantly for our enjoyment. Let them be rich in good works, let them give things away easily, let them share. Let them save up for themselves a good foundation for the future, so that they may lay hold of the true life."*[1050]

So then, brothers, if the apostle was determined to turn away the thoughts of those who appeared to be doing very well in the present life from earthly concerns, and to direct them toward heaven; if he didn't want them to rejoice in the present, but to hope for things to come; if the apostle says such things to people who have all this, how much more should that man stretch out his whole heart and soul to what lies ahead in the future, who has decided to have nothing on this earth? To have nothing superfluous, that means, to have nothing which can be a burden, to have nothing which can tie him down, to have nothing which can hinder him. Because even in this

1050. 1 Tm 6:17–19.

time that saying is more truly applicable to the servants of God, *"as having nothing, and possessing all things."*[1051] Let there be nothing you call your own, and all things will be yours. If you stick to a part, you lose the whole; after all, what would be sufficient if you were rich, must be sufficient if you are poor.

Sermon 368

Sermon of Augustine the Bishop Preached on the Text "Whoever Loves His Soul Will Lose It"

[Date uncertain]

IF NOBODY EVER HATED HIS OWN FLESH, MUCH LESS DID ANYONE EVER HATE HIS OWN SOUL

1. Just now, brothers and sisters, while the divine reading was being read, we heard the Lord saying, *"Whoever loves his soul will lose it."*[1052] This statement seems to be contradicted by what the apostle says. *"Nobody ever hated his own flesh."*[1053] So if there's nobody who ever hated his own flesh, how much less anybody who ever hated his own soul? The soul, clearly, is much more important than the flesh, because it is the inhabitant, the flesh merely the dwelling; and the soul is the master, the flesh the servant; the soul the superior, the flesh the subject. So if nobody ever hated his own flesh, who can there ever have been to hate his own soul?

That being the case, the present reading from the Gospel has landed us with no small problem; because in it we heard *"Whoever loves his soul will lose it."* It's dangerous to love the soul, or it may perish. But if the reason it is dangerous for you to love your soul is that it may thereby perish, the reason why you ought not to love it is that you don't want it to perish. But if you don't want it to perish, that means you love it.

"But because I'm afraid of losing it, that's why I don't love it—and of course, what I'm afraid of losing, I love . . ."

And the Lord says somewhere else, *"What does it profit a man, if*

1051. 2 Cor 6:10.   1052. Jn 12:25.   1053. Eph 5:29.

he gains the whole world, but suffers the loss of his own soul?"[1054] There
you have it, that the soul is to be so loved as to be preferred to gaining the whole world; and yet the one who loves his soul is to observe that if he loves it he will lose it. You don't want to lose it?
Don't love it. But if you don't want to lose it, you cannot not love it.

THE WRONG KIND OF LOVE OF THE SOUL WHICH SPRINGS FROM HATRED AND THE RIGHT KIND OF HATRED OF THE SOUL WHICH SPRINGS FROM LOVE

2. So there are people who love their souls in the wrong way; and
this is what the word of God means to correct—not that they
should hate their souls, but that they should love them in the right
way. It's by loving them badly, you see, that they lose them, and
you're left with an enormous kind of back to front contradiction;
still the fact remains, that if you love it in the wrong way you will
lose it, if you hate it in the right way you will keep it safe. So there is
a certain wrong way of loving the soul, and a certain right way of
hating it; but the wrong way of loving springs from hatred, and the
right way of hating springs from love.

What's the wrong way of loving the soul? When you love your
soul in all kinds of iniquity. Listen to how this wrong kind of love
springs from hatred: *"But whoever loves iniquity, hates his own
soul."*[1055] Observe on the other hand how the right kind of hatred
springs from love: in the same place the Lord went on to say, *"But
whoever hates his soul in this age will find it for eternal life."*[1056] Obviously, you love very much what you wish to find for eternal life.
What use, after all, is what you love for a time? Either you are removed from it, or it is removed from you; when it's you that are
eliminated, what ceases to be is the actual lover, when that thing is
eliminated, what vanishes is what you loved. So where either the
lover ceases to be or the thing loved, it's not worth loving. But what
is worth loving? What can be with us forever? If you want to have
your soul safe forever, hate it for a time. So the right way of hating
springs from love; the wrong way of loving springs from hatred.

1054. Mt 16:26.   1055. Ps 11:5.   1056. Jn 12:25.

THE RIGHT KIND OF LOVE MUST DRIVE OUT THE WRONG KIND

3. What, then, is the right way of loving the soul? Do you imagine the martyrs didn't love their souls? You can certainly see nowadays, if anyone is in peril of his life,[1057] life of this present age, how his friends rush around to save it; how they rush off to the church, how the bishop is begged to intervene; if there is anything he can do, to be quick about it, to hurry up. Why all this? For the sake of a soul. And everyone is agitated, each one decides to drop every other business and get a move on; all haste is applauded, all delay complained of. Why? For the sake of a soul. What does that mean, for the sake of a soul? So that a man should not die. Didn't the martyrs know how to love their souls? And yet all this is for the sake of a soul, so that a man should not die.

A person's real death is iniquity. If you run a hundred miles for the sake of this life, how many miles should you run for the sake of eternal life? If you are in such a hurry to gain a few days, and those so uncertain—I mean, the man delivered from death today doesn't know whether he'll die tomorrow—still if there's all this rushing around to gain a few days, because even up to old age our days are few, how much rushing around should there be for the sake of eternal life? And yet people are so sluggish and slow about taking any steps toward it. You will have difficulty in finding even someone who has suffered making slow, hesitant moves for the sake of eternal life. So there's plenty of the wrong sort of love around; while very few people have the right sort of love. I mean, just as there's nobody who doesn't love his own soul, so too there's nobody who doesn't love his own flesh. So it can happen that both what the apostle said is true: *"Nobody ever hated his own flesh,"*[1058] and that the soul is not truly loved.

So let us learn then, brothers and sisters, how to love our own souls. Every pleasure provided by the world is going to pass away. There is a love that is useful and a love that does harm. Let love be hampered by love; let the love that does harm retire, and the love that is of use take its place. But it's because people don't want to re-

1057. He means from the law—under sentence of death.

1058. Eph 5:29.

tire from that sort, that this other sort can't gain entry to them.
They are full up, so they can't hold anything else. They must pour
something out, and then they can hold some more. They are full,
you see, of the love of sensual pleasures, full of the love of this present life, full of the love of gold and silver, of the possessions of this
world. So those who are full in this way are like jars. Do you want
honey to gain entry into a jar from which you haven't yet emptied
the vinegar? Empty out what you have, in order to take and hold
what you don't yet have. That's why the first step is to renounce
this world, and then the next is to turn back to God.[1059] When you
renounce, you are emptying out; when you turn back to God, you
are being filled—but only if it's done, not merely with the body, but
also with the heart.

THE RIGHT ORDER OF LOVE, AND PROGRESS IN IT

4. The question arises, brothers and sisters, how this love grows.
You see, it has its beginnings, it has its increase, it has its perfection.
And we clergy need to know who are just beginning, so that we
may encourage them to increase; who haven't even begun, so that
we may advise them where to begin; who have both begun and
grown, so that we may urge them on toward perfection. The first
thing for Your Graces to note is this: what people always love and
value before anything else is themselves, and from there they go on
to value other things. If you value gold, you first value yourself, and
from there gold; because if you were to die, there wouldn't be anyone to possess the gold. So with each and every one of us love begins with oneself, and cannot but begin with oneself. And nobody
needs to be advised to love himself; this is innate, after all, not only
in human beings but also in animals. After all, you can see, brothers
and sisters, how not only huge wild beasts and large animals, like
oxen and camels and elephants, but also flies, but also the tiniest
little worms, how they don't want to die, and how they love themselves. All animals shrink from death. So they love themselves,
they want to take care of themselves; some do it by speed, others by

1059. An allusion to the ceremony of admittance to the catechumenate, in which
the candidate first stood on a goatskin and facing to the west (the region of darkness) renounced Satan and all his pomps; and then turning around toward the east
(the region of light), confessed his faith in Christ.

hiding, others by resisting and fighting back. All animals, never-theless, fight for their lives, they don't want to die, they want to take care of themselves. So they love themselves.

Something else also starts being loved. But what is this some-thing else? Whatever it is you have loved, it is either the same as yourself, or it is inferior to you, or it is superior to you. If what you love is inferior to you, love it to console yourself with, love it as something to work at, love it as something to use, not as something to tie yourself to. For example, you love gold; don't tie yourself to gold. How much better are you than gold? Gold, after all, is shin-ing earth; you though were made to the image of God in order to be illuminated by God. Since gold is one of God's creatures, yet it wasn't gold that God made to his image, but you; it follows that he placed gold under you. So this sort of love is to be treated lightly. Such things as these are to be acquired for use; one mustn't let one-self be stuck to them, as with glue, by the bonds of love. You shouldn't make extra limbs for yourself, which will cause you great pain and torment when they start being lopped of. So what, then? Rise up from this love by which you love things lower than you are; start loving things that are your equals, that are the same as you are. But what need is there of many examples? If you want, you can do it very shortly.

A QUICK WAY TO REACH THE PERFECTION OF LOVE

5. In fact the Lord himself has told us in the Gospel, and made it abundantly clear, what the proper order is for our obtaining true love and true charity. This is how he put it: *"You shall love the Lord your God with your whole heart, and with your whole soul, and with all your strength; and your neighbor as yourself."*[1060] So first of all, love God, then yourself; after that love your neighbor as yourself. First learn, though, how to love yourself, and in this way love your neighbor as yourself; because if you don't know how to love your-self, how will you be able to love your neighbor in truth? Some people, you see, assume that they are appropriately and legiti-mately loving themselves, when they snatch other people's prop-erty, when they get drunk, when they make themselves the slaves of lust, when by a variety of false slurs they make unjust profits.

1060. Mk 12:30–31.

Such people as these should listen to Scripture saying, *"Whoever loves iniquity, hates his own soul."*[1061] So if by loving iniquity you not only don't love yourself, but in fact hate yourself, how will you be able to love either God or your neighbor?

So if you want to keep the order of true charity, act justly, love mercy, shun self-indulgence; begin, according to the Lord's instruction to love not only friends but also enemies.[1062] And when you strive to maintain these standards faithfully with your whole heart, you will be able to climb up by these virtues, as by a flight of steps, to being worthy to love God with your whole mind and your whole strength. And when you reach this happy state of perfection, you will reckon all the desires of this world as nothing but dung,[1063] and with the prophet you will be able to say, *"But for me to cling to God is good."*[1064]

Sermon 382

Sermon on the Birthday of Saint Stephen the First Martyr
[Date uncertain]

THE PREACHER ASKS THE CONGREGATION FOR THEIR PRAYERS, AND INTRODUCES THE SUBJECT: "LOVE YOUR ENEMIES"

1. Jesus, the son of Nave,[1065] was fighting in the desert, and Moses was praying. They weren't both fighting and both praying, but one was fighting, the other praying. It was what you would expect, that the one who was fighting did not grow faint, because the other was winning the battle by his prayers. In the same way I too appear to be speaking; but I am speaking while others are praying, in order that by their prayers I may benefit from what the Lord said: *"Open your mouth wide, and I will fill it."*[1066] If Joshua was helped by just one person praying, and was not defeated, how much more shall I

1061. Ps 11:5.   1062. See Mt 5:44; Lk 6:27.   1063. See Phil 3:8.

1064. Ps 73:28.   1065. Joshua, the son of Nun, for us; see Ex 17:8–13.

1066. Ps 81:10.

be helped, for whom not just one but many are beseeching my God? Now my heart will not be afraid of speaking, because *"my mouth will speak the praise of the Lord."*[1067]

Our Lord and savior Jesus Christ commands us to do something and promises us something. What he commands us to do is to be done here; what he promises us is to be obtained elsewhere. What he commands us to do has a limit, because it is to be done in the course of time; what he promises us has no limit, because it is eternal. What he commands is work, what he promises us is wages. Here Your Holinesses should take note of how great is his mercy toward us, in that he set us work to do here which has a limit, gives us wages in heaven that have no limit. And that's why we ought first to do the hard work here, and after that to receive the reward in heaven, rather than wanting to receive the reward here and after that to do the work. There are some people, you see, about whom the Lord said, *"Amen I tell you, they have received their reward."*[1068] But you, perhaps, are all agog for the reward, and lazy about the hard work; how can you have the nerve to ask God for what he has promised you and do not what God has commanded you? First carry out the command, and in this way go on to demand fulfillment of the promise. First, I repeat, listen to his command, and only then require him to keep his promise.

What he commands us to do, you see, is to love your enemies. *"Love your enemies,"* he says, *"do good to those who hate you and pray for those who speak ill of you."* You have heard what the work is, wait for the wages: *"so that you may be,"* he said, *"children of your Father who is in heaven, who makes his sun rise upon the good and the bad, and sends rain upon the just and the unjust."*[1069]

THE EXAMPLE OF CHRIST, PRAYING FOR THOSE WHO CRUCIFIED HIM

2. Look at the Lord himself, who did precisely what he commanded. After so many things the godless Jews committed against him, repaying him evil for good, didn't he say, as he hung on the cross, *"Father, forgive them, because they do not know what they are doing"*?[1070] He prayed as man, as God with the Father he heard the prayer. Even now, you see, he prays in us, prays for us, is prayed to by us.

1067. Ps 145:21.   1068. Mt 6:2.   1069. Mt 5:44–45.   1070. Lk 23:34.

He prays in us as our high priest, prays for us as our head, is prayed to by us as our God. So when he was praying as he hung on the cross, he could see, and he could foresee; he could see all his enemies, he could foresee that many of them would become his friends. That's why he was interceding for them all. They were raging, he was praying. They were saying to Pilate *"Crucify!"*;[1071] he was crying out, *"Father, forgive."* He was hanging from the cruel nails, but he didn't lose his gentleness. He was asking for pardon for those from whom he was receiving such hideous treatment.

They were raging, barking furiously all around him, shaking their heads at him—their far from sane heads—and as one man, like so many raving lunatics, raging on all sides against the supreme physician set there in their midst. He was hanging there and healing them. He was suspended there, and yet dispensing goodness. He wouldn't come down from the cross, because out of his blood he was preparing a medicine for their frenzy. Finally, after his resurrection he cured those whose utter insanity he had tolerated as he hung on the cross. There you have why Christ came; not to destroy what he had found, but *"to seek and save what had been lost,"*[1072] so that by loving his raging enemies, he might make them into believers and his friends.

THE EXAMPLE OF STEPHEN

3. But in case you should say it's too much to expect of you, to imitate your Lord, though *"he suffered for you, leaving you an example, so that you might follow in his footsteps,"*[1073] take a look at Stephen, your fellow servant. He was a human being like you, he was born of the same sinful lump as you, he was redeemed with the same price as you were too, he was a deacon, he used to read the Gospel, which you also read or hear. There he found it written, *"Love your enemies."*[1074] He learned the lesson he read there, he carried it out in practice. When he was being murdered by the Jews under a hail of rocks, not only did he not utter any threats against them, but over and above that he prayed for pardon for those who were stoning him. Kneeling down, you see, he began praying, and said, *"Lord, do not hold this sin against them."*[1075] They were stoning him, he was

1071. Lk 23:22.   1072. Lk 19:10.   1073. 1 Pt 2:21.   1074. Mt 5:44.
1075. Acts 7:60.

praying for them; they were pursuing him with rage, he was peace-
ably following Christ. They were blinded by their malice; for him
the heavens were opened, he saw the Son of God, and he was enlightened by wisdom. They were hurling stones, he was shooting
prayers ahead, as though he were saying, "Lord, if you kill these
enemies now, whom will you later on make into friends?"

HOW STEPHEN'S PRAYER WON THE CONVERSION OF SAUL

4. I mean, to show Your Holinesses how much weight the holy
martyr's prayer carried, come back with me to that young man
called Saul, who while Stephen was being stoned was keeping the
coats of those who were doing the stoning, as though to be seen as
himself throwing the stones with the hands of them all. Later on, as
you know—because I know whom I'm talking to, I'm talking to
my brothers and sisters, I'm talking to my Father's children, I'm
talking as a disciple to my fellow disciples—later on, *"he received
letters from the chief priests, so that whomever he might find to be followers of the Christian way, men and women, he should bring in chains
to Jerusalem,"* to be tortured and punished. *"As he was going on his
way, suddenly there shone around him a light from heaven. He fell
down and heard a voice saying to him, Saul, Saul, why are you persecuting me? And he said, Who are you, Lord? And the Lord answered, I
am Jesus the Nazarene,"* he said, *"whom you are persecuting. It is hard
for you to kick against the goad,"*[1076] because you won't hurt the goad,
but your feet which you are kicking with. What have you got
against me? *"Why are you persecuting me?"* Why are you rearing up
against me to your own harm, and not rather humbling yourself
for your own good? But against all the evils you are committing
against me, for which indeed I ought to have destroyed you long
ago, my servant Stephen has prayed for you.

He was struck down a persecutor, he was raised up a preacher.
Let me say it plainly, let me say it more explicitly; he was struck
down *"a son of perdition,"*[1077] raised up *"a vessel of election"*;[1078] he was
struck down as Saul, raised up as Paul. Because if Stephen hadn't
prayed like that, the Church would never have had Paul. But the
reason Paul was raised up from the ground is that Saint Stephen
was heard when he bowed down to the ground.

1076. Acts 9:1–5; 26:14.   1077. Jn 17:12.   1078. Acts 9:15.

WE ARE INCLINED TO ASK GOD TO PUNISH OUR ENEMIES; HE TEACHES US TO IMITATE CHRIST ON THE CROSS AND PRAY FOR THEM

5. But against these great and splendid examples, this is how you go about it, whoever you are who don't love: Kneel down beat your forehead on the ground, cry out and say, "O God, kill the bad man." You as well, praying like that for a man to die, are a bad man praying against a bad man, and that now makes two bad men. You are crying out and saying, "O God, kill the bad man." He will answer you, "Which one of you?" Would Your Holinesses please reflect, I'm saying things you all know. A human judge doesn't himself kill the man he finds guilty, but he gives the order and the executioner kills him. The judge says "Put him to death," and the torturer does so.

And so you, when you say, "Lord, kill my enemy," are making yourself the judge and expecting God to be the torturer. God will answer you, "Most certainly not; I will not be the torturer of the sinner, but rather his liberator, because *I do not desire the death of the sinner, but rather that he may be converted and live.*"[1079] Because if I had the same kind of will as you have, I would have killed you first, before you came to me uninvited. Haven't you blasphemed me? Haven't you provoked me with your evil deeds? Haven't you wished to blot out my name from the earth? Haven't you ignored me in my commandments or in my servants? If I had killed you then as my enemy, whom would I now be making into my friend? So why are you now, with your bad prayer, trying to teach me to do what I never did in your case? So rather let me," God says to you, "let me teach you to imitate me. Hanging on the cross I said, *'Father, forgive them, because they do not know what they are doing,'* I have taught this to my soldiers, taught it to my martyrs. You too first be my martyr witness, my recruit against the devil. Otherwise you will in no way fight and win, unless you pray for your enemies."

1079. Ez 33:11.

Sermon 385

On Our Love for One Another

HUMAN LOVE CAN BE BAD AS WELL AS GOOD

1. We are advised, dearest brothers and sisters, in the Old as well as in the New Testament, in what way we should maintain perfect charity. This, you see, is what the Lord himself said in the Gospel: *"You shall love your neighbor as yourself."*[1080] So let us deal for a little while with the love of human beings for each other; because there are warped kinds of human love. You love someone else in a warped manner, if you love yourself in a warped manner; but if you love yourself in the right way, you also love the other person in the right way. For example, there are shameful, detestable kinds of love; the loves of adulterers, the loves of corrupt persons, unclean loves. Evil loves are reprobated by all human laws and divine laws. So put away these unlawful kinds of love; let us investigate the lawful ones.

VARIOUS GRADES OF LAWFUL LOVE

2. Lawful love starts from marriage, but that is still a fleshly form of it. You can see that it is shared with the animals; and those sparrows, which are chirping away there, have marriages and build nests, and together sit on the eggs, together feed the fledglings. It is, to be sure, a lawful kind of love among human beings, but as you see, it's fleshly. The second grade is love of your children, but this too is still fleshly. It is not, after all, particularly praiseworthy for people to love their children, but it is abominable when they don't. I mean, am I going to praise as something remarkable in a human being what I can see in a tigress? Snakes love their children, lions and wolves love their children. So don't imagine that it is anything very remarkable that you love your children; with this kind of love you are still on a par with snakes; if you don't love your children, you are letting snakes beat you. I am now speaking about re-

---

1080. Mk 13:31. The preacher, or composer, forgets to point out what he has just hinted at, that Jesus is quoting Lv 19:18.

spectable kinds of love; you see, I have excluded those shameful kinds.

Another grade of love, that of our kindred, already seems to be proper to human beings, if it isn't just a matter of habit. I mean, the love which extends beyond our relations is greater than the love which is confined within the circle of kinship. When you love your relations, you are still loving your own blood. Try loving others who are not related to you, give a welcome to strangers. This love has now expanded very widely. It only grows, though, by extending itself from married partners to children, from children to kinsfolk, from kinsfolk to strangers, and from strangers to enemies. But to reach that final point it has to go up many steps, many grades.

FROM FRIENDSHIP BASED ON HABIT TO FRIENDSHIP BASED ON REASON

3. So consider what I am going to say about friendship. There are friends—excepting always that friendship, which should even be called friendship, being the product of a bad conscience; there are people, you see, who do bad things together, and that's why they seem to be inseparable, because they are bound together by a bad conscience. So apart from that nefarious sort of friendship, there is a kind of friendship which is still merely fleshly, that arises from the habit of living together, chatting together, going around together, so that people feel sad when they are left or thrown over by friends with whom they were in the habit of chatting and getting together. Two people meet, they go around together for three days, and now they don't want to separate. And this pleasant kind of friendship is honest and decent enough, of course; but let us continue to examine it, because we are inquiring about the grades of this love; and let us see how we may arrive at such a love or friendship as I have mentioned.

So there is this friendship arising from habit, not from reason; animals too go in for it. Let two horses but eat together, and they desire each other's company. If one of them goes ahead the next day, the other one hurries after, desiring, so it seems, its friend; it can hardly be controlled by its rider, and goes on challenging him with its impetuosity, until it catches up. When it reaches the one that has gone ahead, it calms down. It was carrying the rider's weight, but it was being urged on by the weight of love; it has come at last, as it were, to its proper place, and has rested there.[1081] This sort of friendship arising from habit is still to be found in animals; let us continue to rise up from this sort too. There is another, higher kind of friendship, arising not from habit but from reason, by which we love a person because of mutual trust and benevolence in this mortal life. Any love or friendship we find which is superior to this is divine. Let people start loving God, and the only thing they will love in other human beings is God.

THE LOVE INVOLVED IN FRIENDSHIP MUST BE GRATUITOUS

4. The first thing, you see, that Your Graces should observe, is how the love involved in friendship ought to be gratuitous. I mean, the reason you have a friend, or love one, ought not to be so that he can do something for you; if that's why you love him, so that he can get you some money, or some temporal advantage, then you aren't really loving him, but the thing he gets for you. A friend is to be loved freely, for his own sake, not for the sake of something else. If the rule of friendship urges you to love human beings freely for their own sakes, how much more freely is God to be loved, who bids you love other people! There can be nothing more delightful than God. I mean, in people there are always things that cause offense; still, through friendship you force yourself to put up with things that offend you in a person, for the sake of friendship. So if you ought not to break the ties of friendship with a human being just because of some things in him you have to put up with, what things should ever force you to break the ties of friendship with God? You can find nothing more delightful than God. God is not something that can ever offend you, if you don't offend him; there is nothing more beautiful, nothing more full of light[1082] than he is.

But you are going to say to me, "I can't see him; how can I love

---

1081. This is elaborating on Augustine's famous dictum, *Amor meus pondus meum* [my love is my weight]. Weight, in his natural philosophy, is the force, not quite gravity, which pulls things to their "proper place"; heavy things like earth downward to the lowest place, light things like fire upward to the top place. Augustine will associate this theme of my love being my weight with one of his favorite texts, Ws 11:20: "You have arranged all things in measure, number and weight." See, for example, *The Trinity*, XI, 18; also *The Literal Meaning of Genesis*, IV, 3, 7–12.

1082. Reading *lucidius* with some manuscripts, instead of the *dulcius*, "nothing sweeter," of the text.

someone I can't see?" Here's how you can learn to love someone you can't see; I am now going to show you how you should strive to see what you cannot see with these eyes. Here you are, you love a friend; what do you love in him? You are loving him freely, gratuitously. But perhaps this friend of yours, to pass over other things, is an old man; it can happen after all, that you have an old man as a friend.[1083] What do you love in the old man? His bent and twisted body, his white hairs, the wrinkles in his face, his sunken cheeks?[1084] If it's just the body you can see, there is nothing more unsightly than old age; and yet you love something, and you don't love the body which you can see, which is unsightly. How can you see what you love? After all, if I ask you, "Why do you love him?" you're going to answer me, "He is a faithful man." So you love faith in him. If you love faith, the eyes with which faith can be seen are the very eyes with which God can be seen. So start loving God, and you will love other people on account of God.

GOD IS NOT TO BE LOVED FOR THE SAKE OF ANY REWARD

5. Listen to a splendid instance. The devil is certainly the accuser of the saints, and because he cannot drag us before the sort of judge he can deceive, he is unable to bring false charges against us; he knows in whose presence he is speaking. So because he can't bring false charges against us, he looks for true ones to bring. That's why he tempts us, in order to have true accusations to make. So this adversary of ours, who envies us the kingdom of heaven, who doesn't want us to be in the place he was cast out of: *"Does Job,"* he says, *"worship God for nothing?"*[1085] So here we are, being challenged by the adversary to worship God for nothing, when in his search for something to object against Job, he thought he had found something serious, because he said, *"Does Job worship God for nothing?"* This was not because he had seen into his heart, but because he had seen how rich he was.

We ought to be on our guard against loving God for any reward.

1083. This wry remark has a genuine Augustinian flavor to it—Augustine preaching as an old man. The theme, however, is one he does touch on from time to time. So our patchwork artist could well have taken this little passage from a genuine sermon.

1084. No dentures in the ancient world!   1085. Jb 1:9.

What's the point, after all, of loving God for a reward? What sort of reward is it that God is going to give you? Whatever else he gives you, it's less than he is. You are worshipping him not freely, not gratuitously, in order to receive something from him. Worship him freely, and you will receive God himself; God, you see, is keeping himself for you to enjoy him. And if you love the things he made, what must he that made them be like? If the world is beautiful, what must the architect of the world be like? So tear your heart away from the love of creatures, in order to cling to the creator, and to be able to say what is written in the psalm, *"But for me it is good to cling to God."*[1086]

LOVING WHAT GOD HAS MADE INSTEAD OF GOD IS A KIND OF ADULTERY

6. But if you forsake the one who made you and love the things he made, by forsaking the one who made you, you become an adulterer. That's what the letter of James says loud and clear, calling them adulterers. *"Adulterers!"* And why adulterers? You ask why? *"Do you not know,"* he says, *"that friendship with this world is enmity with God? So whoever wants to be a friend of this age is thereby consti-tuted an enemy of God's."*[1087] He was expressing what he meant by saying *"Adulterers!"* The soul which forsakes the creator for love of the creature is an adulteress. There is nothing more chaste than love of him, nothing more delightful; once you forsake him, my soul, and embrace the other, you become unclean. In order to be worthy of his embrace, my soul, let go of these other things, and cling to him freely, for nothing. It was in that connection that the psalm said, *"But for me to cling to God is good."* In the previous verse it had said this: *"You have destroyed all who play the whore away from you."*[1088] And as though to show you what playing the whore means, he added, *"But for me to cling to God is good"*; I don't want anything else but him; to cling to him, that is my good, that is my free, gratu-itous good; and that's why it's also called grace, because it is to be had free, gratis and for nothing.

So when you start loving God freely and for nothing, you can throw care to the winds, because you are both loving your friend for nothing, and also loving him to this end, that he may love God

1086. Ps 73:28.   1087. Jas 4:4–5.   1088. Ps 73:27.

together with you. Take a look, after all, at that common friendship we started from, in the course of which we climbed steps or
grades; take a look at that. A husband loves his wife, and a wife her
husband; without a shadow of doubt he wants her and she wants
him to be safe and well. She wants to have him safe and sound, she
wants to have him doing well. She loves him to this end, that she
herself wishes to be safe and sound and to do well; what she wishes
for herself, she also wishes for him. She loves her children; who
would ever wish their children to be anything but safe and well?
She loves her friend; who would ever wish their friends to be anything but safe and sound? To this extent indeed, that should anything happen to your friend you tremble, you're upset, you start
worrying, you rush off to prevent it happening; when it does happen you wring your hands. So what does this show that you want?
To have your friend safe and well. So if all who love anyone or anything wish to have the object of their love safe and well, let them
understand where true safety or well-being is to be found, and they
will start loving that in itself, and be obliged to love this true well-
being or safety in and for their friends as well.

WELL-BEING IN THIS WORLD IS TO BE USED, ETERNAL WELL-BEING OR SALVATION IS TO BE LOVED

7. If you are looking for God with the eyes in your head, consider
the three youths delivered in the fire.[1089] If you are looking for God
with faith, consider the Maccabees crowned in the fire.[1090] That
other kind of well-being or salvation is to be loved, this kind is to be
used; it is, you see, necessary to use it, because it is transitory and
doesn't last long. I mean, what the doctors call health or well-being,
brothers and sisters, is not the real, true kind; it is just a sort of alle-
viation for us, because life in this fragile flesh is a continuous sickness. You imagine, do you, that people are sick when they have a
fever, and in good health when they are hungry? "He's well," they

---

1089. Shadrach, Meshach, and Abednego, in the fiery furnace; Dan 3. Consider
them if you want to see God in this way, because—I presume—there appeared a
fourth figure in the furnace, like a son of God; Dan 3:25. But bringing these three
and the Maccabee brothers into this context is very peculiar. There seem to be several lines of thought tangled up together in the composer's/preacher's mind.

1090. See 2 Mc 7.

say. Do you want to see how bad it is to be hungry? Leave him without medicine for a week, he's dead; but because you set before him the appropriate medicine every day, he stays alive.

The medicine for hunger, of course, is food; the medicine for thirst, drink; the medicine for weariness, sleep. The medicine for sitting down is walking about; the medicine for walking about is sitting down; the medicine for fatigue is slumber; the medicine for slumber is being awake. And notice how feeble the human body is; the very aids I mentioned, if you take them and persist in them, your health suffers. When you were hungry, you looked for the aid of food; here's the aid of food; you eat it, you satisfy your hunger. If you do more than satisfy your hunger, your health suffers. You look for a drink to aid you in your thirst; if you drink too much, you choke, where just now you were being driven by thirst. You've got tired through walking, you want to sit down; sit down perpetually, and see if you don't get tired of that. So whatever remedy you take to eliminate some inconvenience, if you persist in it, your health suffers.

TRUE HEALTH OR WELL-BEING IS ETERNAL LIFE

8. So what is this well-being really, this health, brothers and sisters, so soon to pass, so fragile, so perishable, so vain? Indeed, indeed, it's as it says: *"For what is your life? It is a mist that appears for a moment."*[1091] So *"whoever in this life loves his soul will lose it. But whoever in this age hates his soul, will keep it safe for eternal life."*[1092] What is eternal life? True well-being, real health. And if you now consider your friend, whom you love in this world, wishing him to be safe and well; because you yourself are now eager for that well-being and health which is eternal, you now love him to that same end; and everything you want to do for your friend, you want to do it to this end, that he may enjoy that health and well-being with you. You love justice, you see; you want him to be just. You love being under God; you want him too to be under God. You love eternal life; you want him to reign with you there forever.

Then there's that enemy of yours who, as you are all too well aware, is hounding you; it is, in fact, wickedness that is hounding you. With him you ought to be angry in a compassionate way; he is

1091. Jas 4:14.   1092. Jn 12:25.

suffering from a fever in the soul. So just as a worldly friend loves his own soul by the standards of this world, and wishes to rid his friend of a fever, since he loves him as himself with respect to present health and well-being, in the same way you, whoever they are that you love, should love them with respect to eternal life. When you find them suffering from anger, indignation, hatred, iniquity, do your best to rid them of such diseases of the spirit, in the same way as the worldly friend deals with diseases of the body. Love in fact to this end, that you may make them what you also are, and perfect charity will be found in you.

If you turn out to be like this, then love your wife or husband to this end, love your children to this end, to this end love your relative, your neighbor, the unknown stranger, your enemy, and perfect charity will be found in you. If it is, then you are overcoming the world,[1093] and the prince of this world is being driven out outside. I mean, you have heard what the Lord said. *"The prince of this world has been thrown outside,"*[1094] because he himself was going to suffer, and by his passion was going to reproduce his love in us all. *"Greater love has nobody than this, that a person should lay down his life for his friends."*[1095] So in order to be loved, he first loved; in order that nobody should be afraid of dying for his name, he first died for all. So in order to build up charity in all our hearts, he threw the devil outside. Outside where? From the hearts of human beings. Greed and cupidity bring him in, love and charity put him out.

AS THE LORD HAS RESCUED US FROM THE DEVIL, LET US
TAKE PAINS TO FILL OURSELVES WITH GOOD THINGS

9. We, however, brothers and sisters, should reflect very carefully upon the aforementioned steps or grades of charity, in order to avoid repaying the Lord evil for good. And because he came and tied up the strongman, that is the devil, and removed us all, who were his gear, from his power,[1096] we must by his grace empty ourselves of all evil, and take great pains to fill ourselves with an abundance of good things. We should be afraid of that thing the Lord himself said: *"When the unclean spirit goes out of a person, it walks about through dry places, seeking rest, and it cannot find any; after this*

1093. See Jn 16:33.   1094. Jn 12:31.   1095. Jn 15:13.
1096. See Lk 11:22.

it goes back, and finding the house it had gone out of unoccupied, it brings along with it seven other spirits more wicked than itself; and the last state of that person has become worse than the first."[1097] So in order that nothing like that should happen to us too, let us endeavor as best we can to bring in virtues in the place of vices, so that we may attain eventually to the mercy of God.

Sermon 386

On Loving Our Enemies

HOW WE SHOULD LOVE OUR ENEMIES

1. Turn your minds, please, my brothers and sisters, to that charity which the divine Scriptures praise so much, that nothing else can equal it. When God warns us that we must love one another, is he only warning you to love the person who loves you? That is mutual love, and it is not enough for God. You see, he wanted you to get as far as loving your enemies, when he said, *"Love your enemies, do good to those who hate you, pray for those who persecute you; so that you may be the children of your Father who is in heaven, who makes his sun rise upon the good and the bad, who sends rain upon the just and the unjust."*[1098] What do you say to that? Do you love your enemy? Perhaps you will reply, "I can't do it, I'm too weak." But take steps to make progress, to ensure that you can do it; above all because you are going to pray to a judge whom nobody can deceive, who is going to try your case.

So appeal to this judge, where there is no clerk of the court to scare you, no beadle to remove you, no advocate to be bought to plead your case or utter words which you haven't learned. But the only Son of God himself, equal to the Father, seated at the Father's right hand as his assessor, your judge, has taught you just a few words, which any illiterate person can get by heart and repeat, and in these words he has made your case for you. He has taught you the heavenly law, as to how you should plead. But perhaps you will reply, "By whom am I to make my petition? By myself in person,

1097. Lk 11:24–26.   1098. Mt 5:44–45.

or through someone else?" The one who has taught you to pray,[1099] he is the one who presents your plea for you, because you were guilty. Rejoice, because the one who is now your counsel will then be your judge.

So because you are going to pray, you are going to plead your case in a few words, and you are going to come precisely to these words: *"Forgive us our debts, as we too forgive our debtors."*[1100] You see, God is saying to you, "What are you giving me, so that I should forgive you your debts? What gift are you offering, what sacrifice of your conscience are you laying upon my altars?" Straightaway he taught you what you should ask for and what you should offer. You ask, *"Forgive us our debts"*; and you offer—what? *"As we too forgive our debtors."* You are in debt to the one who cannot be deceived; you also have your own debtor. God is saying to you, "You are my debtor, that man is yours; I treat you, my debtor, in the same way as you treat yours. Offer me a gift from what you have spared your debtor. You are asking me for mercy; don't be sluggish in showing mercy yourself. Pay attention to what Scripture says, *"I desire mercy more than sacrifice."*[1101] Never offer a sacrifice without mercy; because your sins will not be forgiven unless you offer it together with mercy.

But I suppose you may say, "I haven't got any sins." However careful you may be, brother or sister, still while you are living in the flesh in this age, you are acting under pressure and in tight spots, and you find yourself in the midst of innumerable temptations; you simply cannot be without sin. Sure, God is saying to you, "Don't worry at all about sin, don't forgive your debtors, if you haven't got anything for me to forgive you; instead, demand payment from your debtors, if you don't owe anything yourself. If, however, you are a debtor, congratulate yourself on also having someone in debt to you, whom you can treat in the way you want to be treated yourself."

Listen to me, and examine yourself, being doubtless among those few upright people who can truthfully pray the Lord's prayer, truthfully say, "Lord, forgive me, as I too forgive." Do this, not dishonestly, not just pretending, but truly from the heart, so that it may truly be done in your case. If the person, after all, who

1099. That is, has taught you the prayer "Our Father."

1100. Mt 6:12.   1101. Hos 6:6; Mt 12:7.

has hurt you, who has sinned against you, asks your pardon, and you say, "Forget it," you are now in a position to say without a qualm, *"Forgive us our debts, as we too forgive our debtors."* I mean, if you refuse the one who begs your pardon, you in your turn will be ignored when you beg for pardon. You have slammed the door in the face of someone knocking; you will find it slammed in your face when you knock.[1102] Because if you open your heart tenderly to the one who begs you for pardon, God will also open his to you, when you beg him for pardon.

Now, you see, I am addressing those of you who ask their Christian brothers and sisters for pardon, and don't receive it. Look, if you for your part have granted pardon, you will be able to pray without any anxiety. But what about him? If he asked your pardon, and you didn't grant it, how free from anxiety will he be? Whoever you are, though, that may have sinned against another, and not won pardon, don't be afraid; appeal to his God and yours. There are debts at issue; will the servant be able to demand payment of debts which his master has written off? If it so happens, though, that the person who has sinned against you hasn't pleaded with you, if he doesn't pray you to pardon him; if he has injured you, and over and above that is still angry with you, what are you going to do about it? Will you forgive him, or not? Suppose you haven't forgiven him. Why not? Because he didn't ask you to. If the reason you haven't forgiven him is that he didn't ask you to, don't hesitate while saying the Lord's Prayer, say it without a qualm; you needn't beat your breast because you haven't forgiven someone who didn't beg you to. So the one who didn't ask for pardon has remained in debt; payment will be required of him, it most certainly will. However, let's hope your charity will be perfect, and that you pray for the one who doesn't pray you to forgive him, because you will be praying for someone who is in great danger.

THE EXAMPLE OF CHRIST HIMSELF AND OF SAINT STEPHEN

2. Here and now turn your attention to your master and Lord, not seated on his magisterial chair, but hanging on the tree, gazing all round him at the crowd of his enemies, and saying, *"Father, forgive them, because they do not know what they are doing."*[1103] Observe the

---

1102. See Lk 11:9.   1103. Lk 23:34.

master, listen to one who imitated him."[1104] The Lord Christ was hardly praying at that moment, was he, for those who had asked him for pardon? No, it was rather for those who were hurling insults at him and putting him to death. Did the physician abandon his duty, because the frenzied patient was raving? After all, he says, *"Forgiven them because they do not know what they are doing"*; they are killing the savior, because they are not seeking salvation. You, on the contrary, are no doubt going to say, "And when can I do what the Lord was able to do?" Why should you say this? Notice where he did this; notice that he did it on the cross, not in heaven. After all he is always God in heaven with the Father; but on the cross he was man for you, where he offered himself as an example to be followed by all. It was for your sake, you see, that he uttered those words, so as to be heard by all. I mean, he could have prayed for them silently, but then there would have been no example for you to follow.

But if the Lord's example is too much for you, don't let the servant's be too much for you. So you are unable to imitate your Lord, are you, when he was hanging on the cross? Pay attention to his servant Stephen, when he was being stoned to death. First he said, as the servant to his Lord, *"Lord Jesus, receive my spirit; and after that he knelt down and said, Lord, do not hold this sin against them. And when he had said this, he fell asleep"* in the restful arms of love.[1105] He found the most abundant peace, because he desired peace for his enemies. He wasn't praying then either, was he, for those who had prayed him to forgive them? In fact it was for those raging against him, for those who were stoning him and killing him. You have his example; learn from it. Notice how he prayed for himself standing up, and for them he knelt down. Are we to suppose, brothers and sisters, that he loved them more than himself? But he prayed for himself standing up as being a just man, who would readily be listened to; because on behalf of the wicked it was necessary to kneel. So he extended his love even to his enemies who were not asking for his pardon.

So, brothers and sisters, to ensure you can say the Lord's Prayer without a qualm, forgive from the heart those who ask you to do so, in order that the Lord may forgive your sins too in this mortal body and in the future forever, etc.

1104. Meaning Stephen, of course.   1105. Acts 7:59–60.

SUGGESTIONS FOR FURTHER READING

WORKS OF AUGUSTINE

Augustine: Earlier Writings. John H. S. Burleigh, ed. The Library of Christian Classics. Philadelphia: Westminster, 1953.

Augustine: Later Works. John Burnaby, ed. The Library of Christian Classics. Philadelphia: Westminster, 1955.

City of God. Henry Bettenson, trans. New York: Penguin, 1984.

The Confessions. Maria Boulding, O.S.B., trans. New York: Vintage Spiritual Classics, 1998.

The Enchiridion on Faith, Hope, and Love. J. B. Shaw, trans. Washington, D.C.: Henry Regnery, 1961; Gateway paperback ed., 1996.

Letters of Saint Augustine. John Leinenweber, ed. Tarrytown, N.Y.: Liguori Publications, 1992.

Nicene and Post-Nicene Fathers. Vols. 1–8. Philip Schaff, ed. Peabody, Mass.: Hendrickson, 1994.

The Works of Saint Augustine: A Translation for the 21st Century. John E. Rotelle, O.S.A., ed. Augustinian Heritage Institute. Hyde Park, N.Y.: New City Press, 1990–.

    Answer to the Pelagians, vols. 1–4

    The Confessions

    Expositions of the Psalms, vols. 1–6

    Letters, vols. 1–4

    Marriage and Virginity

    On Christian Belief

    Sermons, vols. 1–12

    Teaching Christianity

    The Trinity

    Other volumes are in preparation.

The Rule of Saint Augustine: Masculine and Feminine Versions. With introduction and commentary by Tarsicius J. van Bavel, O.S.A. Translated by Raymond Canning, O.S.A. Kalamazoo, Mich.: Cistercian Publications, 1996.

Note: Numerous other translations of individual works by Augustine exist, but no uniform edition in English is yet available of his complete surviving writings. The editors of this volume have made no effort at a comprehensive list here, preferring instead to give the readers some useful highlights.

SECONDARY WORKS

Arendt, Hannah. *Love and St. Augustine.* Chicago: University of Chicago Press, 1996.

Benedict XVI, Pope. *Deus caritas est* [On Christian Love]. Encyclical Letter of the Supreme Pontiff Benedict XVI to the Bishops, Priests, and Deacons, Men and Women Religious, and All the Lay Faithful. Given in Rome, at Saint Peter's, on 25 December, the Solemnity of the Nativity of the Lord, in the year 2005. *http://www.vatican.va/holy_father/benedict_xvi/encyclicals/documents/hf_ben-xvi_enc_20051225_deus-caritas-est_en.html*

Bonner, Gerald. *St. Augustine of Hippo: His Life and Controversies.* Villanova, Pa.: Augustinian Press, 1997.

Bourke, Vernon, ed. *The Essential Augustine.* Indianapolis: Hackett, 1974.

Brown, Peter. *Augustine of Hippo: A Biography.* Berkeley and Los Angeles: University of California Press, 1969; 2nd ed., 2000.

Burnaby, John. *Amor Dei: A Study of the Religion of St. Augustine.* London: Hodder & Stoughton, 1938; reprinted, 1960.

Chadwick, Henry. *Augustine.* New York: Oxford University Press, 1986.

Clark, Mary T. "Augustinian Spirituality." In Michael Downey, ed., *The New Dictionary of Catholic Spirituality.* Collegeville, Minn.: Liturgical Press. A Michael Glazier Book, 1993.

———. *Augustine.* Outstanding Christian Thinkers Series. Washington, D.C.: Georgetown University Press, 1994.

Fitzgerald, Allan D., ed. *Augustine Through the Ages: An Encyclopedia.* Grand Rapids, Mich.: Eerdmans, 1999. See esp. article "Love," Tarsicius J. van Bavel, pp. 509–16.

Gilson, Etienne. *The Christian Philosophy of St. Augustine.* New York: Random House, 1960.

Groeschel, Benedict. *Augustine: Major Writings.* New York: Crossroads, 1996.

Guardini, Romano. *The Conversion of Saint Augustine.* New York: Crossroads, 1996.

Hand, Thomas A. *Augustine on Prayer.* Villanova, Pa.: Augustinian Press, 1997.

Harmless, William. *Augustine and the Catechumenate.* Collegeville, Minn.: Liturgical Press, 1995.

Kirk, K. E. *The Vision of God.* New York: Harper Torchbooks, 1966.

Markus, R. A., ed. *Augustine: A Collection of Critical Essays.* Garden City, N.Y.: Anchor Books, 1972.

Nygren, Anders. *Agape and Eros: The Christian Idea of Love.* Philip S. Watson, trans. New York: Harper and Row, 1969; first published in Swedish, 1932.

O'Donnell, James J. *Augustine: A New Biography.* New York: Harper-Collins, 2005.

———. *Confessions.* Latin text with English commentary. 3 vols. Oxford: Clarendon Press, 1992.

O'Donovan, Oliver. *The Problem of Self-Love in St. Augustine.* New Haven, Conn.: Yale University Press, 1980.

Pelikan, Jaroslav. *The Mystery of Continuity: Time and History, Memory and Eternity in the Thought of Saint Augustine.* Charlottesville: University Press of Virginia, 1986.

Price, Richard. *Augustine: His Life and Beliefs.* Villanova, Pa.: Augustinian Press, 1997.

Przywara, Erich. *Augustine Synthesis.* New York: Sheed & Ward, 1936.

Rist, John M. *Augustine: Ancient Thought Baptized.* Cambridge and New York: Cambridge University Press, 1994.

Schlabach, Gerald W. *For the Joy Set Before Us: Augustine and Self-Denying Love.* Notre Dame, Ind.: University of Notre Dame Press, 2001.

Trape, Agostino. *St. Augustine: Man, Pastor, Mystic.* Villanova, Pa.: Augustinian Press, 1997.

Wills, Garry. *Saint Augustine.* Penguin Lives. New York: A Lipper/Viking Book, 1999.

SELECTED WEB SITES

http://ccat.sas.upenn.edu/jod/augustine.html Web site for Augustine of Hippo maintained by James J. O'Donnell.

http://www.newadvent.org/fathers/ Web site for letters, speeches, and books from the earliest Christians.

http://www.ccel.org/a/augustine Web site for early Christian literature.

JAMES J. O'DONNELL is professor of classics and provost of Georgetown University. He has served as president of the American Philological Association and is a Fellow of the Medieval Academy of America. He has published widely on the cultural history of the late antique Mediterranean world. His most recent book is *Augustine: A New Biography* (2005).

JOHN F. THORNTON is a literary agent, former publishing executive, and the coeditor, with Katharine Washburn, of *Dumbing Down* (1996) and *Tongues of Angels, Tongues of Men: A Book of Sermons* (1999). He lives in New York City.

SUSAN B. VARENNE is a New York City teacher with a strong avocational interest in and wide experience of spiritual literature. She holds an M.A. from the University of Chicago Divinity School and a Ph.D. from Columbia University.

PRAYER OF SAINT AUGUSTINE

Which he was wont to use after his sermons and lectures

———

Turn we to the Lord God, the Father Almighty, and with pure hearts offer to Him, so far as our meanness can, great and true thanks, with all our hearts praying His exceeding kindness, that of His good pleasure He would deign to hear our prayers, that by His Power He would drive out the enemy from our deeds and thoughts, that He would increase our faith, guide our understandings, give us spiritual thoughts, and lead us to His bliss, through Jesus Christ His Son our Lord, who liveth and reigneth with Him, in the Unity of the Holy Spirit, one God, forever and ever. Amen.